OF THOSE
WE LOVED

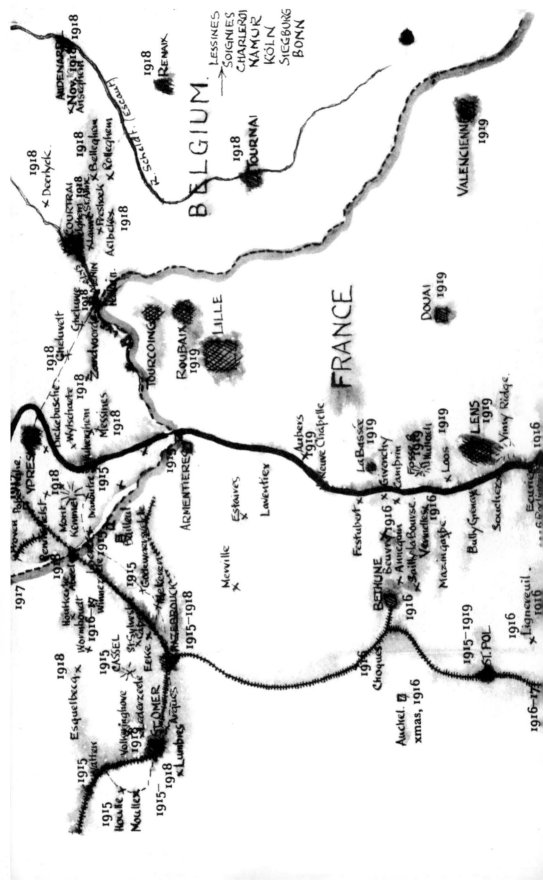

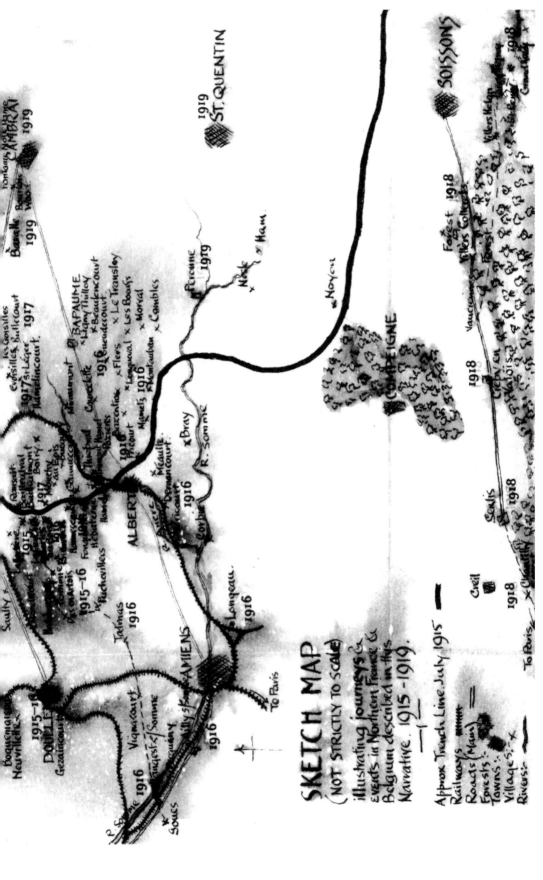

SKETCH MAP

(NOT STRICTLY TO SCALE)

illustrating journeys &
events in Northern France &
Belgium described in this
Narrative. 1915 - 1919.

Approx Trench Line July 1915 ▬▬

Railways ━━━━━

Roads (Main) ═══

Forests 🌲

Towns ◆ Creil

Villages :- ×

Rivers:-

CAMBRAI 1919

Fontaine Notre Dame 1919
× Beaurevoir
Bourlon Wood 1919
Barak 1919

ST. QUENTIN 1919

les Consilles
Ervilles × Butlecourt 1917
1917 St-Léger 1917
Hamelincourt

□ **BAPAUME**
× Ligny Thilloy
× Beaulencourt
1916 Gueudecourt
× Flers × Le Transloy
× Barastre × Lesgueval × Les Boeufs
× Morval
Maurepas 1916 × Montauban × Combles

Péronne
1919

Nesle
× Ham

Noyon

COMPIÈGNE

Forêt 1918
Villers Cotterets
Vauxaillon
1918
Crépy en Valois 1918
Senlis ×
1918

SOISSONS

Villers Helon
× × 1918
× Forest
× Retheuil
Crépy × 1918

To Paris

Boisjean
Neuvillers ×
1915-16
DOULLENS
Gezaincourt

Rainsart
Bienvillers
Bailleulval × Beaumont
1917 Barly ×
Foncquevillers
1915-16
× Buchavilles

Authuille
Thiepval 1916
1916 Bazentin
Picourt ×

ALBERT
× Meault
Dernancourt
Picourt 1916
× 1916
Corbie
× Bray
R. Somme

Scully ×
1915
× × Dainville
Contre St. ×
des Glatois

Talmas
1916

Vignacourt
1916

× Allonville

Longeau
1916

AMIENS

To Paris

R. Somme
× Saleux
× Soues

R. ...
1916

OF THOSE WE LOVED

A GREAT WAR NARRATIVE
REMEMBERED AND ILLUSTRATED

I L 'DICK' READ

Pen & Sword
MILITARY

First published in Great Britain in 1994 by
The Pentland Press Ltd.

Republished in this format in 2013 by
PEN & SWORD MILITARY
An imprint of
Pen & Sword Books Ltd
47 Church Street
Barnsley
South Yorkshire
S70 2AS

ISBN 978 1 78159 101 7

Printed and bound in England
By CPI Group (UK) Ltd, Croydon, CR0 4YY

Pen & Sword Books Ltd incorporates the Imprints of Pen & Sword Aviation,
Pen & Sword Family History, Pen & Sword Maritime, Pen & Sword Military,
Pen & Sword Discovery, Pen & Sword Politics, Pen & Sword Atlas,
Pen & Sword Archaeology, Wharncliffe Local History, Wharncliffe True Crime,
Wharncliffe Transport, Pen & Sword Select, Pen & Sword Military Classics,
Leo Cooper, The Praetorian Press, Claymore Press, Remember When,
Seaforth Publishing and Frontline Publishing

For a complete list of Pen & Sword titles please contact
PEN & SWORD BOOKS LIMITED
47 Church Street, Barnsley, South Yorkshire, S70 2AS, England
E-mail: enquiries@pen-and-sword.co.uk
Website: www.pen-and-sword.co.uk

A NARRATIVE
1914-1919.

REMEMBERED & ILLUSTRATED

BY

I. L. READ,

SOMETIME N⁰ 12819, SERGEANT,

17th. THE LEICESTERSHIRE REGT.,

& LATER

LIEUT. 35th. THE ROYAL SUSSEX REGT.

—|—

FOR MY GRANDCHILDREN.

CONTENTS

CHAPTER I

FOR WHAT PURPOSE?

Our modest garden in Hampshire is a longish, three-cornered piece at the junction of two roads, fringed by mature oaks and ash trees. That winter of 1962/3 it was snow covered after 26th December and still was, three parts through February. Now and then a slight daytime thaw caused a few patches of green under the trees to emerge temporarily—until hidden again by the next fall.

In a bitter east wind, I was sweeping up acorns on one of these patches, which I thought I had raked thoroughly during the previous November. Snow and frost had, I thought, given these acorns a sharper definition against the frozen surface of the ground. Pondering on this somewhat absently, I started at a voice from the other side of the low boarded garden fence:

'Excuse me, sir!'

He was tall, but slightly bent with the years; I judged him about my age, by his pleasant features reddened by the bitter wind and the silver of his hair below the black trilby; his overcoat was in keeping, sober yet good. Politely I bade him 'Good afternoon' and awaited his inquiry—to be directed somewhere in the vicinity I presumed. I was, therefore, the more surprised when:

'I hope you won't think me nosey, but I come by here every three weeks or so to visit my sister who lives up the road there. Every time I go by your gate, though, I wonder about that name you've got on it . . .'

'What . . . Berles?'

'Yes, would it be short for Berles-au-Bois by any chance?'

'That's right! When were you there?'

'Nineteen-seventeen and eighteen—what were you in?'

'Leicesters—we took over from the French and were there all the winter of 1915. I was hit in front of Monchy. What were you in?'

'Coldstream Guards.'

We both laughed as I said, apologetically, 'Ah—real soldiers!'

He continued, 'so you know Pommier, and Bienvillers . . .?'

We reminisced for a few moments, until the east wind brought us back to the present as we removed 'dewdrops' from the blue ends of our noses. He turned to go, 'can't believe it all ever happened sometimes—only when you meet someone who was there. Then it brings it all back . . . and we had some good mates in those days.'

I agreed with him. As he went on his way I started to make for the house, half-turning after a few steps, as he called back to me 'remember Adinfer Wood?'

'Ah! . . .' And as I sat down by the fireside I thought of Adinfer Wood and of the times I'd looked across at it through the matted grasses and the wire from Monchy Mill.

I thought too—before I dozed off—how, particularly when Armisticetide approaches, the TV screens feature short excerpts of scenes filmed during the 1914–18 war, in France and elsewhere. To the youngsters, and indeed to most of the present population of these islands, they seem to show that the soldier of those years jerked along the roads and into battle at an impossibly staccato quickstep, swaying from side to side as a puppet pulled by strings, to the tune of 'Tipperary'!

After watching such a run of old war film shots, one of my grandsons, then aged eleven, summed up his impressions devastatingly thus—'it must have been a silly war, Grandpa!'

Perhaps it was, but at least the British soldier moved about his business and acted like a normal human being, or endeavoured to do so, until bullet, bomb, shell, gas or weather—or a combination of more than one of these—brought him to a standstill. In 1914 the Welfare State and nuclear deterrent were in the distant future. Life was tough, work was hard, hours long, with not much at the end of it for most men, but there was, rightly or wrongly, I believe, a certain pride in being British!

. . . Here goes—before they are effaced from my mind by the quickly passing years and by the necessity for concentration upon the present—I am going to delve into the Long-Ago and re-furbish the fast fading memories of my youth; to conjure up the old scenes; smell the old smells and hear again in fancy the old voices and the old sounds. Already I have forgotten much; fear of forgetting more urges me on, for most of those who survived Ypres, the Somme, Passchendaele and the battles of 1918 have gone long since, or, in the words of the soldiers' song, have 'faded away'; comparatively rarely do they make old bones.

Though it may be pure escapism to forget for a while the shame and grim realities of the Space Age, it may be pleasant to tread once more the pavé of the Route Nationale; with the rising sun in our faces; the 150 rounds in our pouches, balancing the heavy packs upon our backs. Our short-magazine Lee Enfield rifles are new and we are marching at the 'slope'. The colonel on his black horse rides in front with the adjutant. In the centre the band is playing 'Romaika', one of the grand old marches of the Leicestershire Regiment. The smoking field cookers and transport limbers bring up the rear, and last of all the senior major and transport officer look at the long column in front as they ride . . . 'Coming? "C" Company . . . march at ease! You may smoke!'

In July 1915, the 110th Infantry Brigade of the 37th Division lay at Perham Down Camp, near Tidworth. It consisted of the 6th, 7th, 8th and 9th (Service) Battalions of the Leicestershire regiment—units constituted in September of the previous year from men enlisted for the duration of the war in response to Lord Kitchener's call for 100,000 volunteers.

I was a private in 'C' Company of the 8th Battalion, attached to the machine-gun section. Laboriously, enthusiastically, throughout the winter of 1914 and spring of 1915, in camps at Aldershot, billets at Folkestone and on Salisbury Plain, we mastered the intricacies of the Vickers machine-gun as best we could through the media of lectures and wooden models. Then, about six weeks before we left for France, we were issued with four Lewis guns, the like of which we had never seen before, with all their attendant paraphernalia—including heavy Vickers pattern tripod stands on

3

Ⓚ :- KILLED   Ⓦ - WOUNDED

Ted Lineker Ⓚ Bazentin (Somme) 1916

F. Smith   S. Hooton.   C. Cook.   H. Killingley   S. Foxon.   Self.   A. Taylor

Ⓚ Bazentin Ⓦ Berles Lost leg Ⓚ Geudecourt. Ⓦ Bazentin (Somme) Ⓦ Bazentin (Somme)

E. Skelton. du Bois. Bazentin (Somme) 1916 1916.   1916

Ⓚ Bazentin E. Gamble 1915. 1916 (Somme)

1916 Ⓦ 3rd Ypres 1917

W. Vernon.   A. Lyall.

Ⓚ Bazentin   Ⓚ Bazentin.

1916   1916 (Somme)

ALDERSHOT   SEPT. 1914.

W. Johnson E. Withers. A. Lewin. E. Simmonds

Ⓚ 3rd Ypres Ⓦ Geudecourt. Ⓚ Bazentin. Ⓚ Bazentin. 1916

1917   1916   1916

Bourley Camp. Aldershot.

Published by John Drew.
Aldershot & Farnborough

CAMP OF THE 8th BATT. LEICESTERSHIRE REGT.
AT BOURLEY. ALDERSHOT. SEPT. '14.

4

which to mount them. These we learned feverishly; they were real guns at last and we loved them. We knew the recital of their functions and the treatment of their ailments by heart. I have never forgotten—'the boss on the feed arm actuating stud, working in the groove in the tail of the feed arm, moves the feed arm over from right to left,' etc., etc. No Lewis gunner ever will—while he breathes!

After a good many false alarms, order for the division to move overseas came very suddenly and there was no final leave. That evening we watched some of the 7th Battalion serenading their colonel around the officers' mess marquee, the refrain commencing 'you've got a kind face you old bars-tard—you ought to be bloody well shot'. Nothing seemed to happen, except sounds of hilarious mirth, and I suppose it was all taken in good part under the circumstances.

On a beautiful July morning, we found ourselves part of the brigade advanced party at Ludgershall Sidings, helping to load limbers, kicking and bucking mules, panniers of ammunition and anything else that the quartermasters could get us to manhandle on to the troop train. Everything and everyone at length being entrained to the satisfaction of the R.T.O., off we went, and surprisingly quickly were passing the backyards and streets of Southampton, waving to the girls and feeling thrilled generally. As we disappeared into the maze of the docks, we felt ourselves to be real soldiers at last; but our khaki was still very new and our buttons shone in the sunlight.

Our train came to a standstill at a dockside in the deep shadow of huge sheds, and here we detrained and piled arms, divesting ourselves also of our equipment and jackets preparatory to a spell of real hard work, in the course of which we manhandled limber after limber within reach of the cranes on the quayside, which slung them into the holds of a largish steamer which lay alongside. In addition to our own Brigade Transport, horses, mules, guns, limbers and supplies were being loaded simultaneously by other cranes and fatigue parties. it was not until we had paraded and filed up the ship's gangway in the late afternoon that we had time to ascertain her name and take a breather. She was the Ellerman boat *City of Dunkirk*.

Our own kit being stowed in the after-holds, we made ourselves

5

comfortable aft in the lee of a deck house, and took the advice of a friendly old sailor who stood close by, in readiness for recovering the stern wires about to be cast off by the shore gang. We ate our fill of bread and great slices of beef, of which he seemed to have a plentiful supply, and in this I suppose we were fortunate in being comparatively few.

I have indicated the nature of our cargo and we had on board, I believe, several hundred horses and mules when we cast off at, as far as I can recollect, about half-past five in the afternoon. We progressed slowly, but there was much to interest us, and it was not until we were leaving the Isle of Wight astern that the setting sun and freshening wind caused our thoughts to turn to the England we were leaving behind. A sombre mood seemed to settle upon us and first one and then all joined in singing songs we all knew, such as 'Sweet and Low'.

In the gathering twilight of the summer evening the engines stopped; the pilot went down the ladder and jumped into the dinghy which came alongside from his waiting launch. As he jumped, he waved and shouted 'Good luck, boys!'. The engines restarted, and as bells tinkled on the bridge and below, we all sang 'The Anchor's Weighed'. To the sustained farewells of this old song, his little boat and the English coast were lost to view. For many who sang, it was in truth their vale to their native soil.

Meanwhile the wind had risen and already there was trouble with the horses below as the steamer pitched in the choppy sea. On either side of us raced a destroyer, ploughing through the white horses and throwing up great sheets of spray at the bows. At times we could see the length of their decks and the insides of belching funnels as they rose to the waves, by the light of occasional showers of sparks. As darkness fell, however, we lost trace of them, save for an occasional few sparks.

We felt cold in spite of our buttoned greatcoats and at the invitation of our A.B. friend, withdrew to the shelter of the deckhouse, where we attacked more bread and beef. His advice stood us in good stead. We did not feel seasick and became very interested in the twelve-pounder gun immediately aft of the deckhouse, which afforded shelter for the gun's crew not on duty. Once, not feeling tired, we took a walk along the slippery decks, but the stink from the horses'

THE ELLERMAN LINE S.S.'CITY OF DUNKIRK'
ENTERING THE DOCKS. LE HAVRE. JULY 1915.

quarters coming up from below drove us back again, and we thanked our lucky stars that they were not our responsibility. Back in our shelter, we yarned until, one by one, we slept.

I awoke to the cries of gulls circling overhead. The ship was stationary and the sun shone strongly upon a sparkling sea as we stretched the stiffness from our limbs and sat up to take stock of our surroundings. We lay about a mile off shore from a considerable city, and around us lay shipping of many kinds. Just where we were I hadn't the faintest idea, but our A.B. friend told us that we were off Le Havre and that we were going in shortly.

He then pointed to a length of the stern rails which appeared to have been twisted and displaced, and we plied him with questions as to the cause, but he was very evasive and we never solved the mystery, although the general opinion was that we had been fired on during the night.

With a blast from her siren, the *City of Dunkirk* got under way once more, drawing nearer to the forest of cranes and sheds and finding a channel through which we glided by a kind of esplanade into the dock system. We crowded to the ship's side to get our first close-up of France. The cafés with their chairs and tables outside, the quaint tramcars, the blue of the French soldiery and the darker blue of the police—the shuttered windows, the unfamiliar sounds and smells—all these intrigued us immensely.

That was we all we saw, however, of Le Havre. Lost in the labyrinth of docks, evening found us tired out, lying on the hay-strewn floor of our box car, which formed part of the longest train we had ever seen. Horses, mules, limbers, field cookers, officers' kits—we had worked hard unloading all these and getting them on to the train. I recall that just as we thought we had finished, we were detailed to unload another hold containing large parcels, cases of spirits, sauces and other special items for messes and B.E.F. canteens. Very annoyed we were about this and I'm afraid that the goods suffered as a consequence, although the method employed to transfer them to the dockside invited trouble. As we stood in the hold waiting, the crane swung over and lowered to us a thick rope net which we spread on the floor. On went the cases and parcels until we had such a pile that we could just gather up the four corners and fix them over the crane hook. At the 'right-away', the huge string bag ascended to the sounds of ominous creaking and cracking among the contents. Frequently, I'm afraid, the net descended to the dockside leaking at several points.

Our box car, labelled 'Chemin de Fer du Nord—Hommes 40, Chevaux en long 8', stood in a huge shed stacked high with what we were told were bales of cotton from the U.S.A., and lit as evening approached by infrequent electric lights. There were fourteen of us sharing it—we had plenty of room on this, our first experience of continental railway travel—but on pushing back the sliding doors we were assailed by rich smells of the farmyard— 'Chevaux en long huit', as one of us commented. However, ten minutes or so sufficed to cleanse this Augean stable, by tipping it out on the far side of the line and replacing the contents with clean hay, scrounged when the transport drivers weren't looking. Thus installed, we wrote our first field postcards; addressing mine, I speculated on the effect on my parents of the knowledge that I was of the British Expeditionary Force . . .

When I awoke we were on the move—jog-jog-rattle-jog. The night wind, penetrating the sliding doors, was guttering our solitary candle, stuck upon an upturned mess tin on the floor midway among the sleeping forms of my mates. Gingerly, I reached over on hands and knees and moved it away from the draught and lit another from my haversack, but suddenly I felt very cold and snuggled down in the hay again under my greatcoat. With conjecture as to our destination, I slept once more, and it was broad daylight when a mate shook me, holding out a steaming mess tin of cocoa. The train had stopped and he had been along to the engine for some hot water.

Refreshed, I suddenly felt the need for a wash and brush up and seized the chance of obtaining some more hot water by running along the grass-grown track with several mess tins. Many times later on I did this same thing and I cannot recall an instance when either driver or fireman did not oblige—often with a cheery word and a grin. On this occasion, however, I had a longer journey than I bargained for, as the train was such a long one and I arrived breathless beside the huge black locomotive, essaying my first French conversation as the driver looked down on me from his cab. I soon had four tins of almost boiling water, but he gave me to understand that he was just going to start. Halfway back there was a shrill whistle and a terrific clanging and screeching which passed me like an echoing thunderclap as the train resumed its journey. Anxiously I beheld my mates leaning far out, approaching with increasing rapidity. Doing the only thing possible, I turned and ran in the same direction as the train and

CHEVAUX EN LONG 8
HOMMES 40 "

CHEMIN DE FER DU NORD

'WAYSIDE HALT.'
JULY 1915,
LE HAVRE — WATTEN
P. de C.

as our car came level my mess tins and I were seized by several pairs of hands and hauled aboard. Our shaves and mess tin washes were well worth the trouble and, feeling fairly clean once more, we slid the doors back and sat down in the sunshine, dangling our legs over the sides and taking in as much as we could of the French countryside. All day we jogged along thus, living on bully beef, biscuits and tinned butter, and about four in the afternoon passed through Boulogne, then Calais. In the dusk we stopped at a place we made out to be Audruicq and thought perhaps that we were detraining, but another whistle and we were thrown into heaps as we started once again. It was dark when we were shunted into a siding near a station on which we read dimly 'Watten'.

A fine moon had risen when we Leicesters marched out of the station yard at the rear of our column of battalion transport, the machine-gun and transport officers leading the way, and for a while we were quite content to jog along what was a decidedly second-class road, but we hoped that we shouldn't be too long getting to wherever we were going. In the event, however, we were marching or halting for most of the night. Finally, dog tired, we halted yet again in a village street as the first signs of dawn were appearing. We were almost too tired to swear, as wearily we got to our feet again and marched through the gateway of what smelt like a brewery—as indeed it was. Filing into a long empty building, we flung down our packs and equipment. We had had enough of France already!

I had removed my puttees and was unlacing my boots when our sergeant detailed me for guard, telling me that if I did my turn first, I'd get to sleep sooner; whereupon I staggered out to the brewery gateway and stood at ease over the battalion baggage.

A lot of good I must have been as a sentry! Still, I managed not to go to sleep, and the crowing of roosters all around heralded the coming day; soon it was quite light. Occasionally, too, dull reverberations reached my ears from the direction of the scarcely risen sun. In the village, doors opened and shut. Strange to say, I no longer felt tired—only very hungry and very dirty. A door opened behind me, in a house corresponding to the porter's lodge of the brewery, and I heard the clamp, clamp of wooden shoes over the stones of the yard as a girl carrying a pail went to the pump nearby. Straightening up, I watched her with interest and as she returned to the house she saw me and bid me '*bonjour*'. Somewhat confused, but pleased, I returned her greeting as well as I could.

'*Angleterre—hein?*', putting down her pail. '*Ah—oui mademoiselle.*' I told her that we had marched all night from a place called Watten. She looked incredulous. '*M'sieu*—but it is but a few kilometres—how was that?' I told her I didn't know. I supposed we had got lost, but that she could see from the dust on my boots that we had marched a lot. In short, I gathered from her that the village was called Houlle and that there was another called Moulle about five kilometres away. I remembered marching through Moulle during the night and concluded that we had, in fact, marched to the wrong place, but our leaders must have made other mistakes too. A few minutes later she appeared with a basin of hot coffee and a long narrow slice of crusty bread. I don't think I had ever tasted anything more delicious and I told her so with many '*bons*'; whereat she smiled and pointed to my shoulder badges. 'Lei-ces-taires—*hein?* Leices-taire Squairr?' she pronounced awkwardly. 'Long way to Tipperary—*hein*', with a laugh which disclosed a fine set of teeth.

As she disappeared into the house, France was tolerable again I thought; in fact when my relief came, I was not at all anxious to go and 'get my head down', as he put it.

That night the battalion, having crossed via Folkestone and Boulogne, joined us, and the billeting capacity of Houlle was taxed to the utmost.

CHAPTER 2

WULVERGHEM

WE stayed at Houlle for four days settling down, as it were, and preparing for tests to come. There were rigorous inspections of kit, weapons and ammunition and we practised gas drill daily with two kinds of grey flannel contraptions steeped in chemicals which stung the face cruelly after wearing them for a few minutes; also, the heat generated within caused the wearer to perspire profusely and the eyepieces to steam over. We were issued with some stuff to rub over the eyepieces, and I remember there was a special drill for that. Off duty, we swam in the little river, or canal, while French girls and youths on passing barges joked with us and made unintelligible remarks as we dressed or sat about on the grass verge.

Then, one fine morning found us in column of route upon the pavé of the St. Omer road, the towers of which soon became visible through the early haze, and before the sun was very high we had passed through this historic town.

I remember marching to 'attention' and how, anxious to make a good impression, we looked to our 'slopes' as we gave 'eyes left' to a guard there. Beyond St. Omer the blue and white signposts directed us towards Arques and Hazebrouck, and by the time we had marched for another three hours with halts of five minutes at each hour, we had had quite enough, as the sun now beat down upon us unmercifully, loaded as we were and clothed in our thick khaki serge and puttees. Trees there were along the route, it is true, but the lower branches having been stripped they afforded us little shade, while every now and again long convoys of lorries moving either way smothered us in clouds of choking dust. Our faces were streaked with grime and perspiration, while our feet began to show signs of wear. Moreover, although we thought we had husbanded it, most of us had only lukewarm dregs left in our water bottles. Still, by mid-afternoon, the approach to a largish village cheered us. Here, we thought, we shall be billeted. But *no*—we trudged on and on, straight through in the noonday heat, by this time grousing, of course. On the further side we noticed the first odd stragglers—then considerable numbers, mostly from other units of our Division who had fallen out on the march, either through exhaustion, but mostly by reason of their blistered feet.

One or two even we saw at cottage doors asking for water and tendering their bottles. We speculated as to whether it was worth the Field Punishment No. 1 we were warned would be meted out, to men caught, in view of the danger of contracting typhoid and enteric from drinking water so obtained. Most of us were sufficiently intelligent to appreciate the good sense prompting this order. Moreover, we had seen the primitive sanitation prevailing, according to our standards, and already the taste of chlorine in our drinking water and the smell of chloride of lime were necessary accompaniments and guarantors of our daily lives.

Still we plodded on. To our left in the distance, rising sheer above the Flanders plain, we saw the great landmark which we knew subsequently as Cassel—the town upon the hill—but just then we were in no condition to appreciate the scenery. Another halt near another village . . . surely this was our goal! But we were unlucky again. 'Fall in, by the right, quick march' and wearily we went forward once more. A kilometre or so on, the company halted and we sank, rather than sat down, at the gates of a big farm. My feet felt pretty bad; my back ached, and hastily loosened gear and tunic reeked of dried sweat; my rifle seemed to weigh a ton and my tongue and mouth parched and grit-laden. Ruminations were cut short by shouted orders; whereat we struggled to our feet and into ranks again, to march . . . into the farmyard! The clean straw of the barn gave us the best bed we'd ever had in our young lives.

Soon after noon on the following day we reached the village of Eeke, where our company bivouacked in a large field, the officers and senior N.C.O.s sleeping in the farm-house and buildings nearby. Two of us made a 'bivvy' of our groundsheets and slept soundly, being awakened about 4 a.m., however, by several curious cows munching near our unsuspecting heads. We rested here a day and tried to get our feet into something like condition.

During the afternoon the mail arrived and we had our first letters from home. My parents had both written from their different points of view. They could not say much; they tried to hide their anxiety—I could read that much between the lines and wished I could let them know that at that moment I was a long way from shot and shell, and that, save for a blister on my right heel, I was perfectly fit.

That day Field Punishment No. 1 was meted out to two men of our company who had been caught filling their water bottles on the line of march. Each was spread-eagled and tied hand and foot to the spokes of a limber wheel for two hours in the summer sun, under the surveillance of one of the Regimental Police. From our bivouac in the field, we watched with mixed feelings, but whatever else we felt, I'm quite sure that we would think twice before letting ourselves in for a similar fate. Moreover, we knew that as opportunity offered, the two men would be strung up again until the punishment awarded was completed.

Again we took the road, out of Eeke and facing the morning sun. Near the wayside station of Godewaersvelde, by a level crossing, we were ordered suddenly to 'march to attention', and our lieutenant hurriedly adjured us to 'make a good show!'. As we 'eyes lefted' we saw a galaxy of Red Hats and Tabs, slightly in front of which stood a solitary, rather frail figure in a British Warm. Through his glasses he looked at us keenly, and afterwards we gathered that he was General Plumer, commanding the 2nd Army Corps, of which we were now a part. It may be of interest to note that, in the estimation of the troops, by 1918 General Plumer was almost alone among the Brasshats in retaining our confidence, amounting almost to affection, for the 'old gentleman'.

All that day we marched by devious routes, halting at intervals, until in the late afternoon we filed into a neglected field on the outskirts of the village of Dranoutre and bivouacked. We could now hear quite plainly the reverberations of the guns and could see, as evening approached, flashes in the eastern sky. Almost overhead hovered one of our observation balloons, or 'sausages' as they were called, and as we made our little fires we watched it being pulled down beyond a near-by wood for the night. By the remaining light also we watched the black and white puff balls of the German 'archies' pursuing a black speck—white puffs tinged with pink by the rays of the setting sun. Yes, we had a good fire that night, I remember. Even a year later it would have been madness to light such a fire under similar circumstances, for it would have made too good a target for an enemy airman. Later, even the big Gothas, loaded to capacity for Boulogne, Dunkirk or Calais, did not disdain to throw small bombs on any cookhouse fire they saw *en passant*.

We did not sleep well, however. It was not due to the fairly frequent booming of the artillery—or to the intermittent rattle of machine-guns, or to the ghostly pyrotechnics of the not-too-distant Verey lights which hung on the eastern horizon fitfully before expiring into blackness—although certainly these things were very new to us. It was just that we itched so badly, that with morning light we stripped and sat in our greatcoats while we did our best to delouse ourselves by all methods available, the favourite being the glowing end of a cigarette run along the insides of the seams of the trousers or jacket. When accompanied by a steady crackling, the cigarette end was doing its job. Now and again, one of us would exclaim at the size of one detected, such as 'I've got a cap badge!—What a beauty—Match this one!'

From that day to December 1916, when I came on leave and my underclothes were burned in our back garden at home, I doubt whether I was ever free from lice. Although we never missed an opportunity of getting at these little pests, we became used to them. It was Hobson's Choice with us, anyhow.

During the afternoon we were told that we were going into the line that night and from that moment we found plenty to do, including inspection and checking our Lewis gun, spare parts and drums of ammunition.

Amid much briefing and bustle, there was also—let me be frank and confess it—a lot of suppressed excitement and 'wind-up', forgotten perhaps for a few minutes by our first issue of what subsequently was a commonplace—a tin of American pork and beans. As a change from our customary fare, we voted it good.

Afterwards we sometimes joked about it; how our Lewis Gun section followed the rear platoon of 'C' Company in single file across the dark fields; how tense we were and how anxious each of us was not to lose touch with the man in front; how we ducked involuntarily when the first stray bullets whined overhead or rico-chetted; how by the light of a German Verey light we saw, thrown into eerie relief, the British graveyard and the wooden crosses—and how lost we felt in the blackness as the rocket petered out. Then—our first casualty, as we were crossing the last of the fields at the edge of a spinney, just before entering the communication trench. As we passed him we heard the wounded man gasping as the stretcher-bearers tended him. He had been hit in the stomach and subsequently we were told that a sniping rifle was laid on this point by day and fired at intervals during the night. At this period of the war, sniping in any shape or form had developed into a fine art by both sides—with many gruesome successes as the trench war developed.

Our 'wind-up', increased by this incident, subsided somewhat in the comparative safety of the communication trench, and our progress was without incident until we were at the junction with the front line. Then we heard a plop, and saw sparks ascending and then descending in an increasing shower and 'shush-shushing' to our left, followed by an appalling explosion which, catching us entirely unprepared—green as we were—threw us in heaps, while a shower of earth and hot whirring iron pattered down around. As we pulled ourselves together to continue, the acrid fumes of the *minnenwerfer* drifted across on the damp night breeze and, turning right at the junction into the front line of breastworks, we saw a veteran sentry in muddy khaki, on close scrutiny with about a week's stubble on his chin. By the fitful gleam of a distant Verey light we saw his badge in his balaclava-pattern cap—Middlesex. He grinned as we stumbled by. 'Gor—that ain't nuffin' mate!' Our corporal inquired where the machine-gunners were. 'What—you blokes machine-gunners?' he queried incredulously.

'Windy' though we were, we bridled at our corporal's confusion. Perhaps Middlesex sensed this for he grinned again, 'Oh ar—abaht four traverses along. Them buggers've got the only decent shelter along 'ere!'

A crescent moon was rising which, as we followed his direction, disclosed silent sentries standing on sandbagged firesteps looking out over the breastwork parapet. At intervals traverses made also of sandbags intervened. We noticed, too, extensive sandbagged construction of the parados or rear of the breastwork, but came at length to a portion practically open where we halted at a whispered order—passed along.

The lance-corporal of the Middlesex machine-gun section (they were the 4th Regulars) took our corporal under his wing and a few moments later we were sharing a shelter made in a traverse about three feet six inches high, with several sleeping Middlesex men. There appeared to be a kind of front porch consisting of two pieces of galvanised sheeting laid across two sandbag walls, with a few bags laid across the top for added protection.

Their Vickers gun was mounted in an emplacement in the breastworks which had two slits for fields of fire and a steel-girdered roof, but the gunners on duty were doing their turn on the adjacent firestep outside the emplacement; and at this point we found that we were not relieving them, but were with them for instruction.

Personally, I was very pleased to hear this, the more so when I was detailed for immediate duty with one of the Middlesex, taking the place of the two men on the firestep.

As I took my stand with him for the first time, I did not know how lucky we were to have our first taste of warfare under the guidance of such experienced teachers. Many times subsequently had we reason to appreciate that initial tour of duty with them— and with their comrades of the 4th Royal Fusiliers who relieved them. As I have said, they were Regulars, and at the time we met them were recovering from their ordeal in the terrible second battle of Ypres. They still contained a good sprinkling of the real old hands; many of them back with the regiment after recovering from wounds received during 1914 and early 1915. Before we had passed many minutes in their company, we knew ourselves for what we were—absolute novices at the game (if you can call war that), and it is very doubtful whether we as a battalion ever approached these units as a fighting machine, even after we had become inured to hardship and familiar with most forms of frightfulness. Whether it was the effect of contact with 'Kitchener's men' I don't know, but to our way of thinking every man seemed to possess an intangible something which inspired confidence; a calm self-reliance bred of discipline and a constant contact with death over a period of many months.

July 1915.

Breast Works – Wulverghem

Such were the 4th Middlesex and the 4th Royal Fusiliers. At that stage they were old in experience of war, but subsequent events must have demanded further tremendous sacrifices of them. I make no excuse for digressing to pay tribute to these fine remnants of the old British Army of 1914.

I stood upon the firestep with my new pal with no little trepidation, having previously fixed my bayonet and charged the magazine of my rifle as instructed by the N.C.O. of the Middlesex. He, after a few moments, left to show our corporal his Vickers gun, while he, equally, was interested in our new Lewis. It appeared that neither was to be fired unless 'Jerry' attacked, as it would disclose their position and invite trouble—'too bloody right it would!'

The rest of our section got under the shelter and tried to sleep. Everything was quiet save for occasional odd rifle shots and the plop of the Verey lights, although my mate fired off questions at me by the dozen in a low voice. 'What is it like in Blighty now?' and so on, while I in turn made many inquiries about our surroundings.

Apparently our line ran in front of the village of Wulverghem; Kemel Hill and Ypres were to the north—Armentières and La Bassée to the south. I was deep in my subject when my face was smothered with dirt from a split sandbag on the parapet. The cra-crack of the German rifle seemed to come slightly after the dirt, but I suppose I ducked a second or so afterwards, because my partner lay against the parapet laughing so heartily that I had to join in, although I was in no hurry to resume my original position. The realization that a few inches might have made all the difference between that split sandbag and a bullet through my head put me into a cold sweat and for a moment the hair on the back of my head seemed to rise. My neck ached through trying to sink it into my shoulders.

'Meant to tell yer abaht 'im mate—'e lets fly nah and then— soon get used to 'im though as long as yer 'ead ain't sticking right over. Never you mind what the officers tell yer, look between the chinks in the bags—like this. We'll give 'im one back . . . don't do to let the buggers have it all their own way!'

So saying, he pushed off his safety catch and, thrusting his rifle over the parapet, took a rapid bearing of where he judged the sniper to be. Somewhat awkwardly I prepared to follow his example—when cra-crack again and the shower of earth was repeated. I was crouching like a frightened rabbit when my mate, who had scarcely moved, fired, ejecting the smoking case—aimed and fired again. 'Hev that fer supper, you cheeky sod!' he said as, turning to me, he ejected the empty and, putting on the safety catch once more, stood his rifle against the parapet by his side. Seeing me undecided, he encouraged me, 'yes—go on mate—'ave a go—just to the right of that stake, pretty low—Jerry's only twenty-five yards away 'ere!'

This startling piece of news did not assist my aim as I braced up what courage I could muster and went to the corner of the fire bay, with vivid recollections of my two previous peeps. Timidly taking a look, I felt like a coconut at a fair, but as nothing happened I regained a degree of confidence and became intensely interested in what I saw . . . very little beyond a mass of tangled barbed wire mixed with posts leaning at all angles, behind which there was something—but what, I couldn't make out. I was trying to aim as directed when up went a German Verey light some distance away to our right. 'Keep still!' whispered my mate. I kept still by a supreme effort. My head felt as one's head does when walking by a roof of loose slates on a windy day—but the German line lay revealed in a bluey-white radiance. Their rows of sandbags marking their parapet appeared to be larger and whiter than ours, with wire in front which seemed to merge with ours. The light expired and in the resulting blackness I levelled my rifle hurriedly at the point I had chosen—aimed and fired, ejected, aimed and fired again.

The second empty case tinkled on the duck-board below as I reloaded and put on the safety catch. I felt better. It is fear of the unknown which plays havoc with human courage. Now that I knew only a little of the lie of the land—knew something of what I had to expect and what I had to do—I felt something like a member of the B.E.F. again. My mentor must have sensed this, I suppose, because he grinned a 'thet's it mate!' and to pass the time told me in low tones of Ypres . . . and gas . . . 'Them bloody things are no good!'—indicating the two respirators I carried. 'If Jerry sends over gas, piss on a spare sock and tie it over your nose and mouth That's what we did!'

In that manner did I make my first acquaintance with the front line at Wulverghem, and I repeat that I was lucky, for many times as the war dragged on did we see reinforcement drafts fresh from England subjected to terrible baptisms of shell fire, of attack and counter-attack, before they had had a chance to become familiar with day-to-day life in the trenches—literally, as we used to say, before they could 'dump their packs'.

We spent a week in these trenches, the Middlesex being relieved by the Fusiliers on the fourth evening. Nothing of military importance occurred, although to us almost every minute seemed crammed with incident and I trust I may be pardoned for reminiscing for a few moments.

On the early evening of the Fusiliers' relief, one of our Middlesex friends, an out-and-out cockney, was getting his kit together and was searching—unsuccessfully, we noted—for his greatcoat. At length he exploded, with justifiable annoyance, that 'some lousy bastard had half-inched it'. Thoroughly disgusted, he was fixing his almost empty valise to his equipment, before donning the same minus greatcoat, when a youthful lieutenant of the Fusiliers advance party came along and inquired of our corporal the whereabouts of the company bomb store. As the latter prepared to show him, the officer placed the trench coat which he was carrying on the firestep of our bay and followed the corporal round the traverse. As he disappeared, the Middlesex man seized the coat and stuffed it into his valise. Adjusting the straps, he made a respectable looking pack as he patted it down and then donned the complete equipment, leaning on his rifle as he waited for the relief to commence.

We were just venting our feelings of mingled astonishment and admiration when the owner returned, 'cockney' respectfully drawing up to attention and stepping back to let him pass. 'Have you seen a coat lying about here?' he inquired, running his eye along the firestep and obviously nonplussed.

The Middlesex man looked the picture of innocence as, still standing to attention, he countered, 'Why, sir, have you lost your'n sir?' Muttering something unintelligible, the lieutenant passed on. We whistled—this beat anything we had ever seen and we had just gathered round to ask him how he did it when, to our consternation, the officer re-appeared, this time with a sergeant of the Fusiliers. 'I say, are you chaps quite sure you've not seen a coat lying about here?' he inquired with obvious irritation; whereat the cockney sprang to attention again. 'What sort of one was it, sir?' The lieutenant explained. ''Ad it got tabs on the shoulders, sir?' . . . 'Yes' . . . 'and a belt, sir?' 'Yes—why, have you seen . . . ?' 'No, sir, you've lost them as well then, sir!' The lieutenant literally pushed him on one side and, glaring, hurried on, followed closely by the sergeant, who turned sharply to look back as he disappeared round the traverse. The cockney was still wide-eyed and his expression gave nothing away.

We whistled again—whew! What a nerve! "'E won't come back again,' he chuckled at length as we relaxed again . . . and he didn't, but I retain vivid recollections of hunting in the shelter for my own greatcoat—and of my relief on finding it. No doubt we showed very depraved taste in condoning—nay, openly admiring—such conduct, but we did, although we should have regarded such a theft among pals in a very different light and did, whenever an isolated instance came to our notice. Here, a pal had scrounged another coat—the verb 'to scrounge' being very comprehensive, yet elastic, in its interpretation. Roughly, this term covered appropriation of any British, French or Belgian Government property necessary to the execution of the war, and within reasonable limits this was no crime. We certainly were at war; besides, we had gathered already that in the case of the French or Belgian farmer, he claimed, and generally received, more than adequate compensation for any loss he sustained.

Then there was the episode of our interrupted breakfast, whereby we learned a valuable lesson applicable on the whole of the Western Front. The Fusiliers' machine-gun section had come into the line with a supply of fresh eggs, and the following morning proving fine, several of them proposed a breakfast of eggs and bacon. Following a hunt for dry sticks and a few stones, a small clear fire was soon blazing, and a circle with mess tin lids competing for the fire was soon established. In the morning sunlight we could see but very little smoke and the Fusilier corporal, as he cracked a couple of eggs into his lid, observed that if there *was* a bit—well, Jerry was busy with his own breakfast if he had any sense! I had bought a cracked egg and was waiting for my turn at the fire, when we heard a pop, followed by a swish-swishing sound which faded away for a moment. 'Rifle grenade!' yelled several Fusiliers, starting to their feet and scattering. Instinctively we tried to follow this example as . . . swish–swish–SWISH–BANG! As the ringing in our ears subsided and we had started to sort ourselves out, we saw that the grenade had fallen clean into the fire—now non-existent—and that the stones, though now dislodged, had probably saved us from disaster. Ruefully, we hurriedly collected odd bits of bacon and fried bread—and moved away from the spot now that Jerry had the range. From this experience we learned that with the sun in the east and rising to south, on a fine morning the slightest suggestion of smoke showed up white over our lines. As it was, it really seemed a miracle that some of us at least were not serious casualties.

The Fusiliers utilised us for many of their necessary fatigues, and some of us had our first real taste of pick and shovel work. Among other tasks, such as filling sandbags to repair the ravages of *minnenwerfer* damage, four of us were detailed to excavate a new latrine, and dug for the whole of a boiling August day.

Whether or not in our zeal we threw some of the excavated earth too high, I don't know, but just on midday we were treated to several four-gun salvoes of 'whizz-bangs', apparently all to ourselves, which burst above and behind us before we could look surprised and get down in our hole. Fortunately they then left us in peace, while we continued digging and disposing of the displaced earth as carefully as we could. Then we encountered another snag. First, a very unpleasant smell, then a boot and some shreds of red-brown cloth covering the bones of a human leg. A few more shovelsful and more bones and uniform, including the skull with a kepi still on it, were unearthed; whereon we ceased work while our corporal went away to see what was to be done about it, returning with the Fusiliers' 'sanitary man', who sniffed the air and grinned. 'Dead Froggie, eh? Lots of 'em around 'ere—whiffs a bit, don't 'e! Well, we'll see to 'im. Just fill in there again and we'll put up a bit of revetment to hold 'im in. Open aht on the other side a bit further.'

This meant doing much of our job again and here it was that one of our party, a Leicestershire miner, initiated us into the mysteries of under-cutting whereby, given the necessary face to work at, masses of earth can be dislodged with the minimum of effort. By this means we had made good progress when the sanitary man returned with a box lid which he split and, by using the nails still in it, contrived a rude cross. Then, sucking a stump of copying pencil which turned his lips and tongue a vivid indigo, he inscribed first 'R.I.P.' and then 'HERE LIES UNKNOWN FRENCH SOLDAT'. He then sprinkled chloride of lime copiously and placed his handiwork in position with a professional air, remarking as he did so, '*soldat*, that's French for "swaddy"—done quite a few of these lately.' In the atmosphere of chloride of lime and buzzing flies, we went on with the digging.

One other outstanding recollection I retain of Wulverghem is the Bombing Sergeant of the Fusiliers—an enormous fellow, six foot three at least, and broad in proportion, with a tawny beard. Whether he had cultivated this on active service I know not, but we understood that he was a City of London policeman. Several times daily he would pass along our trench, more often than not in his shirt sleeves, a woollen cap comforter on his head, which emphasised his great height. Whenever he went by, the Fusiliers used to tell us of his exploits and of his charmed life. As though lending colour to these accounts, the morning before we were relieved he came walking along the top of the parapet with the grey dawn at 'stand to', inspecting the wire in leisurely yet thorough fashion, taking absolutely no heed of the odd bullets which always spat and whined at that time of day. I know that at the time we thought him a superman, and cast around in vain for a potential equivalent in our battalion. He was the last man of the Fusiliers we saw that night as we filed into the communication trench, standing at the junction with folded arms, watching us, cap comforter on his head, his jacket loosely buttoned. The glow from his pipe threw into relief his rugged features and beard. I wonder if his luck held for the next three and a half years . . . I wonder . . .

Well I recall leaving the trenches for the first time; how nonchalantly we filed down the communication trench—and no longer ducked at the whine of the ricochetting bullets overhead. We reached the cemetery and the ruined farm-house—the aid post was in the cellar—then the belt of broken trees. Beyond was the field and the sniper fired twice, rather high, so jokes were made as we crossed it. He was way off the mark tonight! We didn't have that squirming 'butterfly' feeling in the stomach; in fact, we were learning our trade.

We turned into a lane by another shattered house and the order was passed along 'you may smoke'; at which there was a hurried search for fag-ends in the little tin boxes that many of us had started to carry, in order to preserve every smokeable fragment of the precious cigarettes. In a few moments we were tramping along contentedly in the glow of burning tobacco, while now and again word came along to us from those in front—'mind the wire' or 'mind the hole!' As we passed the messages along we groped for the objects in question—sometimes successful but more often not—but we were a happy crowd that evening. It was rumoured that the battalion had sustained only six casualties and our own circle was as yet intact.

A little further on we halted and formed fours before marching for nearly three hours and passing through several villages where lights glimmered through chinks in shuttered windows, while here and there figures stood silhouetted at their cottage doors in the yellow lamplight behind them.

Strange how welcome these homely sights were to us after a week's absence from them. From behind came the occasional flashes and reverberations of artillery and Verey lights; before us, we hoped, lay good billets and a good night's rest. Tramping on, we searched our pockets and little boxes for fag-ends hitherto overlooked, or begged tobacco for our pipes where possible. At length we halted in a village street, and after some minutes' delay our section marched into a farmyard, and thence into the barn.

Our lieutenant, after seeing us settled round the walls, went across to the farm-house into which his batman was staggering with his kit, retrieved from the transport lines nearby. The open door, lit by lamplight from the room beyond, looked very inviting, but our straw was quite good enough for us that night.

Hot tea flavoured with rum came along and, by the flickering light of guttering candles, the mail was distributed and blankets issued. Minus boots and puttees, we sat or lay upon the straw, swallowing tea, eating bread and cheese, or whatever unexpired portion of the day's ration remained in our mess tins or haversacks, together with cakes from Blighty; handing round cigarettes or throwing across to our pals our bulging tobacco pouches, replenished by the night's mail. We took out our letters again and went through them in detail; newspapers were opened and items of local interest discussed . . . so it went on for some minutes. Then, as the candles flickered out in streams of wax, we began to feel cold, and one by one we rolled ourselves in our blankets. With our heads upon our packs, we were soon asleep.

CHAPTER 3

FRENCH TRENCHES

DAYLIGHT . . . and the sounds of the farmyard. The great double doors of the barn swung open and the morning sun flooded the interior of our dormitory. The orderly sergeant banged on one of the doors with a hay rake. 'Now then me lucky lads . . . we're off the sunny coast of Spain! Rise and shine . . . half-past seven!'

I doubt whether it is possible to convey here more than an inadequate impression of the feelings which moved us to whistle as we stropped our rusty razors and burst into song as we placed pieces of cracked mirror in precarious but advantageous ledges on the barn framework preparatory to our first shave for some days. The thrill of cold water from the yard pump as we pumped it on to one another, stripped to the waist; the rub-down with our already soap-caked and therefore rough towels. Everyone noticed how different and clean everyone else looked. The sheer luxury of it all! And breakfast—unhurried, taken on couches of straw in the glow of a regained cleanliness, with our mess tin lids swimming in hot bacon fat with bread and a good rasher. No biscuit—four into a loaf that morning! To look out and see around the green fields and the routine farm work proceeding, what a change from our outlook of yesterday!

The sun shone from a clear sky as we unearthed our tins of 'Soldier's Friend' and 'Khaki Blanco' from the recesses of our packs and essayed to make our buttons reflect some of its rays— our webbing cleansed of the grime of Wulverghem.

The battalion remained in the village for three days and then marched off south—we machine-gunners, west, with all our impedimenta and complement of transport. Late in the afternoon of a warm August day we came to St. Silvestre Cappel, where we were billeted, and the week following saw us hard at work on various points of Lewis gun training in the neighbourhood of Cassel under the direction of the brigade machine-gun officer.

We did tactical schemes, and at the sound of a whistle, rushed into action against all kinds of imaginary enemies. It was good training and we needed it after the interval caused by our move from Perham Down. The competition among us as individual gun teams became very keen, intensified by the prizes put up for the best performances in such matters as rectifying stoppages, or filling ammunition drums (a drum or pan held forty-seven rounds, running down a spiral track in the hub of the drum). We became expert at these various exercises, which were to stand us in good stead later on. With plenty of food and clean straw to lie upon at night we felt very fit and were sorry to leave St. Silvestre Cappel one morning for what we gathered was a long railway journey. Speculation was rife.

We marched to Hazebrouck and rejoined the battalion on the troop train. As we loaded our trucks we gleaned that they had been digging reserve trenches at Houplines, near Armentières.

There our company commander, Captain McCutcheon—an American and reputedly the husband of one of the original film stars, Pearl White—had given the command 'stack guns' (he meant 'pile arms') in full view of the enemy on one occasion, who were not slow to take advantage of the target offered, to the annoyance of the Northamptons holding the front line, while 'C' Company had sustained several casualties.

There being difficulty in accommodating some of us on the overcrowded troop train, four of us had the idea of getting into the box-like cabin built high on the end of the truck holding our limbers. In those days there were many built thus—for the comfort, presumably, of goods train guards.

From the window of this precarious coign of vantage we surveyed the great length of the train, feeling rather pleased with ourselves until, with a clanging rising to crescendo as it struck us, we were thrown in a heap as our truck jolted forward, remaining thus as the train negotiated in snake-like fashion the many sets of points outside Hazebrouck station.

Somewhat shaken, we saw that by the position of the afternoon sun, we were heading south, and came to the conclusion on

'TROOP TRAIN' —(HAZEBROUCK—DOULLEN
SEPT. 1915

descending to the floor of the open truck that it was preferable. As evening approached and the sun set, we unrolled the nearest dozen of packed blankets from the pile on the next truck and got into them. Night had fallen when we rolled slowly through a dimly lighted station and read 'St. Pol'. Warm in our blankets we slept fitfully, jerked at intervals into wakefulness.

We knew not whither we were bound, the sense of adventure without responsibility adding to our anticipation of the unknown. The war was forgotten. What youth does not enjoy such a chance when it comes his way? Then, no Pullman car could compare with our shabby old truck labelled 'Est . . . Serie . . . Etiquettes' for the peace of mind it gave us as we rattled through the night beneath the stars. What would not I—and many like me—give to do some such journey again, in the same carefree spirit and with the same strength and zest of youth!

We awoke to the shrill note of a shunter's horn; shrill whistles—incomprehensible shoutings alongside and below. Heavy with sleep, we looked from the darkness of our truck upon the white façade of buildings in a street running alongside the lines; white stuccoed fronts thrown into relief against the starlit sky by the street lamps. Interested, we got to our feet, shivering, and moved around to get warm. A shouting railwayman carrying a lamp came stumbling along, and as he passed we asked him where we were. Startled, he shone his lamp on us. 'Doullens! Doullens!' he shouted, and continued on his way, at the same time making signs that we were detraining. We had never heard of Doullens before; still, as he seemed pretty definite, we sorted ourselves out, rolled the blankets and replaced them; buckled on our equipment. It was 11 p.m., but the town clocks struck twelve before we stood in column of route in the main street, ready to march, and hoping fervently that it would be short, for sleep was now heavy upon all of us and we leaned on our rifles for support.

Clear of the sleeping town and into the moonlit countryside, we could read some of the blue and white signposts of the Route Nationale—'Arras—Mondicourt'. On either side stretched the misty fields bathed in the soft light as we tramped along, for the most part in silence, save for the occasional calls of roosters in distant farms, heralding before their time the coming day—a faerie countryside we looked upon, in this, our first night in Artois.

We marched for the remainder of the night. As the moonlight waned, so did our spirits. We were dead tired and hungry when we halted in the village street of Mondicourt in the grey light of dawn, then filed into our customary barn, grousing, but thankful for a couch at last. The barn was a good one—the straw fresh and clean, and we slept long into the morning.

The battalion stayed here for several days. Mondicourt to us was an unspoiled French village and we were among the first British troops to pass through it. Here, we found that we were relieving French troops in the sector ahead, and it was brought home to us how appallingly ignorant we were of the topography of the country.

We gained some idea in conversation with the inhabitants, and we liked these people. Off duty we sat in the *estaminets* and sampled *vin rouge*, *vin blanc* and various combinations with syrups, such as citron and grenadine.

The abundant evidences of French military life also interested us. To our eyes they were not smart and they didn't seem to bother to keep in step on the march; their transport arrangements showed an infinite variety. We were, however, impressed by their physique. Having been brought up on the doctrine that an English-man was worth so many Frenchmen, we were surprised; more, however, by a battery of the famous 75s—*les Soixante-Quinze*—reputed to have a faster rate of fire than our 18-pounders and a better gun all round. Here again, we didn't see the 'spit and polish' of British artillery—but somehow they looked very business-like, the N.C.O.s, especially, tough and efficient. The horses were unshorn, their harness dull, but they looked well fed. In later years we were to find that their ways differed greatly from ours, but they had a way of getting there just the same with, I believe proportionately fewer casualties. Maybe the French learned their lesson in August and September of 1914 when, in their enthusiasm for *l'attaque*, clothed in baggy red trousers, white spats and long blue coats, they had suffered enormous casualties in a series of frontal attacks in mass. I'm afraid the British Command didn't learn until 1918!

The last day of our stay at Mondicourt was marred by a tragedy involving the loss of several lives and terrible injuries to a further dozen men of our battalion.

Months of trench warfare had emphasized the need for trained bombing sections; also, for an efficient grenade for them to use. In this, however, the German stick grenade, as in the case of most weapons, was far superior to the many amateurish devices which our men were called upon to learn. The No. 5 Mills grenade was not issued, to the best of my recollection, until the spring of 1916.

Our newly formed bombing sections were receiving specialized instruction in a field on the outskirts of the village, in the use of the Mexican stick grenade. From what we gathered from survivors, the man under instruction was being shown how to throw it, when he dropped it on a nearby box. The result in a crowded circle can be imagined. It was supposed that, in error, the grenade was

L U. P. P.   CLICHÉ LECLERC - HÉNU

Berles-au-Bois (P.-de-C.) L'Eglise

detonated. Already, although we had seen little of the front line, we were appreciably fewer than when we landed.

At Mondicourt I was fortunate enough to annex a map of northern France from an officer's batman, and from that day was never completely in the dark as to our actual whereabouts. When we marched the next morning, I thought that Arras was our destination, but near the village of Saulty we left the main road, forking right and east and crossing the railway. Saulty was apparently the French railhead for the sector; it certainly became ours. We now heard plainly the occasional rumble of artillery fire, and passed more and more French details marching away or billeted in the farm-houses. At the village of Humbercamps we saw reserve trenches, and at the eastern end of the next village — Pommier, by name—more trenches and a French sentry standing at the sandbagged barricade on the road. In the late afternoon we proceeded by platoons at two-hundred-yard intervals. We machine-gunners went as the battalion section and last of all, this necessitating a long wait in the village street until our turn came. As no wheeled transport proceeded further in daylight, we had to carry much of our kit, and the reason for this was not hard to seek. On the skyline in front we could see, as we passed the barricade, a German observation balloon.

Before us the country road continued level for about three hundred yards, then fell gently away into a valley of neglected fields pitted with shell holes, to re-appear on the further slope about a kilometre or so distant. Sinuously it wound its way among belts of barbed wire and stakes to a cluster of dark trees, above which peeped a visibly damaged church spire, while dotted amid the trees, weathered tiled roofs of houses showed here and there. As we marched toward the village, the late afternoon sun lit the whole scene and the chanticleer on the bent weather vane of the damaged spire reflected it in a point of gold. On either side of the village stretched a ridge of weed-grown fields, bare save for expanses of wire entanglement; beyond, the German observation balloon in the far distance. In the pock-marked valley, we could see a row of gun pits camouflaged with foliage and turfed earthworks.

Twenty minutes or so brought us to the barricaded entrance to the village, and here our officer was approached by a French lieutenant who, after exchanging salutes, led us to the great double gates in an archway leading to the courtyard of a farm-house. Here stood thirty or more French soldiers with all their mitrailleuse equipment, ready to move off. A few minutes' conversation sufficed for our officer and sergeant to look over the billet with their French counterparts and imbibe any information our allies had to

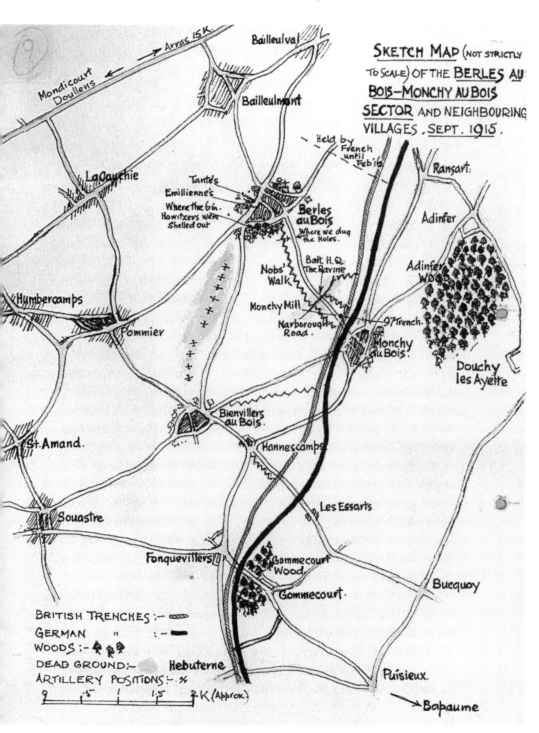

SKETCH MAP (NOT STRICTLY TO SCALE) OF THE **BERLES AU BOIS—MONCHY AU BOIS** SECTOR AND NEIGHBOURING VILLAGES. SEPT. 1915.

Arras 15 K.

Bailleulval

Mondicourt Doullens

Bailleulmont

Held by French until Feb'16

Ransart

La Cauchie

Tante's
Emilienne's
Where the 6 in. Howitzers were Shelled out

Berles au Bois

Where we dug the Holes.

Adinfer

Adinfer Wo.

Nobs' Walk

Batt. H.Q. The Ravine

Humbercamps

Monchy Mill

Narborough Road.

97 Trench.

Monchy au Bois.

Pommier

Douchy les Ayette

Bienvillers au Bois.

St. Amand.

Hannescamps

Souastre

Les Essarts

Fonquevillers

Gommecourt Wood

Buequoy

Gommecourt.

BRITISH TRENCHES :—
GERMAN   "   :—
WOODS :—
DEAD GROUND:—
ARTILLERY POSITIONS :— ×

Hebuterne

Puisieux.

0   ·5   1   1·5   2 K (Approx.)

→ Bapaume

35

give. Then the *poilus* fell in and their transport drivers mounted their shaggy ponies. Called to attention with the knowledge that Frenchmen were watching us, we 'sloped hipe' and came to the 'Present' like a machine, standing like ramrods while the French lieutenant, gravely returning our salute, called on his men to march. So we relieved the 69th Chasseurs in the village of Berles-au-Bois. Our battalion was now there in reserve, the front line having been taken over by our 6th Battalion that morning. As far as we could tell, things were pretty quiet up there.

We now had leisure to examine our billet and make ourselves comfortable, if possible, before night fell. As neither house or barns was inhabited there was plenty of room, and we soon saw that our predecessors had known how to make the best of their good fortune. There was a profusion of wire-netting beds in the room our gun team had bagged, and as we threw down our equipment and stood our rifles and Lewis impedimenta against the walls, we marvelled at the many clever crayon and pencil sketches upon the walls—of girls either in the nude or in various ravishing states of *déshabillé*. There was not any doubt that the unknown artist was a professional; perhaps, we speculated, on the staff of *La Vie Parisienne* or *Pêle-Mêle*. Apparently most of the other rooms had received similar treatment. This alone put everyone in high good humour, and having escaped sentry and fatigue duty, we went outside for a look round while the light held. We found that there was a deep well of first-class water at our door, fitted with brand new winding gear by the French engineers or Genie; also some good cellars under the house, which we examined through narrow grilles at ground level. The kitchen garden and orchard, filled to our disgust with red cider apples, were crossed by a reserve trench protected by a belt of barbed wire, part of reserve defences behind the village. At the end of the garden wall, however, we found an exit through the wire and saw similar exits leading to several cottages which we discovered were in a lane.

At first we thought they were deserted, but almost at once were surprised to see a woman leading a cow emerge from a small paddock which adjoined our orchard, and we walked her way to see where she lived.

Coming up to her, we observed that she was a woman of about

forty, maybe younger, but with features lined by constant toil and exposure to the weather. She wore a poke bonnet with a black shawl pinned across her shoulders, while wisps of straw protruded from her clumsy looking wooden sabots. Returning our greeting cheerily when we asked her whether she lived near by, she replied in the affirmative, pointing up the narrow cart track to which we had come, at the second of the roofs visible among the trees. We walked with her, mentally determining, I remember, to return to our billet with some fresh milk if possible—a very welcome change from the 'Ideal' variety. Arrived opposite her cottage door within a small yard, we noticed outbuildings at the side and rear and heard the grunting of several pigs and the cackling of hens. At these sounds we looked at each other knowingly—here was a piece of luck!

Madame tied the cow to a ring in the wall outside and entered, motioning to us to do the same. As we did so we noticed that there was no upstairs, all accommodation being on ground level, the rooms connected by simple doors. The stuccoed walls were badly pocked and the roof damaged by two shells which had dropped on the cobbles in the yard at different times. The French engineers had repaired the roof with several sheets of corrugated iron. Several hens scratched in one shell hole, and I asked Madame where she was when it dropped. Her face lit up as she pointed to a Windsor-type chair standing to one side of the long, bowl-shaped stove, then to a crucifix and image of the Virgin and Child over the mantelshelf. They protected her and her mother, she said simply, making a quick devotional sign. I remember that we were profoundly affected by her words and, seeming to notice this, she turned and shouted into the recesses of the further room, 'Maman! . . .'

With much shuffling and coughing, Maman appeared within the circle of mellow light cast by the oil lamp which her daughter was now lighting. The old lady walked with difficulty and with the aid of a stick. Age and a lifetime of toil in the fields had bent her almost double, and her features were wrinkled like a dried pea. As Madame assisted her to the armchair on the far side of the stove she made a gesture of introducing us, which the old lady acknowledged with a turn of the head and the ghost of a smile as she sat down; the while we marvelled at the presence of these good people in a spot so exposed to the hazards of war. Then, seeing Madame bustle about with pails, baskets and whatnot, and anxious to assist, we inquired whether we could help her, standing there as we four did before the glowing bowl of the stove—the genial giant Horace Phillips from Uppingham, Ted Lineker from Leicester, Freddy Smith from Shepshed in Leicestershire and myself, from Leicester too.

With an exclamation and a laugh, Madame pushed the blushing Phillips into a chair, thrusting a coffee mill into his lap and making signs for him to grind some coffee. At her direction we put it in a large copper bowl of hot water on the stove as he produced it. We lit our pipes—for this was good—and we took turns with the coffee mill as Madame prepared to go and milk the now-protesting cow. At this, Phillips rose and tried to take the pails away from her, saying that he would have a shot at milking the cow. Shaking with mirth, she put the pails down on the floor behind her. '*Ah! vous brigand!*' she exclaimed amid the general laughter, in which Phillips joined.

'Brigand, am I?' he said, still laughing. 'I can milk a cow, anyhow.' Saying which, he made a quick feint and, seizing the pail, went outside, followed by the now-agitated woman. The door closed behind them and we went on grinding coffee, the while making several ineffectual attempts to converse with the old lady, who seemed to be stone deaf.

Madame returned, all smiles. '*Ah, mais il est bon garçon, votre ami!*' We tiptoed to the window and there, sure enough, sat Horace Phillips, his cap stuck sideways between his cheek and the cow's flank, turning a straw in his lips and milking away as to the manner born. He seemed perfectly happy and so we left him alone.

Madame laid out half a dozen small bowls on the table, returning from the cupboard for the second time with a bottle and some wine glasses.

In the midst of these preparations, we heard voices outside and stamping as of mud from dirty boots. The door opened and three French soldiers in full equipment, laughing apparently at Phillips, came in with many animated exclamations to Madame, who, we noticed, they called *Tante*. Having been very informally introduced, the *poilus* indicated that they could only stay a few moments, but had come to say, '*au 'voir*' to *Tante*, perched themselves on the table, back to back for mutual support, for they resembled Christmas trees, loaded as they were with packs, blankets, spare

WE RELIEVED THEM AT BERLES AU BOIS.
SOME OF THE 69me. BATAILLON CHASSEURS.

Lucien Petitjean
gave me this photo
at Berles au Bois.
He was severely wounded
FRENCH OFFENSIVE IN
CHAMPAGNE
25.9.1915.

"MORT POUR LA PATRIE"

"MORT POUR LA PATRIE"

boots, cooking pots, water bottles, souvenirs, besides rifles and cartridge pouches. They leaned upon the rifles for support, while we asked them all kinds of questions and answered as many.

They told us that *Tante* had been very good to them during their stay at Berles-au-Bois and that we should find her a good friend. They were sturdy fellows of medium stature and in their prime—one fair, the other two dark—their moustaches accentuating the two distinct types. The bugles and figures upon the collars of their long blue coats proclaimed them of the 69th Chasseurs. They told us that they were the last of their regiment to leave Berles.

Here Phillips came in with the milk, greeted on all sides with

TANTE'S COTTAGE —
BERLES AU BOIS. SEPT. 1915.

warm expressions of approval, which he acknowledged with a broad grin as we introduced him. When he gave his name, *Tante* jumped up. 'Phillipe Auguste! Phillipe Auguste!' she cried delightedly, indicating his great stature, whereat the Frenchmen rocked with amusement, in which we joined. *Tante* thrust a glass into his hand and then served coffee and cognac all round. We stood, save for the old lady in the corner. *Tante* gave the toast, holding her glass towards the French soldiers and then towards us, with deep feeling: '*Bonne chance mes enfants . . . et bonne santé!*' Silently we clinked glasses, each with all, and drank. One of the *poilus* searched in his wallet and produced a photograph of his section resting by the roadside. He wrote on the back of it and handed it to me. I have it by me now. Then one looked at his watch and, with a hurried exclamation, reached for his rifle. Hastily they hitched up their equipment and kissed *Tante* and her mother in the French fashion, afterwards shaking hands with us in turn. More hurried '*au 'voirs*' and '*bonnes chances*' and the door closed behind them. *Tante* stood looking at the empty glasses on the table, her eyes suspiciously wet.

Pointing in the direction of the door, she tried to make us understand. '*Partis pour Champagne*' she said, repeating it several times—which showed that her words had not penetrated our thick skulls at first. Actually, we didn't know whether Champagne was ten kilometres away or five hundred and she could see our bewilderment. We had heard of the drink, of course, but none of us had ever sampled any. In 1914 the word 'champagne' conjured up visions of the aristocracy, of rich people, racehorse owners, bookies, actresses—to us almost another world.

Madame thought it was about 150 kilometres and this showed, incidentally, that she was far more conversant with the general scheme of operations than we were, who knew only what was occurring within a few hundred yards or so of where we chanced to be. At the time, her remark conveyed little to us, and certainly we had no idea of the implied import.

Only about a month afterwards, on coming out of the line one evening, we friends went to *Tante*'s for eggs and milk and found her sitting at the table wiping her eyes. When we asked what was amiss, she thrust a letter into our hands which we could ill

'PARTIR POUR CHAMPAGNE'
THE 60+L CHASSEURS A PIED
BID TANTE ADIEU

BERLES AU BOIS, SEPT. 1915.

decipher, but she did not wait for this. With many expressions of
grief she told us that two of our three friends had been killed—the
dark ones—and the third, the fair one, was wounded and in
hospital near Arles. This had occurred in the first onset of the
great French offensive thrust in Champagne in the last week of

42

September 1915, when the British and French attacked simultaneously in the north around Loos.

Before we returned to our billet that evening, she told us that
her husband was in the Argonne with a territorial regiment; that
he was called up on General Mobilization in August 1914; that
she had not seen him for six months; that, as far as she knew,
though, he was well, as she had frequent letters from him.

We stumbled back to our billet in pitch blackness, as the sky
was overcast and the moon had not yet risen. Stray shots echoed
occasionally over the silent countryside—once, the whine of a
spent bullet, like a lost soul. The local artillery was quiet.

If this was a sample of the sector, we said to ourselves, things
looked cushy up there. From far away to the north came the dull
rumbling of heavy guns, but it was faint and intermittent. After a
supper of real eggs, and cocoa with real milk, we retired to our
netting beds very content.

The next morning most of us were detailed for a working party
in the reserve line, and our first job was to collect picks and shovels
from a newly set-up R.E. dump in the centre of the village. Armed
with these, we marched along the road to the eastern exit of the
village to a barricade of cylindrical fascines filled with earth. here
we noticed the start of the communication trench to the front line,
within the barn of a deserted farm-house in a belt of trees, guarded
by a sentry post of our 'A' Company. It was, therefore, with some
apprehension that we followed the officer, who carried a large-
scale map, for about two hundred yards past it, along the road to
a crucifix. Here the road forked, from which the view extended
for several miles to the east, to our left front, to the mass of a
dark and rather sinister-looking wood on the horizon, above which
two German observation balloons had risen. Signs of the trench
lines were in evidence in plenty, the nearest little over a mile away,
where a huddle of broken trees and jumbled roofs marked the
village of Monchy-au-Bois, according to our officer, just behind
the German line.

We took the right fork, proceeding in leisurely fashion down
the road directly toward the trenches for about five hundred yards,
the lieutenant checking off successive belts of wire on his map. In a
few moments we were given the task of excavating pits for two

machine-gun emplacements to command the road from either side. The lieutenant then left us to start another party elsewhere on similar work; whereon we vented our feelings on our sergeant with considerable warmth—grousing which he tried only half-heartedly to check. Nevertheless we dug with a will, and by mid morning, which was overcast, had made a large hole on each side of the road.

Things were very quiet and we were standing in our hole for a breather when we heard two bangs afar off, and simultaneously

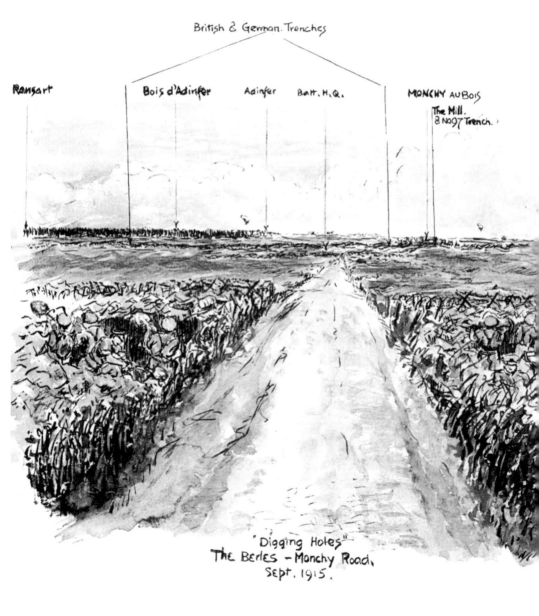

"Digging Holes"
The Berles – Monchy Road,
Sept. 1915.

the rush and explosion of the arriving shells. For registering shots they were a pretty good effort for the German gunners: one burst on the road and one in the air about fifty yards short. We felt that more were coming, and we didn't have to wait long, either, for in about two minutes we had received two salvoes of four shells, which tipped much of our excavation back on top of us, numbed our senses and rendered us partially deaf. The fumes, too, were choking. However, no one had been hit so far, but our position was altogether too warm, especially as we had been put up as targets so suddenly. Two more salvoes arrived. As the smoke drifted away, we needed no second bidding as our sergeant yelled to both parties to get back independently. 'Keep low at the sides of the road and don't leave those damned tools behind!' We were pretty bunched up in our anxiety, I'm afraid, being speeded on our way by two salvoes of shrapnel. Fortunately for us, the fuses were set somewhat too long. This made us scatter in all directions—very happily for some of us, who blundered through some long and dead grass and weeds into a disused communication trench. Here we lay panting, and, after a breather, shouted to the rest to join us. This they did, and, taking our time, we followed the trench back in the direction of the village, emerging eventually quite close to the barricade across the road.

I have said that this was by a farm-house in a belt of trees at the eastern end of the village, and back on the safer side of the barricade we were amazed to see, along a cart track running through the trees, two six-inch howitzers, around which the gunners were building shields of timber baulks camouflaged with green netting. In view of our recent experience, we thought that the enemy had probably spotted them already. We just could not understand the mentality of the staff concerned who had ordered the placing of these pieces in such an exposed position.

We were only privates of infantry, but we could tell that, immediately they fired, they would be seen. It was incomprehensible. Still, we left them to it as we 'fell in' and marched back to our billet. Eventually our lieutenant returned in a bad temper, having visited our position and found no one there. When informed of the circumstances, however, he laughed and expressed his regret, saying that he had only carried out his orders. His representations to Brigade must have been heeded, for that evening he appeared with an amended scheme, whereby we had to construct a reserve emplacement in the trench by which we had escaped in the morning. From his map, this trench had a branch which joined the main communication trench. We had missed this, I suppose, because of the long grass and weeds. So long as we did not repeat the risk we had run already, we did not mind, and early next morning we were on the spot, digging with a will and taking every possible precaution to avoid observation.

We were put in the charge of a sergeant of R.E.s, and by early afternoon had dug a hole sufficiently large for his purpose. During the morning a fatigue party had deposited a number of six-inch steel girders and lengths of substantial timber. We were becoming quite interested, when there was a shattering 'bang' from immediately behind us. We felt the sudden wind from the explosion and distinctly saw the shell speeding towards the German lines like a disappearing pea. Standing up, we awaited the burst and, sure enough, saw a sudden spurt of smoke and brown rubble rise from the gaunt trees and shattered houses of Monchy, which lay two hundred yards downhill from the German front line. Another, then another repeated the dose several times; then all was quiet again. Uneasily, we hoped that Jerry wouldn't retaliate that afternoon, but we were pretty sure he had observed the flash—we saw it plainly. We were lucky, though, and returned to our billet healthily tired, with plenty to talk about. The next morning we returned, reinforced this time by a corporal and sapper of R.E.s to superintend the completion of the emplacement. On the way we were told by one of the gunners that they had the second howitzer in position and were doing a 'shoot' at noon.

He had seen us on the previous day and thought that we were working in a dangerous position, as sometimes they had a 'premature'—a shell bursting at the muzzle. Spurred on by this news, we were hastening to put as many uprights and girders in position before midday, when we heard shouted commands from the rear, followed by the first report.

The shoot then started in earnest, continuing—as shoots did in those days—for nearly an hour at intervals of about five minutes, at the end of which a drifting brown haze partially obscured the village of Monchy. Then all was quiet again and we went on working with added zest, as our efforts were now taking definite shape. Several layers of sandbags were placed on the roof, then some soil was shovelled back on top. From the inside, through the two long slits, we had good fields of fire, and were so absorbed in this that we did not hear the approach of the heavy shell which burst about thirty yards away. When the usual pattering of earth and iron had subsided, we looked out to see the floating pall of dirty grey smoke between us and the howitzer position, and, with no little misgiving, awaited the arrival of the next.

We didn't wait long. Shell after shell hurtled overhead in rapid succession, now apparently right on the target. There was a pause of a few minutes and then another rain of shells, some of it shrapnel and bursting, it seemed, in the village itself, but the majority over the howitzer position. Spouts of red-brown rubble shot into the air and cascades of slates and tiles clattered to earth after almost every explosion.

The shelling ceased, the air slowly cleared. I'm afraid we completed our task in half-hearted fashion that afternoon. We were itching to retrace our steps and find out what had happened. At length, about five o'clock, we filed back into the main communication trench, which ran parallel with the edge of the trees for some yards before tunnelling under the wall of the barn, where it emerged to ground level. We came upon a shambles, and had to pick our way over fallen trunks of trees, baulks of timber, brickwork from the barn and piles of tiles.

We could see where the howitzers had been, although the positions had been battered out of recognition save for a stack of shells and some scattered boxes of charges. We couldn't linger, though, as some artillery officers—one with red tabs—arrived. They were laughing—apparently with some reason, for, by great good fortune only one howitzer had been damaged, and the story went that the battery sergeant major had lost his jacket containing 500 francs when it was hit. The other howitzer had been hurriedly manhandled back into the village street. Three gunners had been hit. The N.C.O. and six men of our 'A' Company doing guard in the barn at the top of the communication trench were full of their troubles, as they no longer had a roof over their heads. All the tiles and some of the rafters had gone.

Back in the village the natives were shaking their heads ominously, and all looking anxiously at the fabric and roofs of their cottages. A lot of fresh damage was apparent. One or two great black and white holes, surrounded by heaps of dislodged material, now showed in the road. From what our mates in the billet told us, we had been in about the best place, for now our barn was minus much of the roof, while a great hole and an uprooted apple tree at the entrance to the orchard were evidence enough of unwelcome visitors.

As soon as we could, several of us ran across to *Tante*'s to see how the two women had fared, and we were relieved to find them unharmed. While *Tante* filled a cap with eggs and a mess tin with milk, we exchanged comments on the day's doings.

She said many uncomplimentary things about the Germans, finally shrugging her shoulders with the remark then usual among French people, '*c'est la guerre!*'. But when we expressed our indignation at the shockingly inept planning of those responsible, she told us, with no little vigour, that French artillery officers had begged our people not to place the howitzers so—but to no purpose. This we could very well believe. At least another two years were to elapse before some of the 'staffs' at least had learned their lessons—and, of sheer necessity, had replaced those who would not learn, even by experiences such as this.

We relieved our 6th Battalion early on the morning of their completion of six days in the front line. The French front line trenches were deep and appeared to be well made, the sides being lined and shored up with wattle and brushwood revetments and fascines. At intervals along the trench floor, deep holes covered by wooden gratings had been dug for drainage (our R.E.s called them 'sumps').

At the point where we relieved the Lewis gun section of the 6th Battalion, they told us we were about fifty yards from the enemy; where, in fact, the road from Berles to Monchy crossed the trenches of both sides. There was no sign of the road. As we peered curiously through a chink between two sandbags, we could see through the morning haze the ruins of the village of

Monchy-au-Bois a few hundred yards away down a gentle slope behind the German trenches. We judged our position to be almost at the crest of this slope, this being marked, as we looked cautiously to our rear, by the ruins of a windmill surrounded by festoons of rusty barbed wire. The disused road was scarcely distinguishable. Our curiosity attracted the attention of the enemy snipers, for bullets began to smack into the parados behind, too near to be pleasant. Discretion therefore curbed our curiosity for the time being.

Our Lewis gun was mounted in a masked emplacement upon its Vickers tripod, the field of fire slits being covered by steel plates which could be moved only in emergency. A fairly sound dugout provided reasonable, if somewhat cramped, accommodation in a short zig-zagged trench actually some ten yards behind, but at least twenty yards to walk. The dugout had four steps down, and we noted that the ceiling was of railway sleepers. On either side of us were men of our 'A' Company, the right company of our battalion. They connected with our 9th Battalion, who had relieved the 7th as we had the 6th. They used their own communication trench, back to the village of Bienvillers au Bois.

By mid morning we had shaken down in our new surroundings, and the single sentry posted at the relief on the firestep at the side of the emplacement was expressing his hope that we had left him a decent place in the dugout. Perhaps because he felt bored, he placed his cap on his bayonet and held his rifle so that the cap appeared above the sandbags. Almost at once there was a sharp double crack and the cap sailed on to the parados behind, while the rifle and its holder were knocked back into the trench, very much surprised—a feeling we shared with him. There followed a general outburst of merriment, during which one chap signalled 'bull' with a French noticeboard he'd found. No shots were fired at this, but we distinctly heard voices and deep laughter, and came to the conclusion that the enemy were trying to read the contents of the noticeboard. The owner of the cap had to wait until nightfall before he could retrieve it, to find that rats had gnawed the peak and lining, in addition to a clean double hole made by the bullet.

Apart from this diversion, that first day—indeed, the first six days—passed almost uneventfully, save for occasional salvoes of whizz-bangs apparently aimed at the mill, which did us no damage. The snipers were no worry in these deep trenches. In fact, we became bored and played a lot of solo, pontoon and brag when off duty. There were endless discussions, too, on dealing with the rats. We did, however, make a start in retaliating to the enemy's sniping activity, and to that end established an observation post near the top of our dugout, amid the tall grass and weeds on the slightly higher ground immediately in rear of our front line trench. This served us well for some weeks, as two men could lie flat here fairly safe, unless Jerry was shelling or sending over *minnenwerfers* or rifle grenades. One could peer between clods of turned-up earth, masked by the rank weeds of two summers, and observe several hundred yards of enemy trenches. By a system of small sticks placed in position relative to a 'master' stick, stuck in the clay in front with infinite care, we marked the approximate positions of several of these gentry. We never fired from this position, however, but checked from the front line in the evening or haze of the early morning.

We were duly relieved by the 6th Battalion and filed out to our old billet in Berles. It was said that the battalion had sustained six casualties, although *Tante* said that the French score was no more in six months. 'If the Boches didn't fire, they didn't—but if they did, then the French—BOUM—BOUM! Two shots for one!' This had been very satisfactory, and the people in the village were not bothered *par les obus*—until the British came.

On the way out we noticed that the name of the communication trench down to battalion H.Q.—'Boyau de Mille Delices'—had been changed to 'Narborough Road', and thence to Berles 'Nottage's Folly' and 'Nobs' Walk'. Rumour had it that Nottage was an R.E. officer—a sapper. Whether the 'folly' was due to the fact that in winter the trench here was always flooded, and whether his men had interfered with the French drainage arrangements, we never did find out. Actually, so many other events occupied our days and nights from then on, that no one bothered very much.

CHAPTER 4

AUTUMN MANOEUVRES

IN the days that followed, our lieutenant told us of an imminent speeding up of operations. Apparently from 'Top Level', word had gone to Division, thence to Brigade, that we could never beat the Boche by sitting down quietly in front of him, as the French in our sector had been content to do. Things were to be livened up considerably. We were out to win the war, as quickly as possible . . . etc., etc. As a start, our brigade machine-gun officer wished us to commence indirect fire at night, at almost maximum range, on the road leading from Adinfer to Monchy—whence came the German ration parties every evening. A firing point had been chosen in the garden of an empty cottage near the south-west end of the village. The section on duty could stay in the cottage. As there were four sections of us—'A', 'B', 'C' and 'D'—and ours was 'C', we figured that our turn would come three nights hence, and in this we were right. Actually, we were all very interested and welcomed some definite action—the more so on the morning following the return of 'A' Company section. Commencing at 'stand to' as evening fell, they fired three short bursts every half-hour until midnight, resuming for an hour, half an hour before morning 'stand to'. They reported that the cottage was a good one, that they had a good fire going all night and plenty of 'char' (Hindustani for tea) and cocoa; also they had cooked welsh rarebit with their cheese ration. Everyone had been keen to fire the gun, which the lieutenant had set on a compass bearing with the range, as I remember, about 1,600 yards. Altogether it had been good fun and we had, of course, heard the rat-tat-tat-tat at intervals; faster than the Vickers or German M.G.S., it seemed to us.

On the third evening, after meticulous checking of the gun, spare parts and ammunition drums, we paraded and marched up

Evening "Stand To" —
No. 97 Trench . Monchy au Bois . Sept. 1915.

the village street in the dusk to the firing point. As we approached
the cottage, we heard a series of peculiar whining sounds, punctuated now and then by sharpish smacks and tinkling as broken
pieces of tile and slate descended from the roofs of adjacent houses.
Then, in the distance, the slow but quite distinct pat-pat-pat. Jerry
was playing us at our own game, but if he was trying to hit our
ration parties, we laughed, he was wide of the mark.

Thereafter we spent a most interesting and enjoyable night, and I well remember my excitement when my turn came to fire the three short bursts about 9 p.m.—the first time I'd fired a Lewis against the enemy. Luckily I had no stoppages—frequent in those days because of the poor quality of much of the ammunition, some of it made, incidentally, in the U.S.A.

Several times that night the bullets whined over from the other side, sometimes like lost souls, and the occasional 'smacks' nearby indicated their descent, but with morning we packed up and returned to the billet well satisfied, anticipating a lazy day after a good sleep. On rising for the midday 'gyppo', or stew, however, we heard that our mates in other sections had faced scorn and open hostility from the 6th Battalion quartermaster's staff and some of our 'B' Company, who had been on ration and stores parties the previous evening down the Berles–Monchy road. Apparently Jerry's ranging was a lot better there. A mule had been hit, and it had been quite a nasty experience for them after the usual quiet.

In the billet we discussed again what *Tante* had told us about the French, and argument became quite heated at times. Which view was right? Maybe the French were wrong, but there was no doubt that our staff, brigade and division, having shaken down in their new surroundings, were now obsessed with the idea of having some positive action against the enemy. Unfortunately, however, with a few outstanding exceptions, our commanders were either Regulars who had risen, because of the war, to heights of command beyond their wildest dreams in peacetime, and therefore were largely unused to the ranks they were filling; or they were 'dugout' officers who had pulled all the strings they could in high places to obtain re-employment. In view of the acute shortage, only too many were successful. After a few months experience of them—without sight of scarcely one of them—that's how we of the rank and file summed up matters. After all, we were only amateur soldiers ourselves, but we were learning the hard way. We were still brimming over with zeal, well primed by the dictum, passed down through several generations, that an Englishman was worth so many foreigners. Our 'Contemptible Little Army' had, in fact, demonstrated the truth of this. If only there had been more of them. Now they were coming over. Jerry—look out!

Today this is as difficult to describe as it must be difficult for present-day youth to comprehend. There is no doubt, however, that at that time volunteers would have rushed forward to take part in the most crack-brained scheme thought up by half-trained staffs. As I have said previously, two years were to elapse before some, at least, of the generals were men trained in the hard school of the war—and not the last—who, before they sent men on errands of death, weighed the risks in the light of personal experience in the field; who, at their level, fought the enemy by tactical means, and not merely by brute force and the bulldog tradition.

I have digressed, in trying to convey to the youth of this generation the mentality and general outlook of mine, but I feel that, in view of the fundamental differences, I should make an attempt, however briefly, to explain some reasons for these. Otherwise some of the events hereafter described may seem beyond comprehension, so fantastic do they appear in retrospect—even to me.

In Britain, the years 1914–1918 saw the beginning of the end of what might be termed a feudally stratified and very sharply defined social order. At the summit were, say, ten thousand largely titled families of landed aristocracy and their connections, whose sons provided the politicians, the Foreign Office, most Established Churchmen of rank, and the majority of the top-ranking army officers, especially of the cavalry and the guards regiments. The remaining Regular Army officers were drawn either from families having a long military tradition, or from those of professional men, such as lawyers, doctors, parsons and bankers.

Although the above classes would have business dealings with the manufacturing and trading sections of the community, there was little social contact. 'Trade' was frowned upon. It was difficult for a grocer's son to be accepted by one of the better known public schools, and practically impossible for him to become an army officer; in other words, he wasn't a 'gentleman' according to the conception of the term then current. (A few years previously King Edward VII had scandalized these circles by encouraging the society of a wealthy grocer and financier. It was unheard of, and stiffened the ranks of high society against further intrusion.) Money in 1914 certainly did not confer with it the status that it would do today; neither did educational attainment, as such. What counted was birth, and the ability to pull strings in high places.

It followed, therefore, that the great bulk of the rank and file of the Regular Army was drawn either from the so-called 'working' or 'lower' classes, or from families with a long military tradition.

For the Territorial Army, re-organized by Lord Haldane from the old Militia in the years immediately before 1914, officer standards were considerably relaxed. Or, rather, they appeared to be, the subalterns being largely ex public schoolboys with O.T.C. qualifications, and this procedure was followed in officering the New Armies, both having, however, their leaven of re-employed officers.

In the matter of the rank and file of both the Territorial and the New Armies, I should make the point that, from about 1909 onward, the growing naval and military might of Germany had roused in the breasts of British of practically all classes, a corresponding ardour to match Germany, come what may. It is most important to comprehend this.

The Boy Scouts, Boys' Brigades and training corps flourished exceedingly. They all had their drum and fife and bugle bands, and were very popular. When the Territorials were mobilized and the New Armies raised, members of these organizations became our first N.C.O.s. Why? Because they could form fours, knew elementary squad drill, and, in many cases, knew the elements of rifle drill. The buglers and drummers were in great demand, and soon were busy forming bands for the newly raised units.

With the leaven in the ranks of time-expired 'old sweats', who soon became sergeants and sergeant-majors if they played their cards intelligently, we enthusiastic entrants from the lower walks of civil life were soon caught up in the military machine. Indeed, we adopted Hindustani terms: for instance rifle (bandook); tea (char); 'What time is it?' ('Khit na budgee?'); 'Quick', or 'Hurry' ('Jaldi'). If we were lucky enough to get a first sip of tea in the morning—the cooks always seemed to get theirs, and who could blame them—we called it 'gunfire', recalling the morning gun at (I believe) Gibraltar. We never questioned the personal courage of our officers, with good reason. They worthily followed the example of selfless sacrifice against overwhelming odds shown by all ranks of our heroic Regular Army at the Retreat, the Marne, Aisne and Ypres, and we submitted ourselves cheerfully to their code of discipline.

From my recollection, the youth of my generation had little interest in the politics of the period. They heard their parents argue endlessly for or against Lloyd George and the measures he had introduced. Certain it was that the landed aristocracy really hated him and his colleagues. This also caused a reactionary closing of the ranks against such impudence by the so-called lower orders.

To sum up: this social order and system had created the British Empire, on which the sun never set. We all learned it at school. Great Britain was *Great*. Her Navy was invincible, and we were going to show the Kaiser that our Army was too! That was the underlying spirit of the New Armies who went overseas in 1915.

Having said this, I return in haste to my narrative.

While in reserve we were kept extremely busy. Besides our duty of indirect firing, rigorous gun drill, rifle exercises and P.T., inspections and lectures filled our days and carrying parties, very often, much of our nights. Scarcely a day passed but that we were paraded to ascertain deficiencies of some article of equipment, or for the issue of another considered indispensable for the future prosecution of the war.

At this period, I remember, most of us received frequent parcels from home, and altogether we lived like fighting cocks. On some evenings, when the mail came up, chaps stuffed with cakes and dainties would be pressed by generous mates with their mouths full, to 'have a bit of Mother's'. Socks and mufflers, all sorts of weird and wonderful articles of woollen apparel began to arrive, doubtless in anticipation of the rigours of the coming winter. Recipients of, perhaps, several mufflers would swap their excess of actual requirements for socks or cigarettes or other available fancies. We presented *Tante* and her mother with two mufflers— one of them five feet long, which could be stretched to well over six. In our few free evenings, although there were two *estaminets* in the village, invariably we went to *Tante*'s and sat around her stove and yarned, and took turns with the coffee mill.

So busy have I been in transporting our battalion to the front, in describing my first youthful impressions of a foreign country and our outlook on first facing the enemy that, so far, beyond naming them, I have done little to describe the mates who sat around the stove with me, and who shared my perils, joys and sorrows. Arrived, and established guardians of a small sector of hitherto French-manned trenches about sixteen kilometres south of Arras, I have time to reflect as, in fancy, I sit once more in that farm-house kitchen one late September evening of 1915, with the wind outside whisking the first leaves from the tall trees around.

Our Lewis gun teams consisted of a lance-corporal and six men. Of these, the N.C.O. and two of the men had left wives and, in one case, children in England. They were considerably older than the rest of us, sharing common anxieties and responsibilities of which we, as single chaps, simply had no idea at that time. Our corporal, in charge of two teams, was an ex-naval gunner and a Welshman. He supposedly had a wife somewhere, but never heard from her. We got along well with him. Indeed, the troubles of the married men were a joke to us, although they had our sympathy and, often, help.

It may appear fantastic, but a private's pay was one shilling per day then. About four months after we had enlisted, the government initiated a Separation Allowance Scheme for married men, retrospective in operation to dates of enlistment. In short, the poor old married men had to contribute by degrees all the back weekly payments in addition to that current, so that for months they only drew one shilling per week, and thereafter three shillings and sixpence, or its equivalent in francs. The consequence was that most of them were 'skinned' after they'd bought a packet of Woodbines and a pint, and relied on us to keep them going for the rest of the period before the next pay day. It is understandable, therefore, that off duty the married men kept pretty much to themselves and we four similarly held together. The trenches and *Tante*'s were the means of bringing to fruition a comradeship which had been slowly ripening in the training camps at home. We four became inseparable. However obnoxious some fatigues or working parties happened to be, they didn't appear half so bad if the four of us were on the same job.

After all these years, how can I put on paper the jovial features of the over-six-foot, fourteen-and-a-half-stone Horace Phillips, 'Phillipe Auguste', as he sits there by the stove, replenishing his pipe with Bruno from an indiarubber pouch. The frail chair looks as though it can scarce support his weight, and creaks every time he laughs, which is often. See his huge red hands as he presses the tobacco home; yet they are capable hands, for he had been a market gardener in happier days. You will recall, too, how he had milked the cow for *Tante*. He sings often, in a clear, if not strong, tenor voice. Snatches of a ballad, very sweet and somehow haunting, so that at odd moments we find ourselves humming the same tune and repeating what we could remember of the words— a song of a minstrel—a great lady, and a knight who wooed her.

> She was a lady, great and splendid
> I was a minstrel in her hall.
> A warrior, like a Prince attended
> Reined his steed by the castle wall.
> Long had he fared to gaze upon her
> 'Ah, rest ye now, Sir Knight' she said.
> The warrior woo'd, the warrior won her;
> In time of snowdrops they were wed.
> I played sweet music in his honour . . .

Laughingly Phillips begs a match; as he turns in the chair, it creaks again. See his great knees and countryman's legs, his size eleven service boots at an angle of more like ninety than forty-five degrees; his blue eyes as he looks at the now-drawing pipe bowl, the glint of the flickering matchlight on his fair, curly hair. Horace Phillips . . . Phillipe Auguste . . . Yeoman of Uppingham, England.

Then there was Ted Lineker—'Lin', we called him—training as a lithographic artist with a nationally known firm of colour printers in Leicester when he enlisted. Standing just on six foot in his socks and well proportioned, he was in no danger of being rejected for bad teeth either; his seemed about perfect, and when he laughed he was good to see. His eyes were grey, his brows finely arched and pencilled, almost like a woman's; his nose, and particularly his upper lip, had what I believe novelists describe as a 'chiselled' appearance, but he had cultivated of recent weeks a fair, clipped military moustache which made him look somewhat older than twenty. He smoked a Dunhill pipe which his mother had sent him and John Cotton tobacco. He carried her photograph in his wallet, and very little else. She looked to us extraordinarily youthful and, we thought at the time, beautiful.

Of a very different type was our third comrade. Try to picture Freddy Smith as he sits in the chimney corner, turning away at the coffee mill on his lap. A shorter, stockily built lad with swarthy features, crisp black hair inclined to curl, and an equally black 'Charlie Chaplin' on his upper lip. He needed to shave twice daily to look presentable in the evening. His father had the grocery business in the North Leicestershire shoemaking and sock-knitting village of Shepshed. In 1914 he was following in father's footsteps in the shop, and the training had alerted and sharpened his senses in many ways. Now watch him. As Phillips asks for a match, see him instantly pick up a spent one and place it in the outstretched hand; listen to his merry laugh at the latter's disgust—the green eyes twinkling under bushy black brows—the white teeth . . . such was Private Smith, F., the perfect campaigner—our champion scrounger. If we wanted anything, 'leave it to Freddy,' we would say, and in due course he would turn up with the twinkle bespeaking success.

Of such stuff, then were my comrades of the autumn, winter and spring of 1915–16; companions alike in moments of danger and of pleasant relaxation such as *Tante*'s cottage afforded us.

The end of September was fast approaching when we relieved the 6th Battalion for another spell in 97 Trench. Their Lewis gunners told us that things were getting warmer, and there was ample evidence of this. Parts of the front line had been blasted away by *minnenwerfers* they said, watching for our rueful reaction to this unwelcome news. 'Every evening, mate, about seven to eight. Last night he got a second machine going! Ta-ta. Good luck!' In addition they had lost three men: one shot clean through his head while on sentry-go, two buried by a *minnie* and sent down the line with shock and bruises. They had also been shelled by five-nines.

On the very first evening following the relief, some of our specialist bombers came up from their dugout at Battalion H.Q. and fixed up a wooden rack contraption in our fire bay, proceeding to fire therefrom two dozen or so rifle grenades—at what we didn't know, and had a shrewd idea that they didn't either. They then 'na-pood' (to use the soldier's corruption of a French expression in constant use at that time), leaving us to face the music—which very soon commenced. A 'pop' and up trundled the first minnie, its course marked by a fiery trail of sparks. We watched it, fascinated, until it commenced its downward course and then, judging its flight in the instant, ran like hell in the opposite direction. To make things worse, the second *minnenwerfer* section started operations, the two producing a cross-fire extremely difficult to dodge. Fortunately our luck held. Twice, while running frantically along the trench, we came into violent contact with chaps running from the opposite direction to escape a falling *minnie* there. Later, when things had quietened down, we stood panting in the remains of our bay—the last *minnie* had fallen clean into it and had given us enough work to last us all night, and we peered around in the darkness at the shattered fascines and torn earth. Luckily the gun emplacement was practically intact, and in taking avoiding action the Number One had run with the gun. As a result of all this, I am quite sure that just then we hated our own bombers more than Jerry.

Strange to relate, as we shovelled feverishly to fill new sandbags, weird sounds floated across from the German trenches: the strains of an accordion and the refrain of a song very popular at the time of the Boer War—'Goodbye Dolly Gray'. Waiting until the singer had finished, we signified our approval by shouting 'hooray' and 'encore', but ceased abruptly when a voice hailed us from the other side—'hallo, Tommy . . . hallo, Tommy!'. Thoroughly intrigued by this development, we called, 'hallo. Give us another song!' whereupon, after several false starts, we were treated to 'Down by the Old Bull and Bush'. We hoorayed again and clapped. 'What's your name, Jerry?' one of us shouted. 'Charlie—you bloody English bastards!'

Filling Sandbags
97 Trench. Monchy au Bois
Sept. 30 '1915.

came the voice of that worthy instantly, which mouthful rather nonplussed us. We were racking our brains for a suitably fruity reply when Charlie called '*gut nacht*', and several bullets in quick succession smacked into the parados above our heads. 'He likes us,' remarked Freddy Smith with some feeling.

The next morning, while still filling sandbags, we saw our first aerial combat, between a French monoplane and a German biplane. As was generally the case at that time, the war on terra firma ceased on both sides for the nonce in the vicinity of the combatants.

Although at this period of the war aerial fighting tactics and machines were in their infancy, this contest was thrilling enough to watch while it lasted. Both planes sped round above the trenches, each trying to gain the advantage of getting on the other's tail. At length the Frenchman succeeded in climbing through a circle and then diving on the German. There was a rattle of machine-gun bullets and we saw a whiff of black smoke shoot from the fuselage of the machine, becoming in a few moments a dense cloud as down he went in a spin behind Monchy, leaving a black cloud which slowly floated away. Overhead the victorious Frenchman circled several times, while a perfect hail of bullets assailed him from the German trenches as he disappeared in a westerly direction. He appeared to have escaped unharmed.

I believe that it was on the following morning, however, that we heard the rumble of a very heavy cannonade far away to the north, which continued with increasing intensity throughout the day and the greater part of the night, the sky in that direction lit with a never-ending display of Verey lights and great flashes. We were told that a 'Big Push' had started north of Arras. That evening we 'stood to', tense and expectant. Iron rations were inspected and increased. Each man was issued with an additional bandolier of fifty rounds, we Lewis gunners with two. More bully and biscuits were distributed. Then came the order to dump our packs in ordered heaps at chosen points, and for the first time we fastened our haversacks upon our backs in battle order. For a wonder, Jerry sent no *minnies* over that evening. Those of us not actually on sentry duty dozed fitfully on the firestep awaiting the order to go forward. Tense and expectant, we waited into the morning of another day . . . and the whole course of it until evening and then . . . nothing! We stood down and reverted to normal trench routine.

The distant cannonade continued in varying degrees of intensity all the next day and then slackened. The Germany artillery opposite then became unusually active, and we had some awkward moments. We heard subsequently that they had some very awkward moments around Battalion H.Q. also, the howitzer shells were falling almost vertically. We remarked ourselves that our own artillery was completely silent during the strafe. Ever since we came to Berles, very little had been heard of our field artillery, much less seen. Occasionally they fired a few rounds. Wags joked and said that they were short of shells; not for some days afterwards did we find that this was only too true. They were desperately short and, worse still, the few shells they had were largely defective.

We were back in our billets in Berles before rumour on rumour, aided by days' old English papers giving some details of the Loos offensive and stressing the gallantry of our troops, convinced us that victory had somehow eluded us. Then another spate of rumours told of disaster succeeding disaster. Two divisions—the 9th and 15th (Scottish)—had been wiped out and two more—the 21st and 24th—fresh from England, were force-marched up to the front from St. Omer and panicked. Poor devils. If that was true, they had our sympathy. We had known the 9th and 15th Divisions at Aldershot and on Salisbury Plain—the finest body of men ever to leave the Highlands. So it went on, until we were due for the line again.

For some inexplicable reason we were not paid until the morning of the relief, to start in the afternoon. Then we privates, passing rich on twenty francs apiece, nipped into the nearby *estaminet* for a quick drink before the midday gyppo was ready—our last meal before going 'in'. Three privates of the K.R.R.s of our division were there. They were on working parties for the R.E. and were sharing a bottle of champagne, respecting which we twitted them good humouredly. We didn't know much about champagne, but the mark 'Moët et Chandon' appeared good enough for Phillips. He called airily, 'Madame—*une* bottle!' As he eased the cork he declined our offers to share the cost, observing with a grunt that we could call next time.

It was very pleasant for a change and we started to compare notes with the riflemen; they had been in a very hot spot called Fonquevillers, a few kilometres down the line towards Albert. The champagne must have induced an unusually cordial atmosphere, for by an unprecedented stroke of luck in 'tossing' our rifleman friends for who paid for succeeding rounds, we had several unopened bottles on the table when an emissary from our billet thrusting his head through the door, yelled 'say—d'you drunken buggers want any dinner? We've kept the dixie waiting about twenty minutes already. The cooks are packing up—c'm on out of it!'

Startled out of our pleasant drowsiness, we rose and made our ways to the door. Outside I noticed that Lineker and Freddy Smith each carried an unopened bottle — smiling that they weren't going to leave them there—as the ground seemed to come up to meet us in spite of our efforts to push it away. In that state we managed to reach the billet, but then we saw the steaming dixie of stew. We looked at it, then at our mess tines, and one by one retired to the orchard. There may be forms of alcoholic excess which produce more shocking effects, but personally I've never tested anything worse than that of champagne. We all felt as though our innards were gripped in a vice, loosened and gripped again, harder. After an hour or so thus we were reduced to a pitiable condition. Then came the order to parade.

As we staggered into the billet I was handed a large parcel from home. This I fixed by the string to the top of my pack, helped by Phillips as I struggled into my equipment and collected rifle and another short shovel which we had 'won', before taking my place in the swaying ranks. For, truth to tell, most of us were really in pretty much the same state, the majority of our mates having patronized the other *estaminet* in the village, where *vin blanc* had been the tipple. Alternately we held on to each other for support and tried to assuage our innards—somewhat difficult through the constrictive influence of a wide belt and six pouches of ammunition. Our Welsh ex-navy corporal, grinning and perspiring as he staggered up to Phillips, told him to take Number One on the gun, the married man holding that job having gone sick. This meant re-arranging the whole team and I was told to take over the canvas bag of spare parts and a pannier of Lewis drums. At this Lineker, seeing me with the spare-parts bag, whispered 'Dick. Those two bottles. Bring 'em with us'—indicating the bottles. 'We'll need 'em to get over this lot!' Phillips heard him. 'Lord, yes, Dick. Get 'em, there's a sport!' Hurriedly, I broke from the ranks and retrieved them from our room, where our erstwhile sick Number One was standing over them, obviously with fell design as soon as we had gone. Shouted commands without precluded argument with him as I grabbed the bottles and dashed out to rejoin the ranks. Before us stood our sergeant. 'Parade 'shun,' he yelled. Turning, he saluted our lieutenant with 'all present and

' The Parcel ·····flew over my head ····!'
(Parade for the Trenches. Berles au Bois Sept. 1915)

correct, sir'. As he did so I endeavoured to hitch up my pack with a great effort. My parcel and I parted company and it flew over my head, landing on the pavé of the yard in front of the swaying parade. Over the stones oozed a brown stream from a wrecked bottle of H.P. sauce.

Everyone seemed to be smiling, or trying to stifle it. Furtively, I looked at Lieutenant Millburn who, it seemed to me, maintained his parade demeanour with difficulty as tactfully he gave the order, 'carry on, Sergeant'. Looking back on the events of that afternoon, as we did subsequently, we decided that he did the only thing possible in the circumstances. In the long run, he didn't lose anything by his tactful handling of the situation; he must have seen at once that we were all pretty far gone. The parcel remained where it fell.

We managed to get as far as Battalion H.Q. before our loads, and the necessity for continuing our journey, began to get the better of us. At this point individual gun teams separated, joining the respective company sectors by their own communication trenches. Our lieutenant left us there also; whereon our crew, suffering from acute alcoholic poisoning, managed to get a hundred yards or so further on our journey up Narborough Road towards 97 Trench before beseeching Corporal Jones to call a halt for a few minutes. He was in no great form himself, oozing beer from every pore and crimson with exertion, but he had nothing to carry beyond his rifle and equipment.

We could, however, understand his anxiety to get us to our position without being reported by an officer of the outgoing battalion, or, for that matter, by one of our own. Moreover, as I have said, he was an ex-naval man and prided himself on being something of a disciplinarian. He was not feeling very pleased, either with himself or with us. He therefore speeded our faltering steps with various salt-water exhortations, commencing 'me hearties . . .' and concluding '. . . and carry your liquor like the f. . .ing Englishmen you are'. He, of course, was a Welshman!

Under the lash of his tongue we staggered on until Phillips temporarily put an end to our torture by catching his toe upon a loose sump cover in the trench bottom and sprawling headlong. In an effort to break his fall, he had pushed the gun barrel foremost into the clay, and when extricated it was useless as a weapon until it had been dismantled and cleaned throughout—our first task when eventually we reached our position.

Our colleagues being relieved asked us to keep quiet, as rifle grenades were becoming a daily nuisance there. Additional damage by *minnies* told its own tale—but by that time all we wanted to do was to sleep and we all had to watch and prod one another to keep awake, especially after the evening stand-down, when Lineker and I took the first turn of two hours.

For some reason unknown to us no *minnies* came over, for which we were profoundly thankful, as listening for the reports of these as they were fired was about the only thing that kept us awake. At 10. p.m. Phillips and Freddy Smith relieved us, rubbing their eyes and shivering. Corporal Jones was snoring like a pig, they said. 'What about a hair of the dog?' So as soon as Lin and I had reached the dugout we eased the cork from one of the bottles, the resounding 'pop' failing to wake the occupants. We each took a pull from the bottle and Lin went along to Phillips and Smith with the remainder, after which we two were soon snoring like the others; with the result that several rats, who used our recumbent bodies as a springboard, were able to jump on our sandbag of rations (which, to escape their attentions, we had suspended from the roof) and work without interruption for the next two hours. By that time a yawning hole had all but replaced a loaf in the bottom of the bag, while I was covered with breadcrumbs, raisins and chewed strands of sandbag.

CHAPTER 5

DOWN THE LINE

As things turned out I did not miss my share of the rations a great deal. It was a fine morning and just after midday, as Lineker and I were filling sandbags in leisurely fashion in the warm sunshine to repair the length of trench adjacent to our dugout, rifle grenades started to drop in groups along the front trench. We did not worry over much about this, as the nearest yet had fallen about thirty yards away; we went on with our job.

I had gone a few yards for some good shovelsful of loose earth to complete the bag that Lin was holding, when I heard a grenade coming. Before I could shout, I felt a sharp stinging sensation in my right thigh and momentarily blacked out. Half-stunned and with singing ears, I struggled to my feet and realized that Lin was helping me. I told him I had stopped something. He asked me whether I could walk. I hadn't thought of that and was relieved that I could, although I could feel the pain and a warm trickling sensation. Lin cut my trouser leg open and we tied my field dressing over the hole. There didn't seem much of it and we laughed ruefully at the ruin of my trousers. Lin said he'd better tell Corporal Jones and I'd better get down to the aid post at Battalion H.Q., but as he went, a grenade fell smack on the sandbag he had been holding before I was hit. We were smothered with earth, and our faces in particular felt bruised and painful. He had a very lucky escape, but came back with my kit, accompanied by Corporal Jones who told me what a lucky so-and-so I was to get such a nice 'Blighty' one, and told Lin to help me down to H.Q.

Lineker waited while the M.O., his mouth full of lunch, removed the field dressing and probed the hole. He thought at first that he could extract the piece, but finally he gave up the attempt, telling me I'd have to go down to C.C.S., whatever that was

(I soon found out). I now felt depressed at the thought of leaving my mates, as I gave Lin the news and he wished me luck. I told him I'd be back before long; actually I was away for nearly two months.

That early October evening I rattled up the road to Berles from Battalion H.Q. in an empty returning ration limber. At the dressing station there an orderly gave me an anti-tetanus injection and wrote something in indelible pencil in the palm of one of my hands. Three chaps lay beside me, wounded by shrapnel in 'C' Company's sector that afternoon. Early next morning tickets were tied to our wrists and we were put into a Ford ambulance, the curtains were drawn and off we went, jogging along on and off the pavé for the best part of two hours. I think I dozed for some of the time. At length we stopped, the curtains were pulled back and we were lifted out onto the ground, from which we could see around us several large marquees, some huts and some tents. An R.A.M.C. corporal came up, looked at my ticket and the indelible pencilling. He shouted and two orderlies approached and carried me into one of the marquees, where an army nursing sister, wearing gum boots and carrying a hurricane lantern, directed them to put me in a vacant place on the grass at the far side. By now my leg had stiffened, and throbbed whenever I tried to ease the pain by movement.

Our old soldiers had told us tales at odd times of the treatment sometimes received in India and other 'outposts of Empire' at the hands of army nurses, and, truth to tell, I regarded the red band around her cape with some apprehension, as another nurse joined her and they proceeded to inspect the new arrivals.

Lying there, I became conscious for the first time of my helplessness, although my hurt was comparatively trivial and I felt rather ashamed of myself in their company, the majority of whose wounds were obviously more serious. They came to the stretcher in front of me, and as I watched I could just see a white bandage round a dark head and the outline of blanketed feet as she of the hurricane lamp shone it upon him and her colleague bent over with busy fingers. The soldier groaned and half-turned his head, putting his hands to the bandage. 'There, that's better, sonny. They'll put you right.' As they turned towards me his hands

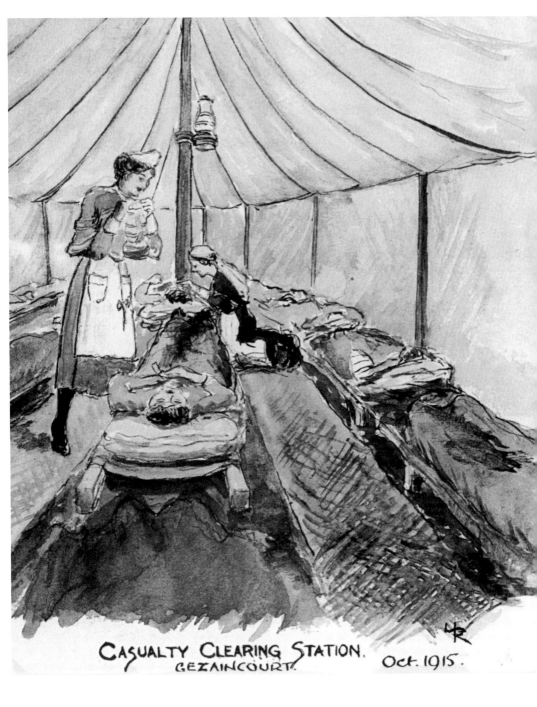

CASUALTY CLEARING STATION.
GEZAINCOURT.
Oct. 1915.

groped in the air. I heard him say, 'nurse, nurse, shall I see again?'
The nurses looked quickly at each other and then one pushed his
white-swathed head gently onto the pillow and his hands beneath
the blanket. 'Don't worry, sonny, they'll get you right.'

'Now then, young man!' As the tall sister shone her lamp upon me, her colleague looked at the ticket, pulled back the blanket and removed the bandage. She examined the hole and prodded all round it, said that it was going septic but there would be a train to the base next day and they would put me right there. An orderly followed and re-dressed my leg, and while he was doing this I watched the sisters attending to the case on my left.

The lad looked pretty bad. It was evident that he had lost a good deal of blood. The R.A.M.C. man whispered to me he had been hit in the privates. 'If only he'd lie still he might have a chance, but while he keeps moving about the bleeding won't stop.'

The M.O. strode up and all three knelt beside the stretcher. The R.A.M.C. man said something about a saline injection. After some minutes they moved on, and as they did so the lad caught the eye of the sister with the lamp. I heard him say, 'want to write'. She admonished him kindly and told him to lie still, but he tried to raise himself, repeating his request. The sister then took a memo pad and knelt down by him and wrote, I believe, a few sentences at his dictation, after which he lay back, quite still. I thought he slept.

Some hours passed and it was getting dark. We were fed and physicked. The lad still slept, and as I looked at him I reflected as I had never done before on this aspect of the war, and on the terrible nature of his hurt. I dozed and dimly saw, in the light of lanterns now lit, another nurse and a corporal come and look at him, turning back the blankets and, after a quick glance, replacing them. Shortly afterwards, two orderlies came and carried him 'to another ward' (as they put it).

I must have slept, but opened my eyes to see several figures at my side. They had just deposited a stretcher beside me, from which came groans and mutterings. Seeing the orderly who had dressed my leg, I inquired of him what had become of the boy they had moved. At my question he turned his thumbs down in a significant gesture as he bent down to me. ''E's passed out mate. This chap's a field artillery driver. Pitched off 'is 'orse. Got concussion pretty badly.'

I didn't get much rest for the remainder of the night, as the newcomer made sleep impossible. He rolled off the stretcher twice, vomited and wetted his blanket in his delirium, uttering a stream of obscenities in addition which, naive and ignorant as I was of the after-effects of concussion, really shocked me, because the night nurse heard much of it. However, my red face gave way to surprise on seeing that she took no notice whatever of his ravings and did what she could to make him comfortable, calling him 'sonny' or 'old chap'. Although beyond my comprehension then, in the weeks that followed I began to understand.

The next morning we were taken to the station of Gezaincourt near Doullens, and put on a hospital train of an improvised type, being placed one above the other in three tiers which corresponded with the positions of the seats and partitions in happier days. I found myself on the equivalent of the luggage rack, and a little while after the train started felt just about as comfortable. In the hot vitiated atmosphere of the roof of the carriage I could scarcely breathe at times; moreover, my leg was becoming increasingly painful, so that I didn't enjoy the run down to Rouen, where we were whisked off to one or other of the big base hospitals on the outskirts of the city.

I was taken to one on top of the hill, which I believe was called Bonsecours. The exact name and number of it I have forgotten, but it doesn't matter, anyway. The wards were in large wooden huts. I recall being bathed and having my leg dressed; the clean hospital shirt they put on me; the sheer luxury of the fresh-smelling white sheets; the soft pillow! I was revelling in this when the night sister came up to my bed in the dimly lit ward, telling me to sleep well and they would look at me in the morning.

They soon put me right at Rouen. I was X-rayed, and the segment of rifle grenade located and removed. The hole they kept open until certain it was clean, when it then healed rapidly. I was soon hobbling about the ward helping those not so fortunate as I was, shaving and washing them, in fact doing anything I could to assist the nurses and make myself useful.

Most of the cases went off to Blighty as soon as they were fit to move, and I was only struck off at the last minute, when one list was being prepared. It was a disappointment at the time, but I couldn't complain, as there was no real need for me to return to England. The whole staff were very kind, and we lived on the fat of the land here in Rouen. Our breakfast eggs, I recall, often had the names of Devonshire farms scribbled on them, while presents of fruit and chocolates were showered on us in profusion.

The nursing staff appeared to be drawn from many branches of the nursing profession. I believe the matron to have occupied a similar position in a large hospital in England—she was efficient, firm, yet kindly. Immediately subordinate to her were several sisters of the Army Nursing Service, in charge of wards. Their nurses, from their uniforms, came from several services or hospitals. All with whom I came into contact were fine women. Finally, there were a number of probationer nurses—I think they were V.A.D.s—again, grand girls, and I hope I may be excused for an incident I recall concerning the probationer in our ward and a Grenadier Guardsman occupying the next bed to mine.

He had been shot through both thighs at Loos and his progress had been retarded by a number of complications, one at least being the wounds having gone septic. The daily dressing was a long and often agonizing ordeal for him, and the smell appalling. Rubber tubes inserted for drainage purposes, and leading into 'Winchesters' at the bedside, were removed for dressing and then re-inserted—the crucial moment. In those days antibiotics and penicillin were in the far future. When gripping the frames of his bed with both hands in an endeavour to bear the awful pain without flinching, beads of sweat stood out on his forehead above half-closed eyes.

The girl had done this dressing several times before and they got on well, but on this occasion his iron self control gave way as she was re-inserting the tube, and in his agony he swore at her terribly—personally. She, too, had reached her limit. She put down the tube, bit her lip and rushed down the ward in an endeavour to hide her tears while the Grenadier, exhausted but already ashamed, looked round wildly.

The girl came back. Each looked at the other quickly, then she said, trying to smile through the tears, 'let's have another try, shall we?' I heard him say, 'sorry, gal!' and she completed her task. I am not being sentimental, but after that there was an understanding and a mutual respect between those two which, I felt at the time, nothing else could have established.

One more anecdote of that Grenadier who, just before I left the hospital, had improved enough to be moved to England.

The people of the West Indies apparently had collected a lot of money for comforts for the troops which took the form, in our case, of the distribution in our ward of boxes of Cadbury's chocolates, in which the nurses took a deal of pleasure. The guardsman looked at his, saw what it was, and with an effort threw it across to me with the withering remark 'I'm a soldier!' Surprised as I was, the implication was not lost on me. It was clear in his eyes that I wasn't.

At the time this incident made a great impression on me. Lying there, I had plenty of time to think and pass in review my own youthful progress (?) to date, in an atmosphere of terrible wounds and, in some cases gangrene, which devoted women were working selflessly to heal. In retrospect it was invaluable for the insight it gave me into human nature—its frailties and the capacity for quiet heroism.

In this backwater of war it seemed years since I had run down the Humberstone road in Leicester at 6.25 every morning, at the first note of the warning buzzer. In my blue overalls, or sometimes dressing as I ran, I had crowded through the great iron gates of the engineering works with the apprentices a few moments before Horace, the timekeeper, swung them shut with a loud clang, locking out the unfortunates who had arrived too late. He admitted them a quarter of an hour later, after jotting down their names. They 'lost a quarter', as the saying went. Two such lapses in a week were regarded as serious and, in the case of the men, were tantamount to getting the sack. How far off my bench seemed, and the vice at which I worked and filed! My foreman, Alf Haining, inspecting parts which I had finished, spitting tobacco juice all around from his quid of twist. 'What d'you call this—it's a thou out 'ere!' Should I ever go back to it? What was going to happen before it was all over?

I gave up wondering, resigned myself to the life of a soldier and thought increasingly of Berles and of my mates there . . . of *Tante*. I found myself wanting to be back with them, and asked the sisters when I could go to what I had heard was the convalescent camp on the other side of the river Seine in Rouen, as a first step back to the line. They kept me a week or so after this, during which time I did all kinds of odd jobs for the nurses, including putting in two window-panes, for which they provided the necessary glass and putty.

Then one afternoon I drew my kit—including a new pair of trousers—and off I went on a lorry to the convalescent camp. My right leg was still pretty tender, but after I had reported myself, drawn ten francs and had obtained a pass-out for the evening, I tested it by walking down the mile or so of tram route towards the town. I was glad enough, however, to board one to complete the distance to the bridge over the Seine, which passes through the very centre of Rouen. There I sat down in the first *brasserie* I came to after I alighted, feeling tired but glad to be about again, fairly sound in wind and limb.

Several days passed. It was said that it was the custom to let men rejoining their units have two or three passes-out into the town before sending them up to their base depots; most of which, in the case of infantry, were gathered around Étaples, not far from Boulogne on the Channel coast. Then, thankfully, for I had spent practically all my money, I saw that I was listed for 37th Division Infantry Base Camp. I well remember the last night in a tent there with ten others, including a Scot who told us his was the first V.C. of the war. As he had imbibed too freely, we didn't take him seriously; but, to our surprise, he showed it to us by a feeble candlelight—the only V.C. I have ever seen to examine closely. Unfortunately, he persisted in telling us his hardluck story, to which perforce we had to listen as we couldn't get to sleep, although it was not without interest, and perhaps threw a sidelight on Britain's alleged shabby treatment of her heroes.

As far as I can recall, he told us that he was a Regular and that he had gained his decoration for taking a German machine-gun single-handed, killing several of the enemy. Part of his reward had been special leave and a visit to his native city of Edinburgh, which no doubt had suitably welcomed him, a collection being made for him which realized a considerable sum of money. He told us the amount, which staggered us at the time, but which I have forgotten. All this adulation apparently turned his head for, on his own confession, he had scarcely been sober since for many hours on end and had spent most of the money raised by admirers of his deed. At the expiration of his leave he had been given a plum job at the regimental depot, helping the recruiting campaign, but had given so much trouble that authority there lost its patience with him and had sent him back to Rouen Base. Here, apparently, he had enjoyed an equally easy job, but again his habits had caused him to fall foul of the C.O. who, according to his account, never gave him a chance.

Listening to him and putting two and two together, we surmised that he had been so impudent, and his conduct generally so ill-devised to ingratiate himself with the officers in charge of the camp—the C.O. apparently had told him that he was a bad influence—that he was being sent up the line again. We concluded that everyone was heartily sick of him—as, indeed, we were rapidly becoming. As we, and he, subsided into sleep, we heard him saying that he was going to see that the guard 'turned out' to him when we marched down to the station. This privilege—if, indeed, he could exercise it—certainly impressed us, and re-awakened us for some moments. There were subdued mutterings and chuckles all round the tent.

On the morrow we were literally itching to see what would happen, but in the event he stumbled by the camp guard at the entrance, supported by one of us on either side, and it was not until we were entraining in a siding in Rouen that he realized dimly what had happened. After that I never saw him again, but years afterwards, on the front page of a leading daily paper, I saw a photograph of him selling newspapers in Edinburgh with the caption 'V.C. hero living in poverty'.

In the cold cheerless dawn of a late November morning we detrained at the great base camp of Étaples—'Eetapps', as the British soldier called it. We were marched off to our respective divisional camps on the windswept hillside and I duly reported with several others at the 37th Division Camp, our 110th Leicestershire Brigade forming a part of this.

Here the shivering canvas of rows of white tents presented a chilling aspect to the newcomer and a few hours afterwards, as I stood peeling potatoes in the lee of a field kitchen to escape some of the icy blast from the North Sea, I prayed fervently that my stay in this inhospitable spot would be a short one. Regretfully I contrasted my present position with the warm comfort of the hospital ward which I had fretted to leave, and cursed myself for being such a fool. Still, it was too late now, and after all, I thought, one had to learn by experience. I consoled myself with the thought that at any rate there were no shells or *minnies* flying about, and that no doubt thousands of poor so-and-sos up there would be only too glad to change places with me.

I remained at Étaples for a week or so, while drafts were prepared for the battalions of our brigade, and a few of my recollections while there may not be devoid of interest.

The town itself was quite small, and was completely smothered by the forests of huts, marquees and tents which surrounded it. In addition to being the reinforcement base for most of the infantry of the B.E.F., hospitals of enormous extent abounded, stretching for miles along the Camiers road and towards the river mouth. Their attendant cemeteries, which even then had assumed staggering proportions, are now all that remains of tangible proof that they ever existed. Before these hospitals made their appearance, I should say that the windswept sand dunes were singularly uninteresting. From our camp upon the hillside, we could look down upon some of them and beyond, across the estuary, to the wooded tongue of land, capped at its extremity by the lighthouse of Paris Plage.

One day we were taken there on a route march. Well before we reached the group of hotels forming the sea-side resort of pre-war days, long since converted into hospitals, my leg started to give me trouble, and I had endured quite enough when we halted on the sandy shore close to the Hôtel Atlantic. Here we piled arms and fell out for a breather, the captain in charge of us saying, with an attempt at humour, that anyone who wished to bathe could do so. Needless to say, the bitterly cold north-east wind proved a sufficient deterrent. I spent the time resting my leg, but when the order came to fall in again, I was not feeling in very good form. My discomfiture was completed when, as we stood there, the order was given 'slope arms'. As I lifted my rifle, I made a mess of things, principally because my hands were half-frozen, and the butt fell clumsily against my barely healed thigh. I finished the route march in a passing lorry.

Close to our camp, along the Camiers road, two lorries passed us, crammed to capacity with swaying, singing and hilariously happy soldiers—a most unusual sight! The explanation was supplied by the driver of the lorry giving me a lift. A small vessel had gone ashore a mile or two along the coast and a salvage party had been sent to the spot to collect and guard portions of the cargo washed ashore. Unfortunately, most of this turned out to be casks of spirits, with the result that the party was soon 'incapable'. Military Police, sent hurriedly, were also quite incapable of dealing with the situation, for which a strong party of troops had been needed, and the two lorry loads were the result. I do not know what happened to them, but over forty years afterwards, at the bar of a well known hostelry in the Bethnal Green Road, I heard this incident described by one of the rounding-up party. He said that the local engineers rigged up a special cage for them of stakes and barbed wire.

Two days before I left Étaples to rejoin the regiment I was detailed for guard duty in the main detention compound. We duly paraded under a sergeant of our 9th Battalion, recovered from an arm wound, and marched past the base hospital huts in the teeth of a bitter north-easterly gale and across a desolate stretch of sand dunes towards the high barbed wire fence surrounding an isolated collection of tents and huts by the sea shore. Shortly after we relieved the outgoing guard, snow started to fall, and it was my luck to share the first spell of two hours with three more chaps.

Our lot was not an enviable one. With heads sunk deep in the turned-up collars of our greatcoats, and with rifles slung, the better to keep our hands from the icy blasts, each of us stamped up and down one side of the square of the barbed wire perimeter fence surrounding the lines of now-silent huts under a mantle of snow, thus meeting a comrade for a moment at each extremity of our beat. After a minute or so of grousing, we stumbled off in opposite directions, our ways dimly lit by small electric lamps at infrequent intervals, which threw the falling snowflakes into relief. From the blackness beyond came the ceaseless crash of the breakers on the sea shore, followed by the surge of the receding undertow. It was something to be on land, at all events, on such a night.

Relieved in due course, we made our way back to the guard

ON 'GUARD'-COMPOUND PERIMETER.
DETENTION CAMP—ETAPLES. DEC.1915.

hut with the sergeant, in the cheerful atmosphere of which the snow on our persons started to melt before we could divest ourselves of our equipment and greatcoats and shake it off outside. The huge coke fire in a brazier rendered the air positively unhealthy, but no one bothered about that as the sergeant produced a water bottle of rum and invited us to take a swig. We needed no second bidding, but neat rum should be taken with discretion. We were some minutes recovering, although in the process of gasping, spluttering and wiping our eyes we certainly got warm.

I have recorded this twenty-four hours of guard duty chiefly on account of my recollections of the unfortunate prisoners themselves, and the rigid discipline to which they were subjected. It is not for me to say whether or not some of them deserved what was meted out to them. No doubt, too, such places were necessary. The very nature of the national call to arms ensured a certain proportion of ne'er-do-wells in the ranks of every unit, but I doubt whether many of those I saw behind that fence were of that category. From what transpired, they soon had our heartfelt sympathy. As for the punishment acting as a deterrent as well, opinion in our guard hut was unanimous that the treatment—as we saw it, at least—did not make them better soldiers. We could imagine a man released from this place returning to his unit with the iron in his soul, a smouldering hate warping his best instincts, ready to burst into a fierce flame of revolt against recognized military discipline at the first favourable opportunity—with increasingly dire results for him, and perhaps for his comrades.

Awakened for a further turn of duty, we staggered from the guard hut, shivering and trying to open our eyes, which were gummed up and heavy-lidded by reason of the coke fumes within. Snow was still falling but was now fine and powdery. The December dawn was just breaking, disclosing the desolate white expanse around the camp, broken here and there by the black islets of tufted and withered grasses reaching above the snow. The sky was as yet dark and leaden, with a faintly lighter hue towards the north-east. Our beat was inches deep in snow, which had drifted in places by the fencing to much greater depths, while the thickly woven wire itself was festooned with accumulations of patterned snow.

As I relieved my man, we noticed signs of life among the tents. Whistles shrilled and figures appeared outside, running. In a surprisingly short time the large tent flaps were rolled up and secured, the sectional wooden floors stacked outside each tent, the blankets neatly folded and each kit in orderly piles within. Everything, in fact, was done 'at the double'. Even the men detailed to empty the latrine buckets endeavoured to run with their burdens, supervised as they were by a shouting N.C.O. We observed, too, with bewilderment, that the buckets were being scoured and polished— aye, burnished! The floorboards were actually scrubbed and piled again by these poor shivering fellows with pinched faces and blue hands, working in the morass of snow and slush made by their efforts. All this time the wind was blowing the powdery snow under the folded flaps of the bell tents and on to their kits.

At a word they doubled to form several squads, two deep. Rolls were called by N.C.O.s of the Military Police, the slightest move in the shivering ranks calling forth stern reproof, which made our gorges rise and, in my case, engendered a loathing of that branch of the army which I have never been able to eradicate since, although in subsequent years their duties have become far more diverse and, I believe, humane. I think it true to say that within the fighting portion of the British Expeditionary Force, no one had a good word to say for them, good fellows though some of them doubtless were.

In this case it was the thought that they were in a position to torment, almost beyond endurance, men who in all probability had faced death many times, while they themselves may never have been within ten miles of the line unless by sheer accident. At that time, also, I was but a youth with all the impulsive feelings of an inexperienced youth.

I watched through the wire the parade for breakfast after the squads had doubled round and round and performed some arm-and-leg P.T., ostensibly to warm them up. What a breakfast on such a morning—a hunk of bread, some jam and some stuff that I hope was butter, and a mug of tea, eaten in the doubtful shelter of a tent open to the bitter wind. After breakfast more parading and doubling and polishing—more inspection.

By the time I was relieved I had seen quite enough to make me think pretty deeply but, being tired, I slept most of the morning and when next I went on duty the prisoners were all lined up preparatory to being marched by an escort to the fumigator, carrying with them their blankets as well. Apparently they had complained about the camp being 'lousy'. As I marched along my beat one of them came staggering from a tent near me with a roll of blankets and seeing me, looked round furtively. Seeing that the line of tents hid him from the assembled parade, he paused and beckoned to me. Involuntarily, I went close to the wire. 'Mate!' he called in little more than a hoarse whisper, 'got a fag to spare?

Don't matter if it's only a nob end!' It was strictly against our orders to hold any conversation with the prisoners, but the hunted look in his thin, pinched face decided me in the instant. Hurriedly I felt in my greatcoat pocket and found a squashed Gold Flake packet with six or seven in it and, pushing it through the wire, marched on. I saw him seize the packet as though the cigarettes were gold sovereigns, and put them in his blow belt as he staggered forward again with the blankets. I do not remember, before or since, having done anyone at any time a so-called good turn which gave me more real satisfaction.

The last I saw of the prisoners was the procession of fumigated men with their blankets returning under escort in the gathering twilight of the winter day, shortly before our relief. Their clothes were in thousands of creases caused by the steam treatment of the process. In the bitter wind which still blew the powdery snow like dust about the dunes, the sorry procession of pinched faces presented an unforgettable picture of misery as it entered the compound.

CHAPTER 6

WINTER, 1915

ON returning to camp that evening, most of us found that we were listed on a reinforcement draft due to leave for railhead the following afternoon; and indeed I was not sorry when the crowded freight vans into which we were packed jerked into motion. I have recently described the average British soldier's attitude to the Military Police; that afternoon we relieved some of our bitter feelings on an M.P. lance-corporal on duty in the siding where we entrained. As we were there about two hours before the train started, he, no doubt acting on orders, came along the train shouting that no one was to leave it. Before long, first one and then another had to obey the call of nature. As we couldn't get down on *his* side, we alighted on the other side. By the time the train started he was the butt of about two hundred jeering men, against which he could nothing, for all his shouting. As the train started and our vans came by him with increasing speed, he was assailed by a perfect hail of tins, among them an open tin of jam. Well content, we closed the sliding doors and got our heads down.

The following evening the 6th and 8th Battalion drafts marched into Berles and I was told to report to the Lewis gun section once more. Feeling glad to be back, I encountered one of them in the village street and we shook hands. He damped my spirits considerably, however, by informing me that we now had another billet and, what was far worse, a real bastard of a sergeant from the 2nd Battalion. Retracing his steps for my benefit, he showed me the way, and in due course I reported myself to Sergeant Rose at his billet.

There are some men who, when first encountered, inspire confidence; others produce an instinctive aversion, and Rose was one of the latter—very much so, as I was soon to discover. A reservist, I believe, at the outbreak of war in 1914, he had blossomed into a drill sergeant in England, and we used to say among ourselves that someone who could pull strings must have hated him sufficiently to get him drafted to France. Arrived at our battalion, none of the companies wanted his services, and so it was decided to foist him on to the Lewis gun section. That's how it seemed, anyway, and unfortunately we'd got him.

As I appeared before him that evening, ushered in by Corporal Jones, he was in the act of putting on his tunic. I noticed with some dismay that he had turned one of our mates into a batman, who regarded him anxiously as he inspected the buttons one by one as he fastened them upon his short, stocky figure, affecting to ignore us entirely. He proceeded to button his shoulder straps, first one, then:

''Ere, me lad!' to the batman. 'D'you call this clean?' The unfortunate, by name Simmonds, changed colour. 'Well?'

He turned to us with a really malignant leer of pleasure at having humiliated Simmonds publicly. 'Wait till I've finished with these people!' Deigning to notice us, he sat down, with the agitated Simmonds behind him. Preparing to deal with me, he assumed a look of penetration, his black gimlet eyes boring up and down. His mouth set in a line, beneath a huge bristling moustache which gave him the appearance of being top heavy.

Corporal Jones stood to attention while he recited my name and pedigree, etcetera, and asked whether I should rejoin the section. Sergeant Rose relaxed somewhat; his face again had the beginning of the leer which I had seen lately fully developed.

'Yes, Corporal Jones. Get the others to make room for 'im. And remember, my lad', addressing me, 'the Lewis gun section 'as smartened up since you were 'ere last.' The beady eyes fastened on my buttons. 'Don't come on parade like that in the morning! Simmonds!'

Outside, Corporal Jones exploded, clenching his fists and glaring back fiercely at the door.

'The cocky little bastard,' he said, between his teeth. '*Me*—standing to attention before him—*me*—a chief petty officer. *Me!*' Words failed him and I did my best to console him as he led me toward the billet. Here I met my comrades and for the moment

Sergeant Rose was completely forgotten in the pleasure of reunion. They took me to a near-by cottage—next door, in fact to the sergeant's billet—from which came sounds of singing and much laughter. As we entered the air seemed stiflingly hot and blue with tobacco smoke. Two rooms seemed full of our mates, drinking café, cognac, eating chocolate or biscuits. Through the smoke we saw two women by the stove attending to their wants and Phillips pushed his way through to them.

'Émilienne!' he called, exuding geniality as he looked around. '*Café pour comrade*. Quick. *Vite!* Émilienne, where are you?'

In response, a buxom girl emerged from an inner room with a coffee pot, proceeding to replenish it from the steaming bowl on the stove.

'Aal right, Phillipe,' beaming at him, then at all of us. 'New comrade?' she inquired, indicating me, her voice low and husky, but somehow pleasant.

'*Non, non,*' replied Phillips with emphasis. 'Dick, *blessée, tranchée*— Monchy, come back from hospital *ce soir—compris?*'

Such was my introduction to Émilienne, the high colour of her naturally rosy features heightened by frequent proximity to the stove. Her hair was, if anything, fair and wavy but was pulled back and coiled into a bun. Her eyes at times seemed blue, at others green, and she had a lovely smile; oft times when a smile must have been very difficult to raise. When we met her, she would have been about twenty years old.

Her younger sister, who already appeared to answer to the name of 'Skinny Liz', was precisely her reverse in build—tall and thin—with a shrill girlish voice. Their mother, whom everyone called 'Maman', seemed to be a very good natured soul and appeared to enjoy the jokes of the soldiers and to take everything in good part. The other two members of the household were 'Papa' who worked either in the fields near the gun pits at the rear of the village, or in the garden at the rear of the house, and Étienne, their little son, who was in bed on this, my first visit. I suppose he was trying to sleep, poor little beggar. After all these years, and with experience of my own family, I realize how almost impossible it must have been for him, with all that row going on until 10 p.m. in the next room.

Émilienne served what we termed good coffee and my mates were recounting everything of note that had happened during my absence, when a sudden hush seemed to descend on everybody. To our consternation, Sergeant Rose appeared in the doorway and in a shrill agitated pipe, meant for a whisper, Skinny Liz announced, '*Le Sergent Rose!*'

My mates swore under their breath—as I believe everyone did. Rose evidently noticed the impression his entrance had made and leered his satisfaction, allowing his gimlet eyes finally to come to rest upon Émilienne who, to my utter surprise, had come forward with a chair. She seemed to share the general fear which his presence occasioned—fear of the humiliating sneers which his displeasure would bring forth and the cunningly conceived indignities which he had the power to inflict on us if he so desired. As we watched him while Émilienne poured out his coffee, we knew why he had violated a cardinal rule of the British Army code—sergeants did not consort with privates, much less drink with them. Hurriedly, we four bade Émilienne and her folks 'goodnight' and made our exit. Outside, Phillips expectorated twice noisily on the pavé yard. 'My God, it makes you want to . . .' Words failed him, as we picked our way through a sleeting rain to *Tante*'s cottage.

Tante gave me a warm welcome—'ah, Dick!'—and produced the glasses. We spent the remainder of the evening there, saddened as she told us that, because of her mother, they were leaving Berles and going to live with her sister at a village near Doullens—in a few days she thought, but it depended on the authorities and when transport for their effects could be arranged. This, in any case, would have to be under cover of darkness.

Our new billet was not nearly so commodious as the former one had been, but still, the netting beds weren't too bad, and the broken windows had been repaired with sacking, pieces of corrugated iron and boxwood. The rain came in via the damaged roof at one corner—the only real defect—and many were the times after this when the shelter our room afforded us, fresh from the line, seemed the height of luxury. The thought of it when we were in up there was the sole thing to which we looked forward on our relief.

The next morning I had my first taste of Rose as a drill

sergeant. After a minute inspection outside the billet, we were marched to a clearing in the rusty barbed wire defences behind the village in the lee of some tall trees. Here our lieutenant appeared and inspected us, followed by Sergeant Rose. As the lieutenant came to me he seemed genuinely pleased and gave me a cheery word or two before passing on. He then handed over the parade to Rose to do his worst—which he certainly did, for two solid hours, at the end of which we did things mechanically to an accompaniment of intermittent sarcasm between bawled orders. Possibly this smartened us up after a fashion, but it was the thought that we were being made the puppets of this little beast—to double at his whim over this shell-pocked stubble field, to wheel, to halt, to quick march, trail arms, extend, to assume the prone position (which last, as he well knew, meant that our knees and elbows at least were soaking wet)—all this made us long for the great day when we should witness his discomfiture. Such is the difference between the cheerful compliance with orders given by a real leader, and the subservience enforced by an inferior intellect dimly conscious of his own shortcomings, but endeavouring to hide them by the ferocious abuse of the little authority entrusted to him.

His downfall happened sooner than any of us expected. Our lieutenant appeared and was approaching when one of the nearby batteries fired a round. Taken completely off his guard, Rose ran like a rabbit for the trees. Just then a second gun fired, at which he pulled up short in a welter of indecision, and in the same instant saw our lieutenant. He realized that he had been seen. All this happened in about ten seconds; and utter surprise at what we had witnessed had precluded any other action on our part. We watched Rose recover himself and step up to the lieutenant as smartly as he could and salute. Rose's back was to us, but we saw that our officer's unease was ill disguised, as he could see our reaction. Evidently he told Rose to march us back and dismiss us, and this he did. We, on our part, by keeping absolute silence in the ranks, gave him no chance of recovering his aggression.

Back in the billet, Freddy Smith summed up our feelings neatly. 'That's the best thing the artillery's done since we came here!' Of course, the good news soon spread in the village and we had our

GOING "IN" – BERLES AU BOIS.

DEC. 1915.

legs pulled unmercifully. It was too much for Rose; he was not in evidence for the rest of that day, and in the morning Simmonds told us he had reported sick.

Meanwhile we had pouring rain, followed by a hard frost in the morning. We had to go into the line, but thoughts of Rose

The Ravine and site of Battalion H.Q. dugouts, Berles–Monchy road, photographed in September 1966. The parapet of the road bridge indicates site of Nottage's Folly, now a drain. Nobs' Walk, the communication trench from Berles, ran on the right of this road to the Ravine dugouts. From there, Narborough Road ran up the hill to the front line, beyond the crest.

were put clean out of our minds by the issue to us of natural skin coats—with the hair on. As it was very cold we revelled in their warmth, and the village street looked like a scene in Lapland or Alaska. When the warmth engendered reached the skin coats, the smell became almost too strong for our stomachs in the billet. Nevertheless, notwithstanding the thaw and drizzling rain, we all wore our coats under our equipment as we set out to relieve the 6th Battalion once more for a four-day tour of duty. We, under the supervision of Corporal Jones, were indeed a cheerful party until we had gone a hundred yards or so down Nob's Walk. It was then evident that we were in a muddy, squelching quagmire, in which we had to stand for minutes on end because of holdups of the troops in front of us. Every now and then, huge slices of the trench sides slipped down to the bottom, loosened by the alternate frosts, rains and thaws of the previous few days. But

Site of Monchy Mill and 97 Trench. Ramsart Church and north end of Adinfer Wood in the distance.

worse was to come. The heavy rain and the thaw had flooded the trench floor, and in places the duckboard sump covers had floated off. Where earth from the sides had fallen, we unsuspecting unfortunates blundered in up to the waist.

In this fashion we emerged from Nottage's Folly, near Battalion Headquarters, over an hour behind time; in a sorry mess indeed, and apprehensive of what we should have to encounter in tackling Narborough Road, up to 97 Trench. After a breather we started off again, and found the average depth of the morass knee high, while every few minutes one of us blundered into a sump and had to be rescued by his mates. Eventually our progress stopped altogether and, dilapidated and wet through as we were, our spirits were, I suppose, at their lowest. We cursed and cursed, louder and longer at each fresh setback, although we couldn't help laughing wryly at times at each others' comical efforts to surmount immediate difficulties. One of us, whose watch was still accessible and readable, said that it was nearly twelve o'clock midday. Then Corporal Jones, saying that getting shot wasn't much worse than going on as we were doing, led the way up the slippery side of the crumbling trench and, one by one, we followed. As we paused to get our bearings and ascertain whence the first bullets would probably come at us, we were astonished to see groups of figures moving like ants all over the landscape in front of us. Evidently they had reached the same conclusion, but considerably earlier, and had almost reached the front line. No one molested them.

We gazed incredulously at the scene, now lit by wintry sunshine, but our amazement was complete when we observed a snake-like trail of German soldiers approaching their trenches from Monchy in full view of everybody. Needless to say, no one fired at them— or, I may say, felt like doing so.

As we stood there and kicked and scraped the worst of the mud from our persons, we just had to laugh, warmed as we were by the excitement of this new experience. 'What a war! What would some of our armchair military experts at home advise now?' In that moment the tremendous truth dawned on us: that men find it next to impossible to hate or fight when they are cold and wet. Someone echoed our feelings with, 'what are we fighting for, anyhow?' Truth to tell, just then we had forgotten.

The Truce
8th Leicestershire (Regiments
73rd (Hanover) Fusiliers
Dec. 1915

Looking around, we saw the road just to our right which we knew led past our position in 97 Trench to Monchy. It had not been used for nearly a year, and grass and weeds, now withered, had grown upon it. The surface was further pock-marked with shell holes and it was crossed at intervals by masses of rusty barbed wire entanglements. Still, we made for it, and from that point our progress was comparatively easy. Arrived on the brow of the hill and at the grim ruin of the mill, we looked down upon the German trenches and, incidentally, saw occupants, a dozen or more of whom were walking about smoking, or shouting to each other in the open. Of us they took not the slightest notice, probably because already they could see several hundred khaki figures away to our left, and almost the same number in *Feldgrau*.

We therefore took the opportunity of having a good look round. In Berles we had been told of the fight at the mill in November 1914, and here we saw abundant evidence of it, including the rotted horses and now-tattered uniformed skeletons of some French cavalrymen. Apparently the trench lines had been stabilized in their present position after this fight. We turned away from the gruesome sight, resolving to bury the remains at night if we could. In the meantime we were hailed by the 6th Battalion Lewis gunners we were reliving, who, hearing us approaching, had climbed out of their trench and were coming to meet us. Then handover took place on top. They were in a better state than we were, not having struggled through over a mile of mud as we had done. They said that the dugout was still O.K. and that things had been very quiet. We advised them to keep to the road if they could, and after looking at us they needed no encouragement.

As they left we heard shouting opposite, and saw a group of German soldiers trying to attract our attention. Hurriedly, there-fore, we dumped our kits, cleaned up the gun, mounted it in the emplacement and got on the top again to see what transpired, our sodden feet and clothes forgotten. In the bright sunshine the scene before us was of enthralling interest. From the top of our actual trench we could not understand what the Germans to our front intended to convey to us, as the thick wire thrown out by both sides largely obscured our view of one another. But about 150 yards to our left, where the distance between the trench lines increased and there was a distinct no-man's land, we saw a number of our men clear our wire and advance to meet a party of German soldiers there. They met, and groups were soon deep in conversation, gesticulating and laughing in efforts to understand one another. We saw the Germans stroking the hairy coats worn by our chaps, mud-encrusted though they were. Cigarettes were exchanged, and we observed several Leicesters smoking cigars. The Germans offered their water-bottles which, we were told afterwards, contained Schnapps or coffee.

Some minutes went by and then a shrill whistle sounded. We saw one of our 'A' Company officers—a well-liked lieutenant, Wratislaw by name—sign urgently to our men to return to their trenches. He appeared to meet a German officer in one of the groups, as salutes were exchanged, and they talked for some moments. Then they parted with more salutes, and both sides streamed back to their own trenches—regretfully, it appeared.

We, indeed, were disappointed, as we were about to hazard a foray through our wire to reach our opposite numbers, and fancied sampling German cigars and cigarettes. Also, we wished particu-larly to see in the flesh 'Charlie' and another German, 'Paul', who

"STAND TO"

DECEMBER EVENING 1915. MONCHY MILL – 97 TRENCH
'COCKNEY' NEWMAN conducting Salvationist service thus: –
"Nah that Sister Mary there 'as testified (several 'Allelujahs!')
we'll all sing together number Two Twoty Two in the Red Book –
JOYFUL WILL THE MEETING BE!' . . . Then . .
     "ANOTHER SHILLING ON THE DRUM BROTHERS!" . . . .
. . followed by distinct sounds of laughter from the German
73rd. Fusilier Regiment of Hanover – (25/30 Yds. away in the
Trench opposite), and two quick bullets into our parapet.

94

spoke English even better. These two still shouted across to us at 'stand to' in the evenings and sang (very abusive) songs in a light-hearted way, revelling in all the swear words. In this we were baulked, however. A minute or two later the dreary landscape was empty again. Cautiously we peered through chinks in the sandbags for signs of movement. The silence was the more impressive by reason of the previous shouting. Then we saw a German almost opposite get on top of his trench and relieve himself on the wire in leisurely fashion. He prepared to get down again when a shot echoed over the fields and the German fell back. We saw him struggle to his knees and disappear into the German trench. This wretched shot had been fired by one of our 'A' Company, and we all felt ashamed for our side; the more so when, a few moments later, 'Paul' shouted across, 'Tommy, you don't play the game!'

After that the merest suspicion of movement above our parapet brought an immediate 'crack'—perhaps several—and we dreaded a *minnenwerfer* or rifle grenade strafe with our trench in such a terrible state. We could not have run a yard to dodge them. Fortunately for us the enemy forbore to do this; probably they had troubles similar to ours. Their trench was lower than ours, and that night we heard sounds of pumping for some hours. Ruefully, we wished we had a pump, too. We certainly could have used it. The water was level with the top of the firestep. Mercifully however, the weather turned fine and frosty again and we worked hard all day filling bags, building them up at night. By dint of continuous baling, the water level was lowered to a muddy quagmire over our boot tops, which didn't matter much in our case as our feet were long since soaked, and our spare socks also. When we were relieved after four days, our front trench didn't look too bad, but a horse and cart could have been driven down it, as the top was so wide. It no longer afforded us the protection it had formerly.

As may be imagined, it was with feelings of thankfulness, and anticipation of a good sleep in dry blankets, that we filed once more into our billet and threw down our kits on the beds before going to Émilienne's for coffee and a warm before her stove. In retrospect, those nights when we came out of the line stand out

CANDLES

Chocolat
Menier

Evening at Guillienae's
Berles au Bois.
Dec. 1915.

as memories to be cherished, when good fellowship reigned and our cares for the moment were forgotten.

I see again my comrades standing there, mud-caked from head to foot, slinging their accoutrements one by one upon the netting beds, shoulder straps unbuttoned and flapping; finding, by the light of several guttering candle-ends, nails on which to hang their rifles, wrapped around as they were with discarded socks or mufflers in an effort to protect them from the mud. Phillips leans over our best candle to get a light for his pipe, and as tobacco ash drops on to the grease in profusion, the flame, alternately rising and subsiding as he draws, throws into relief the clay-encrusted stubble on his otherwise rosy features. Several voices are raised in protest from the dim corners of the room.

'Hi there . . . Who the . . .? How the . . .?'

But Phillips shakes like a great jelly and stands back, puffing contentedly, his happy laugh echoing all round. The candle, fouled with tobacco ash, gutters and splutters terribly, but nobody cares. 'Plenty of candles tonight . . . let's go to Émilienne's!'

We troop into the darkness without, our goal a few shafts of light issuing from the closed shutter a few yards away. A burst of sound and warm smoke-tinted yellow light assail us as we make our several ways to the stove in the centre of the crowded throng.

'*Ah, bon soir messieurs!* . . . *Ah—vous Philippe, ah Freddie—faites s'asseoir*—one minute!' As Émilienne greets us, beaming as she prepares to preside over the coffee pot, the other women hurry about, Maman jabbering, Skinny Liz piping shrilly. Soon we are sitting round the stove, baking hard the mud upon our clothes— terribly shabby—but at last thoroughly warm and happy. More of our mates come in and the air gets even bluer with tobacco smoke. Everyone is in a good humour.

'Émilienne—*avez-vous* candles—*un* packet, *s'il vous plait?*'

'Émilienne—matches, *alumettes, chocolat* . . . biscuits.'

She does a roaring trade. From the mantelpiece she produces a school slate and prepares to write thereon, smiling broadly. 'On *der* slate, you say—*hein?*'

'*Oui, oui* Émilienne—pay *demain matin*—tomorrow!'

'All right, Tommy—you not forget!' and, a sudden thought striking her, she singles out a man through the smoke and makes a significant note on the slate. 'Jacques—Jack—you pay to-morrow—you not pay me—*beaucoup fâché avec vous!*' There is a roar of laughter and shouts of 'We'll see that he pays Émilienne!'

Then we troop out into the darkness and to blessed bed. We take our boots off, then our sodden socks—these with difficulty, as we notice that in places the skin is embedded in the sock and comes off with it. Between our blankets, we read our letters by the light of a dozen or more fresh candles and yarn awhile. Then, one by one, the candles are extinguished, and in a few more minutes all is quiet save for occasional echoing reports from the front line, or the whining ricochetting of spent bullets overhead.

In the morning, to our dismay, our feet felt burning hot and were swollen, so that we got into our boots with considerable difficulty, but managed to march it off in an hour's drill in the stubble field under the direction of Sergeant Rose—who, we noted with considerable satisfaction, was looking very seedy. His stand-ard of barking had also deteriorated, and we gathered the impres-sion that he was glad after an hour to march us back to the billet and direct us to 'make and mend' (in the words of our ex-naval Corporal Jones) as our afternoon task.

Our four-day respite passed only too quickly. One afternoon, to our disgust, we were all (including several recruits to our Lewis gun section) roped in for a fatigue party, carrying girders for the R.E. from Bienvillers church to the line in front of that village—a march of three kilometres from Berles.

On the journey up St. Cross Street (the communication trench) with a girder, I partnered a chap who stammered when excited, and whose first name was Sam. Just about then an American ragtime song was quite popular, which started 'Let stammering Sam sing'; accordingly Sam's leg was pulled quite a lot. Just as we reached the junction with the front line—thankfully, for we felt pretty well exhausted—we heard several ominous 'pops' fol-lowed by the swishing that presaged the arrival of a shower of rifle grenades. Hastily dropping our heavy load, we crouched in the trench; even as we did so, with a resounding 'Whoosh' a grenade buried itself in the soft mud between us and beside the girder, the protruding rod smoking, the mud steaming. We looked at it fascinated—speechless. At length approaching footsteps brought us to our senses. I suppose I said something blasphemous, but Sam struggled ineffectually to articulate.

The corporal of the 7th Battalion, who were in the line there, stopped by us for a moment. 'You want to take that to our bombers—they'll see to it!' This was too much for Sam, who nearly choked in giving tongue.

'Y-y-y-y-y-y-you-yu-you . . . take-the-bloody-thing-yourself!' So saying, he got to his feet and picked up his end of our girder, which we dumped at its destination as soon as we could.

We had two new men in our section, one a Leicester youth named Collins (of whom more anon), the other a blue-eyed lad from Market Harborough whose name I forget but who, on arrival with us, gave the impression of being more than usually naïve. When he produced a Crown and Anchor board, and spread it in the yard of our billet after our midday stew on the morning we were paid twenty francs apiece, a crowd of us soon gathered round him in anticipation of easy pickings. Being a mess orderly that day, I watched from a distance while cleaning out a dixie, but from disgruntled mates who left the crowd one by one, I gathered that he was rapidly skinning all of them. This is, in fact, what occurred, and when we went in again we realized every time we were close to him that somewhere on his person he carried several hundred francs. In particular it infuriated Corporal Jones, to whom, among others, I had lent three francs.

Talk among us in the village centred on the recent truce, and we listened to several individual accounts from 'A' Company men who had been more fortunate than ourselves in making contact with our opposite numbers. Apparently they were the 73rd Fusilier Regiment from Hanover, and on their caps had the word 'Gibraltar'—an honour gained when the regiment fought with the British at the Siege of Gibraltar in 1781–83.

The weather had now broken up in earnest and we were issued with whale oil with which to rub our feet before going in. By the time we reached 97 Trench we were wet through from the waist downward and plastered with mud. Our spell of four days was one of unrelieved misery, but I recall several events, including the sniping—clean through the head—of one of 'A' Company on sentry in the next bay to ours, as he stood on the firestep with his

F.O.O. R.F.A. 9ᵗ Trench Berles-Monchy Dec. 1915.

back to the parapet, talking to two of us one morning. He must have forgotten momentarily, and stood up to his full height. He fell forward almost on to us, but there was nothing we could do: he was dead, and two of us carried him down to Battalion H.Q., which took us the whole afternoon.

By contrast, the lad from Market Harborough had a truly miraculous escape when we were standing to the following evening. We were cleaning our rifles and he, with another, was on the firestep. A crack and he fell back, and in a moment blood was pouring all over his shoulders. Getting to him, we removed his cap, and it was quite clear then what had happened. The bullet had been deflected in some way by his cap badge and had, literally, parted his hair down the middle, gone over the crown and halfway down the back of his skull.

Naturally he was very frightened, but we made as good a job of him as we could, assuring him at the same time that he'd got a lovely 'Blighty'. Corporal Jones detailed Lineker and Freddy Smith to take him down to Battalion H.Q., and, taking them to the end of the bay before they started, whispered audibly and fiercely, 'don't you come back without his blow belt—or what he's got in it—all our spendin' money for Christmas! Besides,' he added, 'the poultice wallahs down there will get it if we don't.' He was dead right. Naturally, therefore, most of us awaited their return with more than usual interest, and in view of their protracted absence there was an atmosphere of tension in our shelter. Just before two of us were relieving those on sentry about 9 p.m. they appeared, and Corporal Jones sat up abruptly, eyeing, as we were doing, the sorry mess they were in. Each leaned over the candle and lit a cigarette. At length—'Well?' from Jones. The two looked at each other and Lineker grinned. 'You tell 'em, Freddy.' Whereupon Freddy unbuttoned his top pocket, produced a wad of dirty notes and threw them down on Corporal Jones' blanket. 'Should be a hundred and fifty there, Corp.'

Corporal Jones wetted a finger and counted the notes lovingly. 'Oh you little beauties—you little beauties.' Then suddenly, 'where's the rest, Freddy?' Lineker then spoke. 'We left him a bit, he's a good lad at heart. We'd never have got anything if we'd tried any other way; the orderlies down there at H.Q. were busy with him all the time so that he could go back on the ration limber, so we tried moral persuasion and Freddy almost had him crying at the last minute. He took out his wallet—he'd got an inside pocket sewn in his shirt—and coughed up what you've got there. There was nothing in his blow belt as far as we could see except a few cap badges stuck round it.'

Jones had to be content. As far as I know he shared out about 25 francs apiece to our augmented section, admonishing each of us not to let on to any of the other sections. For obvious reasons, I did not participate in this share-out, but only recouped the few frances I had lent.

I recall, too—with some relish, even now—the arrival in our trench one dismally dull afternoon of a field artillery subaltern. (We came to know his kind well subsequently as forward observing officers, or F.O.O.s, when on similar errands.) He was accompanied by a signaller trailing a reel of telephone wire and with the requisite outfit for using it. We were agog to know what this portended, particularly when, after a few moments' conversation with Corporal Jones, they went to our 'secret' observation post off the trench leading to our dugout and latrine. Here the officer climbed into position, the signaller at the same time squatting on the trench floor below and testing his line.

It should be realized that, we had never before witnessed the procedure of an artillery battery registering. We had held our trenches for several months—in the face of daily salvoes of whizz-bangs and five-nines, in addition to the liberal plasterings we received almost nightly from the *minnenwerfer* sections—without any practical assistance from our gunners, and were anxious to see whether the shell shortage was over, and whether aid (in the form of retaliation) that our officers assured us they had repeatedly, but fruitlessly, requested, would be forthcoming. Those of us not on duty, therefore, drifted to where the signaller was transmitting to the battery, range and direction, type of shell, as ordered by the F.O.O. Fascinated, we waited for the magic order 'fire!', and fidgeted as he took a last long look through his binoculars at the target and checked with his protractor. This seemed to be something on the north-eastern flank of Monchy, slightly left of where we stood. Then. . . 'No. 1 gun, fire!'

We heard the signaller repeat the order and shout to the F.O.O. 'No. 1 gun fired, sir . . . No. 2 gun—No. 2 gun', but we were knocked all of a heap by a sudden rushing roar, half-stunned and smothered with debris and choked by picric acid fumes as the shell burst just behind the trench a few yards from us. For what seemed an age our singing ears listened to the thump and patter of disturbed earth and iron falling around. Freddy Smith broke the tension. Scrambling to his feet, and with an attempt at a grin, he remarked significantly, 'What goes up, must come down!'

We followed his example and noted that the signaller was badly shaken. He hadn't gone through the breaking-in by shell and *minnenwerfer* that had been our lot. Glancing upwards, we saw the haggard and worried features of the F.O.O. as he scrambled down from his perch and took the phone from the signaller, saying to us as he did so, 'it's this bloody American stuff they're giving us.' He then unburdened himself to his battery for ten minutes or so, after which he seemed to recover his equanimity. 'Sorry about this, you chaps,' and he scrambled up to his vantage point again. 'Better luck this time, I hope!'

The battery then fired at intervals for corrections three pairs of shells, one each of H.E. and shrapnel, two of which latter the F.O.O. told us were duds. His news really shocked us, and it was pretty disturbing to learn that, after sixteen months of war, our shells either wouldn't carry accurately or wouldn't burst. In the meanwhile we were relieved when, as dusk approached, the signaller packed his gear and they both departed, as we put it rather bitterly, 'back to tea'. For we rarely had a hot meal under the conditions then existing. The dixie carriers could only reach the front line at night over the top, and then we had to send two men with our mess tins to a central distributing point. Frequently they staggered back with the contents spilled or fouled with mud and, by the time they arrived, quite cold.

That evening, whether by way of retaliation we knew not, the enemy produced a new form of frightfulness—throwing over two *minnenwerfer* 'rum jars', many times the size of those to which we had been accustomed hitherto. Truly appalling crashes followed the sparking arcs that the great cylinders made as they tumbled over and over through the air. We were thankful when relief came at length and we found ourselves once more in Berles.

It had been a tour of duty that, in many respects, we should have liked to forget. What was worse, we found that another battalion had come to Berles for instruction with us—the 19th Battalion of the Manchester Regiment—and the billeting capacity of the village was taxed to the utmost.

Just before the 6th Battalion relieved us, we determined to cut off the long skirts of our greatcoats, as we had seen done by many men already. The added weight when caked with mud, and the additional obstacle to progress this caused, was the reason. To do this we used an old razor, which made a tolerably clean cut; but one of our recruits, Collins, cut his so short that the sack pockets hung down well below the hem on either side. Behind, his coat tails extended but a foot or so below his waist belt, giving him an altogether ludicrous appearance, the stump protruding from his backside in a manner reminiscent of a cockerel's tail feathers.

When eventually we removed our foot gear once more in Berles—and, by the way, the first operation was to remove the sandbag wrapped around each leg to keep out the worst of the mud: a filthy business—our feet were sodden and numb, and looked it. Patches of skin came away with our socks when, gingerly, we eased them off. Within an hour or so of getting between the blankets we were forced to thrust our burning feet beyond them, and on the following morning not one of us could get his boots on. Fortunately two mates who had not gone in with us (one had just been to England on compassionate leave) were able to wait on us, and we heard then two pieces of news as we held out our mess tins. First, that Sergeant Rose had gone down the line 'sick'—wonderful if true—and second (which caused within my immediate circle a real feeling of sadness), that *Tante* and her mother had gone, and the cottage was now full of Manchesters. They, of course, had no clue to her address.

Lieutenant Millburn was very considerate when he saw the state of our feet and cheered us up when he told us that we were all being issued with gum boots; but the next day he dismayed us with the news that, as there were only enough for the troops in the line, the 6th Battalion had them and when we went in we should take them over. As we surmised, this was a most unfortunate and stupid piece of staff work, well-meaning as, in all probability, it was. We got our feet and legs wet going in, and had to take over boots already sodden inside with perspiration and from the fact that the original wearer's feet were wet when he put them on. All very unpleasant. Luckily, when we went in for our last time before Christmas, I managed to take over a pair a couple of sizes too large for me, and, with the aid of my remaining pair of

WHILE SHEPHERDS ···AND THE 73RD.FUSILIER REGT. ····· WATCHED !
ON WIRING PARTY. CHRISTMAS NIGHT, 1915
MONCHY AU BOIS.

dry socks I was tolerably comfortable for a while; but the weather turned cold, and then my troubles began. My right foot began to burn and throb so much that wet mud on the outside of the boot dried in a few minutes, while that on my left remained—well, wet mud! At this period shells, bullets, *minnenwerfer* were minor considerations with us. Our enemies were mud and water, and their avowed object—our feet.

By superhuman efforts we managed to manhandle a hand-pump of the type used for emptying cesspools, together with the intake and delivery hoses, up from Battalion H.Q. Several of us crawled out into our wire and threaded the delivery pipe as far as it would go through it, and covered it as well as we could. It sloped downhill towards the German trenches, and once it was started relays of us pumped almost continuously, cheered by the distinct fall in the water level. This spurred us on to renewed efforts, and we persevered until all that was left was the thick ooze. This we shovelled as well as we could on to the parados. Here I would observe that there was a distinct knack in mud-slinging; the inexperienced exponent found that the greater part refused to leave the shovel, with the result that he pulled his arms almost from their sockets and plastered himself with catapulted mud.

The following night we had to go out with our Lewis gun and give cover for a wiring party.

I retain one other recollection of that turn. Two days before Christmas we were relieved as dusk fell. For some reason unknown to us, our mail came up at midday—Battalion H.Q. had kept it all night. With Christmas imminent, practically every man had parcels. We tied these on to our equipment when the relief came, and were anticipating an uncomfortable struggle in the dusk down Narborough Road, when Corporal Jones announced that he was going to wait a few minutes and go over the top. We needed no encouragement to follow him when he started, one after the other, but it couldn't have been dark enough, as we were spotted. We went to earth as quickly as we could after the first bullet arrived, and the next minute provided one of our worst experiences for a long time. Several rifles were potting at us, the bullets striking sparks from the mass of rusty wire around Monchy Mill, which didn't help matters at all. I was crawling on my stomach with my parcels tied to the pack on my back when I felt a jar. When we reached Berles—thanking our lucky stars, as it was a mercy none of us was hit, I found that the bullet had gone right through two one-ounce packets of Chairman tobacco and a cake.

We found Émilienne's full of Manchesters, but they were a very good lot of chaps and we liked them from the start. I believe a prominent Mancunian had raised them, and I recall that many of those we met worked in banks, insurance and other offices. What staggered us was what they told us about their salaries: their employers were making up their army pay to what they were getting when they enlisted.

Christmas came—1915. In our billet we suffered an absolute surfeit of good things from home; whenever mail came up there was another avalanche of parcels. Phillips' sister, a buyer at Marshall & Snelgrove's, sent him a hamper from Harrods with enough preserved ginger and Turkish Delight to stock a shop. Ted Lineker had another, from his mother, via the Army & Navy Stores, with all sorts of delicacies, including a tongue, wonderful apples and pears wrapped like china, nuts and preserved fruits. Of cigarettes and tobacco there was a glut; also of socks, mufflers, Harrison's Pomade and divers other lice destroyers. The air was redolent of cigar smoke, and when we went into the line again the day after Boxing Day most of us resembled Christmas trees, so many parcels and odds and ends had we tied to our kits. I don't think we touched our rations, and unopened tins of jam, bully beef and so on lay stacked on the mantel-shelves of our billet.

On Christmas night, however, we were out on a wiring party in front of our 7th Battalion, south-west of Monchy Mill and quite near our 97 Trench. As can be imagined, we groused a lot on the way at our disgusting luck, but the march cleared the Christmas fug from our heads—and anyhow, we managed to complete most of our task before the moon rose over the mist-covered frosty fields, whence floated sounds of song, including '*Helige Nacht*', across the fifty yards or so of jumbled wire and stakes separating us from a watchful enemy.

In those days there were no screw pickets. Each stake had to be driven into the frozen ground with a maul, the impact noise muffled by a folded sandbag on top of the stake. We were sniped at intermittently by an enemy who knew we were there but could not quite locate us, and once we were sprayed by machine-gun bullets from a flank, which whizzed past knee high, striking sparks as they hit the festoons of wire we were putting up. Instinctively we dared not crouch, on the principle that one in the leg was preferable to one in the stomach or head. When Verey lights went up we stood stock still, the smoking and spluttering remains twice falling quite close to us. Some of our stakes weren't driven in very firmly, I'm afraid, but we managed to get back without mishap. One in the stomach didn't strike us as a fitting conclusion to the festive season. I recall that, no doubt acting on orders from above,

Our First "TIN HATS"

Monchy au Bois. Feb.1916.

our guns of all calibres (such as they were) strafed Fritz for ten minutes early on Christmas morning. The general opinion expressed among us was anything but complimentary, for two reasons: because there was a wish to leave Fritz alone for a day; and because, when our officers had called for retaliation from our artillery when our trenches were being flattened by *minnenwerfers* and five-nines, the reply was invariably, 'we're short of shells! Sorry!'

With the New Year 1916 winter really arrived, and frost was

general, with very occasional thaws during the months of January and February. I recall that we took over a further sector of French-held trenches to our left in front of Bailleulmont, and that the mitrailleuse section we relieved left us some fairly fresh French bread, which we voted good and a pleasant change. These trenches had not been hammered as ours had been, either, and apparently it had been a quiet war there till we arrived.

About this time, too, we were issued with the first tin hats; initially, to the men in the line, who handed them over to those relieving them. They couldn't have been more unpopular, and it took the repeated threats of court martial treatment to get us to wear them. In the event, it was something else to carry and for weeks a subject for grousing.

Throughout these first months of 1916, however, our over-riding and ever-present concern was our feet. The constant standing in mud and water in December had done its fell work only too well: the bitter cold of January and February completed the ruin. In spite of the lavish use of whale oil and the fact that every man now had his own rubber thigh boots, these amenities seemed to do little to mitigate the ravages of what soon became known as 'trench foot', and occasionally of frostbite. To provide ease from the bitter cold, tours of trench duty were shortened from four days to forty-eight hours, but on each morning after relief the battalion sick parade in Berles lengthened, assuming proportions which caused our officers grave anxiety. From high up came a stream of instructions and threats: strange as it may seem, serious attempts were made to rate trench foot as a crime. However preventable it may have been in the case of new troops, we took the view (with blasphemous feeling) that 'the stable door was being shut after the horse had bolted' and that those responsible had no experience of standing in the mud and water for days at a time, as had been our lot, or of exposure afterwards to the frosts.

For the cold *was* intense. No one who has not done sentry-go under the same conditions in the watches from midnight to 'stand to' can have an adequate idea of the numbing effect on the senses of such a January dawn. Stamp our feet and flail our arms as we might, the cold gradually gained on us. Our ears, deprived by instructions from above of the protection of ear-flaps or balaclava helmets (as these were held to prevent sentries hearing a creeping enemy), had long since ceased to have any feeling in them at all. We nudged one another frequently to keep alert. A muttered word or a cough, and the breath made a miniature cloud of steam in the frosty air. With 'stand to' and first light, we would cock our frozen ears in an effort to catch the first faint footfalls of the dixie carriers coming up the communication trench from the cookhouse in the ravine, their load of hot tea well laced with rum, and the bacon—alas—sadly congealed. The very sound quickened our numbed senses, and as the dixie drew nearer, though still at a distance, the aroma of the rum reached us across the now-white-topped sandbags. How welcome, when eventually it arrived and put new life into us to face another day. If we could, we used to stand over the steaming dixie and breathe in deeply through our running noses, until the carriers replaced the lid and, stolidly shouldering it again, staggered off around the traverse.

In my own case my weakness was my right leg. With each change of weather my thigh, where I had been hit, ached un-accountably, and in mid February my right foot started to throb, swell and get hot. I managed to keep going, however, realizing that several mates were in worse case than I was. We all longed for the coming of spring and better weather, in the hope that our troubles would pass.

No longer we went into the line at 97 Trench; instead we manned a trench and emplacement in the middle of the battalion front, extended by taking over the French trenches. The enemy was about 150 yards from us, but as we had patrols out every night, often covering them with our Lewis gun, things were quite lively, although there weren't so many *minnenwerfers*. When we reached Berles on one occasion, I was detailed for a four-day course on Lewis gun work and a new respirator at St. Amand. Congratulating ourselves on our good fortune, a mate from 'D' Company's section and I set out early the following morning, but on reaching Pommier we had to rest because of our feet. Even-tually, with more rests, we reached St. Amand, where our billet and schoolroom were adjoining barns, the entrance to one on the village street. Our billet was warm and dry, and about twenty-four of us were on the course from battalions of our division. It was a wonderful feeling to lie down in the straw and pull our blankets well around us, and feel that with the morrow we had not to journey once more up the communication trench.

St. Amand, although only six kilometres or so west of our front line, gave us our first glimpse of that other world of back-area soldiers. Our Divisional H.Q. was at Pas-en-Artois, a few miles further to the rear, and transport and headquarter details were coming through our village at all hours, many of them despatch riders on motorcycles. There were also lots of well-dressed officers, some with red tabs and highly polished boots and belts, which entailed much saluting on our part. I remember St. Amand chiefly because one evening we saw our divisional concert party perform in a converted barn there. It was newly formed then, and the organizer and producer was, I believe a very popular and talented young actor by the name of Nelson Keys, a lieutenant in one of the Royal Fusilier battalions in our division.

The divisional band played the accompaniments to what were, more often than not, parodied versions of current London revue hits, the words strikingly topical and appealing to we front line soldiers, away from it all for a few days. Recruited as they had been from units of the division for their various talents, they knew that their audiences regarded them with envy. One of them, 'Sandy' Reeve by name, from our 'C' Company, had a fine bass voice. In camps in England he had often elicited thunderous applause for his rendering of 'Asleep in the Deep'. He repeated it that evening as an encore, but the great attraction at this and all such concert parties I saw subsequently was the 'girl'—a likely lad with unusual acting ability, made up regardless of expense, who sang quite girlishly and looked very pretty. 'She' was a real success.

The final number by the assembled troupe was to the tune of a current London hit song, 'You're here and I'm here, so what do we care?' The words, however, differed greatly, and I quote from memory:

> You're here and we're here
> We hope you've been amused
> Now you've seen what we've done—well
> We hope you won't abuse us

'Cause we'll tell you straight and true
That we are soldiers just like you—
And though
We're not in the trenches just now
It's because our gallant Staff
Has sent us around here
To try and make you laugh
But one and all
We're ready at the call
To join our Regiments!

We enjoyed that evening, and, indeed, our stay in St. Amand, very much, although I remember little of what we did on the course, except that the 'respirator' turned out to be a mine rescue apparatus made by Siebe Gorman Ltd. which included a small oxygen cylinder at 1,500 lbs/sq. in. pressure, carried on the left side. Leading from this was a bellows slung round the neck on a harness, connected also to the face-piece. The intention was to issue the Number One of each gun with these, to give immunity from the deadliest gas attack. It was beautifully made, but we wondered what would happen if a bullet hit the oxygen cylinder. The general opinion seemed to be—rightly or wrongly—that the wearer would be incinerated. However, shortly after our return to Berles, one per gun was issued. I had to carry ours, and give instruction to other teams. After a few weeks, although we never had an opportunity of testing their worth, they were recalled; for which relief I, at any rate, was grateful.

The thoughts of many of us at that time were centred on the stupendous German attack on the fortress of Verdun, and on the heroic efforts of our French allies to hold on. We, of course, derived our information from newspapers nearly a week old, or from accounts handed on from visitors from back areas, but it was plain to us all that the carnage on both sides was unprecedented, due largely to the heavy concentrations of artillery. We did some very serious thinking and arguing amongst ourselves. Early in March the weather improved, and one morning the sun shone warmly on our trench, making the wet sandbags steam. Several larks sang overhead, high above the expanses of withered brown grass, tumbled earth and rusty wire. It was good. Wet socks were laid out to dry; fellows shaved in cracked pieces of mirror and gave their hair more attention than for many months in the past. In the afternoon the sun still shone and birds—I know not what kind—cheeped at intervals. From a gap in the bags on the parados of our bay, we could look back over the desolation towards Berles. The sun glinted on the damaged spire, and by the churchyard wall we could discern the burial ground where quite a few of our mates lay already. Looking thus, a discussion started as to what the odds were that we should be pushing up the daisies before long. Grim jests were made in light-hearted fashion, the general purport of which were that (indicating the graves) *their* troubles were over; for them the war was finished . . . and anyway, when you came to think of it, it wasn't such a bad spot to be buried in, after all.

Yes, the future just then for us could not have been more obscure or uncertain . . . this stalemate of the trenches could not continue indefinitely . . . it might last for years yet . . . at least another winter . . . so we argued. At this last conjecture, a wag remarked that by that time we should have no feet left. Suppose we went forward in some grand attempt to break through . . . what would be our luck? . . . another Loos?

Pondering thus upon possibilities and probabilities, while the sun shone and the birds chirped, the strains of a military band playing 'Michigan' came across to us quite distinctly from the village. We looked at one another, pleasantly surprised, yet somewhat apprehensive, for we wondered what the enemy thought of it.

CHAPTER 7

OVERTURE

SPRING came to Berles-au-Bois. With the better weather and the lengthening days, we noticed the arrival of heavy artillery behind our front, with what seemed to be a fair supply of ammunition.

At intervals we heard the shells chortling high overhead towards the German back areas, and when in the line they gave us a new interest as we listened for the sounds of the explosions. These, when they occurred, seemed to travel a long way to reach our ears. When there was silence, it was broken by our mutterings of 'Dud!' Somewhat uneasily, we argued that Jerry would retaliate, and hoped that Berles would not be the target.

The damaged school building near the church housed a dry canteen, which opened for an hour at midday and in the late afternoon for the sale of toothpaste, condensed milk, candles, chocolate, Woodbines, etc. When the divisional band came, it played in the school yard, as it did one sunny afternoon in late March. In our billet one of our mates, by name Frank Mee, put his head through the doorway of our room, where we were lying on our wire-netting beds. 'Anyone want anything from the canteen?' We gave him our various requirements and the requisite francs where possible, and he went . . . and that was the last we ever saw of him. As he reached the school, the first heavy German howitzer shell hurtled down with terrible effect. succeeding shells for the next ten minutes completed the carnage, and I believe there were between thirty and forty casualties, including some civilians. More than a dozen were killed on the spot, among whom was poor Frank Mee. He was buried with others by the churchyard wall in what became, in after years, the Berles Franco-British Cemetery. Frank was twenty and a favourite of Émilienne's. When we came back to Berles in 1917, we found that she and her mother had tended his grave.

Corner of Franco-British Cemetery, churchyard extension, Berles-au-Bois,
Pas de Calais, photographed in September 1966.
Frank Mee's grave is third from the right.

My right foot still gave me a deal of trouble; indeed the generally bad condition of our feet may have been the reason why the division was relieved temporarily by the 4th (Regular) Division—we by the 2nd Battalion, the Essex Regiment. From Berles we marched to a village a few kilometres to the west, the name of which now escapes me. Here most of us found our legs again by means of the easy treatment prescribed—plenty of rest, not too many drills, and now and again a short route march. In the evenings we played 'House' in the *estaminets*, but on one occasion visited the next village for a most enjoyable performance by the 4th Division concert party. I recall the rousing singing of the current hit 'And when I told them how wonderful you are—They wouldn't believe me'.

The enterprising lads who started schools of 'House' reaped rich rewards, and soon became expert at calling the numbers by various humorous pseudonyms, which all of us soon learned: 'clicketty click, 66', 'legs eleven', 'Kelly's eye', 'Kaiser's downfall' and others followed, until the teller's voice was drowned by the sudden shout of 'House!' across the hot, smoke-laden room.

It was too good to last, and we soon found ourselves back in the line, where my right foot let me down badly and I had to report sick. I was sent down to a temporary hospital for trench foot cases in a large school at Doullens. Here I stayed for about three weeks—part of the time with a wire cage over my feet in the bed—but by then I had recovered sufficiently for the M.O. to pronounce me fit to rejoin my unit, which was now going to a rest area. This, at any rate, was cheering news, but when I went to draw my kit my boots, apparently, had been lost and I was issued with a pair which had already been worn and repaired with a clump sole of incredible thickness.

For information as to the whereabouts of the battalion I was told to inquire at the R.T.O., Doullens, and by the time I had found this my right foot was already giving me trouble. By lorry jumping and humping it alternately for two days, I located the battalion at length at the village of Warluzel and literally dragged myself to the barn where my Lewis gun section was billeted. Here I found room to dump my kit in a hay-strewn farm cart which stood in the arched entrance, and duly reported myself. I was ordered to report sick the following morning, owing to the really bad state of my right foot; which I did, causing our M.O. to inquire 'why the devil they had let me out thus'. He had half a mind to send me back, but eventually decided to put me on light duty, which suited me very well. I sat on the cart-tail of a morning in the spring sunshine, peeling potatoes or cutting up meat for the stew, the while I listened to the shouted sounds of drilling in the nearby field.

Invariably, as mid morning approached, an obliging brown hen would flutter into the cart behind me and lay an egg, amid much cackling. While it lasted it was a good life! By dint of stuffing my offending boot with wads of tightly packed paper, and wetting the upper, I managed to erase the furrows made by the previous owner, and achieve a reasonable degree of comfort as my foot healed. There came a day when I could dodge parades no longer, and did my drill and exercises with the rest. On returning to the cart, however, my egg generally awaited me.

While at Warluzel we were issued with four more Lewis guns, making the battalion's complement eight. The machine-gunners

'Peeling Spuds'
WARLUZEL (P de C.)
Apr 1916

ceased to be a separate section, and came under the direct control of their companies; thus our 'C' Company now possessed two Lewis guns, and we recruited a second team from their ranks. At the time we thought we had received the worst throwers of Mills grenades, as the platoon sergeants guarded their bombing sections jealously, but the newcomers mastered the intricacies of the Lewis gun surprisingly quickly, and compensated us in some degree for the loss of Horace Phillips and others.

At about this time, too, the newly organized Machine-Gun Corps, equipped with the Vickers, took over the purely defensive part of our duties when in the line.

One afternoon, our recruits were under instruction in the barn, clustered around one of our Lewis guns. One of them, sitting in front of the gun, received a bullet in the groin, from the effects of which at such short range he died in a few minutes. The tragedy cast a gloom over all of us. Of course, it was strictly contrary to orders to use live rounds at all, and in the event the N.C.O. responsible narrowly escaped a court martial. There were many extenuating circumstances, however. A supply of dummy bullets being unavailable, we had to make our own from live rounds to expedite training in correcting stoppages and loading drums of ammunition. The tip of a bullet was used as a tool in dismantling and assembling the gun, and this, we surmised, was how the live round had crept into circulation.

Having been thus thoroughly rested and reorganized after a winter of considerable hardship—a great deal of which, we judged, could have been avoided had our general staff possessed a more intelligent outlook—we moved to Bouque-Maison and Neuvillette, in the neighbourhood of Doullens, where we trained hard in 'attacking' exercises for a fortnight or so, in beautiful weather. By lorry hopping (for we were near the Doullens–St. Pol road), some of us managed on one occasion to sample what the town had to offer: *vin rouge, vin blanc,* malaga, grenadine. In conversation with other troops, it was understood that a 'lady' living in a certain cottage on our way back to camp was available for a consideration. Led by two of our married mates, therefore, we hastened to the spot in the gathering dusk of a lovely May evening. Prolonged knocking on the door at length caused the upstairs window to open. A torrent of abuse greeted the expectant upturned faces, and the window closed with a bang. Undeterred, the two knocked again . . . and again. Suddenly the window opened, a large white chamber pot thrust forth, and a deluge descended upon the two unfortunates below. The six or so of us who were spectators were so convulsed with mirth that we laughed all the way back to Neuvillette, to the added discomfiture of the now-stinking victims.

Once more we set our faces towards the line, and two evenings afterwards we marched through the familiar village of Bienvillers to the ruins of Hannescamps, which lay but a few hundred yards behind our front trenches. Here we relieved some Warwicks of our division, who told us that there was plenty doing, and that a few nights previously one of their parties on patrol had vanished completely. At the point we took over there was no danger in looking over the top in daylight, as eight hundred yards or so separated us from the German trenches. For almost half the distance, the tangled weed-covered ground beyond our wire sloped away gently before us and in the shallow valley lay a big bed of osiers, the surface of which rippled in the breeze. Here the Warwicks' patrol had disappeared, presumably surprised and captured by a stronger party of the enemy. Beyond the osiers the ground rose again to the German wire and their line, continuing to the horizon a kilometre or so beyond, bare save for the battered hamlet of Les Essarts.

The road from Bienvillers to Bucquoy and Achiet-le-Grand— now a grass track barricaded at a dozen points—crossed our trenches near our gun position, but we could follow its course into the valley along one side of the osiers, then into and past the German trenches up the slope to Les Essarts, where it disappeared behind the ridge. At night we could hear what at first we took to be the German ration limbers trundling up on the reverse side; but as May turned to June, we felt pretty certain that new German batteries and their attendant ammunition columns were responsible for at least some of the nightly rumbling over the pavé. Looking across to our left, we could see the broken trees around Monchy, and beyond, at a new angle, the dark green mass of Adinfer Wood; to the right that of another wood, the more sinister because of its close proximity to the trenches there—the Wood of Gommecourt—of terrible memory, as I shall try to tell.

From our position towards Gommecourt, the trenches gradually approached each other to a point opposite the ill-omened German 'Z' trench, where only a few yards separated them.

When in reserve, we lived in dugouts in the ruins of Hannescamps, but we didn't have much rest by day or by night, for we were generally on carrying parties for the R.E., humping all kinds of material to dumps near the front line.

On one occasion we had just deposited our loads in the front line, at that point about three hundred yards from the enemy, when an excited sentry drew our attention to a message on a blackboard being hoisted high above the German trench. We could not quite read the words, but as we were endeavouring to do so an officer observing for a field battery came round the traverse. He was soon looking at the blackboard through field glasses. Gathered below him in the trench, we listened as he read slowly, ' "British Fleet" . . . they can't spell British'—pause—'looks like "sunk—*Queen Mary, New Zealand, Warrior, Black Prince, Bulwark, Defence* . . ." ', finishing with ' "twelve hundred *gefangenen*" . . . what the hell's that?' He jumped down from the firestep, putting his glasses in their case. No one spoke until he exploded suddenly: 'blasted Boche propaganda! Take no damned notice of it!' and he went his way. But of course, apprehensive speculation was now rampant. Returning to Hannescamps, our fatigue party no doubt helped to spread the story. That evening we gathered from two artillery linesmen that there had been a big sea battle, but they had no details.

It is history that the first British accounts of Jutland substantially confirmed what the blackboard had told us, and days passed before news trickled through of the German losses and retirement, lightening somewhat the general depression. Then we heard that the blackboard had been hoisted again. This time the message was 'Kitchener is dead'. It is difficult to convey adequately the dismay this caused among us, for we ourselves were of the 'First Hundred Thousand' of Kitchener's Army. For months at Aldershot we had worn 'Kitchener's blue' in lieu of khaki. We recalled one pouring wet afternoon in October 1914, when thousands of us, drawn up on the Queen's Parade, stood for several hours in ankle-deep mud and water in our makeshift civvy overcoats, soaked to the skin. At length there were shouted commands from somewhere in front, then more shouting. Our new officers drew their new swords and stood at the 'present'. We had no arms; we just tried to stand to attention. No one had the faintest idea of what it was all about. Then, through the driving rain, we glimpsed the bobbing upper portions of a cloud of what must have been horsemen passing in front . . . and they were gone. Officers sheathed their swords through the slits made for the purpose in their new, soaking wet greatcoats— all except our platoon officer, Ward. He pushed the point of his sword through the side of his coat, thus making a new slit several inches long. It was the only bright spot in our day. Later we learned that Kitchener had been showing the French War Minister, Millerand, some of his New Army.

In the event, we must have known many hours before the news was released to the British nation, that H.M.S. *Hampshire, en route* for Russia, had been lost off the Orkneys with practically all hands, including Lord Kitchener and his entire staff. We had no time to ponder on this, however. Even when in the line we were constantly carrying or digging, or checking equipment and supplies. That a great offensive could not be much longer delayed was obvious to all. Even we could see that the preparations being made were on an immense scale. New batteries, many of them 'heavies', were constantly registering targets, some far in the enemy rear, as the dull red flashes at night showed. South African heavy artillery arrived in our area—grand fellows! Likewise, the German artillery fire increased greatly in intensity from early June onward, and casualties were frequent.

It was about the second week in June that thirty of our company, including our Lewis gun team, went on a special wiring party, attached to the R.E. Instead of occupying our usual dugouts in Hannescamps, we marched to a farm-house near Bienvillers, presumably to get better rest during the daytime. The barn was a good one, and in one corner we found a pile of kilts, evidently discarded for some reason by Highlanders of the 4th Division a few weeks previously. One of our number, a cockney named Newman, drafted from the cavalry to us at Warluzel, dressed in one, making such an impression that several more followed his example. We were in the charge of a well-liked sergeant—Gamble by name. When those in kilts begged to be allowed to wear them on the coming night's work, he was so amused that, reluctantly, he agreed.

An eventful night followed, cockney shouting down front-line dugouts in tolerable Scots, deceiving many gullible Englishmen who, in the dark, surmised that the Jocks had arrived to make a raid—especially as we disappeared over the parapet into the wire. Before we reached our barn again, Sergeant Gamble had been threatened with court martial proceedings by an irate major, awakened from sleep by a report that some Jocks were out in front. This sobered us, and when, on the way back, the kilted ones complained of violent itching, the truth dawned upon us that those kilts had been dumped for a very good reason. When discarded again, they were found to be alive with lice.

These nightly wiring parties played havoc with our hands, boots and clothing, and before we bid the R.E.s adieu we had sustained three casualties. On one occasion a bullet knocked a coil of wire from my hands as I held it on a stick, to unwind it; on another, the steel picket I was just screwing in was hit by a bullet, with a flash of sparks.

I can assure you that, by daybreak, when we slid back into the trench with our task more or less completed, we breathed thankful sighs of relief that our luck had held for yet another night. Filling our pipes and lighting our fags, we would survey ruefully our scratched boots, torn puttees and trousers—results of blundering over hidden strands in the darkness; our hands, too, with the skin off them in places, in spite of the gloves we wore. Then we would march back to our barn and sleep until well after midday, after a good breakfast.

We rejoined the battalion in the line, and our Lewis team was out around the osier bed nearly every night, providing cover for our patrols. It was a change from trench routine. One night six of us lay in two shell holes near the osiers when a party of Germans filed by, talking in low tones and laughing. Afterwards, we said we could hear our own hearts beating. Our corporal ordered us not to fire, as they were too many for us, but in our opinion we missed a great chance (confirmed by subsequent experiences), for the devastating effects of machine-gun fire opened unexpectedly at close range, would have more than compensated for our lack of numbers. On the other hand, our patrol in the osiers beyond would not have known what was happening.

As June progressed our situation became more hazardous with each succeeding day. To add to our discomfort, the enemy commenced operations with what was to us a new type of mortar, dropping shells into our front line with uncanny precision at a range of eight or nine hundred yards. We felt safer out on patrol around the osiers, but one night these came to an end. Then we formed strong covering parties for our 6th Battalion who, under R.E. direction, started to dig advanced trenches, with the necessary communication trenches, much closer to the German positions.

The first night was largely occupied in marking out operations, and from our trench we could plainly see some of the pegs. I suppose they must have been as plainly visible to the enemy, who now redoubled his efforts to make life difficult for us. Indeed, save for an occasional few moments the day before, when a parcel from home reminded me of it, I had forgotten then my twenty-first birthday was imminent. On the 26th—*the* day—first light disclosed a lovely June morning with the rising sun rapidly dispersing the night mists. It was my turn to fetch the section's breakfasts from the point along the trench where the dixie carriers dropped their loads from Battalion H.Q. I made my way thither with the mess tins and lids—I gave my birthday not a thought. I duly filled the tins with tea, the lids with bacon and fat. On the way back to our dugout, a sudden salvo of whizz-bangs caused me to spill a little tea but, this being nothing fresh, I continued to within about twenty yards of our dugout, situated in the side of the chalk embankment, where the road crossed our line. Then I heard the report of a heavy gun from behind the German lines, and stood listening momentarily, waiting for the shell to chortle over as usual. It did until almost overhead, then it seemed to drop suddenly. I started to run . . . 'Crash!' . . . the hot wind of the explosion lifted me down the steps, where I spilled most of the tea and scattered bacon in all directions.

It also awaked my mates not on sentry duty, who had got down to it again after 'stand to', pending the arrival of breakfast. Ruefully I relit the candle, picked up the pieces of bacon and was scraping them, when . . . 'Crash!' again. Out went the candle and a shower of chalk and other debris descended from the dugout roof, followed by choking fumes. We relit the candle, which spluttered feebly in the settling dust cloud, and two of us climbed over the debris at the entrance, to find that Ted Lineker, on sentry-go, was unhurt but badly shaken. He was standing in our bay about twenty yards away. Fortunately neither gun nor ammunition drums were damaged. As we were speaking to him we heard another coming and all ran round the nearest traverse to get further away, if possible. Then a great spout of black smoke, flying chalk and timber at the dugout entrance made us wonder whether the worst had happened to those inside. An answering shout to our calls reassured us, but before we could wriggle through the damaged entrance, the now-familiar report of the distant gun made us get away quickly.

From our bay we saw the German balloon standing out sharply above the eastern horizon and had no doubt at all that it was directing the gunners. I suppose another half-dozen shells landed either above or around the dugout before there was a lull, during which those still inside emerged. Coming, blinking, into the bright sunlight, they couldn't understand why we were laughing, until they saw that they were white from head to foot with powdered chalk. Hastily removing the worst obstacles from the entrance, we lit several candles and made hurried examination of the dugout roof and supports. Two were badly splintered, and the crossbeams had bowed, allowing the loose chalk above to fall. As I have said, it had been driven into the side of the road embankment leading to Les Essarts, about ten yards back from the front trench—an easy map reference for the enemy gunners.

I managed to salvage a bit of bacon, but no tea, and was munching it between two pieces of bread, when Jerry started again. We were trapped inside, and for the next half-hour or so were wondering whether the next one would be the one with our names on it. Then the range seemed to lengthen about fifty yards, as he plastered the communication trench which ran along the base of the road embankment. We found afterwards that a number of men coming up on a working party were killed outright, including a padre, a lieutenant, and the lad who played the big drum in our band.

In the meantime we had started to move tons of displaced chalk and baulks of timber, mixed with barbed wire festoons thrown from the obstacles barring the road. We could only move it sideways, however, to make the barest way; for the balloon was still there. While we worked against time, our company commander arrived. Looking at the balloon, he ordered all, save doubled sentries posted on flanks, to evacuate the immediate vicinity for the time being—a very sensible suggestion. What we didn't realize in doing this, however, was that the morning seemed to have gone. Twice more Jerry pummelled that spot.

About four in the afternoon, as Freddy Smith and I went on sentry-go, I felt in my pocket for pipe and tobacco and pulled out a new packet of Chairman tobacco and a new pipe which a girl I'd met when billeted in Camberley had been good enough to send me. Then I remembered it was my twenty-first birthday. When I told Freddy Smith he pointed out that I'd had a hell of a lot of presents—a 'Brocks Benefit' of fireworks and a bloody good party, which must have cost Jerry thousands of pounds!

Certainly there seemed a grim humour in the day's events; the celebrations had been distinctly novel in character, and of a nature to remember in after years. To mark the occasion further, Freddy and I decided to have a shave after we had been relieved. In the event we worked up a lather in the remains of some lukewarm tea. This, of course, was before the safety razor had come into general use. We had heard of them, but I doubt if many of us had seen one. Our razors were 'issue', of the cut-throat variety, and therefore not of the highest quality, but they sufficed for our needs. These we stropped on the leather belts which most of us wore beneath our tunics. A mate was holding one end of my belt as I stropped my razor, and Freddy had just started to shave, when a salvo of four whizz-bangs skimmed the top of our trench. Freddy cut his face; I cut my belt . . . a memorable day!

A continuous cannonade was now in progress to our right. In the few hours of darkness, while we cleared our trench, most of the battalion were out as covering parties for the 6th, who were digging the forward trenches. The gun flashes beyond Gomme-court lit the night sky. All the next day we wondered what the German reaction would be, but, strange to relate, they didn't bother us unduly. On the following morning the 6th Battalion relieved us and we returned to the Hannescamp dugouts. In turn we were relieved by the Warwicks of our division, marching back to the village of La Cauchie, via Bienvillers and Pommier on 27th June. This village was about two kilometres west of Berles. Here, to my surprise and disgust, my name appeared in Battalion Orders as promoted to acting lance-corporal, attached to H.Q. Company, to take over duties of battalion range finder—of all things.

The rumble of the bombardment to the south was still continu-ous. We gathered that the guns were ours. Soon the artillery around Bienvillers joined in, and we noted the frequent reports of heavy guns behind us.

On reporting to Regimental Sergeant-Major Cattell, I found that Private Johnson, A., also of 'C' Company, was to be my assistant. Seeing him, I remembered that both of us had attended a course on the Barr & Stroud rangefinder at Tidworth. We groused at our luck, and together returned to our company billets to fetch our belongings. I groused again to Ted Lineker and Freddy Smith, but they told me not to be such a b. . . fool and to get on with it! However, I hated the thought of leaving them and of taking a stripe, which was contrary to our unwritten code of ethics, and departed sadly for the other end of the village. I derived some comfort from the thought that Jackie, my new mate, was, from what I had seen and heard of him, a thoroughly good lad. I was not mistaken, either. In England he had held the rank of sergeant, but his outspoken comments at times, and his determination to take unofficial leave on one occasion, resulted in the loss of his stripes. He said he was much happier without them, and I believed him. He had a pull with the N.C.O.s of our company which stood him—and, afterwards, us—in good stead.

He was short and sturdily built, with blue eyes which challenged; he appeared to stare so at anyone to whom he was talking, especially in argument. Fellows used to pull his leg about it: 'easy now, Jackie, don't look so wild!' and so on, to which he would reply, 'damn a man who can't look a pal straight in the face!'

I don't think the rangefinder had been used since the battalion landed in France. 'What good can we do with this b. . . thing?' I asked Jackie a dozen times a day. 'What's the use of it in this sort of war?' 'Open country fighting soon, Dick,' he would opine sagely; then, facetiously, 'Lance-Corporal (unpaid) Read, give me the range please to Berlin'; then, seriously, 'let's make the most of this now we've got a cushy job.' He told me that his firm in Leicester, who were making rangefinders and other optical requirements for the Admiralty, had been trying to get him back, but the Army wouldn't release him.

As we talked, the artillery fire from Gommecourt southward grew in intensity, and now seemed quite continuous; moreover, the heavy artillery in rear of us provided crashing explosions of considerable local effect, as the great shells went whistling high overhead. It was said that they were twelve-, fifteen- and eighteen-inch howitzers on railway lines.

On the last day of June, Jackie and I were on a fatigue party which reported at a dump near Bienvillers church to carry up sixty-pound 'toffee apples' (mortar bombs) to the front line near Monchy. The village was now under continual shell fire and we were glad to get on our way from the dump, and up St. Cross Street, as the communication trench was called. We managed to dump our loads without mishap, although the front line there was now truly a hornets' nest. Rifle grenades and mortar bombs were coming over all the time, but the artillery fire from both sides rendered it quite impossible to hear their approach.

Near Bienvillers on the way back, we met some 4th Leicestershire (Terriers) of the 46th Division. They told us they were going over the top the next morning at Gommecourt. A few hundred yards further on we passed a motor car in which sat a general, talking to two staff officers. The sergeant in charge of us dutifully made us march to attention and 'eyes left'. It was said the general commanded the 46th Division. It wasn't ours, anyhow. Our division—the 37th—was commanded by Major-General Count Gleichen, said to be a relative of the royal family. We hadn't seen him since Perham Down Camp days, but no doubt he was around somewhere. As we passed the car, we saw to our amazement that the general was holding up two little toy dogs for the officers' inspection. Both had light blue silk ribbon bows round their necks. Many were the bitter comments made as we plodded on back to La Cauchie. His seemed to be a different war from ours. In after years, however, I think that perhaps his little dogs may have helped him to keep his sanity when faced with the hell that followed shortly after we saw him.

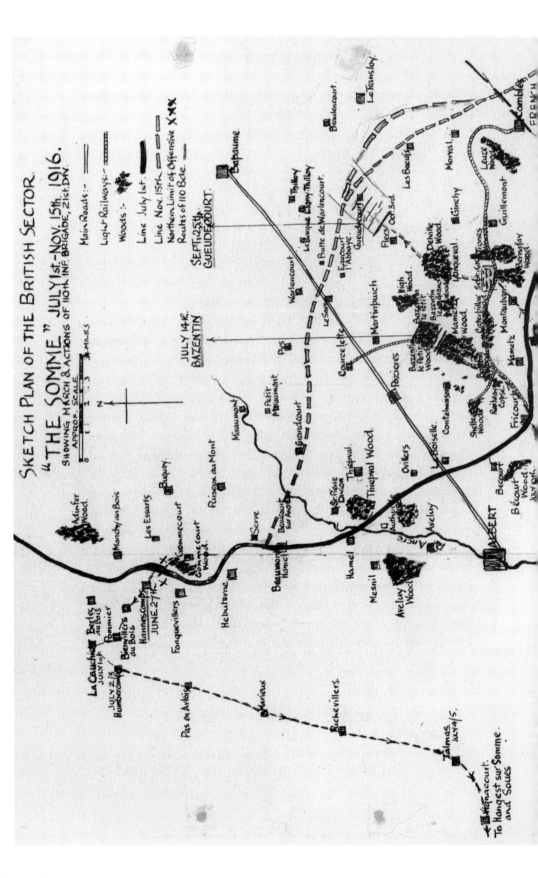

SKETCH PLAN OF THE BRITISH SECTOR.
"THE SOMME" JULY 1st - NOV. 15th. 1916.
SHOWING MARCH & ACTIONS OF 110th INF. BRIGADE, 21st DIV.

APPROX. SCALE.

0   1   2   3   MILES

Main Roads :-
Ligr Railways:-
Woods :-
Line July 1st.
Line Nov. 15th.
Northern Limit of Offensive XXX
Routes of 110 Bde.

N

Adinfer Wood.
Mondy au Bois.
Les Essarts
Bucquoy
Commecourt
Ruisseux au Mont
Miraumont
Pet. Miraumont
Grandcourt
Beaumont sur Ancre
St Pierre Divion
Thiepval Wood.
Thiepval.
Ovillers.
La Boiselle.
Contalmaison.
Shelter Wood.
Fricourt.
Railway Copse.
Mametz.
Montauban.
Mametz Wood.
Caterpillar Wood.
Bazentin le Grand Wood.
Bazentin le Grand.
High Wood.
Bazentin le Petit Wood.
Bazentin le Petit
Martinpuich.
Courcelette
Pozieres
Le Sars
Eaucourt l'Abbaye.
Flers. OCT 3rd.
Gueudecourt.
SEPT, 25th.
GUEUDECOURT.
Butte de Warlencourt.
Ligny-Thilloy
Le Barque
Thilloy
Bapaume.
Warlencourt.
Pys
JULY 14th. BAZENTIN
Delville Wood.
Longueval.
Ginchy.
Guillemont.
Bernafay Wood.
Trones
Bazentin
Sebastopol
Le Transloy.
Beaulencourt.
Les Boeufs.
Morval.
Leuze Wood.
Combles
FRENCH

Serre.
Hebuterne
Fonquevillers.
Foncquevillers
Commecourt Wood.
JUNE 27th.
Hannescamps
Berles au Bois
Bienvillers au Bois
Pommier
La Cauchie
JULY 1st.
JULY 2/5.
Humbercourt
Pas en Artois.
Beaumont Hamel
Hamel
Mesnil
Avеluy Wood.
Aveluy
Authuille
Ancre
Becourt
Becourt Wood.
JULY 9th.
Becourt Wood. JULY 9th.
ALBERT

Bavieux
Rubeville.
Talmas. JULY 14/5.
Vignacourt.
To Hangest sur Somme. and Saleux

CHAPTER 8

THE SOMME

To Our Comrades of The Somme, 1916

For some we loved, the Loveliest and the Best
That from his Vintage rolling Time hath prest,
Have drunk their Cup a Round or two before,
And one by one crept silently to Rest.

The Rubáiyáat of Omar Khayyám.

AT dawn on the next day, 1st July, which broke fine and warm, we heard for the first time what we afterwards knew by the term 'drum fire': a continuous pulsating rumble, punctuated by the frequent reverberating reports of heavy artillery in our vicinity. Looking across at Bienvillers from our billet in the village street of La Cauchie, the view was obscured by a heat haze and by the smoke of the bombardment. At Berles the cannonade was sporadic and feeble by comparison. At any rate, we thought, they are not going over the top there. Then, for a few minutes, the firing increased to an unforgettable, indescribable intensity. Looking from one to another, we knew what was happening before Gommecourt Wood and in front of Fonquevillers. 'They've gone over—good luck to them!' was our one fervent wish, and as we speculated upon the 46th's and other divisions' chances of success, we wondered what *we* were going to do.

After breakfast, in general parades, each man received five pieces of yellow material about 2½ inches square, and was shown how and where to sew them on his tunic: one square on either side of the collar, one on each upper arm immediately below the shoulder strap, and one on the back below the collar. We spent most of the morning getting these fixed—it certainly gave us something to do, but we could not really settle to anything. Our thoughts were with those who had gone over. The guns were comparatively quiet and speculation was rife as to the reason for this.

We watched the Pommier road, standing that hot interminable afternoon in groups outside our barns in the village street. Anyone who came from that direction faced a barrage of questions, with the result that, by early evening, all kinds of rumours were in circulation. 'They had broken through' . . . 'The South Staffords had been held up by wire' . . . 'They were going over again shortly' . . . 'The South Staffords and Notts and Derbys had been cut up in Gommecourt Wood' . . . 'The 4th and 5th Leicesters had been wiped out' . . . and so on.

In the absence of any news of a definite nature, we became vaguely depressed and apprehensive. Evening came, and with it a crop of fresh rumours. Then, about 9 p.m. in the gathering dusk, we saw some transport limbers in the distance. As they approached, we could discern figures walking here and there between the limbers. At length, by signs on the limbers, we saw that they were South Staffords. The drivers looked spick and span, in violent contrast to what we could now see was a mass of about eighty men. In the dusk, as they tried to keep a step, they looked dishevelled, dirty, hollow-eyed and grime-streaked, their sandbag-covered tin hats chalky, muddy and dusty. Every now and then the step broke and they seemed to march anyhow, with heads bent, either looking straight before them or at the ground. It was impossible to tell if there were officers among them. We sensed somehow that these men had seen hell, and none among us dared ask *the* question, until one of us shouted, 'how d'you go on mates?' No one took the slightest notice, save a corporal carrying three rifles, who was bringing up the rear of the party. He half-turned, and, indicating the weary straggling figures before him, shrugged expressively. 'General f. . . up in command again!' and he went on. Then he turned again. 'Back where they f. . . well started!'

We thought of the red-tabbed general and his beribboned toy dogs and did the best thing we could. We turned in.

Early on the following day the battalion moved in artillery formation to Humbercamps, H.Q. Company bivouacking in a cider apple orchard on the western outskirts of the village. The orchard also contained a twelve-inch howitzer on railway lines, which had been laid from Saulty on the Doullens–Arras line. The crew were all giant City of London policemen, who worked stripped to the waist. Every time the howitzer fired we were deafened. Green apples and leaves fell off the trees in showers, and tiles from neighbouring farm buildings, loosened by previous explosions, descended in cascades.

We understood that we were going up to relieve the 46th Division before Gommecourt. Arrangements were, in fact, made for us to dump our valises—or, as we called them, packs—including our greatcoats and blankets, and dress in battle order; that is, our haversacks with bare necessaries and iron rations, taking the place of our packs.

Lewis gunners were warned that each would have to carry two extra bandoliers of cartridges in addition to the usual loads. Bombing sections likewise would have to carry extra Mills grenades, and so on. Then, with morning light, fresh orders came. By midday we were on the march with full packs, in column of route, heading south-west. The whole 110th Brigade, in fact, the 6th, 7th, 8th and 9th Battalions of the Leicestershire Regiment, were on the move. During one of the hourly halts we heard that we were leaving the 37th Division and joining another. Before we left Humbercamps we gathered that the attack on Gommecourt on 1st July had been a ghastly fiasco. Apart from the failure of our artillery to cut the wire adequately, hundreds of South Staffords, Notts and Derbys and Leicesters had been cut off by the Germans, who came out behind them through underground tunnels in Gommecourt Wood. Casualties had been very heavy, and the attackers were back in their original front line, harassed now by increasingly accurate German artillery and mortar fire.

We recovered our good spirits, however, as we tramped along, no doubt relieved by the thought that, at any rate, we were not going to have another smack at Gommecourt, whatever awaited us at the end of our journey.

It was late that evening that we marched, aching and tired out, into the village of Talmas. Here we slept in a barn which had recently housed troops. The straw wasn't too clean, either.

Our first day's march via Pas-en Artois and Puchevillers in a souther-westerly direction had been roughly parallel with the line, but towards Talmas had veered away from it, so that the continuous rumble of the battle now sounded somewhat more distant. From conversations with various details encountered *en route* or in Talmas, it seemed clear that 1st July in this sector of the front had been a day of unrelieved disaster. We gathered that, going south from Gommecourt, the 56th (London Territorials), 4th (Regular), 36th (Ulster) and 29th (Regular) Divisions had suffered terrible losses and had made no headway. Uncut wire, and the hail of machine-gun bullets were given as reasons. In several instances, reserves had been decimated by the German counter-barrage while moving up in support of leading waves which had broken through in the initial rush. These had been compelled to relinquish their gains.

On the straw in the barn we found a *Daily Mirror* of 2nd July. It was silent on these matters, but told of brilliant advances further south-east of Albert, and featured a sketch map showing the gains at Ovillers, La Boilselle, Fricourt and Montauban in heavy black lines. On the British right the French had also started an offensive, which seemed to have made considerably greater gains of ground, guns and prisoners.

This paper, picked up by chance, showed how little we knew of what was going on. We guessed that we were destined for some hot spot on the recently captured ground, but this was mere conjecture, and why we were now going away from it all was a mystery to us.

We were on the move in good time on the following morning, having drawn constituents of a haversack dinner. The day promised to be hot and sunny. After marching for four or five hours through Vignacourt and Flixecourt, with the usual 'fall out on right of t'road' for five minutes every hour, we began to feel the strain—principally, of course, in our feet—and our officers did their best to help us to keep going by frequent words of cheery encouragement. Colonel Mignon rode to and fro along the ranks continually, joking with us and exhorting us to stick it for the honour of the regiment. Heartened by him, we determined grimly to keep going. By mid afternoon, however, our feet were getting really sore and human endurance could not have kept us in ordered ranks much longer, when we halted near the bridge crossing the river Somme at Hangest. Although we were not in a condition properly to appreciate it at the time, we could not help noticing that the countryside hereabouts was extremely interesting in character, contrasting sharply with the rolling expanses we had lately traversed. Hangest-sur-Somme appeared to me to be a charming old-world town, sleeping in the July sun, on a river amid surroundings having real scenic quality. I could not help thinking—although lying wearily on the roadside verge, propped up by my heavy pack—that here was a peep at the real France that I had read about in books.

Beyond Hangest we made slow progress. Our colonel and other mounted officers now shepherded us continually, each riding with several slung rifles. Even though carrying several rifles, Colonel Mignon made a fine figure of a soldier, sitting his horse as though part of it, his iron-grey military moustache upturned at the ends, almost Kaiser-fashion.

We would have dropped in our tracks that day rather than have straggled. It would have been letting him down. Such an attitude may seem näive and outdated to the youth of fifty years after. We knew in those moments that in Colonel Mignon and his officers we had real leaders. We all helped one another to get along, so that at length we hobbled into the village of Soues, where we found clean, sweet-smelling straw in a lovely old barn. We washed, ate . . . and then slept. Soues seemed a thousand leagues removed from war, or thought of war, and we made the most of our six days' stay there. There was a tacit acknowledgement that we were for it shortly, and for that reason were given an easy time. The weather was beautifully fine and warm. Rambling in the woods and fields around the village, we were able to forget and look out for once upon 'the Fair Land of France'—almost the first time that we had seen views which, in our opinion, justified the term.

I met Horace Phillips, Freddy Smith and Ted Lineker again; indeed, we spent most of our spare time together. There was good swimming, too, and in the cold black water, amid the tall and overhanging trees, sparklingly diamonded by the bright sunlight above, we vied with one another in showing that, although we

Soues (Somme)
July 8th. 1916.

had been in the trenches for almost a year, we had not forgotten everything. In short, Soues was so good to us that we feared to leave it, hoping inwardly that something would happen to postpone the evil day.

On the morning of 11th July, however, the battalion paraded in a large field on the outskirts of the village, looking spick and span and in fine fettle. The summer sun glinted on the polished bugles and brass of the battalion band standing near the open gate to play us in. For some time we carried out various exercises under the command of our colonel, who afterwards inspected us at considerable length. The battalion then formed four sides of a hollow square and we were told to sit down. In the centre, now mounted, were Colonel Mignon and the adjutant, Captain Popham. For a minute or so the colonel looked at us keenly, quieting his horse the while, as it was somewhat fresh and restive.

He then addressed us, making sure that all heard him. Speaking slowly and deliberately, he told us that the 110th Leicestershire Brigade was about to take part in the great offensive on the Somme now in progress, and that he felt sure that we should uphold the honour of our regiment and of our country. He then proceeded to give us a short history of the Seventeenth Regiment of the Line and hoped that, with our comrades of the 6th, 7th and 9th Battalions, we should be instrumental in adding another honour to those already inscribed upon the Colours. He asked us to remember that we were fighting as Englishmen, for all that Englishmen held dear, and that as we were a unit of the New Army, the eyes of all would be upon us; for although we had done well so far, we had yet to be put to the test of battle. Finally, he told us that the Leicestershire Regiment did not know the meaning of the word 'retreat'. The battalion would entrain that night; and as this would be, in all probability, the last opportunity he would have of addressing us for some time, he wished us good luck and Godspeed.

Whatever else we felt or thought as we listened to him, it was obvious that all were profoundly moved by his stirring words, and the manner in which he delivered them. We knew that in him we had a real leader, who inspired confidence and made us feel that we *could*—come what may. The foregoing may seem naïve and outdated, and we fools to believe in such an appeal to our conception of honour, ideals, tradition—in general, what was worth fighting for. But no matter!

We marched late that afternoon in the general direction of Amiens, taking the road along the Somme valley, parallel with the railway, which ran alongside for much of the way. It was almost dark when we passed through the quaint little town of Picquigny, and the horizon before us was now illuminated by a

March to Ailly sur Somme
Evening. JULY 11th 1916.

constant succession of flashes, as of summer lightning. As yet we could hear little and were still a long way off. Intent upon the spectacle, which prompted much serious thinking among us, we tramped along, mostly in silence. At the next town, Ailly-sur-Somme, we entrained and slept fitfully while we were jolted at intervals over the interminable maze of points and junctions about Amiens. We rattled on through the night with frequent halts until we reached railhead—what had been, in happier days, the small country station of Dernancourt. Now, evidences of vast military activities were on every hand: new sidings, camps, huts, wagon and horse lines, lorry parks, huge dumps of supplies and munitions. Criss-crossing the occasional stretches of arid brown landscape between, were festoons of telephone cables. Amid it all, constantly moving ant-like masses of infantry, artillery, horse and mechanical transport, threaded at times by convoys of motor ambulances, each unit in its particular cloud of dust.

We took the road to the line; another dust cloud in this huge hive of activity, overwhelmed and obscured at intervals by other storms of dust churned up on the overworked road by the never-ending succession of solid-tyred three-ton lorries which passed us, going up, or returning for more—Karrier, Albion, Tilling, Pierce Arrow. We were soon coated thick with it, and as, at length, we entered the skeleton village of Méaulte, engulfed as it was by the machinery of war and the German long-range effort to destroy it, we noticed that what remained lay under a thick, dirty, whitish coating—everything was smothered, even the few wretched inhabitants—dust! We thought of Soues and the dark, cool water, the pleasant fields and woods of yesterday, and now—desolation.

Near Méaulte we turned off the road into a field thick with dust-coated stubble and trampled, uncut hay, withered by the hot sun and the thousands of marching feet that had preceded us since 1st July.

Here we halted and made our final preparations. We rolled the single blankets, issued the previous evening, in bundles of twelve; stuffed souvenirs, our letters and all that was not absolutely necessary, including our greatcoats, into our packs, and dumped them in piles by companies at a tent hurriedly put up by the battalion quartermaster's staff. We dressed in fighting order, our haversacks on our backs, and taking but the barest necessaries: rations and extra iron rations. Each man received an extra cloth bandolier of fifty rounds, Lewis gunners two. Bombing sections were issued with Mills grenades to which, for a time, they were busy fixing detonators—always a tricky operation. We were issued with goggles against tear gas shells. Jackie and I were told by the R.S.M. to report to 'C' Company with our rangefinder, which we did

MÉAULTE. - EVENING JULY 12th 1916
Ready to move up ....
Blankets stacked in bundles of twelve ..
Packs dumped by Compinies.
"Battle Order."

DAWN -FRICOURT (SOMME) JULY 13th 1916.

and, in effect, augmented the strength by two 'handicapped' rifle-men.

At dusk we moved off, leaving behind a small cadre of officers and men per company—in order, as one wag remarked with feeling, that we couldn't be completely wiped out. Already the eastern sky was sparkling and glowering, and the reports of great guns and howitzers nearby echoed and re-echoed over the fields. They were planted thickly, as the red flashes as they fired showed, stabbing the darkness and sending their vomit roaring into the beyond.

Every few seconds we saw and heard the explosions of German shells, searching for them—at times too near to be pleasant; heard, too, the stealthily whistling approach of their gas shells, seemingly wandering overhead like lost souls; the soft 'plops' as they burst in the fields around, so that the night air became charged with the unmistakable odours of tear gas and chlorine. However, although our eyes and noses ran at times, we were not worried overmuch.

We progressed slowly, moving frequently to the side of the track to allow returning horse and mule transport to pass, and entered the zone of the field artillery—our eighteen-pounders and 4.5-inch howitzers. Before them lay the inferno of Verey lights, exploding shells, and the incessant rattle of machine-gun fire. The heavies had been planted pretty thickly, but their lighter brethren seemed almost wheel-to-wheel. They spoke in desultory fashion as though to show that they were awake, the reports sounding staccato and hollow, stabbing the night with flashes which threw into vivid relief the shell-torn skeletons of trees and the battered brickwork around them; occasionally, too, the bloated corpses of horses and mules, legs distended in the air, the smell even penetrating the now-intensified tear gas and chlorine. These batteries, too, were being subjected to a feeble searching fire by the enemy, and a few shells, doubtless intended for the road on which we were marching, gave us some near misses.

At length, by the gun flashes, we could see that we were crossing a complicated trench system with all the attendant defences of barbed wire and obstructions. We passed more corpses of horses and mules, which stank abominably. The road had been repaired in parts with railway sleepers as we entered the ruins of the village. The drivers of some returning limbers shouted to us, on inquiry, that this was Fricourt, taken on 2nd July. A working party was spreading road stone and stood by their shovels to let us pass, with a few 'good luck, mates!' About halfway through the village, as we judged it, we were ordered to fall out on the right. For some minutes we sat down amid the debris of bricks and splintered timber and a sickly, sweetish smell, thankful for the respite after the march. At length, finding that there appeared to be no immediate prospect of moving on, we wrapped our waterproofed groundsheets around ourselves and slept the sleep of oblivion.

CHAPTER 9

BAZENTIN

WHEN I awoke it was light. I had not slept so very long, for the nights in July are of short duration. I felt stiff and cold and stood up, stretching my aching limbs and breathing in the chill and tainted air. In doing so I stopped short, overcome by a sudden combination of fear and awe at what I beheld. I had been resting my head on the side of a huge unexploded twelve-inch shell lying half-buried in the mass of bricks and earth. Jackie's head still rested against the other side. I suppose we hadn't noticed this before, as we lay down to sleep tired out, in our tin hats. Two yards away a dead German lay on his back, staring to heaven and dreadfully swollen, a large bluebottle buzzing noisily round his face. I looked further—there were others, also some of ours. Not so many, perhaps as there had been, as I surmised that many of our dead would have been buried by this time. I turned away to the sleeping forms of my mates, lining the roadside, then to Jackie. He was stirring uneasily. I thought I wouldn't wake him; he would see it all soon enough! I shivered in the early morning air, wondering, too, at the comparative quietness, for the guns of both sides seemed to be still.

For something to do, I set about the task of making some tea, using a little water from my bottle. At any rate it was an easy matter to make a fire without much smoke, for there were masses of dry, splintered woodwork around everywhere. As the little fire crackled I positioned two bricks on which to stand the mess tin. Jackie roused and sat up, rubbing his eyes and greeting me with a yawn and a shiver as he rose uncertainly to his feet. I invited him to look behind him and was interested to note his reactions, which were pretty well the same as mine had been. He stood for perhaps two minutes, wide-eyed, his mouth half-open. Then, turning to me: 'Christ! Let's have a drop of that tea, quick, Dick—here!' producing his water-bottle, 'have a drop more water.'

The hot tea, together with a bit of biscuit and cold bacon, made us feel a deal better, and helped us to become accustomed to our surroundings. We followed with no little interest the lines of the German and British trenches on 1st July and, as most of our mates still slept, we clambered over the debris for a look round and a scrounge.

The preliminary British bombardment, which had lasted for six days, had been terrific in its intensity and effect, but it was only too clear to us that it had failed in one of its essential objects—that of cutting the German wire. In many instances the trenches themselves had been obliterated by the explosion of huge shells, each making an excavation the size of an average room; on the other hand it was obvious that some strong points remained virtually untouched.

The dugouts were so deep that, in the main, they had weathered the rain of shells, except for here and there a blown-in entrance. Indeed, the whole terrible story of 1st July here lay before us like an open book. There, were the khaki figures cut down in swathes by the German machine-gunners and hanging on the wire, or on the ground nearby; looking, even in death, as though they were trying to get through it. And then, in the German trench behind, we came on the gruesome sequel. There lay the German corpses, slaughtered by the infuriated remnants of the assailants, who had seen their mates mown down and at length had won through to get to grips with them. We looked down one dugout steps, now choked with shattered and swollen bodies, two with their machine-gun belts around them and their gun and tripod—damaged, perhaps, by a Mills grenade—on top of them. We could picture them, knocked, shot or bayonetted into the entrance and the Mills being thrown among them to finish them off. Perhaps, a few yards further on, these British lads had met their own fates.

Here was war as we had not seen it—or smelt it—hitherto. We knew now what to expect when our turn came. Looking around at it, we braced ourselves instinctively in anticipation of our coming ordeal; found ourselves hating those dead machine-gunners as we looked again upon our poor fellows on the rusty wire, and arguing, with a fierce satisfaction, that they had got their deserts.

After that we went scrounging in the dugouts, finding much to interest us, such as German officers' helmets, newspapers, letters, paybooks: only the thought of being left behind caused us hurriedly to return. As we clambered back to the road and joined our mates who, by this time, were astir, our natural instincts dulled, blunted, so that these horrors no longer surprised us. In those few minutes we seemed to have developed an outlook, half callous, half fatalistic. Our feelings of apprehension had gone, had somehow given place to the feeling that, 'up there is the enemy— let's get on with it now and get it over; if we are for it . . . well, we shall get it'.

Shortly after we rejoined our mates, the battalion moved, and as we formed up the word went round that the brigade now formed part of the 21st Division. We went forward by platoons up hill beyond the village to some chalk trenches at the side of a small but terribly shattered wood, where we were comparatively safe from the heavy shelling at frequent intervals throughout the day; although on several occasions we made journeys lasting an hour or more, carrying ammunition and stores to our support line near the western edge of Mametz Wood. At the eastern edge and towards Contalmaison, the shelling and rattle of machine-gun and Lewis gun fire was practically continuous, and we constantly met driblets of our walking wounded, stretcher-bearers with serious cases and groups of dishevelled prisoners coming down. Without exception, they bore evidence of the ordeal through which they had passed a short time previously, their unshaven faces pinched and with a yellowish tinge, their eyes red-rimmed and hollow.

The prisoners wore no equipment and their field-grey uniforms were stained and dusty. Hardly any wore their steel helmets, but many their round forage caps. Only their boots looked worthwhile; although dust-coated and scratched, they appeared more suitable for soldiers' work than our own footgear and puttees, which were regarded by many of us as relics of the South African War. There is no doubt that the pre-1914 army Blücher boot (of which I was lucky enough to be issued with a pair at Wigston Barracks on enlistment) was hard to beat as a marching boot and for general comfort, but the wartime substitutes which followed were far inferior in the view of most of us.

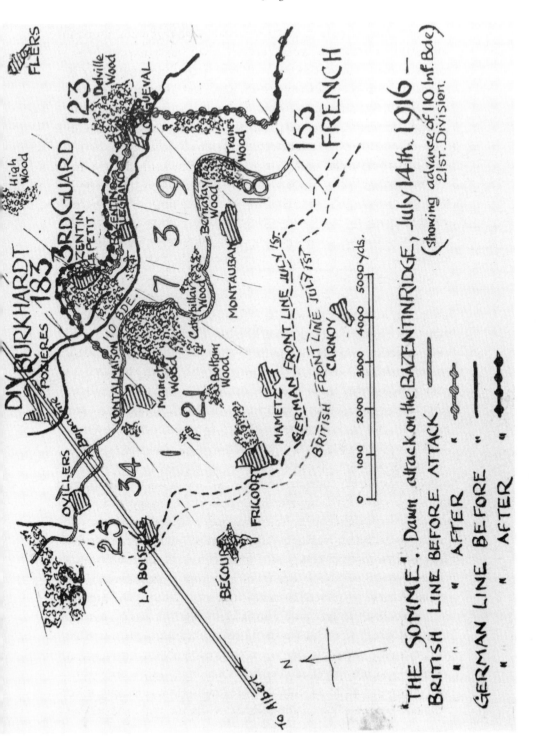

"THE SOMME". Dawn attack on the BAZENTIN RIDGE, July 14th 1916 — (showing advance of 110 Inf. Bde) 21st Division.

BRITISH LINE BEFORE ATTACK ——————
" " AFTER " ———o——o——
GERMAN LINE BEFORE " ——————
" " AFTER " ●●●●●●

GERMAN FRONT LINE JULY 1ST.
BRITISH FRONT LINE JULY 1ST

FLERS
High Wood
Delville Wood
3RD GUARD 123
LONGUEVAL
DIV BURKHARDT 183
POZIERES
BAZENTIN LE PETIT.
BAZENTIN LE GRAND
7 3 9
Trones Wood
Bernafay Wood
153 FRENCH
OVILLERS
110 BDE.
CONTALMAISON
Mametz Wood
Caterpillar Wood
Bottom Wood
MONTAUBAN
25 34
21
1
LA BOISELLE
FRICOURT
MAMETZ
BÉCOURT
CARNOY
0 1000 2000 3000 4000 5000 yds.

To Albert

N

145

These fatigue parties served to enable us to get the lie of the land and to accustom us still further to the inferno around us. I retain a vivid recollection of our field artillery ammunition columns running the gauntlet to their guns over an exposed portion of road, along what soon became known to us as 'The Happy Valley'. One of our fatigues took us across this road on our way to a dump between the shattered ruins of the village of Mametz and the wood of that name.

The Happy Valley. I wonder how many men of both sides—and, for that matter, how many horses and mules—died along its length during the first fortnight of July 1916. What irony in that strangely haunting name; yet how easily the words came upon the tongue, and what a flood of memories they recall among those who knew it in those days.

The artillery drivers—I can see them now, approaching the danger spot at the trot with their double teams, set of face under their steel helmets, getting ready, tense. Then, of a sudden, a mad hell-for-leather ride of five hundred yards or so, the heavily loaded caissons behind jolting and swaying crazily upon the shell-torn track, while the shrapnel burst above and around them, with here and there a great black crump of a five-nine in which the team would be lost to view momentarily, to re-appear with the foam-flecked and sweating horses rearing madly . . . but not always.

On the occasion of which I write, as our party, heavily laden with mortar shells, approached the road, we saw a rushing team all but obscured by a sudden huge spurt of dirty grey; saw black objects tossed high above the smoke and, twirling in the air, fall; then several madly plunging horses, traces trailing, with drivers struggling to control them and, yards behind, as the acrid smoke floated slowly away, the overturned caissons of ammunition. A few moments later we crossed the road at this spot—hurriedly, I remember, every man turned dumb and sick at what he looked upon. At a slow double, for our loads were heavy, we tried to get away from it, but a few yards further on encountered another revolting reminder—a naked torso, scorched and steaming. As we stumbled on with our loads of Stokes bombs we realized that, a minute before, this had been a soldier in the saddle, exhorting and encouraging his two horses past the danger point. And now . . . that.

Early that evening our officers confirmed that our 110th Brigade was now part of the 21st Division, replacing a brigade which had sustained very heavy losses on 1st July and succeeding days. They told us, too, what we now had to do. The 62nd Brigade of our division—mostly Northumberland Fusiliers—had just cleared that portion of Mametz Wood to its front, completing its capture, as the remainder had been finally occupied on the previous day by the 38th (Welsh) Division. The task of the Leicestershires was to carry by assault the German defence line between Mametz Wood and the wood and village of Bazentin-le-Petit beyond. The 7th and 8th Battalions were to lead, the 6th and 9th to follow up. Zero hour was to be 4.35 a.m. the next day, and detailed instructions were given to us regarding the preliminary bombardment, and the creeping barrage which we were to follow closely immediately it lifted from the German front trench. The divisions on our right would also be attacking, their objectives that part of Bazentin Wood in the vicinity of Bazentin-le-Grand, together with the village. The assaulting waves had positions and duties allotted, and I remember that from the point of view of Jackie and myself there seemed no place for us in the scheme of things, so that I worried our company sergeant-major so much, asking to go back on a Lewis gun team, that finally he told us to march with the Company H.Q. signallers and runners, and that probably he'd send us to Battalion H.Q. later on. Vague enough, but something! It was now nearly dark and Verey lights from the front line rose fitfully over the dark mass of Mametz Wood. I remember spending the last few minutes before we started, in having a few words with Freddy Smith and Ted Lineker, who were busy checking their Lewis ammunition drums. After wishing each other the best of luck and promising ourselves a good booze-up when we came out, we parted and took our places in the assembling company.

We moved off in silence, no smoking being allowed from the start. For some time we made steady progress in the darkness, but after a while, as we neared the wood, frequent halts of varying duration were the rule. Meanwhile the enemy, apprehensive, perhaps of coming events, started shelling the wood intermittently with five-nines. Every now and then, as a shell burst, we heard the tearing and splintering of timber as a big tree crashed down,

MAMETZ WOOD (SOMME)
DAWN - JULY 14th 1916.

and the whistle of shell splinters or shrapnel through the thick foliage. After skirting the wood for some distance, we entered it and started to follow a broad white tape laid for our guidance along what had once been a ride; now, alas, littered with fallen timber, over which we had to clamber.

The wood smelt strange and dank in the night air, the natural odours of the churned-up undergrowth blended with a mixture of high explosive, tear gas and chlorine fumes. There the halts became more frequent as companies at length arrived at their allotted positions along the eastern edge, aided by the ghostly radiance of the German Verey lights which also outlined the thick, opaque ground mist which obscured their line, a few hundred yards away, and the intervening ground, as by a white wall. I remember that 'C' Company extended immediately in front of us. At this point we discovered that the company signallers had disappeared, but we worked our way along the line to where we were told Company H.Q. might be. This we found, but the officers and the sergeant-major were busy with their men, and we judged it best to wait. Just then, however, the German artillery, alerted, perhaps by a listening enemy, commenced a heavy bombardment of the wood which soon caused casualties. Shouts for stretcher-bearers mingled with the cries and moans of wounded men. Every now and then a great tree, or a portion of one, would crash down into the mass of tangled undergrowth beneath, sometimes claiming yet another victim.

Seeing the uselessness of going further for the time being, we crouched behind a fallen tree until things had quietened down somewhat. Then, as we prepared to move, we noticed that dawn was breaking. As we spoke a thousand shells seemed to whistle over our heads at once, then . . . pandemonium indescribable, as the preliminary bombardment of the German positions commenced. The enemy retaliated, but such was the noise that we could not hear their shells coming at all, saw great bursts quite close, and were smothered and bruised several times with earth, leaves and tree bark. To speak to Jackie I had to cup my hands and shout into his ear. Just then we saw Colonel Mignon clambering over the fallen trees in our direction, ash plant in hand, with which he thrust aside the undergrowth, bending low here and there and shouting encouragement to the men as he passed.

He came to us. 'Not long to go now lads—stick it!' Then, seeing the rangefinder, he exclaimed, 'what the devil are you two doing with that thing here?' I stood to attention and shouted to him above the din and he shouted back, telling me, not unkindly, to dump it at Battalion H.Q. (for which he gave me a direction) and bring back some S.A.A.—we should want it soon—and look sharp!

We set off as instructed and came to the twisted rails of a light railway track which ran through the wood. The growing light made things easier, although the noise beggared description, and

THE LIGHT RAILWAY TRACK-MAMETZ WOOD 14.7.16.
.... They said he was the Prince of Wales.

once we were stunned for some seconds by a shell which burst just in front of us. We tried to speak and couldn't, our ears roaring, our senses numbed. I don't exactly know how long we lay there before struggling to our feet. Perhaps the stinking smoke or the tear gas in our eyes and nostrils stung us somehow into activity again, and to put on our goggles. They helped, but our eyes streamed and they seemed to fill with tears, half-blinding us.

We stumbled on two of our H.Q. signallers testing their line. They told us to follow it, and this we did, but before we reached Battalion H.Q. we found that a shell had parted the line as it emerged from the wood. A signaller who had come to find the break directed us to Regimental Sergeant-Major Cattell, about thirty yards away, in a German trench littered with bodies. Two signallers and a runner were trying to improvise a shelter across the trench with some fir saplings and sandbags left by the enemy. Near by was a dump of about a dozen boxes of S.A.A. and another of Stokes mortar shells.

The falling shells and the noise were not quite as bad here, and I was able to explain matters fairly coherently, although the reports of our forward field batteries, now almost in line with us, were ear-splitting as they fired salvo after salvo. They were completely in the open and one battery appeared to be straddled already by the German gunners. We dumped the rangefinder, and the R.S.M. seemed very relieved to hear from us that, as yet, the colonel was all right. He gave us permission to take one of the fir poles. This we threaded through the rope loops at either end of a box of S.A.A. and, lifting together, Jackie and I shouldered our load, the R.S.M. shouting, 'good luck' as we set off back. We managed to re-enter the wood, seriously bothered only by the tear gas, the state of our goggles rendering it very difficult at times to see the breaks in the ground and railway track.

A stream of walking wounded was already coming down— some actually laughing, in spite of their injuries, at the thought of having a Blighty one and leaving the inferno so soon. One such, Taylor by name, a fellow apprentice with whom I had enlisted in Leicester, had been hit in the left lower forearm. As he came towards us, holding it and his useless dangling left hand with his right, he extended it to us, shouting, 'put it there, Dick, better born lucky than rich!' and on he went. I met him in Leicester after the war. He couldn't grip anything with that hand. Years of special treatment and several operations were partially successful and he got a job as a handyman carpenter.

Finally he took a pub in Syston. His hand continued to give him hell.

Suddenly the noise reached a crescendo of intensity. Instinctively we stopped for a few moments. They were going over! Anxious to know how our mates had fared, we shouldered our load again and stumbled on, past the edge of Mametz Wood, on to what a few moments previously had been no-man's-land, met three pairs of stretcher-bearers with wounded officers but couldn't see who they were—saw the first still khaki figures lying here and there.

On to and over the hurriedly thrown up and wired German line, now a shambles, pocked with still field-grey bodies; the first column of German prisoners, their hands held high above their heads. Between here and the corner of Bazentin Wood we encountered a succession of very unpleasant bursts of heavy machine-gun fire, apparently coming from the open country to the left of the wood, two bullets of one burst striking our pole and causing us to stagger and fall in a heap. Recovering, we crawled along the ground as best we could, dragging our box and pole behind. Gaining dead ground near the edge of Bazentin Wood, we sat in a shell hole and removed our goggles to clear them and regain our breath. 'That was bloody close, Dick!' Jackie remarked with feeling, and I remember being shocked at his face. I suppose he felt the same about mine. Pressing on, we found some of 'D' Company extended along the rough track along the northern edge of Bazentin Wood. They were digging holes in the bank at the side with their entrenching tools and said they had been told to expect a counter-attack from their front. The heavy machine-gun was already bothering them, and as we were speaking to them a salvo of shrapnel burst above and hit three. One was past aid immediately.

As we left them for Advanced Battalion H.Q., which the R.S.M. had told us would be in the centre of the wood, we came upon many more German dead, and some of our lads, and more prisoners with their hands up. Met some 'C' Company men and were glad to see them, but they couldn't give me any news of Freddy Smith or Ted Lineker. They were lining a shallow trench in the wood. Heavy firing and bombing was in progress in front and in the direction of the village. Just then a young subaltern, whose name I forget, came along and made us dump our box of S.A.A. 'Just what they wanted,' he shouted. 'Get some more as quickly as you can. The Boche will probably counter-attack in a few minutes!'

A gust of shrapnel swept down the trench, killing two men outright and hitting the lieutenant in the shoulder and leg. We half-carried and supported him back to the edge of Mametz Wood. He fainted, but here we met a party of R.A.M.C. men with stretchers coming up, and two of these took the lieutenant away to their aid post, which they told us had been set up by the light railway beyond the wood.

Back at R.S.M. Cattell's dump we couldn't tell him any news of the colonel and, seeing his annoyance, resolved to find out on our next journey, and to get out of his way—quick! We levered a long angle-iron stake out of the trench in lieu of a pole and shouldered another box of S.A.A. We had noticed a sizeable dump of red petrol tins had appeared, and as we moved off he shouted to us to take one each. I'm afraid that his joke—well meant, perhaps—that they would be thirsty up there, was lost on us just then, and until we established a sort of rhythm as we moved, we had considerable difficulty in getting forward at all.

On the way we went by the aid post. Around the Red Cross flag and completely in the open, although shadowed by the trees, three doctors worked among the dozens of stretchers lying around, and at several trestle tables. Near the corner of Bazentin Wood we went very warily and slowly, and thought we had managed to get to dead ground unmolested, when a sudden burst nearly got us.

Either a bullet, or a splinter of a shell which burst nearby immediately after, punctured Jackie's tin of water, a jagged hole through which the water slopped as we stumbled forward in a kind of stupor.

We found the numbers of the men holding this flank sadly depleted, although by this time they had dug deeply into the bank. I remember calling to the first one I saw sitting in his excavation, his rifle and bayonet held as though he was just getting up. As there was no reply, I looked again. He was dead, and there was a round hole in the top of his tin hat. Shrapnel, we supposed. Several of the others begged us to drop a water tin there and we let them have Jackie's, which they seized on eagerly, but spat out in disgust. It absolutely reeked of petrol. We were furious, and if at that moment we could have got at the Service Corps wallahs responsible . . . ! Throwing down the other tin, we trudged on to the centre of the wood as previously, and, finding the trench deserted except for the corpses, we went forward towards Bazentin-le-Petit village where heavy fighting was obviously in progress.

The trees echoed to the constant rattle of rifle and machine-gun fire, punctuated by frequent explosions of grenades in the direction of the village. The shelling had slackened, probably because neither side knew where their opponents were with any accuracy. For some time it had been clear to Jackie and myself that communications had broken down completely, the signallers either casualties or endeavouring to repair lines damaged by shell fire. Casualties among the company and H.Q. runners had also been very heavy: they were sent out and did not return. In short, definite information was very hard to get, and rumour was rife.

Here, near Bazentin village, we found that we were being sniped at from behind and took cover hurriedly in the undergrowth. A few moments later the sniper fired again, at some figures coming our way through the wood. Two 7th Battalion men, recognizable as such by their red 'flashes', were shepherding a line of German prisoners who stumbled forward with hands clasped over their heads.

Jackie and I spotted our man in the same instant, sitting in a tree barely a 130 yards away. He appeared to have forgotten us, and was pointing his rifle at the leading 7th man when, having had ample time to aim, we both fired. The German toppled over backwards and fell to the ground, his steel helmet following his descent through the branches. We both rushed to the spot, as one does after potting a rabbit. He was quite dead.

Meanwhile the 7th Battalion man and the leading prisoners had seen what had happened, and the latter were looking apprehensively at one another. It seemed to have unhinged the 7th man. This, and the strain of the last ten hours had evidently proved too much for him, for he started to laugh in a strange fashion, pointing his rifle first at the corpse and then threateningly at them. They immediately held their hands high, several shouting, '*kamerad, kamerad!*' His mate came up, his rifle slung, but holding a Mills grenade in his right hand and the drawn pin in his left. He, too, looked scarcely responsible for his actions, as he glowered and shouted at them 'c'mon yer bastards. Keep those f. . . hands up. C'mon!' and the sorry procession moved on. We left them, not giving much for the chances of the unfortunates, although just then I'm afraid we shouldn't have minded much.

Near the outskirts of the village we met the survivors of 'A' Company and dumped our load of S.A.A. with the C.S.M. who had taken charge, as all their officers, apparently, were casualties. Near by were some of 'C', among whom we recognized the giant figure of Sergeant 'Tiny' Gamble. None had seen either Freddy Smith or Ted Lineker, but Jackie was delighted to see his cronies Sol Sharpe and Ted Donohue from Loughborough. They had heard that the colonel was dead, killed leading some bombers down a trench in Bazentin Wood. They had one officer left, Lieutenant Warner, a boyish figure who now looked ten years older. We promised to bring them some ammo on our next trip, also some water if we could find some uncontaminated tins.

Near by, practically in the village—now terribly shattered— were 'B' Company, one of whom told us that Captain Beardsley was now commanding the battalion. Beyond them were the 7th, 6th and 9th in and on the far side of the village.

Having had a good look round, we retraced our steps by a direct route, meeting one of H.Q. runners coming up with a message for Captain Beardsley. He pointed to some bushes by a shallow trench where, among other motionless khaki and field-grey forms, Colonel Mignon lay, apparently still clutching a rifle. Hurrying on, we reached R.S.M. Cattell, who knew already about the colonel. He was furious when we told him about the petrol tins, and we tried a number before selecting two which didn't reek so badly.

Balancing our new load of S.A.A. and water, we set out again for 'C' Company, strung around also with divers extra bandoliers, each of fifty rounds. We were approaching the edge of Mametz

Wood when two R.A.M.C. stretcher-bearers with a wounded officer passed us, one calling out, 'The Prince of Wales is just up there'. I heard Jackie behind me muttering something obscene about the Archbishop of Canterbury; but, sure enough, about two hundred yards further on, we came upon a slight figure at the side of the track, red-tabbed and tin-hatted, holding a long stave on which he leaned as he surveyed the scene around. Certainly, he tallied with the descriptions we had gained from photographs, and he actually smiled at us as we stumbled past. A few yards on Jackie called, 'if he was expecting a salute, he was bloody unlucky!' Still, we reflected, it wasn't exactly a healthy spot where he stood, and it confirmed reports we had heard that he wanted badly to fight with the troops, but couldn't for reasons of State.

Our artillery had apparently silenced the machine-gun nuisance around the corner of Bazentin Wood, firing from a strong point towards Contalmaison known to us now as 'The Switch', and our journey was uneventful. We found three Lewis gunners of 'D' Company with their gun, and left some badly needed bandoliers of fifty rounds with them and a tin of water. Inquiring about Horace Phillips, I seemed to know by their faces in the instant what they would tell me. 'Didn't you know, Dick? Poor old Horace was knocked out before we started—corner of Mametz Wood, when they shelled us.' I remember feeling very depressed, and as the shelling started again we pressed on with the rest of our load, which we dumped without further incident.

On the return journey we supported a man hit in both legs. We did our best, as he cursed and entreated us by turns as we jolted him unavoidably, clambering over or around the many obstacles to our progress, in a concentration of tear gas. Having reached the comparative shelter of Mametz Wood once more we halted to get our breath, and it was then that we heard a hoarse cry from the bushes nearby. Wiping our eyes and goggles, we peered into the undergrowth and saw a khaki sleeve and out-stretched arm a few yards away, moving feebly. Pushing our way in, we found a Welshman of the 38th Division who had obviously been lying out for some days, although he was too far gone to tell us. Kneeling by him, we saw that both his legs were shattered and he was now unconscious. Leaving Jackie with them, I made for the aid post as fast as I could and, explaining about the Welshman, prevailed on an R.A.M.C. corporal and one of his men to come the few hundred yards with me. We took a couple of stretchers and a blanket with us and had our first lesson in practical first aid as we assisted the corporal to get both cases on to the stretchers. His know-how and quiet efficiency impressed us greatly at the time, I remember, and as Jackie and I left them at the dressing station we thanked him, mentally revising our estimates of the 'poultice wallahs', as the old soldiers called them.

On reporting to R.S.M. Cattell again, he told us to act as runners, and asked us whether we had seen the brigadier up there, as he was reported to be in Bazentin village. Our signallers there seemed to have established communication with 'B' Company which, we surmised, might save us some more journeys in our new role.

Perhaps the R.S.M. thought we looked about dead beat, as he left us alone for a spell, in which we seized the opportunity of mashing a mess tin of tea. We opened a tin of Fray Bentos, but the tea reeked so strongly of petrol and chloride of lime that our appetites vanished, although the hot liquid, coupled with the break, seemed to do us a world of good. We were loath to move. Sitting there in that shallow chalky trench, we discovered that we had lost all sense of time and were astounded to find by our watches that it was around four in the afternoon; twelve hours since the brigade had gone over, and eighteen or so since last we had eaten. The latter thought seemed to renew our appetites, and we set about the Fray Bentos and bread and cheese in spite of the petrol fumes which rose in our throats between mouthfuls.

I looked at Jackie—we had both removed our goggles. He seemed years older and the thick coating of dust and grime covering his unshaven face was streaked with tear tracks, his blue eyes bloodshot and red-rimmed, outlined by a ridge of grime made by the edges of his goggles.

Seeing me looking at him, he grinned, staring at me as was his wont, through the dirt. 'Why look at me? You ought to see yourself!' So saying, he got up and suddenly came beside me, looking at the back of my neck. 'Take your hat off a minute.' I tried, and found it stuck to my head. 'Here, hold still!' He poured some water into his mess tin and, with his handkerchief, started rubbing and swabbing at the back of my head. After a few minutes I felt a sharp twinge at the back of my head as he pulled the inner lining clear. He ran his fingers up and down my hair near the tender spot. 'It's a bad bruise and the skin's busted, I think, Dick. It's bled a bit and caked.' We looked at my tin hat, which, under the slightly torn sandbag covering, had a considerable dent in it. I couldn't remember feeling anything hit me there, although several times we had been bowled over by explosions. I got out my field dressing and used a bit of it, wetted, for a pad. Jackie helped me to get my headgear on again without disturbing it. As soon as I could find one suitable, I made up my mind to change my tin hat, as I could now feel the dent through the lining. Just then, though, that was a very minor matter.

We made one more journey to the front line that day, taking slung bandoliers of S.A.A. and a water-tin each of better quality (as another lot had come up by a carrying party); also several messages.

It was clear that Captain Beardsley now commanded the survivors of the 8th, with three or four subalterns, two company sergeant-majors and a few sergeants. By this time remnants of companies had been sorted out and assigned definite positions in the line, which was now being consolidated as far as possible. I found no clue as to the fate of Freddy Smith and Ted Lineker and instinctively, somehow, I knew that I should not see them again. The brigade had indeed suffered terrible losses, and those that remained—at least among the 8th—were woefully few to repel any counter-attack which might be launched against them. Many inquired eagerly whether we had any news of relief, or of reinforcements, but we could not tell them anything.

When we reached Battalion H.Q. again it was nearly dark. The shelling was sporadic and aimed apparently at ration parties and suck like, and areas immediately to our rear; indeed, it was almost quiet by comparison with the inferno which had raged through the greater part of the day. Back in our trench once more, we held a kind of summing up of the day's events, as hurriedly we put some poles across it and covered them with some of the German groundsheets lying around—which, incidentally, were much better affairs than ours in every respect. Examining them more thoroughly, we selected one each from the kits of dead Germans lying nearby, for keeping out the night chill; also a greatcoat from a dead officer, beautifully lined with lamb's-wool, for a blanket.

Under our shelter we made a small fire and mashed some tea, which put new life into us, by the firelight examining a German's paybook picked up in the trench. I forget all the details, except that it was of a private of a Bavarian regiment, and this reminded me that we had no idea of the identity of the enemy regiments our brigade had encountered that day. We made mental notes to find out if possible, and get one of the beautiful spiked helmets which we had seen lying about near the village, if they were still there when next we went up.

On inquiry it seemed that we should only be wanted in emergency. We watched a fatigue party bringing up our rations, dumping piles of bulging sandbags on the ground near us, and this set us running through the names of our mates we knew already to be killed, wounded or missing. Both of us had lost all our best pals, and we sat there with leaden hearts, lost in our thoughts. Eventually Jackie broke the silence. 'Plenty of rations tonight, Dick!' nodding towards the pile. 'Enough for the whole battalion, eh? About six times too many.' He added bitterly, 'Christ, there'll be hell to pay in Leicester and Lough-borough . . . and Coalville . . . and Melton . . . and Upping-ham . . . when they know about this. The Leicester Brigade, eh? Bloody well wiped out!' And he trailed off into silence again, immersed in his thoughts.

So we sat, until I suppose sheer fatigue started to get the better of us, and we were dozing when we heard sounds of cursing and heavy breathing nearby at the back of our trench. Starting to our feet, we made out in the dim light a soldier stooping over a figure on the ground. Alerted by the noise we had made he turned and, seeing us, stood upright and then came towards us. By his badges we saw that he was of the Northumberland Fusilier Pioneer Bat-talion of our division, and we caught the strong whiff of rum as he approached. 'Hey, what about this, mate?' he inquired hoarsely, holding out something for our inspection. 'Dunno.

What?' said Jackie sleepily. 'Why, that b. . . there—I got 'is teeth—thet's gold, mate!'

We were at a loss, and, truth to tell, could scarcely believe that we were really seeing and hearing him aright. We watched him pocket the gruesome object and stumble away, noting that he had taken them from the dead officer whose coat we were using.

We got back into the trench feeling physically sick. 'Why didn't we shoot that b. . ., Dick?' exploded Jackie.

A minute or so afterwards . . . 'Why didn't we?' When we came to think about it, lying down under the groundsheets and great-coat, we concluded that it depended on one's outlook on life in general, and this was determined by the circumstances of one's upbringing. Was there really any difference between taking the coat and taking the teeth? We slept.

The next morning was fine, but we shivered as we unstuck our bleary eyes and came to our senses about 5.30 a.m. No one else had bothered us during the night. Over a mess tin of tea we speculated on what the day would bring forth, and essayed some welsh rarebit in a lid—melted cheese on some bread which, toasted on the end of a bayonet, had fallen in the embers of the little fire several times. Still, we were hungry.

Now fairly awake, we approached our signallers for news—warily, as we didn't relish being given a walk to the front line so early. They had lines working to Captain Beardsley and back to Brigade. They said that their mates up there kept inquiring about relief, as there was a strong rumour going around among the 7th and 6th. Here, however, there was no news of this kind.

About 9 a.m. two padres put in an appearance, and after some moments' conversation with them the R.S.M. called to us, telling us to go with the chaplains and help them as much as we could. We departed with them to a huge shell hole, about two hundred yards away, in which several of our Pioneers were working with shovels to lengthen and deepen it. Here one of the padres told us to relieve two of the men. About ten minutes after we had started digging the grim purpose of the hole became evident from the approach of a party carrying bodies on stretchers, which they deposited in the excavation, departing afterwards for more. The padres then knelt and carefully and reverently removed the identity discs from a score or more of dead, who properly should have been buried at least a week previously. Many uniforms still bore the flash of the Red Dragon of Wales. Another layer was added and then the padres motioned to us to stop digging. One of them then read reverently a short service as we stood with our shovels, watching, in spite of ourselves, the motions of his colleague who, we concluded subsequently, must have been a Roman Catholic padre. At the time he made a certain impression on us, and somehow brought us face to face with the fact of death and the hereafter in a way that we could not remember considering before. But there was no time for reflection then.

A short pause after the service, and the padre motioned to us to fill in, which we did, the while he and his colleague made more notes and checked map references. One of the Pioneers wrote something in blue pencil on a piece of boxwood which he stuck in the ground. Then the padres thanked us and the party moved on, doubtless to continue its grim work, of which, unfortunately, there was more than enough.

We had just returned to R.S.M. Cattell, when a shout from one of the signallers drew the attention of all. He was pointing to Mametz Wood, where groups of men from the battalions of our brigade had appeared at several points. As we watched, our mounted, red-tabbed brigade major galloped across our trench towards them, closely followed by the staff captain, gesticulating frantically and shouting, 'go back—go back!' to the now-halted men. They, for some moments, appeared undecided. Then, I suppose, the habit of discipline asserted itself and they turned, and in a few moments disappeared into the wood again, followed by the brigade major and staff captain.

A few minutes later an artillery driver came up, inquiring about his horse. Was the officer coming back? Apparently the brigade major, seeing the incredible situation then developing, had borrowed it. Eventually, an hour or so afterwards, we did in fact see his horse returned to him. For many a long day to come, reasons were advanced for what had happened to cause many front line troops to leave their posts in the belief that relieving troops were in front of them, the most likely being the presence of a large working party in Bazentin from another division. In any case,

Names of missing officers, Leicestershire Regiment, Somme,
Thiepval Memorial, 1916. Photographed in September 1966.

neither Captain Beardsley nor Lieutenant Warner, nor the men in their vicinity, moved and the whole thing in retrospect was inexplicable—yet it actually occurred. Fortunately the enemy did not take advantage of the lapse, and I doubt whether the incident has a place in the official histories.

In fact, three more days passed before we were relieved, of which I can remember little except an incident late the preceding evening. Apparently R.S.M. Cattell's post had been chosen as a Brigade Headquarters by the relieving formation. I retain a vivid recollection of the arrival of the brigadier with staff, and of him strafing all and sundry some time later as he strode to and fro along the top of the trench in the darkness—and

MEN OF THE LEICESTERSHIRE REGIMENT MISSING.

Pte. H. Matts. Send news of him to Mrs. Matts, who lives at 11, Alexandra-terrace, Leicester.

Pte. W. Jarvis. Write to his mother, at Ivy Cottage, Laindon Common, near Billericay, Essex.

Cpl. E. S. Swift. Address letters to 65, Barrington - road, Crouch End, London, N.

Pte. Alec Whitlock, wounded and missing. Write to Miss E. Whitlock, at Tugby, Leicestershire.

Pte. H. M. Taylor. Write to Mr. J. B. Elliott, who lives at 3, Garrick - road, Northampton.

Pte. Mattock. Send news of him to Mrs. Mattock, who lives at Fleckney, nr. Market Harborough.

Pte. F. W. Smith, wounded and missing. Write Mrs. Smith, Charnwood Stone, Shepshed, L'estershire.

Pte. D. J. Smith. Write to Miss Smith, his sister, at Sindlesham, Wokingham, Berkshire.

'Freddy Smith.

particularly his batman, because a jar of rum which we had seen the latter deposit earlier on top of the miserable shanty had mysteriously disappeared. We had no idea as to the identity of the culprit, but the spectacle so amused us that for some minutes we quite forgot the war.

At length, at dusk on the fourth day, the survivors of the Leicestershire Brigade trooped wearily down through Mametz Wood and back to a fairly sheltered spot near Fricourt, where we bivouacked, only too glad to be on the way out. I remember seeing our brigadier, Hessey, dirty and bedraggled as the rest of us, walking slowly down the light railway track with the aid of a long stick, head bowed like a weary old shepherd. Our acting 'C' and 'B' Company commanders: the one a boyish figure of a subaltern, no older than ourselves, who had taken over the company in the heat of the action from his wounded captain, and who had aged ten years in the last four days; the other, Captain Beardsley, martial yet, though dirty and unkempt, his left hand bandaged. He had gone into action with his sword, and now it was sheathed at his side, but he strode proudly at the head of his remnant—a pitiful few—who followed him like faithful dogs.

Such are my recollections of Mametz Wood and Bazentin-le-Petit, where so many of Leicestershire's finest sons fell: the last resting place of my good friends Phillips, Lineker and Smith. So far as I know, no trace of the two latter has ever been found. Horace Phillips was buried at the corner of Mametz Wood and the spot marked, but no trace of his grave remains. His name appears among the 'missing' on the Thiepval Memorial. The song he used to sing to us still lives . . . 'She was a Lady, great and splendid, I was a minstrel in her Hall . . .'

Before we left Fricourt I returned to the Lewis gunners, who now numbered six, all told. Jackie also returned to company duty. We dumped the rangefinder with the battalion quartermaster, who told us to put it on one of the ration limbers. It had not been of any practical use, but, as Jackie remarked with some feeling, it had perhaps saved *our* bacon!

We marched off at dusk and left the Somme with very mixed feelings—of sorrow at the thought of those we had left behind, and of individual relief at being out of it, if only for a time. As we tramped along with our faces to the sunset, songs were attempted by a few bold spirits, and presently we all found ourselves joining in.

> The roses round the door
> Make me love mother more
> I'll see my sweetheart Flo –
> And friends I used to know.
> They'll be right there to meet me
> Just imagine how they'll greet me,
> When I get back—When I get back
> To my home in Tennessee!

or

Ah've got a sneakin' feelin'
Round ma heart
That ah wanta settle down!
Ah'm goin' tear pack ma grip
An' take a trip
To some good ol' southern town . . .

and the chorus:

Back home in Tennessee
Just try and picture me
Upon ma mother's knee
She thinks the world of me . . .

and so on. The songs of the Somme, which only they who marched along those roads under similar circumstances can appreciate.

I suppose that, in wild flights of fancy we imagined, as we sang, our loved ones meeting us at the end of our march—a kind of mental mirage, perhaps, conjured up by the sentimental words and the witchery of the tunes, but strangely comforting to war-weary men.

THE GENERAL

"Good morning; good morning!' the General said
When we met him last week on our way to the line.
Now the soldiers he smiled at are most of 'em dead,
And we're cursing his Staff for incompetent Swine.
'He's a cheery old card!' grunted Harry to Jack.
As they slogged up to Arras with rifle and pack . . .

. . . .

But he did for them both by his plan of attack.

Siegfried Sassoon

. . . . Visiting the iniquity of the fathers upon the children
unto the third and fourth generation of them that hate me . . . . .

EXODUS 20. V.

CHAPTER 10

ARRAS

VERY late that evening we reached the village of Méricourt, footsore and pretty tired. How pleased we were, though, I recall, to see our C.Q.M.S. Peach, with a shaded hurricane lamp, at the approach to the village. He guided our remnant of 'C' Company along the silent street into a barn redolent of fresh hay and clean straw. Lying there were our blankets, ready to unroll, and through the barn doors came the whiff of hot soup and the smell of the company cooks' field oven at the rear. One of the cooks brought in a dixie of tea and was greeted by us all with a cheer. An old soldier with the Boer War ribbons, he looked round at us as we flung down our equipment, stood our rifles and Lewis gun against the walls, and sat down to unwind our puttees and unlace our boots. He was pleased enough to see us, but when he saw how few we were he became grave, his face eloquent with unspoken questions. We guessed why. C.Q.M.S. Peach was anxious, too, to do all he could for our comfort, and agreed to leave his lamp as we could scarcely muster a candle-end between us.

Sergeant Chesterton asked Peach and the acting C.S.M. 'Tiny' Gamble whether we could have the mail and they went off to fetch it, returning shortly with two bulging bags. It was then that we suddenly realised that we had neither heard from home, nor had our boots off, for over a week—since we left Soues, in fact.

It was a fine night and we made a ring around Sergeant Chesterton as, with the aid of the lamp, he called the names on the letters and parcels. More than two-thirds of them lay unclaimed afterwards: in response to his call 'Private So-and-So' a voice would shout 'killed' or 'Blighty', or two or more would confuse the issue by shouting both. We helped Sergeant Chesterton put these sad reminders into the mail bags and then turned

THE MAIL —AFTER BAZENTIN
LATE EVENING
MÉRICOURT-SOMME - 19.7.'16.

our attention to our own letters, foraging in our haversacks and
pockets for scraps of candle by which to read the news from home.

Comfortably full of soup, tea and bread and cheese, I recall
feeling very pleased at getting an unexpected letter from a girl in

England, with her photograph, and went to sleep for the first time with rosy visions of leave which, I reflected, might now be considerably nearer. As a single man I hadn't dared to give the subject a thought previously, as there were still many names of married men on the roster before mine. Now, it might be different.

Next morning we recovered our packs and swapped greatcoats and other items from the piles of those unclaimed. Then, as far as we could, after the luxury of a shave at leisure with hot water we brushed and spit-polished away the wear and tear of our recent experiences. In the afternoon we paraded with the rest of the brigade for inspection by our 21st Division commander, General Campbell, who thanked us 'for our splendid effort on July 14th'; but this parade demonstrated more clearly than anything had done previously, the terrible losses sustained. We were a mere handful.

That night we entrained, and were taken to a back area, west of Arras. Where actually we detrained now escapes me, but in the village of Wanquetin the battalion re-organized, receiving several considerable drafts. I was made an acting corporal, and spent the hot summer days with the reconstituted Lewis gun teams, inculcating in the many newcomers the elements of the weapon. Among these were several veterans of 'C' Company whom I was very glad to see with us, among them Lance-Corporal 'Fatty' Briggs (of whom more anon). He told me he wanted to join us because he had seen at Bazentin what a Lewis gun could do.

One July evening a week later we marched into the battered and silent city of Arras by way of Dainville, bedding down for the night in the deserted Caserne, in happier days barracks of the 33rd French Regiment of Engineers (Genie).

At dusk on the following day we marched in artillery formation out of the city and through the residential suburb of St. Nicholas towards the line—a desert of partially roofless villas surrounded by gardens now overgrown with brambles and climbing roses run riot. High overhead droned a flight of our bombing planes returning from the direction of Cambrai, and with the darkness the shell-pitted frontages of the houses became bathed in a soft moonlight. At length the houses and the road gave way to a weed-grown vista of chalky overturned earth and rusty wire. Into a gap in this we filed and down into a communication trench

labelled 'September Avenue', now assailed by the smell of putrefying grease or fat, which worsened as, in the moonlight above
the trench, we saw the gaunt outline of a battered, roofless factory
building and, through gaping holes, or thrust into the sky, the
twisted shafting and rusting machinery. Between it and our communication trench the ground was strewn with great barrels and
other debris protruding through the two-foot high weeds—the
source of the stink. We hurried on to get away from it, our feet
ringing on what seemed to be an iron trench bottom. Later we
found that these were a kind of tray originally used in the factory
and that, when wet, they became very slippery.

We passed the support line with dugouts, whence sounds and
faint illumination issued from within the curtained entrances. Momentarily, we wished we were stopping there—afterwards we knew
it as the Nicholls Redoubt and Battalion H.Q.—but pressed on
along what seemed a never-ending trench to the front line. It was
quiet, only an occasional Verey light or a rifle shot from afar
disturbing the peace, although to the south we could hear faintly
and see in the night sky the flickering flashes of the guns of the
Somme battle. When dawn came, we found that we were holding
part of the rim of a large weed-grown mine crater. Subsequently
we found that there were three of them, called Cuthbert, Clarence
and Claude after the characters in a song from a popular wartime
revue. Ours, I believe, was Cuthbert, and my abiding recollection
of these Arras trenches was chalk, powdered, chunky and wet; of
mine craters, mines and miners, the latter the New Zealand
Tunnelling Company, assisted by Pioneers from our 14th Northumberland Fusiliers, themselves miners.

When holding the front line here, we always had the very
unpleasant knowledge that, in all probability, the enemy was busy
tunnelling beneath us. Indeed, the New Zealanders told us cheerfully that he was, and that as long as they could hear Jerry
working, there was nothing to be afraid of. It was when he stopped
we had to look out, because the mine was probably ready to
detonate—perhaps *underneath* the other mine (or *camouflet*, as it was
called) that the New Zealanders were making. Listening, according
to them, was a vitally necessary part of the job; and, perhaps for
this reason, our own hearing faculties were frequently strained to

the utmost when in the front line. In the daytime we would hear frequently a thumping sound, like that which a dog makes with a hind leg when scratching behind his ears, which came invariably, however, from the enormous mangy rats with which these trenches were infested, as they made their toilets among the tangle of weeds and wild flowers on our parapet. They were the largest and most voracious we had seen, and our friends the New Zealanders said that they had come out of the honeycomb of tunnels and sewers beneath Arras.

While we were in these trenches, the enemy blew a *camouflet* one evening in the side of Clarence crater, burying a number of New Zealand tunnellers and some Pioneers of the Northumberland Fusiliers who had been assisting them.

A week or so later a picked party from our battalion made a night raid on the German trench opposite to obtain identification of the unit holding it, following a short preliminary bombardment by our artillery. Apparently forewarned by this, the enemy vacated the area and our men found no one, returning disappointed and empty handed.

We held these trenches for about six weeks. I believe that our 64th Brigade was on our left in the villages of Ecurie and Roelincourt, and the 62nd Brigade covered the eastern suburbs of Arras and the river Scarpe. Heavy fighting had taken place once, but not since the British had taken over the sector from the French Army in the spring. After our spells in the front and support lines, we would file down September Avenue, past the demolished *stéarinerie* (candle factory), and back into Arras to billets in the Caserne. Every afternoon the Germany artillery strafed the city, presumably aiming at the much-damaged cathedral, although once a shell carried away a portion of the roof of the barrack block we were occupying. As this always occurred about 4 p.m., we did any coming and going before or after and became quite used to it.

When off duty in the line, while not neglecting all necessary precautions, we passed the hot summer days amid the lazy buzzing of bees and bluebottle flies among the wild flowers and matted weeds, playing endless games of solo, pontoon and brag. We were on good terms with our friends the New Zealanders, and our fatigue parties moved many hundreds of filled sandbags of excavated chalk from their underground tunnelling beneath the enemy, assisted by a rope-and-pulley arrangement of little trucks on a light railway running into their shaft. They used to bring us eggs and fruit from Arras, and wouldn't take anything for it from us. We used to marvel at their pay, while they, on the other hand marvelled at ours—theirs being about six times ours!

I vividly recall, however, an incident late one night when, while in support around Nicholls Redoubt, I was N.C.O. of the Battalion H.Q. guard there. We had a new colonel, by name Harvey; a violent contrast in every way to our much-loved Colonel Mignon. He was a pale, dandified, effeminate-looking type, with a high-pitched falsetto voice, his pallor and sharp features, black hair and eyes accentuated by a heavy, sharp-pointed black moustache. Frankly, no one liked him; perhaps for the very reason that he suffered so much by comparison with his predecessor. On the occasion of which I write, I was visiting the sentry on duty as he stood upon the firestep of a bay a few yards to one side of Battalion H.Q. mess dugout. His duties were to note the direction of the wind in case of a gas attack, and any untoward occurrence. It was then that we heard an officer issue from the dugout and come in our direction. The night was fine and starry, and at the officer's approach the sentry challenged him clearly and firmly. He received a blurred sort of reply and I hurried along the firestep to get a better view of the newcomer, seeing then that it was Colonel Harvey. I managed to preserve a respectful attitude as, steadying himself, he climbed on to the firestep beside me, redolent of whisky and perfume of some kind. To his inquiry as to whether there was anything of interest to report, I replied in the negative, and he remarked on the wonderful night in his curious falsetto voice. It was then that I concluded that he had dined and wined rather too well. Surprisingly, he then took a cigarette from a slim case and proceeded to light it, standing head and shoulders above the firestep. From the reflection of the lighted match in his cupped hands I had a glimpse of his flushed features. Although we were several hundred yards from the enemy, I began to be apprehensive of what he would do next, but we stood in silence for some moments, the sentry meanwhile departing to the far end of the bay. Far to the south, the horizon flecked with Verey lights which, at that distance, resembled burning iron filings in the night sky, there rumbled the distant drum-fire of the Somme battle.

At length the colonel spoke, waving a hand in that direction. 'Still killing the Boche down there . . . belch . . . killing 'em and being killed, eh?' then, turning to me, 'are you afraid to die, boy?' and, seeing me taken aback by his question, 'pooh—pooh! Why, what are we but a lot of poor fish . . . belch . . . just like the fish in the sea, boy? What do a few thousand more or less of us matter. If it's our turn to be taken, boy . . . *kaput* . . . phut! . . . that's all there is to it,' snapping his fingers to emphasise his point. This conversation I have given verbatim, as it remains in my memory so clearly after all these years.

After a pause to collect my thoughts and suppress my first angry reaction, I answered that I supposed he was right, but that I didn't want to die—not yet—because I was young and had not really started to *live*, what with the war and having to leave everything. There were so many things, too, that I didn't want to miss, before my turn came. He laughed indulgently at his own interpretation of my reply and blundered down into the trench once more. 'Quite so, boy, quite so, Corporal . . . a lot of fish . . . that's what we are!' Taking a few steps, he disappeared behind the mess dugout curtain, where I've no doubt he told them in there what a lot of fish *they* were.

Standing outside there under the night sky, we sniffed at the mixed odours he had left behind—a combination of whisky, scented soap and Turkish cigarettes. In the ignorance of youth, we gave tongue to some very uncharitable observations and were ruminating thus when the battalion signalling officer, Lieutenant Dixie Smith, came out of the dugout and stood looking up and down the trench before spotting me. He then inquired whether I had seen the colonel. I told him he had asked for our report and then returned to the dugout. 'Huh!' was Dixie Smith's comment. 'Oh, Read,' he continued, 'I've got something for you, wait a minute!' and he dived back into the mess dugout, issuing in a few moments to hand me a large envelope. 'I've noticed you sketching, Read, and as I had a day's leave in Avesnes-le-Comte yesterday I bought this little sketch book for you. Good pictures with it!' I stammered my thanks and he bade me 'goodnight' as he went off to his own hideout near by. It was a very kind thought, characteristic of him. He was a well known Leicester businessman and all-round sportsman, and had missed Bazentin through being on a signalling course.

A few evenings before we left the Arras trenches for good, we were witnesses of a remarkable escape from what appeared to be certain death. As a flight of our bombing planes was returning from the direction of Cambrai the German 'archies' opened a furious cannonade as usual, but on this occasion it was soon obvious that one machine was in difficulties, starting to lose height as a long white plume of smoke trailed behind it. Then, as we watched, the nose dropped and the whole plane started to fall in a sickening corkscrew motion, the white changing to a cloud of black smoke. Seemingly within a few hundred feet of the ground, the pilot appeared to get out of the spin; the machine, while still rapidly losing height, levelled off. He crash-landed, I believe, in no-man's-land on the front of our 62nd Brigade. We saw the billowing smoke from the burning machine and heard the fusillade of rifle shots from the German trenches, but our officers told us that the pilot staggered out and made the British trench safely. We liked to believe that this was indeed the case, but apparently the remainder of the bomber's crew perished.

All good things must come to an end and, as I have said, the division left Arras for good, marching to back-area villages around Avesnes-le-Comte. We bedded down in the pleasant village of Lignereuil. Here we trained hard and received another considerable draft, which included several of the original battalion, lightly wounded at Bazentin. We Lewis gunners were issued with hand trucks in which to carry our stuff when on the move—a welcome improvement in our lot. Long since, our pack mules with great leather portmanteaux like panniers for drums of ammunition, had been abandoned, our mules used to replace casualties in the transport lines when the enemy shelled them at Pommier, Humbercamps and near Méaulte.

In a way, the sylvan surroundings reminded us of Soues, but the training and inspections indicated some hard task ahead. I remember that I chummed up with a Corporal Jack Quincy of 'D' Company, a young schoolmaster at Ashby-de-la-Zouche before 1914. He was of a studious disposition and, in my loneliness, save for Jackie, I was attracted to him and liked his company and conversation. Like us, he had lost all his pals at Bazentin. Together we wrote to Émilienne at Berles, telling her of our mates killed at Bazentin, most of whom she would remember quite well. Before many days had elapsed, Jack received a very well written reply from her, partly in English.

I remember well her comments on our news that one of her favourites, Tommy Butler, had been killed. At every opportunity he used to 'pull the leg' of her sister, Skinny Liz. '*Pauvre* Tommy Butler', she wrote, and we could imagine her saying '*pauvre* Tommeee'. She told Jack, too, how grieved she and her family were to read our bad news; that things were quiet at Berles; that she and her family wished us *bonne chance* and would always be glad to hear from us. As Jack put the letter into his wallet, I rather fancied that it wouldn't be long before he replied to it himself, but I don't think he did, because on the following morning we paraded with the rest of the brigade in a large stubble field about a mile from Lignereuil, the four battalions each forming one side of a huge square. Here General Campbell, mounted on a fine black horse and followed by his staff, also mounted, rode on to the parade. A composite band played the 'General Salute' as the whole parade, with fixed bayonets, presented arms—without any exaggeration a stirring sight, as no doubt it was intended to be!

We then unfixed bayonets, grounded our arms and were told to sit down. Through a loud-hailer the general then called, 'gentlemen, you may smoke!' After a short pause, while many lit fags and pipes, the blow fell. Leaning forward between his horse's ears he addressed us all in clear ringing tones. 'Gentlemen, the 21st Division, which I have the honour to command, has been chosen to take part in the Somme offensive for the third time . . .'

We heard him continue as though in a dream, thinking that it was hardly possible that we were really hearing this. He continued, impressing upon us the value of thoroughness in all that we were about to undertake, illustrating his point by telling us how he, as an amateur, rode the Grand National winner 'The Soarer' at Aintree in 1896, attributing his success to attention to detail coupled with the will to win. He stressed, too, the necessity of keeping direction in the coming operations: 'direction, gentlemen—direction! Direction!' Then he told us that he had a pretty good idea of the perils we were about to face, and that it was through no wish of his own that he could not be with us in the forefront; in August 1914 he had been wounded by lance, bullet and shell fragment. Very earnest and inspiring words, spoken by a general who was no 'dug-out', but a fine leader. Since the opening of the Somme battle on 1st July there is no doubt that the 21st Division had proved itself the equal of any in France, and subsequent exploits under General Campbell were to earn for it a splendid reputation. It never let him down.

Well, we had heard the worst, and we marched back to Lignereuil—I will not say like condemned men, but like men who had just heard a momentous decision affecting the whole future course of their lives and were trying to take a dispassionate view of things, each man busy with his own thoughts for a while.

We were paid—I got twenty francs, I remember—and in the afternoon attended a brigade boxing tournament near the village, sitting around a ring made in a natural bowl of grassy slopes, with trees around the fringe. In the course of this our heavyweight hope, Sergeant Brotherhood, received a broken jaw in the second round from one 'Cock' Howard of the 6th Battalion, which probably saved his life. Anyhow, we all envied him as we watched him being carried off on a stretcher.

Evening saw us congregating in the *estaminets*, forgetting, for the nonce, and getting tight in the process. Actually, until fairly late I was busy with the two lance-corporals who were the Number Ones on the Lewis guns, checking the packing of our new trucks, and by the time I pushed my way into the singing crowd filling the nearby *estaminet*, they had only malaga—a sweet raisin wine. Many, therefore, mixed their drinks pretty badly, but I had too much malaga too quickly. Then the Regimental Police cleared the *estaminets* and we went down the village street arm-in-arm singing 'Oh . . . the old red flannel drawers . . .'

The only people who were quite sober appeared to be the orderly sergeants and orderly corporals of the day, who flitted about in the dusk, busy with returns and messages to and from the orderly rooms. From all the barns we passed issued sounds of harmony, choruses with mouth-organ accompaniments. No sooner had we reached our billet, however, than we had to parade in the farmyard for an inspection of respirators, steel helmets, iron rations and field dressings. In vain C.S.M. 'Tiny' Gamble and the C.Q.M.S. Peach, helped by Sergeant Killingley, tried to maintain a proper semblance of order; the ranks swayed up and down amid snatches of song and outbursts of alcoholic elation. During the inspection of respirators, which we had to put on, one unfortunate was sick in his, which evoked much merriment.

Down in the village the bugles blew the 'Last Post' and the parade dismissed as the last notes echoed plaintively in the surrounding trees. Thoroughly fuddled and happy, we lay down in our straw, some drawing on a last fag, redly illuminating themselves and their mates on either side. A few joyous spirits still sang. Then the bugles sounded 'lights out'. As from afar, we heard the orderly sergeant: 'now then—put that bloody light out there!', and we slept.

CHAPTER 11

GUEUDECOURT

WE were early astir next morning, but almost all of us retained legacies of the previous evening in the form of splitting headaches and an aversion to food of any sort; feelings which we endeavoured to dispel by putting our heads under the farmyard pump. When we moved off, after standing on parade for half an hour or so in full kit, we felt far from well, and the (to us) considerable march which followed—to the railway station at Frévent—proved a severe test of our powers of endurance.

Luckily, we Lewis gunners were able to dump our packs upon our new push carts, which ran fairly easily when everyone pulled or shoved, but we had good loads of guns, spares and ammunition pans, and uphill the going was hard. Had we been in condition, we would have laughed at the march, but as it was we struggled into Frévent feeling pretty well washed up. Here the battalion piled arms in a field near the station, while the sky became overcast and it began to rain, lowering our spirits still further. Eventually we entrained and jogged through the night, detraining, I believe, at Méricourt.

We soon found ourselves traversing the familiar brown wastes and scenes of desolation, but this time we left Fricourt well to our left, and by a night march across country gained the high ground behind the ruins of Carnoy, where we bivouacked in the open for two days.

By the continuous shell fire to the east we surmised, correctly, that a major battle was in progress—actually the capture of Flers on 15th September, when the tanks made their début. From here, looking north west, we could see the town of Albert, and through field glasses the 'Tilting Virgin', with the intervening vista of derelict horse lines, camps, battery positions and trenches; also

The "Tilting Virgin" of ALBERT (SOMME) IN 1916. AS THE SOLDIER KNEW IT.

Fricourt, La Boiselle and Ovillers, with the trenches and a mine crater outlined in chalk. The sun scarcely shone at all, and fitful and sometimes heavy showers didn't improve matters. One afternoon, I recall, one of our observation balloons which had broken loose sailed overhead, aided by a westerly breeze as it headed towards the German lines, gaining height rapidly. We watched it until it was a mere speck, surrounded by tiny black balls of bursting shells from the German anti-aircraft batteries. We didn't think the basket was occupied.

At length we moved further forward on a rainy mid September evening: through the ruins of Carnoy; then of Montauban, taken on 1st July and now bristling with great eight-inch howitzers, to which more were being added as two Fowler traction engines, puffing and pulling, blocked the roughly repaired road at intervals, while sweating gun teams and the battery officers shouted above the prevailing chaos. Past these, we made our way slowly down

TODAY —

"OUR LADY" OF THE
BASILICA OF NOTRE
DAME DE BREBIÈRES
HOLDING THE CHRIST
CHILD ABOVE ALBERT.

AT NIGHT HER GOLDEN
FLOODLIT FIGURE HANGS
IN THE SKY, VISIBLE FOR
MILES AROUND.

the hill of Montauban, past more heavy artillery, the road skirting the mangled trees of Bernafay Wood.

At the eastern edge of the wood at the bottom of the hill we halted and, spreading out, bivouacked in the shell holes near the north-east corner. By nightfall two infantry brigades of our division were occupying the valley between Montauban and the rubble heap of the village of Longueval, which lay in the shadow of Delville Wood. Our third brigade, we heard, was in the front line somewhere near Flers. As we rigged our groundsheets I remember that, before darkness obscured it, we had a long look at the gaunt leafless stumps of Delville Wood, for we had read much about it and how, at length, it had been taken after many attempts. To our right lay the similarly shattered remains of Trones Wood, bounding our view in that direction save for a small gap through which, we learned, lay the track to Guillemont and Ginchy, now in British hands. Past our bivouacs and along the valley towards

DELVILLE WOOD & LONGUEVAL.

as at JULY 26/29 1916.

British Line 26/27 July
" " 28th
" " 29th

Waterlot Farm

GINCHY ½ m.

GUILLEMONT 1½ m.

TRONES WOOD

24 R.

XIII

2

90th

South St.

King St.

Campbell St.

Rotten Row St.

Buchan St.

Bond St.

Regent St.

Strand

Prince's St.

Delville Wood

8 Lr. Gr.

⁸/₂₃rd (12 Div.)
29/30 July

5

52

1 X Rrs.
¹¹/₂₃ 12 D FLERS 1¾ m.
28/9 July

17 R

95th

High Wood

Picadilly

Duke St.

Pont St.

Claroes St.

Bazentin
Le Grd ½ m.

Sloane St.

15th

Down's St.

Dover St.

Montauban 1½ m.

XV

5

1

0   50   100   yds   1000

Guillemont, ran the rusty twisted rails of a light railway. Along this track passed a constant stream of transport: guns and limbers; fatigue parties of the Guards and 20th Divisions, who were fighting hard up there; walking wounded, and stretcher parties bearing casualties to an R.A.M.C. advanced dressing station just off the Montauban road nearby, the furthest point reached by the motor ambulances.

The rain really started to fall on the following day and the German heavy shells to plaster us at intervals; one, I recall, falling on the field cookers of the 2nd Lincolns. From the meagre shelter of our groundsheet bivouac we watched the procession on the churned up track—Coldstreamers, Grenadiers, Scots Guards, Devons, Cornwalls—sliding, sticking in the whitey-yellow mud, the whole making way for the patient teams of steaming bespattered horses and mules, drawing heavily loaded caissons of shells for the field artillery, which bumped and swayed between the shells holes, the drivers set of face with necks sunk deep in the upturned collars of their greatcoats, while the raindrops ran off their sandbagged tin hats in cascades on to their hunched shoulders. Many of these men were unsung heroes in those far-off days, working like galley slaves to feed the guns, snatching sleep when and where they could, and invariably tending to the needs of their four-footed friends before their own. I recall seeing two large shells fall in succession near the track towards Trones Wood, but as the dirty grey smoke drifted away I saw the procession moving on quite unaffected by the occurrence, so completely had men and beasts become inured to shell fire.

Along the valley and upon the brown slopes toward Longueval, ant-like khaki figures of regiments of our division moved to and fro during fine intervals, digging holes deeper, baling out, improving shelters with battlefield flotsam and tending little smoky fires of damp sticks to get a hot drink somehow, while the going was good. We had ours—even putting twigs in our pockets to keep them dry until needed.

That evening we were of a party which went up into Delville Wood carrying duckboards, which we endeavoured to lay there, and in all my experience before or since I am quite certain that I never saw such a rotting scene of slaughter. After such an interval

Above: Longueval Cemetery and Delville Wood (Somme), photographed in September 1966. Graves of Rhodesia Regiment men are in the foreground.

Part of Longueval Cemetery and South African National War Memorial, Delville Wood, photographed in September 1966.

of time there seems no point in trying to describe what we looked upon in that dusk of pitiless rain, but the shattered stumps of Delville Wood, and what lay within, remain indelibly printed on my mind. In fact, each year passed in the comfort of civilian life renders the recollection the more terrible. It was not the number of dead, but their manner of dying which awed and sickened us. The German infantry and machine-gunners had fought to the last man for every inch and I cannot say how many regiments—British and South African—struggled for weeks to take this wood, or which of all those finally drove an heroic enemy into the open ground beyond. As for us, we slithered about in the downpour, to the methodical attentions of German five-nines which caused several casualties near the north-east corner. As best we could, we levered the dead aside—English, Scots, South Africans and Germans, inextricably together in death, sometimes crushed anew by fallen timber and fresh shell bursts in the churned up undergrowth. I recall now the gruesome sight of a Scot and a German, each on his knees with his bayonet thrust into his opponent, and our efforts—unsuccessful—in separating and moving them to one side.

The same half-sweetish, sickly smell persisted as at Mametz Wood, of dank, turned up undergrowth and earth mixed with a combination of chlorine, tear gas, the stale fumes of high explosive, and putrefying flesh. Is it strange that now, even after all these years, whenever I walk through an English wood in the summertime involuntarily I picture it as I once saw other woods then; the blackened greeny-white crusted pits amid the corpse-strewn brambles; the great trees torn asunder, uprooted and stripped of their leaves, splintered and gashed—and all those other things. The natural smell of a wood recalls it all and sets me the task of blotting out those ghosts of other days.

Before we set out that evening we saw four Guardsmen approaching from the direction of Guillemont, taking turns at bearing a laden stretcher. By their manner of walking, somehow they interested us and we surmised (as it happened, correctly) that their burden was no ordinary casualty. One of us inquired of the Grenadier N.C.O., and I recall the sense of shock we experienced, even in those surroundings, at being told that the body was that of Lieutenant Raymond Asquith, Grenadier Guards. He was the, then, prime minister's son. We watched them deposit the stretcher at the dressing station. I do not know for certain whether or not he was buried there, but I have a clear recollection of the considerable number of graves which appeared there during the days that we passed in the vicinity.

I saw Jack Quincy several times; his Lewis gun section lay in shell holes quite near us. Late one afternoon, between the showers, we explored the nearest portion of Bernafay Wood together as we talked of various things—of England. I recall that he continually whistled part of a tune familiar to me, although I was ignorant of its title. Seeing me looking at him, he apologized with a grin. 'Sorry, old man, but that keeps running through my head today. Dunno why, but tunes do sometimes, don't they?' On asking him what it was, he described it to me as the 'Barcarole' from the opera *Tales of Hoffman*, and I remember we hummed it together once more as we made our way slowly through the wrecked trees. At one point I spotted two German boots which, although creased and dusty, on examination were almost new; moreover, they were a pair. For the fun of the thing, as they looked my size, I took off a boot and tried one on. It felt so comfortable that I was tempted to try on the other boot, when, to our consternation, we saw that it contained a withered foot.

Back in our shell holes we made tea. One of my section brought me two letters and a parcel—which latter, by the writing thereon, was from my Aunt Minnie. On opening it I pulled out a beautiful new shirt which was at once the envy of Jack and the others around, who felt the material as I read the short note. With the shirt on my knees I opened the first of the two letters. It was from Horace Phillips' sister, to whom we had written after Bazentin. She was a buyer at Marshall & Snelgrove and she concluded her letter by adjuring me to inquire for her at the number she gave in Vere Street when I came on leave. I put the letter away to read again more privately—if an opportunity ever presented itself, I thought ruefully—and slit open the other letter, postmarked Blackpool, from which a photograph slipped into the mud. It was from a lad I knew in Leicester. He was working on munitions and had snatched ten days' holiday in Blackpool. Probably I was most unfair to him in reading the letter aloud to Jack Quincy and the others, but just then we were in no mood to read that his digs weren't too good, that the food might be better and the weather had been rotten. Our gorges rose as, furiously, I read that the shows weren't as good as in previous years.

Quincy reached over and picked up the photograph, depicting the writer on Blackpool sands. Wiping the worst of the mud from it, he remarked with considerable feeling that some people back in England seemed to have a rum idea as to what war meant! We looked out on the scene before us . . . the dusk settling down once more upon desolation; felt the chill creeping through our damp clothes; thought, as we looked across at Delville Wood, of what was yet to come . . . and Blackpool! Each of us became immersed in his thoughts, but I saw my shirt and my mood changed as I hastened to put it on while it was yet dry.

My section was detailed for a carrying party that evening, and as we fell in the drizzling rain started once more. As Jack Quincy left us, I heard faintly the strains of the 'Barcarole' as he picked his way back to 'D' Company across the shell holes.

The following day, 24th September, showed some improvement in the weather, and we spent most of the morning drying ourselves and cleaning our gun and ammunition—in short, a much-needed overhaul of essentials. Our officers told us that we would move up shortly, and the impression was strengthened when the padre came among us, announcing a short voluntary service at 4 p.m. near the edge of Bernafay Wood.

While we were cleaning our gun we heard a sudden shouting and looked up to see a number of staff officers gallop by on the track in the direction of Trones Wood, headed by a slightly-built red-tabbed figure about ten yards in front. Then our own officers suddenly emerged, shouting like mad, and we saw our mates emerging from shelters and struggling to their feet, endeavouring to stand to attention in the mud. As we tried to do likewise 'Nobby' Clark, our platoon officer since Bazentin, told us that the Prince of Wales had just gone by. Afterwards every N.C.O. and man in the battalion knew that two men, at our new colonel's instigation, had been hurriedly charged, remanded for his jurisdiction and punished by a harsh stoppage of pay for not standing to attention. In retrospect there is little doubt that details of this affair were magnified in transit across the shell holes, so that by the time the story reached us it was said, rightly or wrongly, that one of the unfortunates had left the colonel, in his paybook will, the amount of the pay stoppage he had received. At all events, the general impression created among us was one of disgust with what we considered to have been a brutal and quite unnecessary action, and thousands of unprintable adjectives registered the battalion's increased dislike of the author of it.

A good number of us attended the padre's service that afternoon, and many more, hearing from afar the singing of well known hymns, drifted over to listen to the short address. I say this in no 'goody-goody' spirit, but I believe this service benefited those who took part in it. Most of us went and sang and listened because, I think, we felt that it was a chance to make a peace—to compose ourselves for the ordeal ahead. In my own case, the padre's text from the 121st Psalm recurred to me many times in those next days, and has done at times over the years: 'I will lift up mine eyes unto the hills, from whence cometh my help'. Just then, with some previous experience to give me a fairly good idea of 'what we were about to receive', I found a wealth of cheer in those words. Indeed, where else, or from whom, in these frightful surroundings, could a man obtain the wherewithal to move and act calmly?

Late that afternoon operation orders were issued. N.C.O.s were called together and briefed by companies. Roughly, the 110th Leicestershire Brigade, advancing on a two-battalion front of which the 8th was one and the 9th the other, had to storm two lines of trenches east of Flers, known as Gird Trench and Gird Support Trench. Then, after a pause of forty-five minutes to enable our artillery to concentrate upon it, capture the village of Gueudecourt. The 6th and 7th Battalions would move up in support to consolidate. We would march at dusk that evening, following several tapes laid for our guidance. Further orders—details of barrage, times of lift, zero hour, etc.—would be issued later.

Breaking off with our tidings, we N.C.O.s explained them as well as we could to our men. Our battalion was to go over in several waves and it therefore devolved upon the other Lewis gun corporal of my company and myself to decide between us which of our two teams was to go over in the first wave. To settle this

THE SUNKEN ROAD. FLERS-GUEUDECOURT.
NIGHT of 24th SEPT. 1916

I spun a coin with Lance-Corporal Hewitt and lost, whereupon he—a very good sort, by the way—explained earnestly that he was sorry, but that as he had his chaps to consider, he would go in the second wave. This decided, I well recall that we shook hands on it, and wished each other the best of luck, our lads doing the same amongst themselves, before we parted. Our section then got down to a final pow-wow and, looking at them, I knew that I had five good mates: Fatty Briggs and Arthur Wise—September '14 boys—and Wild, Poynton and Hughes. Fatty Briggs was married and had just returned from leave in Leicester. Only years after, when married myself, could I realize what must have been passing in his mind as we moved off that evening. I carried the gun and all the others were equally heavily loaded, either with ammunition drums, spare parts, or bandoliers of reserve ammunition, shovels, rations and water-tins. We followed our tape in silence down into a depression beyond the wood and up the succeeding slope to the Flers Ridge. Here the going was heavy, owing to recent rain, but rendered considerably more difficult by the vicious searching shell fire from the enemy, seeking the thickly planted batteries, which replied at intervals. By the flashes we made out the corpse-littered scene with all the wreckage of a battlefield and, worming their way through it, long strings of heavily laden mules, loaded pack-fashion with shells, struggling and splashing their ways towards the waiting guns.

Progress now became slow, and in the darkness we were completely dependent upon the tape and upon those in front to maintain contact. At length, with Delville Wood now far behind us, our company moved forward with seemingly a definite object in view, and from then on we scarcely stopped until we were on our final position. We were enjoined by our officers to maintain absolute silence and cursed ourselves every time one of our members tumbled and banged, perhaps, a shovel and a petrol tin together. It was easy to see by the Verey lights, being sent up by an apprehensive enemy about every minute, that we were in a cart track or sunken road, littered with dead of both sides and the debris of a wrecked German battery position, including two damaged field guns.

We moved along and slightly down this track for perhaps two hundred yards and then filed off to our left on to what was once a field, only halting to find ourselves close to another line of crouching figures immediately in front of us, who turned out to be of the Pioneer Battalion of Northumberland Fusiliers of our division. With the coming of night they had preceded us, digging the outline of a shallow jumping-off trench. They were now kneeling in the separate holes each had dug. Nobby Clark then came along our line, whispering to us to get into the holes and dig like hell. This we endeavoured to do, and the Pioneers, hurriedly shouldering their shovels and with whispered 'good luck,

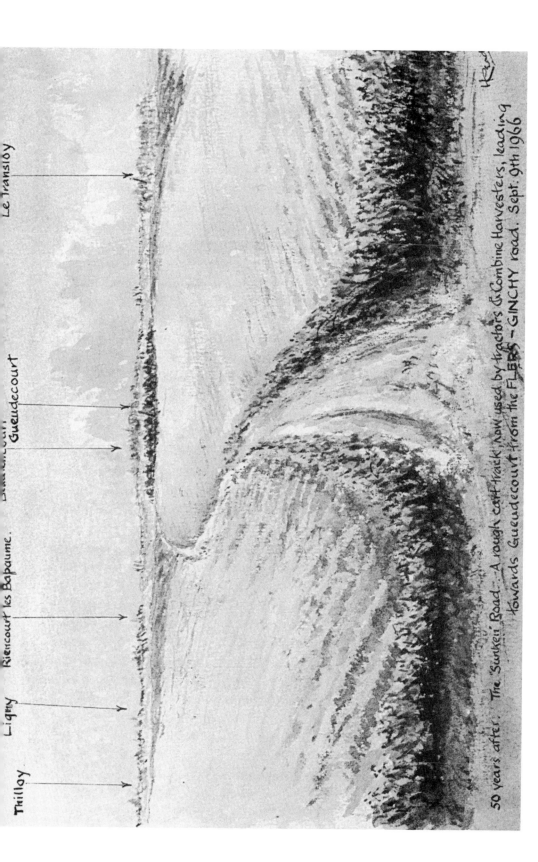

Thillay   Ligny   Riencourt les Bapaume.   Gueudecourt   Le Transloy

50 years after. The "Sunken" Road— A rough cart-track, now used by tractors & Combine Harvesters, leading towards Gueudecourt from the FLERS — GINCHY road. Sept. 9th 1966

mates!' disappeared one by one into the night the way we had come. In a few moments we were left to ourselves.

We hadn't the slightest idea where we were, but as the enemy Verey lights ascended, we judged our distance from him at 250–400 yards. Spurred on by this, and the more frequent showers of shrapnel, we dug feverishly, both to link up our holes and to get another yard of depth, at the same time raising some kind of crude parapet before daylight came. In this manner the night passed all too quickly, and the dawn found us in a fairly good jumping-off trench. In the enemy side we now worked hard to scoop niches in which to crouch as further protection against the shell fire we knew we would draw as soon as our efforts of the night were seen. We were not mistaken, either, and as soon as the morning mist had cleared away the German 77mm batteries started to pepper us in earnest; but by this time we were so tired out and hungry that we actually slept a little by turns and managed a meal of cold bacon rasher and bread, washed down by tea made with infinite pains from a tiny fire of wood chippings cut with our jack-knives from pieces we had brought with us. Our hands were bruised and skinned in places, our nails broken by the exertions of the night, as there had not been enough shovels for all and we had used our entrenching tools with a will, often scraping up the loosened earth with our hands rather than waste a minute. Still, our efforts were rewarded by the comparative shelter thus obtained, as we were practically safe from the 77mm shrapnel and nothing short of a direct hit from a whizz-bang could harm us. Five-nine howitzer stuff was another matter, but I don't think our front wave had more than a dozen casualties before we went over.

With sunrise, our heavy artillery commenced a sustained bombardment of the German trenches, batteries and communications, along what seemed to be our whole front for miles on either side of us. The German reply, as yet, seemed sporadic and feeble by comparison, although we ourselves were subjected incessantly to salvoes of whizz-bangs and shrapnel. Occasionally we peered across at the German positions, over which a haze of smoke had settled, but nevertheless we could see plainly enough the wire in front of the first of the two lines of trenches; also, at the end of the long gentle slope, the (as yet) only partially destroyed

Barrage-Zero +
GUEUDECOURT
SOMME Sept.25/19

trees and houses of Gueudecourt, perhaps a kilometre or so distant.

As the morning wore on, tension increased. Lieutenant Nobby Clark came crawling along the top behind our trench, telling us that 'zero' was at 12.45 and that we were going over at 'zero' plus—I forget how many minutes, now—but after a slight interval to let the barrage move forward. We set our watches by his, and as he left us voted him a good sort and one to be relied upon after this, our first real impressions of him in action. Previously, we had known him as a stocky, cheerful, chubby-faced lad and as a good boxer, but there had been no opportunity in the Arras trenches of seeing him in battle conditions.

Several of our planes droned overhead, undeterred by the German 'archies', machine-gun and rifle fire, but not as yet the contact monoplane. This, we had been told, would wear two black trailing streamers behind. No doubt those we saw were observing for the heavy gunners. I forget now what the arrangements were for giving recognition signals to the contact plane—N.C.O.s with special squares of coloured material, I believe, were to lay them out in certain ways—but in any event, as far as we were concerned, the scheme was a complete failure.

Nobby Clark came back. 'Not long to go now, boys!' He took up his position about fifteen yards to our right so that we could all see him, almost head and shoulders above the trench level. The sun had risen higher and the morning now was brilliantly fine and warm, causing the wet earth to steam in the bright sunshine. At length, it wanted but three minutes or so to 'zero'. The long wait was beginning to tell on us and we scarcely spoke to one another. As much as anything for the sake of something to do, I remember that Fatty Briggs handed me a drum which I placed on the magazine post of the gun. His hand had trembled. Mine had. Instead of putting it on in 'one-two' fashion, smartly, I bungled it and had to thump and coax the drum down into position. I kept trying to swallow and was conscious of a feeling of cramp in the pit of the stomach.

Then, like a terrific thunderclap, the field batteries at our rear spoke as one, and a tornado of shells screamed over our position and burst just beyond us, the shrapnel luckily, for the most part, well in front. Nevertheless, some of our men were hit in the first instant by the comparative few falling short.

The show was on!

As though by magic, I felt calm again, saw that my mates were the same. Rising almost to our feet, we held our kit in readiness. I pulled back the cocking handle of the gun. We grinned at one another and wished each other the best of luck, our eyes now on Nobby Clark, almost standing now, intent on the second-hand of his watch while he rubbed his whistle to and fro on his lips. Then he started up, looked to his men on either side and blew on his whistle. We couldn't hear it, but saw him wave his revolver arm. As we scrambled up over the freshly turned earth of our parapet I heard him yell, 'direction lads—keep direction!' At the double we stumbled forward across the churned-up field behind the barrage, which was now falling beyond the first German trench and shrouding everything in thick smoke. We hurried, for our orders were to keep

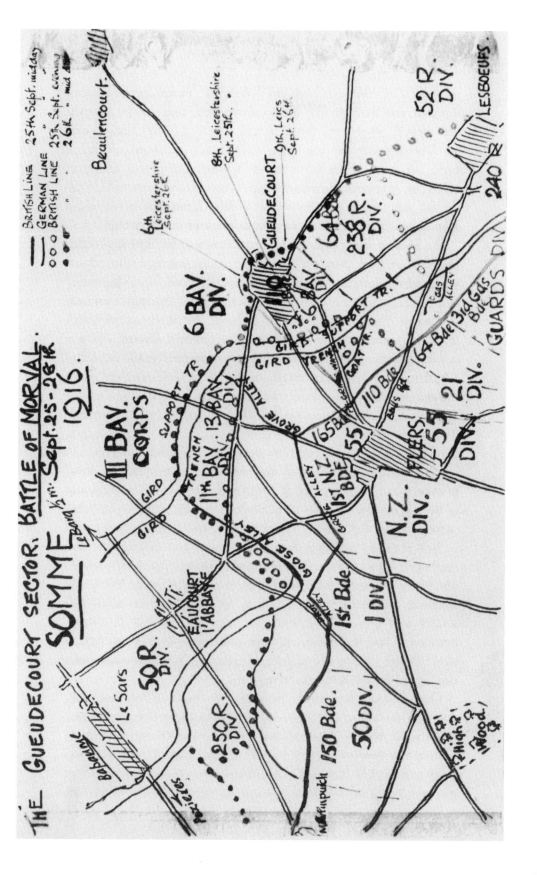

THE GUEUDECOURT SECTOR, BATTLE OF MORVAL.
SOMME Le Bard 1/2m. Sept. 25-26th. 1916.

British Line — 25th Sept. midday
German Line ——
British Line ooo 25th Sept. evening
•••• 26th " mid day

Babœuf
Le Sars
Pozières
Martinpuich
Beaulencourt.
Eaucourt l'Abbaye
Gueudecourt
Flers
Lesbœufs.

6th Leicestershire Sept. 26th.
8th. Leicestershire Sept. 25th.
9th. Leics Sept. 26th.

III BAV. CORPS
50 R. DIV.
250 R. DIV.
6 BAV. DIV.
6 BAV. DIV.
64 R. DIV.
238 R. DIV.
52 R. DIV.
240 R. DIV.

11th BAV. 13 BAV. DIV.

GIRD TR.
GIRD
GIRD TR.
GIRD
GIRD TRENCH
SUPPORT TR.
GOAT TR.
GAS ALLEY
GROVE ALLEY
GROVE ALLEY
BULL'S RD.
165 BAV.
110 Bde.
55
55
64 Bde 3rd Gas Bde
GUARDS DIV.
GUARDS DIV.
21 DIV.

1st N.Z. BDE.
N.Z. DIV.
1st Bde.
1 DIV.
150 Bde.
50 DIV.
High Wood.

up with it as closely as possible. I fired two bursts forward as we tore our way through the tangle of wire and leapt down into the first trench, where we found several Germans with their hands up. Guessing that the oncoming waves behind us would attend to them, we made them throw down all their equipment and start off to the rear with their hands up. This done, we scrambled up the far side of the trench to find Nobby Clark and most of his men about thirty yards in front of us towards the next line.

We tried to hurry, but the many shell holes and our heavy loads impeded us. Just then the German counter-barrage came down with frightful intensity and effect, and we stumbled forward blindly in a numbing inferno of explosions which, after perhaps a minute, we passed. Fatty and Wise were still with me when, a few yards from the German support trench, Wise pitched forward. It was strictly against orders, but we stopped instinctively and saw that a bullet or shrapnel had struck him in the mouth and had come out on one side of his neck. Fatty and I put a small stone on the spurting hole in his neck and bound it with his field dressing. Telling him that those coming along behind would see after him, although I think he was scarcely conscious, we hurried forward to see Nobby Clark and what was left of his men taking some prisoners and bombing along the trench. Just as we arrived, out of breath, Nobby told all of us to get forward another 150 yards or so towards the village, telling us that the Boches would shell us heavily while awaiting our second jump at Gueudecourt. Accordingly, we scrambled forward again into the open and noticed our heavy shells reducing the village to a rubble heap. We could distinctly see many of them falling like black bottles amid the houses and trees. Occasionally a huge shell would fall short, between us and the village, in a great fountain of earth and flying steel. Others, failing to explode, ricochetted for a mile or more, shining in the sunlight like flying fish.

Once beyond the trench, however, we could not help noticing that we were alone; there were no British troops on our immediate left or right. Scarcely had we observed this, when our mates started to drop like flies and bullets started to smack into the earth round Fatty and myself. Nobby Clark rushed across to us, shouting that we were being sniped from behind and to take cover where we stood. He ran on as we dropped into the nearest shell hole. Looking back hastily over the edge of it, we saw the length of Gird Support Trench to our left alive with the enemy. Turning to see the whereabouts of Nobby Clark, we saw him gasp and fall to his knees, hit in the legs. He dragged himself into a shell hole. As we were wondering whether we should go to his assistance, the gun, which I had laid on the edge of the shell hole, was almost jerked from my grasp and another bullet filled my eyes with earth.

Here was a pretty situation. Crouching there, scarcely able to move an inch, we nevertheless made efforts to attract the attention of the contact monoplane which buzzed up and down the Gird Support Trench line and circled above us more than once, the black pennants streaming behind. We could see the pilot looking down, but doubted whether he saw us. Fusillades of shot were directed at him from the German-held portion of the trench, but in those moments we would have changed places with him gladly.

We started to weigh our chances and came to the conclusion that, failing the arrival of help pretty soon, the best we could hope for was a German prison camp. Prompted by this thought, we turned round and peered cautiously in the direction of Gueude-court and to our left flank, successive bullets and thuds, accom-panied by showers of earth, indicating that we were being watched.

We were cheered, however, by seeing no sign of any enemy issuing from Gueudecourt; I, the more so, by observing Fatty, cool as a cucumber and grinning in derision at each near miss. In that shell hole I first learned to appreciate him—his smooth, plump, boyish face, portly figure, blue eyes and fair curly hair. In billets he had seemed to be somewhat of a butt for the rude, though good-natured, wit of his mates, especially since returning from leave not long since as a married man, and that at the age of twenty-two. He had only been a Lewis gunner since Bazentin and, as he told me afterwards, had only joined the Lewis gunners to get away from his mates in his platoon.

After a few minutes, Fatty stuck his tin hat on his bayonet and moved it cautiously along the ridge of the shell hole. Immediately we felt the jar as a bullet buried itself in the ground in front of his hat. Our man was still waiting for us.

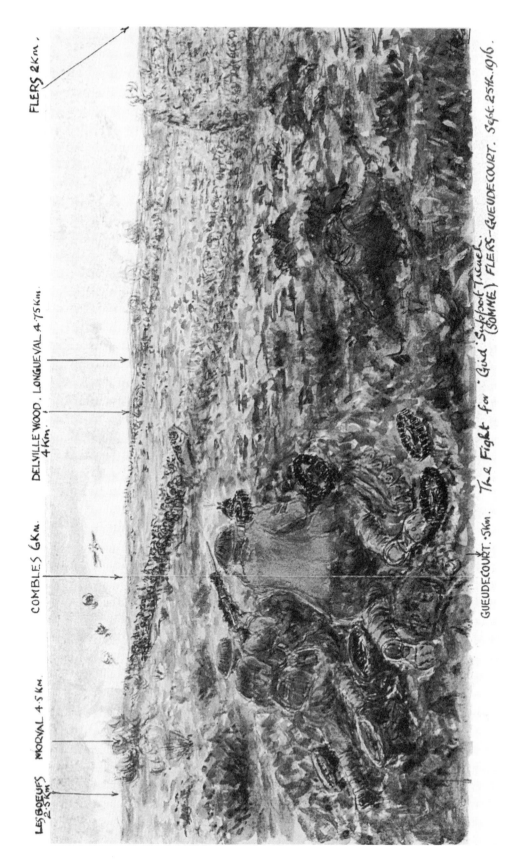

FLERS 2 Km.

LES BOEUFS
2·5 Km.

MORVAL 4·5 Km.

COMBLES 6 Km.

DELVILLE WOOD. LONGUEVAL 4·75 Km.
4 Km.

GUEUDECOURT. ·5 Km.   The Fight for "Gird Sugarloof Trench".
(SOMME) FLERS-GUEUDECOURT. Sept. 25th. 1916.

Then I had an idea. It seemed to me that one man, particularly, had us spotted, and our first job was to find him. Fatty agreed so, shoving the gun up quickly, I fired several short bursts in the general direction of the Germans in the trench while Fatty took a hurried look round. Two bullets all but struck the gun as I got it going, but after that there were no more. Fatty, shouting glee-fully, 'that's made the b. . . get down,' rose to his knees. Suddenly he pointed. 'Hi—give it to him, Dick. There the b. . . is, behind that barrel . . . back of the trench!' Raising myself, I got the butt of the gun properly into my shoulder, peering through the sights and firing short bursts as I endeavoured to spot the barrel. As I saw it, to my disgust the drum came to an end. In the same instant I saw the German appear from behind the barrel, raise his rifle and steady it against the side to fire at me, but Fatty, bless him, was too quick for him. Unknown to me, he had taken careful aim with his rifle at the barrel and, almost as the German appeared, he fired. I remember well, still looking along the sights, seeing the puff of dust spout from the German's chest as he fell over backwards.

Jubilant at regaining comparative freedom of action we saw, behind and to the left of the German we had put out of action, a stretch of a hundred yards or so of the Gird Support Trench, from near where the sunken road crossed it to the crest of a gentle rise in the ground, crammed full of the enemy, the sun actually glinting here and there on the tops of their steel helmets. Seizing our opportunity, we raked this trench with three complete drums at two-to three-hundred-yards range and had the fierce satisfaction of doing frightful execution there, for at that distance it was almost impossible to miss. We were just congratulating ourselves that we had 'about laid 'em all out' when a fresh lot of Germans appeared over the crest of the rise and appeared to be stepping over their fallen comrades. Something knocked me clean over on to my side as I lay at the gun, just starting to fire again. I felt an acute burning sensation between my shoulders and told Fatty I'd stopped one.

Hurriedly he loosened my equipment and helped me remove it, together with my tunic. Next he literally tore my new shirt off my back. I heard him laugh and then swear heartily. The burning sensation was almost gone. With an effort I struggled to my knees, stripped to the waist, scarcely crediting my good fortune. Fatty, holding it first in one hand then in the other, because it was still pretty hot, showed me a large curved shell fragment about two inches long and an inch wide. 'Well, I'll be blowed, Dick, you're a lucky b. . . You'll have a jolly good bruise there—that's all.' So saying, he helped me on with my tunic, apologizing for ruining my shirt. 'Hey, come on, Dick—let's have a go,' and seizing the gun he fired several short bursts at two Germans who were mounting a heavy machine-gun on the parapet of the trench near the crest of the rise, no doubt intending to deal with us. Fatty soon stretched them on the ground and I started refilling drums from our bandoliers as he again raked the length of trench visible to us until there was no sign of movement there. The gun was now very hot, but just then I saw several more Germans appear around the machine-gun, which had not been properly mounted. Fatty rolled one of them over, with the gun portion in his arms; then his mates, afterwards firing a long burst into the gun itself to damage it well and truly.

In the lull which ensued I thought I had better try to get my equipment on again, and it was then that we found that the piece of shell had smashed through my haversack and my hold-all containing my knife, fork, spoon and razor. They were bent and broken, but their presence had probably saved my back. I found I just couldn't bear the weight of the haversack, so laid it aside again. That machine-gun seemed to be a tempting bait, as we bagged several more Germans who were attempting to recover it.

It was soon after this that we were overjoyed to see, above the shell holes directly behind us, the steel helmets of one or two of our mates; although a number, unfortunately, lay around. We waved to each other, and in doing this noticed also that there were now khaki figures in the Gird Support Trench on either side of the sunken road—on our side about 150 yards towards the German-held portion where, on looking more closely, we saw that bombing was in progress from both sides. While speculating as to how best we could assist, we observed a considerable party of Germans creeping along the back of the trench and holding stick bombs ready to throw, each, besides, having a plentiful supply hanging round his waist. Seeing they were intent on surprising our mates in the trench, we quickly lay down again and got the old gun into action, giving them a nasty surprise. A number lay still, while others dragged themselves back into their portion of the trench.

We remained out there for another ten minutes or so, in case another foray was attempted; then, gathering up our belongings, we made our way back to our comrades in the trench, many of whom turned out to be men of the 1st/6 King's (Liverpool) Regiment—of the division to our immediate left.

We looked for Nobby Clark on our way, but evidently he had dragged himself back. My back now gave me considerable pain but, like Fatty, I was thankful we had extricated ourselves for the time being. We asked our own fellows in vain for any news of the main body of our battalion. Where were they? Why hadn't they supported us? Why was the Gird Support Trench, a little way away, still crammed with Germans full of fight? Who was going to take Gueudecourt?

There were no officers, and when we arrived Leicesters and King's Liverpools, both remnants commanded by sergeants (ours, we found, commanded by Sergeants Chesterton and Kirk of 'C' Company) were sorting themselves out into some semblance of order in a trench littered with enemy dead and dying. Sergeant Chesterton was glad to see us; they had all seen us firing drum after drum, and when we explained what we had been doing he took control of the situation and ordered us all, with what men he could muster as bombers in front, to work up the trench towards the brow of the hill. This we started to do, and progressed for some distance without serious opposition, to a little beyond the cement barrel on top of the trench where our erstwhile tormentor now lay beside it. Just here was a German strong point in the trench which had been blown in by a big British shell. We had noticed the timbers protruding at all angles when we were firing from the shell hole. Our bombers started to clamber over, and I remember well Fatty and I following behind them when there was a 'crack' and the back of the leading man's head seemed to fall away as he pitched forward. Another 'crack' and another fell, shot through the chest, apparently at point-blank range. The rest of us stopped still until Sergeant Chesterton, grabbing a couple of Mills grenades, set an example by hurling them well and truly, for the explosions were followed by screams. At this we made a concerted dash, sometimes firing from the hip and progressing about thirty yards, picking our way over a mass of dead and wounded Germans. Many were terribly hit by our Lewis fire from the shell hole. One sat in the trench bottom, literally trying to put back his insides. Seeing Sergeant Chesterton, he stopped and, reaching for a nearby Mauser automatic, intended to take a shot at him, but couldn't, and fell back, unconscious with the effort.

They were a Bavarian regiment and their packs were of natural cowhide with the hair still on. I remember the tawny and white mottled shades. We continued for perhaps another fifteen yards to a fall in the trench, bombing and dodging the German stick grenades, which knocked us silly and made our heads sing more than once. Indeed, the opposition became so determined that we could get no further, and Sergeant Chesterton resolved to hold the trench at this block with bombers and riflemen. He ordered us to go back to the junction with the sunken road, collect all the Mills grenades we could find and pass them to him, get our Lewis ammunition drums reloaded and generally get ready for an emergency. It was only then that I realized that I had left my equipment there when regaining the trench. It was still lying there, but my back was so stiff and sore that I didn't try to put it on.

There seemed to be a lull; for a time no more stick bombs came over the block. No doubt the enemy were in pretty desperate straits just then, as were we.

Gueudecourt still lay before us, apparently deserted but as yet untaken. Overhead droned the contact plane again, black identification pennants trailing behind, up and down, endeavouring to sum up the situation accurately. Whenever he passed over us we waved, but no doubt the observer was at a loss to understand the trench full of the enemy, who fired at him continually.

Of one thing we were quite certain, we could go no further towards Gueudecourt because of this holdup on our right flank; also there appeared to be fewer than fifty of we 8th Leicesters left of the five hundred or more who had gone over. Looking at my watch, I was amazed to see that it showed half-past four. As I sat there beside Fatty, refilling our drums, with no shirt, a torn undervest, a sore back with a rising bruise, a familiar voice cried, 'what ho, Corporal! 'Ere we are at last—better late than never, eh?'

Looking up, we saw the tall, ungainly figure of Hughes slipping down into the trench and grinning broadly beneath his grime. It was good to see a mate come back, as it were, from the dead, and we welcomed him, at the same time asking him where the hell he had been putting himself. To our amazement, he bent down and thrust a pocket Bible into our faces by way of an answer. He read, '"I will lift up mine eyes unto the hills, from whence cometh my help." See that, Corporal?' I nodded. I had, indeed, thought of it several times that day. 'Well, Corporal, look here!' Half-turning, he showed a scorched and ripped trouser leg with the puttee hanging in blackened tatters. 'See that? . . . well a shell did that, I reckon, when it went by. Pretty close war'n't it . . . eh?' and he repeated the text.

We could not help but agree with him, and he then told us that it had happened between the Gird and Gird Support Trenches. Following behind us, he had been knocked down and dazed. When he picked himself up he found himself among the remnants of the following waves, on which the German counter-barrage was falling with terrible effect. He said that he passed Jack Quincy, lying with a hole in his forehead, and concluded his story by telling us that eventually he came across some King's Liverpools.

I was glad enough to see Hughes, but terribly sorry and embittered to hear his news of Quincy. I thought of the 'Barcarole'.

As things were comparatively quiet, I asked Hughes to see if he could brew up some tea. There were plenty of wood splinters and we had matches, but little water. In an effort to get more, Hughes scrounged among the dead Germans and got three water bottles of cold coffee, which wasn't too bad. There wasn't much tea, though.

After the drink I fancied a smoke but, on taking my pipe from my pocket, found that half the bowl was missing. I certainly hadn't noticed the bullet or shell fragment responsible. The pocket was a ruin and the remains of the pipe and the packet of Chairman tobacco had somehow hung in it.

Some strange things had happened that day, but more surprises were to come. As we rose to our feet, I was looking up the sunken road. I turned to Fatty. 'Do you see what I see?' Fatty's comment was, 'good God! Can't we tell them to go back? They'll all be shot before they get here!' But, strange to tell, they weren't. In retrospect, I think that the Germans along the trench shared our amazement and did not fire as, crouching as low as I could, I went up the track towards them.

They were Indian Cavalry and were headed by a fine turbaned figure of an N.C.O. I tried to tell them to go back, indicating the nearby enemy, but as I walked beside his horse the N.C.O. told me he had orders—'The King Emperor's Orders!' A mounted Hotchkiss machine-gun section and a dozen more troopers walked their magnificent black horses steadily behind him.

It was evident that their orders were to reconnoitre Gueude-court, and as they passed beyond our trench we watched them, fascinated, as at length some of them dismounted by the fallen trees and brickwork on the fringe. Then firing began from the ruins. Within moments a few horses were galloping untended among the shell holes until they were hit. We of the 8th Bat-talion never knew what became of these brave men. I have often thought I would like to have known the name of their regiment and who, that day, was responsible for sending them on this errand of death. In those few moments most of us gave vent to our feelings. We looked around. I think then we hated our red-tabbed gentry, well behind the fighting, much more than we did the litter of dead, dying and wounded German soldiers, with our own lying among them.

I remember, as we passed the last of our drink round, that a badly wounded German, leaning against the trench side and seemingly as good as dead, opened his eyes and made a faint gesture with a terrible hand. I don't know why—perhaps we were ripe for the reaction—but I do know that, as he raised his mangled hand, he seemed to wash out all traces of our fury. Fatty, nearest, held the mess tin for him to drink. We bandaged his hand and arm, but he was far gone and we could do little for him. We started looking among our own men, too, who lay near, but all seemed past any aid that we could give them. Several, we noted, held rosaries.

As dusk came on the enemy started to bomb us again at the

block and we were all kept on the alert against surprise from any direction for the remainder of the night. Fatty, Hughes and my-self—indeed, every man there—stood or lay straining his ears for sounds of creeping attackers with their stick bombs.

It would have been about eight in the evening when we heard footsteps approaching down the sunken road from the rear. I had annexed a German Mauser automatic pistol and, levelling it at the intruder called, 'halt, who are you?' The answer came '8th Battalion Leicestershire—who are you?' Vaguely recognising the voice I replied, still holding my pistol, '8th Leicesters — come on!'

'Thank God!' exclaimed the newcomer, stepping out of the blackness. Hastily I lowered my pistol and tried to stand to atten-tion. It was Major Beardsley, with a runner following behind. He commanded 'B' Company at Bazentin, where he went over car-rying his sword. Since, he had become our second-in-command, and a very popular one, too. At the sight of him we felt like lost children who have been claimed at long last, after thinking them-selves forgotten.

I told him briefly of our situation and then took him along to Sergeant Chesterton, where Major Beardsley told us he had come up to take command and that he had been searching for us for hours.

We were all immeasurably strengthened by his presence. He promised to get some rations and water to us, and when eventually he set out to return to what I supposed was some attempt at a Battalion H.Q., telling us to hang on, we felt that help would soon be forthcoming. It was only after he had gone that I realized that I was wearing a German greatcoat to keep out the chill night air as, having no shirt, I had soon found the need for extra protection after the sun had set. Shortly before daylight we found ourselves dozing off every few minutes and we three, therefore, decided to take turns to sleep. All seemed quiet just then, so Hughes and I stood back-to-back, keeping each other awake and staring out into the half light. We gave Fatty about an hour and a half and then Hughes insisted that I take the next turn, I suppose because of my aching back. I did, and I was asleep directly. I awoke to find Fatty shaking me and shouting in my ear, 'come on, Dick . . . get up; look at what's happened. Be quick—you'll miss it all!'

It was full daylight, and getting to my feet—painfully, as my back was now very stiff and sore—I heard strange sounds amid the general shouting and 'rat-tat-tat' of machine-guns. Looking where Fatty and Hughes were pointing excitedly I saw, for the first time, a tank in action. It was a Mark I (MALE), halfway up the slope, parallel with the trench, and strings of German soldiers were standing with their hands up, being shepherded by Sergeants Chesterton and Kirk and their exultant men. The roar of the tank's exhausts were accentuated as its snout rose in the air, taking the protruding beams of a strong-point in its stride, to fall with crushing frightfulness on the next obstacle. More Germans rose from the trench beyond with arms held high, as, at length, we saw it disappear beyond the crest of the rise—going strong.

We heard that nearly four hundred prisoners had been taken as a result of this tank's action, when Sergeant Chesterton's men returned from following behind it; also that the Grenadiers of the Guards Division were at the Les Boeufs end, several hundred yards beyond the crest. The way having been cleared, we saw our 6th Battalion, moving in small driblets, occupy in force the shattered stumps and ruins of Gueudecourt. To our right the survivors of our 9th Battalion, together with the 7th Battalion and the 64th Brigade of our division, now went forward towards the ridge south-east of Gueudecourt, beyond which lay the village of Le Transloy.

As soon as we could, we collected all our wounded who were lying out, and were glad to hear that Nobby Clark had managed to crawl in and had been taken down. The German whom we had bandaged the previous afternoon still lay propped against the trench side, but his steel-helmeted head now sagged forward on his chest. For him the war was finished, his sufferings over. In his undamaged hand he held a rosary. I remember we stood for a few moments looking at him, deep in our own thoughts.

That evening we gathered up our belongings and moved back in the dusk up the sunken road, to a trench several hundred yards to our rear, situated on the high ground to the south-east of Flers. Here, in the last of the light, a roll was called by Sergeant-Major Gamble who, in the wave behind us, had survived the counter-barrage with several of his men. With remnants of these following waves, who had trickled in during the day, we numbered just eighty all told out of the five hundred or so who went over.

I remember standing on the top with Fatty, Hughes and the others, being counted. He had counted seventy-nine, when a lad asked him if he had counted himself. He hadn't—giving us the first real laugh for days. Then we filed into the now-neglected, deep and battered trench, hanging our equipment on the nearest convenient projection. Reaction had now set in badly with us although, hurriedly, groups for sentry duty were detailed. Sergeant Major Gamble said some rum had just come up with the rations, of which there were literally piles.

We soon made little fires, which we shaded very carefully with some of the debris lying around, and sat in the trench bottom eating pork and beans and biscuits, and passing round a blackened mess tin of scalding tea, well laced with rum. Then we slept, covered with German groundsheets, which were far more practical than ours.

Morning light and the sun breaking through the haze beyond Gueudecourt caused us to get early astir and take stock of our new surroundings. The trench commanded a fine view of the landscape in front, to the left and right of the country beyond Gueudecourt, which from here lay in a shallow valley, now just another collection of tree stumps and rubble, whence issued reports of desultory rifle and machine-gun fire. Occasionally several fresh spouts of red and grey rubble would rise over it, as the enemy artillery searched for our 6th Battalion men there. Behind it and to the right stretched away a long gentle slope of cultivated fields, culminating in a low ridge upon which nestled the village of Beaulencourt. To the right of it and beyond, we could discern the trees and buildings of Le Transloy, both villages as yet still standing. Along the ridge to the left, our view was bounded by the villages of Ligny-Thilloy and Le Barque, with a wooded mound before them which a map showed as the Butte de Warlencourt. Beyond Ligny-Thilloy and Le Barque lay the goal of all these months of British effort—Bapaume.

Suddenly we felt we just had to shave and, if possible, clean up. Water from petrol tins which came up with the rations was poured sparingly into mess tins, little fires were lit again, and cracked pieces of mirror from haversacks were stuck in the trench side. It was then that I remembered that the entire contents of my holdall had been smashed by the shell splinter. As I went to my equipment, hanging there along with Fatty Briggs', I called to him—his features now covered with lather—and indicated the peg on which it hung. 'D'you see what I see, Fatty?' He looked and drew back. 'Poor b. . . !'

In the dusk of the previous evening we had hung our stuff on the protruding bones of an arm, shattered at the wrist; whether of friend or enemy we never knew, but almost three feet of clay were above it, so we didn't move our kits. Fatty lent me his things when he had finished. My towel, such as it was, had escaped damage, but it was stiff through with dried soap and dirt from many previous washes. Opportunities for washing towels were few indeed.

We remained in this trench until 2nd October, in reserve, furnishing carrying parties supplying the units in front or, at dusk, searching for wounded and burying those beyond aid. These were mostly youthful privates of the King's Royal Rifles, caught by machine-gun fire from this trench on 15th September and mown down in swathes. As may be imagined, it was very difficult indeed to make thorough searches in the half-light, especially in view of the churned up state of every inch of ground. Wounded men generally made for shell holes if they could, but because of this were apt to be overlooked. I remember finding, when out with Fatty one evening, one of our 'A' Company who had been lying out there for over four days. Quite by chance we spotted him in a shell hole. He had been badly hit in the groin and was in a terrible state, some idea of which may be gathered from the fact that he had drunk his own urine in an attempt to quench a raging thirst.

We collected the paybooks and identity discs of the K.R.R. boys who had lain there for three weeks, the evidence of their documents showing that they had received one payment only in France, at the base depot, and had formed part of a reinforcement draft arriving just before the battalion went into action.

While occupying this trench, our division and that to our left, which included the New Zealanders, improved their positions around Gueudecourt, and several field artillery officers observed for their batteries from it, providing barrage fire and breaking up counter-attacks as required. One fine afternoon we became particularly interested, as one of them explained the rudiments to us as he worked at his map with protractor and other tools of his trade. On several occasions he illustrated the points he made by actual demonstrations, but his great difficulty here was that his battery was firing at extreme range since the advances of 25th/26th September.

Once we helped him in putting down a barrage for an advance towards Ligny-Thilloy by repeating his orders to the telephonist in the trench below. Shortly afterwards, while he was busy registering on another target beyond Gueudecourt, we noticed a German counter-attack developing against the position which, an hour or so previously, we had seen our men gain. Immediately we pointed this out to him he rapped out his orders, sharp, clear and unmistakable. We shouted them to the telephonist who repeated them to the battery. After the lapse of over fifty years I still recall snatches of them: 'all guns fifteen degrees left . . . five thousand two hundred . . . report when ready.' I recall, too, the telephonist's 'ready, sir!', the lieutenant's 'Number One, fire!', echoed and re-echoed by us and by the bombardier below at the 'phone, then his 'Number One fired, sir!' . . . and so on until, incredibly quickly it seemed to us, the range was bang on. With a final 'add fifty—repeat', the battery, now with many others, hurled salvoes of H.E. and shrapnel upon the attackers, who seemed to melt away before it.

On the day we were relieved, 2nd October 1916, I made a rough sketch of the landscape, as seen from this trench, on the only blank piece of paper I had—the letter I had received from Horace Phillips' sister Winnie just before we went into action. It is almost the only souvenir that I now retain of the Somme.

That evening some Buffs of, I think, the 12th Division relieved us, telling us that they were going forward beyond Gueudecourt to the far ridge. We wished them 'the best of luck, mates!' as, in the dusk, we filed out and picked our way across the brown desolation to the corner of Delville Wood once more and thence to our old shell holes by Bernafay Wood, where we bivouacked for the night, our task made much easier by the German groundsheets we brought back with us. Here we yarned with those of our mates who had been left behind as the battalion cadre before we went into action, drinking rum-laced tea and smoking, glad to learn that we were marching further back. They gave us news, too, of many of our wounded mates, who they had seen either walking or being carried down, including our commanding officer, who had been wounded slightly and had gone down the line. We were content to have Major Beardsley.

I managed also to obtain a new grey-back shirt from our quartermaster sergeant, Peach, who forbore to ask the customary questions which his kind delighted in generally, convinced, apparently, by my torn jacket and by the now-blackened bruise on my back.

The following morning we set out in drizzling rain, marching all day through the devastated countryside by way of Montauban and Carnoy to Méaulte, most of us now enveloped in our green German groundsheets, which were convertible into tolerably good waterproof coats. In any case, we did not mind the rain at all; we were getting away from the Somme, and sang for a good deal of the time. At Méaulte we halted for ten minutes or so in the street, where a gang of German prisoners were re-metalling the road. As we stood there, the driver of the steam roller stopped his charge and called upon some of his mates to observe our badges and shoulder brasses. All stopped work and crowded round us, asking whether we were the same Leicesters who used to be in front of them at Monchy au Bois and Bienvillers. When we replied in the affirmative, we chatted as with old friends until we fell in again. They were of the 73rd Infantry Regiment, and when I mentioned 'Charlie', who sang the English songs, several laughed excitedly with many '*ja! ja!*'s, but said that he had been sniped through the head one morning, just before the regiment left the sector for the Somme. 'Boum . . . Charlie *kaput!*' As we fell in again they said they had been captured at Ginchy and grinned as they made us understand that for them the war was finished. They certainly had got something there, and looked well fed and contented. Just then we would have changed places with them gladly!

I forget where we spent that night but, marching by easy stages, we entrained two days later at Longeau, a big railway junction on the outskirts of Amiens. When the troop train jolted into motion, none of us had the faintest idea as to our destination, but we were leaving the Somme—for good, as it turned out, at least as far as I was concerned.

CHAPTER 12

VERMELLES

As I have said, we entrained at Longeau, having not the faintest idea as to our destination. After our recent experiences, however, this did not worry us unduly. We were away from the war—all that mattered. As we jogged along leisurely with frequent halts through the Picardy countryside, recovered to a certain degree the British soldier's traditional outlook on things in general in those days—an attitude very difficult to explain in detail now, but which enabled us as a battalion to carry on once more.

We detrained at Choques, near Béthune, and here the view around us differed vastly from any we had seen in France; great colliery slag tips, with twinkling winding wheels in latticed steel towers near by, where wreaths of steam and smoke rose, also, from the powerhouses beneath. Marching the few kilometres over the familiar pavé to billets and huts in a mining village near Béthune, we noticed that, when we stepped aside to allow lorries to pass, we tramped through black mud. Between the road and the mines stretched flat fields of roots and vegetables on either side, the monotony of the landscape relieved only by occasional farm buildings or by huddled rows of shabby miners' cottages. From the eastern horizon, lined with distant slag heaps, came fairly frequent echoes of dull explosions, reminding us of our proximity to the line. Loos, it was said, was over there—a sobering thought.

I cannot recall now the name of the village in which we were billeted, but we were very comfortable there, doing little for two days beyond erasing evidences of the recent fighting where possible, and consuming prodigious quantities of fried eggs and chips, washed down either with *vin blanc* or with coffee. Here the male population consisted of elderly or middle-aged men, with a sprinkling of boys. The majority worked in the mines, and many of the womenfolk were employed around the pitheads. The remainder toiled in the fields until dusk, whatever the weather.

With the arrival of several drafts of officers and men, the battalion began to take shape again. Some of the newcomers had been wounded at Bazentin and there were some joyous reunions among old mates, but leisure soon gave place to hard work. I received my third stripe, and in addition to shouldering a sergeant's duties started to train twelve more men as Lewis gunners. Fatty Briggs became a corporal, which gave me much pleasure at the time. Notwithstanding our reinforcements, however, we were still far below strength when we moved up to the line, our company—now commanded by Captain Warner, a youthful platoon leader before Bazentin—numbering fewer than a hundred of all ranks. The strength of the other companies was similarly depleted, and when marching in column of route the battalion appeared pitifully small in numbers, its transport section proportionately large.

Still, we did our best as we tramped through Béthune, a novel experience for many of us, who had not seen a town of this size for a year or more. To us Béthune seemed to afford excellent billets for a good many Category A1 officers and men in well-brushed khaki, highly polished buttons and leather. We remarked on the beautifully cut breeches and wonderfully wound puttees on specimens we passed with – to us – soft jobs in a back area. Sour grapes, of course, on our part—but try to imagine how we felt, barely out of one hell and on our way to another. Still, by and large, we took the good luck of these people philosophically and dreamed secretly of one day realizing our own ambitions. Mine was that of a town major's clerk, or batman, in a fair-sized back-area village, miles from any fighting, plenty of good food and drink, unlimited scope for romance . . . The war could go on indefinitely then!

Such were some of our thoughts as, trudging eastwards out of Béthune, our company wit (a cockney drafted from the cavalry) suddenly raised a real laugh, telling the files around him, 'don't I wish I was a millionaire's bastard'—pause—'livin' in New York'—pause—'ten tharsand a year'—pause—'lyin' in a tiger skin rug with me fancy piece'. His next sally was drowned in a gale of wry mirth.

We tramped on along the Béthune road, moving frequently aside into the black mud to allow lorries to pass, to Sailly-la-Bourse. Before us were more slag heaps, and, judging from the proximity of the reports, we were getting close to our heavy artillery positions.

We marched from Sailly-la-Bourse by platoons in artillery formation and soon saw belts of rusty wire covering grass-grown reserve trenches, stretching across the untilled fields on either side of the road. A mine to our left was still working, a plume of white steam rising from the pithead, though some of the buildings appeared to have been damaged by shell fire.

As we trudged on, our horizon became somewhat limited by a low ridge on which straggled the gaping roofs and brickwork of a large village about a kilometre distant. Half-left, however, the landscape stretched away to a large slag heap, with which shortly we were fated to make much closer acquaintance. Leaving the main road, we made for the centre of the village, halting near the ruins of the church, I remember, where, from direction notices displayed, we read that we were in Vermelles, of sinister reputation. I say 'sinister' because we recalled reading the name in newspaper accounts of the Loos battle a year previously.

Sitting there, the trundling roar and explosions of a five-nine shrapnel and H.E. behind the church seemed to tell us that Jerry had spotted us. As the clouds of rubble dust and dirty black smoke drifted away on the October breeze, we speculated uneasily and welcomed the order to move on, but after two more Jerry left us alone as we threaded our way in single file past faded shell-pocked enamelled wall signs—'Pneus Michelin', 'Chocolate Menier', 'Du Bonnet', 'Vin Quinquina'—pathetic reminders of what was . . . once!

An hour or so afterwards we found ourselves in reserve, herded in a collection of rat-infested shelters along what went by the name of 'Lancashire Trench', some distance east of Vermelles. From there we worked our way up to the front line by several stages of support trenches designated O.B.1, O.B.2, etc. (O.B. meaning 'Old British', i.e. before Loos), a two- or three-day interval occurring between each move. In this manner we found ourselves eventually, by way of a battered communication, Bart's Alley, at the infamous Hohenzollern Redoubt, manning the salubrious spots known as

'Northampton Trench' and 'Cobden Trench'. These two trenches ran along the rims of two huge mine craters, rejoicing in the names of 'Hohenzollern' and 'Potsdam'.

The trench system here was extremely complicated, due primarily—without doubt—to the heavy fighting in the area from 25th September to 13th October. Finally, the Hohenzollern was stormed and held by the 46th Division at enormous cost in lives. For months prior to our arrival, the front and immediate support and communication trenches had been blasted almost out of recognition, rebuilt, blasted again and again by the explosions of enormous trench mortar shells resembling oil drums in flight—of which Jerry had plenty. We called them 'rum jars' and they trundled over with alarming frequency at times, with shattering effects. The unfortunates holding the line then spent the night following making good the damage as far as possible: that is, if they were still alive.

To afford protection for men not actually on duty, and to give them a chance to get some sleep, there were two deep dugouts some distance apart. Each had two entrances shrouded by gas curtains. When in the depths of one of these, the damp, foetid, candlelit air alone was bad enough for morale, and the occupants 'rested' in constant dread of rum jars exploding in the entrances. On the other hand, when such a strafe was in progress, relief sentries dreaded equally emerging into the open air above—with the possible dire consequences.

When, shortly after arrival, we peered in the dusk through a slit in the bags of the Northampton Trench parapet, we saw, some hundreds of yards behind the reverse rim of the crater, the vast and overpowering bulk of a colliery slag heap—to wit, Fosse 8—which we had first seen in the distance when leaving Sailly-la-Bourse. It dominated the British positions here completely and, I recall, did not exactly help us to become reconciled to our lot. Back in the support trenches, we could see away to the right two damaged high latticed steel towers, presumably the German line near Loos. They went by the name of 'The Tower of London'.

We very soon found that it was courting sudden death to look over the parapet, except under exceptionally favourable circumstances. The enemy snipers were amazingly alert and were excellent shots. To raise a trench periscope generally meant that within a few seconds it would be smashed. Crawling over the debris caused by a rum jar strafe was therefore a very hazardous undertaking and not to be attempted unless absolutely necessary. Frequently the junction of Bart's Alley with the front line also became completely blocked in this manner, and it had to be cleared before we could get any rations up or contact the companies on our flanks.

Our company strength was so depleted that we garrisoned these two trenches with several isolated posts in saps running out to the rim of the crater. In daylight it was a tricky business visiting them at all, and sometimes, after a strafe, an impossibility without being sniped while clawing and wriggling over the torn earth. The latrine problem in these, as may be imagined, was a constant and very real one.

I well remember visiting one of these posts at 'stand to' one late October dawn. It was held by a Lewis gun section and the lance-corporal in charge motioned to me to look through the rusty tangle of wire over the crater rim to the reverse side, to the spot he indicated. I could scarcely believe that I was looking into a German post about twenty-five yards away. The occupants were standing to also, their backs half-turned to us. The lance-corporal whispered, 'what should I do?' After I had recovered, I whispered back, 'nothing—but watch 'em if you can. Don't fire unless you have to!' He looked very relieved, for just then our policy was 'live and let live'. We argued, if we shot these Germans from this post, we invited annihilating retaliation from rum jars, to which we had no adequate reply. Subsequent events justified our attitude at that time, and I remember one instance, at least, where a well-intentioned but newly joined subaltern ordered a Lewis gun section to fire at a German wiring party. The Germans were no fools. They marked flashes, doubtless verified the spot by daylight, and over came half a dozen of those horrors which cost us three good men we could ill afford to lose.

In this sector, shortly after I put up my third stripe, the winter of 1916 descended upon us in downpours of cold, driving rain, alternating with occasional fine, still days followed by starry skies and sharp frosts at night. Our experiences of the previous winter were repeated, with the important difference that now every man possessed a pair of rubber thigh boots and, if he was wise, several pairs of dry socks.

Communication trenches, front line and saps alike crumbled and slithered into the form of ditches of various depths of glue-like, chalk-laden mud, and our posts were virtually isolated by day. In the long and tortuous communication trenches especially, men frequently lost one or even both thigh boots under the dire necessity of stepping out of them to free themselves from the bogs in which they had stuck fast. Sometimes ration carriers in particular could not even step out of their boots until rescuers slung a hefty pole across the trench on which the unfortunate could pull himself clear. Then there was a dig until the boot or boots were recovered—if possible.

After each spell in the front line we used to make our way back following relief to either of the support trenches O.B.1, 2, 3 or 4, from which we furnished various fatigue or wiring parties. Rum jars rarely reached us here and there wasn't much shelling, but the rats were enormous. After three days we would go back to the delights of Lancashire Trench, where the rats were even larger and more numerous. From here small parties went daily to a shattered house with a roof patched with camouflaged, galvanized iron sheets and boarded-up window frames, near Vermelles church. Here were the 'baths', and, in what had been the back garden, several low-category grimy figures tended cauldrons of hot water and stoked the fires carefully in order not to make too much smoke. Within, there were rows of large tubs—if one could see through the steam arising from them—and after undressing near the wall, we watched for a vacant tub. Then two or three of us would step into the warm, grey, curd-laden water used by numerous previous participants and reach for the nearest cake of army soap.

If one was lucky, one of the sooty staff appeared through the steamy haze and, with a grunted warning, poured in a large bucket or dixie or near-boiling water. To us it was sheer luxury, but amid exhortations by the N.C.O. in charge to hurry up, we stepped out at length onto the wet duckboards and scoured, rather than dried, ourselves with our already dirty, soap-caked towels. Then we queued up in a state of nature at a far window with our wet towels,

THE BATHS. VERMELLES.
Nov. 1916.

underwear and socks. Here, in due course, a bundle of clean replacements was proffered, with but scant consideration as to size. Protests were unavailing, and served only to raise shouts from those behind to 'get a move on!'

Outside once again, the newly clean mingled for a few moments with unclean comrades awaiting their turns to enter, the former showing off their clean underwear or grousing bitterly at glaring misfits. Marvellously refreshed, each party, when complete, filed

218

back through the ruined village to the communication trench and Lancashire Trench again. There is no doubt that these baths put new life into us and were a creditable effort on the part of those responsible. Much was made, too, I remember, of the clean towel exchanged on the occasion I have mentioned. Incidentally, I forget just how frequently I managed to wash my own towel, but I can say with certainty that it was not often enough. The fact that we used, somehow, to shave with the old cut-throat razor, when humanly possible, contributed largely to the generally disgusting condition of these items of our equipment. Often we would achieve a wash and shave in half a mess tin of water, and, on more than one occasion, a shave even in tea. The resulting soap-caked towel, even after just a few such treatments, can be imagined.

One November afternoon, I recall a wild stampede for clothes and cover at these baths following the arrival of two five-nines unpleasantly close, quickly followed by two more. Mercifully no more came and we were left, shivering by this time, to return to our rudely interrupted ablutions where, after a few minutes, the mirth at our recent discomfiture waxed loud and long. Too long, perhaps, because the laughter ceased suddenly as several men sought, loudly but unsuccessfully, for their underclothes. This prompted others still in the nude to check on their own, with varying results, but the man at the window stubbornly refused to issue more clean items without the soiled equivalents. With truth, he maintained that the victims all came in with shirts, pants, vests, etc.—where were they? It was easy to see, however, that some bright lads, returning sooner than others, had been scrounging, particularly socks. Happily, however, I was able to end this little impasse by getting one or two who had dressed to go outside and lift some dirty stuff from a pile I had seen quite unguarded in the yard, awaiting transport to the laundry near Béthune. This was presented and duly exchanged. By this simple expedient I obtained an extra pair of socks for myself and was then under the painful necessity of preventing the remainder of my party overdoing it.

The bad weather descended upon the armies particularly early in the autumn of 1916, and among those who professed to know, portents heralding a severe winter were not lacking. Mud and frost brought the Somme battle to a finish, and after the final effort at

Beaumont Hamel in mid November matters there were pretty much the same as with us.

With the onset of winter, we worked unceasingly to keep communication trenches clear. Having now attained the rank of sergeant, I was no longer under the necessity of handling a shovel myself, but often did so, either to keep warm or to pull my weight with our fellows. Indeed, I had begun to appreciate the fact that with stripes—in these trenches, at any rate—youth assumed considerable responsibility. We were so far below our normal strength that all ranks were fearfully overworked. Although most of the men could, with truth, be described as veterans and thus were not in the habit of grousing without good reason, it required all the tact and force of example which we, as N.C.O.s, could command to get done, somehow, the arduous and constantly recurring tasks which perforce we had to detail them to perform.

To add to our troubles, there was a spy scare; apparently not without some justification. The story went the rounds that a German officer in British uniform and trench coat had been walking round the sector apparently unhindered until, finally, when challenged, giving the wrong number of the battalion in the line. Even then he had got away before the real significance had dawned on the sentry. What did actually happen, though, was that a party of enterprising Germans raided the trenches to our right held by Northumberland Fusiliers of our division, and carried off upwards of thirty men under cover of darkness. Some of the raiding party penetrated far beyond the support trenches before the alarm was given—some said to the outskirts of Vermelles. The surprise had been complete but, under the circumstances, understandable. As may be imagined, however, we were apprehensive of a similar effort against our own posts, and when holding the front line were constantly on the alert, doing our utmost also to strengthen our wire at night by every means available, and repairing damage made by rum jars at the earliest possible opportunity.

A system of passwords was instituted, each company being assigned a new password at sunset. I'm afraid that this gave rise to several alarming challenges, especially at first when, for one reason or another, men had not been apprised of the current password. One, I recall, amusing in retrospect but not at all funny

"GUMBOOTS"
Northampton Trench. Dusk. Dec. 1916
Hohenzollern Redoubt.
Hulluch.

at the time. The password was 'Jellicoe'. As N.C.O. on duty I had just visited our sentries at the junction of Bart's Alley with Northampton Trench and had stopped for a few moments' conversation with them before going on. It was a vile black night, with rain falling in a steady downpour, the only other sound just then being the 'plop, plop' as lumps of trench side slithered into the morass below until, from away down Bart's Alley, we heard squelching and stumbling sounds which gradually increased, with muttered curses alternating. Slowly the newcomers approached, until gasps of laboured breathing in the pitch black darkness now drowned all other sounds.

'Halt! Who are you?' challenged the sentry, raising his rifle. A pause, then from the darkness the answer, 'Jellicoe—f. . . you! Stuck in the . . . mud. Now we've stopped, we shan't be able to . . . well move again—you lousy . . .!!' He was right too, but with the aid of a fir pole and my torch we were able at length to extricate both of them; also the welcome four sandbags of rations they carried slung round their necks.

So trench life went on, but in the midst of all this I was twice sent for by Company Headquarters. On the first occasion Captain Warner wished to speak to me and, on reporting to his shelter in the support trench, he asked me with a smile across the candlelight if I would care to go in for a Commission; if so, he would be pleased to recommend me. Completely taken aback, I tried to recover my wits. He saw this, and with a friendly grin told me to take it easy.

I could only consider his proposition from two viewpoints. It meant England again—after nearly eighteen months. It would be much longer, probably, before I went if accepted, but what an opportunity to grasp. Then, too, I thought to myself, my brother was a lieutenant on the Somme with a six-inch howitzer battery. He had made the grade via public school O.T.C. and the Artists Rifles. I had not these opportunities but, on the other hand, had more experience of war. Standing there I tried to weigh the odds sanely, and finally told Captain Warner I'd like to have a shot, but there were many difficulties to overcome. He just said, 'good man, I'll do what I can.' Whereat I thanked him, saluted and went back up Bart's Alley and soon forgot all about it in the midst of many cares and day-to-day events.

On the second occasion, about a fortnight later, in the first week in December, Company H.Q. presented me with a leave warrant. I had not seen my parents for twenty months—indeed, not a long absence by standards of those days. How tenderly I handled that precious warrant, the care with which I placed it, together with a wad of ten-franc notes of my back pay, in my wallet! I remember going back to get my kit and handing over various duties to wryly joking fellow N.C.O.s, all the while hoping that no unlucky rum jar or five-nine would fall before I could make my getaway. Walking on air, I remember ploughing through the mud back to Lancashire Trench, where I joined two more chaps going on the same errand as myself. We hurried through Vermelles in the gathering dusk, to Philosophe Corner and as far as Sailly-la-Bourse. There we paused in the frosty evening to eat great plates of eggs and *pommes de terre frites*, washed down with *vin blanc*. Coming outside into the night air, we were lucky enough to get a lift in the back of a lorry to Béthune. Here we waited until dawn on the freezing station for the leave train, but nothing then could have dampened our spirits.

The journey to Boulogne was painfully slow, but nobody cared. On the outskirts our train came to a halt for the umpteenth time, remaining there nearly an hour, during which time we walked up and down the track, cursing French railways in general and buying chocolate, oranges or biscuits from various little urchins who had appeared from nowhere at the prospect of doing business. Eventually a piercing whistle recalled the scattered groups to the train, which was well under way when the last stragglers were hauled aboard, out of breath and limp with relief now that the fearful possibility of being left behind—on a leave train of all trains—had not materialized. In our compartment a kilted Jock and a Canadian sat opposite each other in the corner seats, puffing and blowing thus, quite heedless of the open door swinging to and fro as the train gathered speed. We heard other doors banging, too, in similar case.

Having recovered his breath, the Canadian rose to shut the door, when the air suddenly darkened. We heard splintering crashes in front and then our door hit the side of the tunnel entrance with terrific force. In we went, unable now to shut out the choking sulphurous fumes pouring in upon us through the open doorway, while below, now hanging by a leather strap and one twisted hinge, our shattered door bounced about like a thing possessed to an ear-splitting accompaniment which ceased only when it became detached.

In this fashion we crawled into Boulogne, but before it came to a standstill and into the baleful gaze of the local railway officials, the train had practically emptied, and all were in an eager crowd anxious to be first on the leave boat. No doubt an all-suffering British government paid ample compensation, eventually, for the stricken carriages. However, our hopes of getting on to the boat sustained a rude shock when we formed up and were marched away to a building where we had a vapour bath, a clean change of underclothes and a certificate to the effect that we were free from vermin.

I can remember little else after all these years, except the approach to Victoria Station in the dusk of a December afternoon and, a few minutes later, the sea of faces at the barrier. Some of those on the train living near London had sent telegrams from Folkestone, and dear ones were there to greet them. We envied them, I think, as we passed through the scrutinizing curious crowd, fringed by a sprinkling of unattached ladies. From beyond the booking hall came the sounds of the London traffic, like music, and outside, the familiar smells of London: petrol, manure, soot, stale scent, rotting vegetables—and the combination went to our heads like wine.

My ten days' leave was divided into two parts, the first lasting for five days, filled with the simple joy and excitement of greeting and being with my own folk once more; of looking up old friends and old scenes—in short, of all the things I had often thought could never happen in my case. The almost ceremonial immolation, in the back garden, of all my underwear the morning after my homecoming, as I stood in a mixed lot of clothes belonging to two of my brothers. My mother then dumped my uniform trousers, puttees and tunic into a tin bath of hot soapy water. Then followed the somewhat painful extrusion by her loving fingers and thumbs of the many blackheads which, allegedly, adorned my forehead, ears and neck. Nearly three days of a wondrous existence passed before I dressed once more in cleaned and pressed khaki and, with a silk scarf of my mother's round my neck at her special request, was judged to be tolerably presentable.

It was grand, too, to look again upon the scenes of my boyhood at Eastbourne. I well remember trudging up to Beachy Head with my brother Alfred, and standing with him in the chill December wind looking at the expanse of English Channel sparkling in the winter sunlight. Many had been the time when I had wondered

On leave with my brother at Eastbourne, December 1916.

whether it would be my luck ever to look on this again—and here it was! In truth I had a great deal for which to be profoundly thankful, and the realization, I think, really hit me hard in those minutes up there.

The second part started on the sixth day with the first faint disturbing reminders, thoughts which I endeavoured to dispel, but which would not be completely denied, although visits to theatres and calling on friends in the company of the girl who had sent me her photograph after Bazentin helped a lot. I'm afraid I knew very little about girls, though, and I must have appeared to her very rough and gauche; perhaps the more so from the company I had soldiered with and my experiences of two years and more of war. As the time for my return drew near I got the impression, wrongly perhaps, that somehow I hadn't added up to her expectations—and this persisted. The last day was one of rather enforced cheerfulness and my leave terminated at Victoria on a foggy December morning—a pretty miserable business.

I was positively thankful to step ashore at Boulogne. Béthune, two evenings later, seemed welcoming, the native somehow understanding of the soldier's lot. At Sailly-la-Bourse, after a final plate of eggs and *frites*, I was quite ready to set off with the battalion ration carts for Vermelles and Lancashire Trench. Of my ten days in Blighty there remained just a dull ache—and that was all.

At Battalion H.Q. I passed a dugout whence issued strains of the hit of the current George Robey revue, *The Byng Boys*—'If You were the Only Girl in the World and I was the Only Boy'. Then that dull ache became an emotional rush of memories of those ten days, and I think that then I reached my nadir of depression as I stumbled on with the ration carriers and the company mail up to O.B.1, where we were in support.

I think they were pleased to see me again, if only for the fact that I could ease the sergeants' trench duty rota. It was amazing, however, that after a few commonplace answers to inquiries made by mates about the state of things in Blighty, I seemed to fit into my groove once more in this sea of desolation, where morning light once more showed Fosse 8 through driving rain, and, barely discernible, the Tower of London.

So life went on—front, support, reserve and back again. We had been at the Hohenzollern for seventy-seven days when, at length, on 22nd December 1916, we were relieved and we marched out a dusk through Vermelles in artillery formation like schoolboys on holiday, via Philosophe Corner, Mazingarbe and Sailly-la-Bourse; thence, after a halt to rest our poor feet, which were sadly out of condition, in column of route to Béthune. Here, after standing about in the night air of the deserted street for some time, our company filed into an empty factory. We were on the first floor. By then it was pretty late, but most men either possessed or borrowed sufficient money to obtain enough stimulant in the local *estaminets* to account for the uproarious scenes at 'lights out'. Although I had but recently enjoyed the pleasures of leave, I shared and appreciated the general feeling of relief at being out of it for a spell, especially at Christmas.

The next morning we were paid—generously, according to standards then current, for, having been in the line continuously for more than two and a half months, everyone had accumulated some back pay. The majority of us had not been loose in a town of this size for very many months, and it was not surprising that

the first call for many was the 'Red Lamp'—the brothel some distance up a side street, whence the queue stretched as far as the main road. On the further side stood several red-tabbed Brass Hats of our divisional staff, watching the scene in amused amazement. Before 'lights out' that evening it was said that the general had been among those watching, and he was credited with the remark, 'My God—if those Leicesters f. . . like they fight, God help those poor women in there!' Probably a complete fabrication, of course, but amazingly morale lifting at the time, I recall. Judging, however, by the conversation before the candles were doused and the snores commenced, one of the women, by catering for the needs of about 80 per cent of our company, had earned the soubriquet of 'the baby elephant'—an amazing performance by any standards.

We left Béthune in good time the following morning, marching almost due west, and the knowledge that we were getting further away from the trenches with each succeeding step put everyone in a good humour. To a man we were imbued with but one definite object—to enjoy Christmas, whatever happened. In boisterous mood we passed one after another of these mining villages, singing lustily, cracking jokes and vying with one another in rude sallies of doubtful wit at the expense of the womenfolk, young and old, who stood at cottage doors as we passed. Most of them took the shouted invitations to *'promenade'* or *'voulez-vous coucher avec moi ce soir?'* in good part, replying with a laugh, *'après la guerre!'* or with some such evasive jest. Here and there, however, one would take exception to such invitations and gesticulate wildly with virtuous indignation, whereupon she would be mimicked unmercifully until, unable to continue the unequal contest, the outraged lady would retire into her domicile, generally closing the door with a final *bang* of disgust.

In this fashion we came, around midday, to the large mining village of Auchel, of blessed memory, noticing on the outskirts an airfield with hangars and huts. Drawn up in line thereon were several Handley Page bombing biplanes, which impressed us considerably, I remember, giving most of us our first close-up of the machines which droned high over the line on fine evenings at dusk. As yet we did not know that we were stopping at this place, but as we progressed, the sight of our company quartermaster, Sergeant Peach, saluting Captain Warner raised our hopes. We knew he had gone ahead to find our billets. Immediately, then, we began to study every house critically, and within a few minutes saw our 'A' Company filing into houses. We, however, seemed to march almost through the village before arriving at our billets. These, as we three sergeants saw the fellows settled in, seemed to exceed our wildest expectations, and together we tackled Peach as to whether he had found us a good billet. He told us somewhat sourly to have a bit of patience, and eventually, having fixed up the Company Sergeant-Major Walker (C.S.M. Tiny Gamble had gone home for a Commission in November) and the officers to their satisfaction, he returned and led us to an *estaminet* at the junction of two roads almost at the village end, with fields opposite but dominated by several great slag heaps. A cheery, buxom, middle-aged woman answered Peach's knock, and after introductions with many *bons* on our part, we followed them through the bar and up the stairs, filled with a pleasurable sense of anticipation. Neither were we disappointed as we entered a large bedroom containing two double beds in addition to a wardrobe, dressing table and all the usual bedroom furniture.

There and then we divested ourselves of our packs and equipment, signifying our emphatic approval both to the smiling Madame and to the slightly supercilious Peach, who remarked with a grin, 'now then, you lot, don't tell me again that I don't see after you. I reckon you've got the best bloody billet in the village!'.

'You're a damned good sort, Quarter,' enthused Kirk. 'I'm not coming on parade again 'til we leave here. Fancy Cheg,' slapping Chesterton on the back and indicating the *estaminet* below, 'we can get beer all day here if we want it . . . We can have it brought up in bed . . . I say, Quarter, how many in the family here?'—this with a glance at Madame—'any young stuff about?'

'*Qu'est qu'il dit?*' inquired our hostess, somewhat anxiously, plucking at Peach's sleeve. Peach seized his opportunity delightedly, indicating Kirk: 'him—*le Sergent* Kirk—*pas bon*, Madame—*marié Angleterre*—six piccaninnies *Angleterre*', holding up his fingers to emphasise the point. Chesterton and I sat on the bed, while Kirk jumped up and blushingly refuted the accusation. He patted the laughing woman on the back. 'Don't you believe him—*le Sergent* Peach so—*comme-ça*', and he put one finger to his head in a corkscrew movement. '*Compris?*' whereon Madame, by now almost helpless with mirth, stood aside as Peach, with a, 'well, I'm busy . . . Got something else to do besides waste time with you ungrateful so-and-sos!' clattered down the stairs into the street below.

The short silence which ensued as we mutually inspected one another was broken. 'Madame,' inquired the still-perspiring Chesterton, '*avez-vous* three—*trois* pints *bière*—*tout suite s'il vous plait?*'

I managed to explain 'pint' to Madame, who beamed and informed us that there was a room downstairs behind the bar where we could sit in comfort and take our drinks. At this news I recall that Chesterton and Kirk danced up and down the room, kicking my tin hat about, while the good woman feared for her furniture. 'Come on, Madame, lead the way!' And we followed her joyously.

Well, there was no doubt that this was the finest billet we had come across so far in France, and on going downstairs for our drinks soon found that Madame also provided the finest eggs and *frites* it had been our lot to sample. We found, moreover, that there were three young women about the house, and were informed by Madame that one was her daughter, but that the other two were refugees from Lens. They were only there during the day time. Madame's husband, together with their son, temporarily released from the army, and three other men lived in the house, and all worked in the mines nearby. While we were there they returned about half-past four in the afternoon, covered in grime from their arduous toil at the coal face. Soon after three thirty Madame and the girls were always busy setting out five large tubs on the kitchen floor and heating lots of water. As the sabots of the miners were heard approaching on the cobblestones outside, Madame and the girls partially filled the tubs, so that the room was so full of steam that it was difficult to see the length of it.

After their baths the men would eat an enormous meal, then taking their ease for a little while, smoking and talking before getting off to bed, for they were due at the pit again at a very early hour on the following morning. In conversation with them we found that Madame's son had been wounded at the Mort Homme, Verdun, and that the three other men had been released from the army to work in the mines. They told us that the local pits were working under great difficulties owing to labour shortages. We took an immediate liking to all of them. They were good types, and on closer acquaintance their army background became very apparent. Occasionally they would sing snatches of marching songs, the words of which we understood not one jot; at some, Madame and the girls affected to be shocked—all the same, there followed sounds of stifled giggles from the kitchen.

SUPPER WITH THE FAMILY IN OUR BILLET. XMAS EVE 1916. AUCHEL, P. de CALAIS.

We would have been quite content to have had all our meals with these good people after having supper—by invitation—with them on Christmas Eve, although somehow we three were restrained and on our best behaviour at first—being inspected, you could call it—Madame having paired us off with the three girls. Gradually, however, the atmosphere thawed and by the time we parted to attend Company Headquarters and various duties, we felt that we had made some real friends.

At Company Headquarters we were told by the C.S.M. that a battalion sergeants' mess was being started as from Christmas Day and that we would have our dinner there, after we had assisted the officers to wait upon the men at their dinner, in traditional fashion. We three didn't like the idea one bit, not least because the mess was about twelve minutes' brisk walk from our billet.

I don't remember much about Christmas Day. After a church parade we adjourned to the new mess, but we felt too much under the eyes of the R.S.M. and the company sergeant-majors to be at ease there. After a very late dinner we seized the first opportunity of getting away to an inter-company football match, in which I functioned at left back (after a fashion), as everyone taking part had either eaten or imbibed too much beforehand. I cannot recall who won, but we were all thankful when 'time' was blown and a chance came of lying down on one of those glorious beds in the billet and sleeping it off.

I was awakened by persistent knocking on the door, and on rising accepted a smiling invitation from Madame for the three of us to dine with the family again that evening. In doing so I apologized as gracefully as I could for the snoring Chesterton and Kirk.

It was getting dark when we heard the miners come in and the subsequent splashing and singing downstairs. We descended after a wash and brush-up to find the kitchen and adjoining room still full of steam, but preparations for a savoury meal were in progress, the aroma causing us to look at one another appreciatively: 'the R.S.M. could stuff his battalion sergeants' mess . . . !!'

At table, twelve of us managed to squeeze ourselves in, we three being paired as on the previous evening, but we had scarcely started when a large portion of plaster fell from the ceiling onto the laden board, disintegrating into powder and many small pieces. No doubt the continual steaming from the tubs was responsible. However, the ladies having regained their composure and most of the plaster having been retrieved from the eatables and tablecloth, the meal proceeded and was an unqualified success.

In between the many toasts I recall that I held my neighbour's hand under the table and that she dug her heel into the toe of my boot—all very pleasurable. For the first time I realized that she was quite good looking and that her black velvet dress became her well. Her name was Nöelle; very appropriate, I thought at the time. She told me that Georges Carpentier, the boxer, was a cousin of hers.

No doubt Chesterton and Kirk were equally pleased by their partners, for as soon as we were by ourselves again the three of us were obsessed by conjecture as to where the girls went after the *estaminet* closed for the night. They would not tell us, and we plied the menfolk in vain. We could not get an answer, only a lot of evasive smiles and shrugs, with occasional sallies which we didn't understand. All that we could gather was that Nöelle and her sister Louise were refugees from Lens.

Two afternoons later, however, as we were reclining on our beds after a hard morning's drill followed by a bout in the sergeants' mess, I heard a faint knock on our door. As before, I opened it, but this time was astonished to find the three girls standing in some confusion outside in the half-light of the landing. Recovering from my surprise, I was about to burst into delighted greetings when Nöelle held up a warning finger, at which I subsided. We all tiptoed into the room and I pushed the door to. My mates were snoring peacefully, causing stifled giggles from the girls, and I was still at a complete loss as to the reason for this unexpected visit, when Nöelle started to explain. Would we, she whispered, care to come and *boire café* with them that evening after the *estaminet* shut? Momentarily I found myself without words; it seemed too good to be true! Half-doubting that I had understood her aright, haltingly I asked her to repeat her invitation. She did so and I hastened to tell her how delighted we would be to come . . . 'but where are we to go?' They would not tell us where they lived.

'*Écoutez, monsieur* Dick,' whispered Nöelle, clutching at my sleeve; and she asked me whether I had noticed a caravan at the far side of the field opposite. She didn't say 'caravan', and I remember that I was some time in understanding what she was driving at, but once I comprehended that, the rest was easy, although I was astounded at what she told me. It appeared that she and her sister lived with their mother in the caravan and that, as we had gathered already, they were refugees from Lens. Two days previously, however, their mother had gone to Paris to see their brother, seriously wounded but now convalescing in hospital there. They, Nöelle and Louise, were now alone, but Marthe had permission of her parents to stay with them for company while their mother was away.

So that was where they lived!

I said that we would try and come across as soon as all was quiet, around 11 p.m., or sooner if possible, without arousing the family's suspicions. As they tiptoed down the stairs and I closed the door, I could scarcely believe that I had not been dreaming, but the faint perfume that they left behind reassured me. A drowsy voice from one of the beds grunted, 'who's that?' and the sleeper turned over and was dozing off again as, full of my news, I went to them in turn and shook them violently. 'Hey, wake up, you beggars . . . Hey!'

Lying there, dishevelled and sleepy, they refused to believe my story for some time; agreed that either I must have dreamed it or was drunk; told me to lie down and I would feel better. By degrees, however, I managed to get some credence attached to my tale, and on going downstairs, the covert glances of the three girls convinced them more than all my arguments had done that I was not indulging in any wild flight of fancy. Holding an impromptu council, we judged it best to stay at the mess all the evening, and before going out acquainted Nöelle of our intention. She nodded approvingly, and as we went outside whispered to me, '*à dix heures et demi* . . .'

That night we bid the old folks an ostentatious 'good night' soon after 10 p.m. and made much noise upstairs. Shortly after 10.30 we crept downstairs in our socks, with no little trepidation, and slipped out of the back door into the yard, where we put on our boots. Crossing the yard and getting through the double gates to the street as quietly as we could, we found ourselves in almost pitch darkness outside, the only gleam of light coming through the shuttered windows of the kitchen, where Madame and her husband presumably were still washing glasses and cleaning up after the night's business.

After getting our bearings as well as we could, we crossed the road and came to the poles barring the way to the field. There we stood again in the blackness to decide our course before striking out towards where we judged the caravan to be. We had gone fifty yards or so and my mates were beginning to mutter audibly when, by good luck, I spotted a pinpoint of light almost directly in front. We made tracks for this and were soon standing by the steps of the caravan. Kirk and Chesterton pushed me forward, the latter saying in a fierce whisper which symbolized the thoughts of all three of us, 'you go first, Dick. If we're having our legs pulled, we'll b. . . well murder you when we get back!' It was bitterly cold.

I mounted the steps and put an ear to the door. Hearing sounds within, I knocked but, truth to tell, my heart thumped wildly as I waited for something to happen. The glimpse of light disappeared as I heard a key turn in the door and a low voice inquire, '*c'est vous, monsieur* Dick?' I answered in the affirmative and whispered to my mates to come on. Gingerly we stepped inside. All was dark, but the warmth within seemed to enwrap us as we heard the door close behind us and the key turn again.

Nöelle spoke quickly in French and a match was struck, which revealed Louise holding it with Marthe standing beside her, removing the glass from a hanging lamp. They re-lit it and as Marthe turned up the wick the whole interior of the caravan unfolded before our astonished gaze. It was a revelation to us—a marvel of neatness, compactness and cleanliness. The little stove halfway down one side shone in the lamplight, as did the polished cutlery on the snowy white tablecloth, half-hidden as it was by the array of gleaming bottles and glasses thereon; the tasteful curtains over the window and over the bunks at the far end; above all, however, the laughing faces of the three girls, who could see our surprise and were gratified by it.

Nöelle took me by the arm. 'You like it, eh?' We all hastened to tell them that we thought it all wonderful—especially themselves—and I recall that in my elation I kissed her, French fashion, on both cheeks, and that the faint perfume she affected rather went to my head. I make no excuse for that, as for the preceding two years the prevailing scents in my case had been chloride of lime, gyppo (stew), or worse—frequently much worse.

The other four laughed at us while Nöelle blushed as she explained that they had put out the light before opening the door so that no one on the road should see us enter. This brought them renewed bouquets from us, in the course of which they made us sit down at the table while they busied themselves with the little larder, the stove and the bottles.

I shall always remember those bottles and the first cork popping to the roof, and the 'mark'—'Deutz et Gueldermann'. Nöelle filled the six glasses. We stood and toasted our hostesses, each looking across the wide top of bubbling, sparkling champagne in his glass at his fair neighbour, while on the stove the savoury repast gently frizzled, awaiting their pleasure.

So started the first of what, in latter days, we used to designate 'the better nights'—a night which compensated us for all the mud of the Hohenzollern; much more than that—a night such as I had vaguely pictured that summer evening up at Arras, when I told our colonel that I didn't want to die just then, as I hadn't started to live—in the fullest sense of the word. Here was the realization it seemed of a legitimate youthful longing rudely interrupted and stifled by more than two years of war—but the 'reason why'.

Even the chilly business of getting back undetected to our room before dawn was not without its thrills, but as at length we lay down on our beds to snatch an hour's sleep before reveille, life to us seemed really worth living at last; for were we not going across to the caravan again at '*dix heures et demi*'? Just then we envied no one!

Buoyed up by anticipation and the keen pleasure of these nocturnal excursions which we managed to keep a close secret, our stay at Auchel passed all too quickly. Came 1st January 1917, and with it the commencement of a spell of bitterly cold weather.

On our exercises and parades, we were hard put to it to keep reasonably warm unless we did P.T. or took part in frequent organized games. The ground became too hard and frost-bound to play football, although matches continued until it became too dangerous a sport. We were short enough of men as it was, without sacrificing more through broken legs and collarbones and wrists. One evening we went to Miss Lena Ashwell's Concert Party, then visiting Auchel; on another to our own 21st Divisional Concert

Party, which provided hilarious entertainment of a somewhat riskier type. In addition, one of our 'C' Company was a popular member. He had a fine bass voice and his songs, such as 'Drinking' and 'Asleep in the Deep', always went down well with the troops.

Towards the end of the first week in January the mother of Nöelle and Louise returned from Paris. Nöelle gave me the news with what I fancied were a somewhat wet pair of eyes. We tried to laugh these tidings off with a shrug, saying, *'c'est la guerre'* but, certainly for us, life was no longer spiced with the same feeling of pleasures to come, and of adventures. It had lost much of its savour.

Apart from seeing the girls in the course of their daily work, and occasional chats in the evenings over drinks, we regretfully reverted to regimental life. Nevertheless, the change which the rest had worked in the battalion seemed little short of miraculous. To see our company on parade, now indeed strengthened by a goodly draft consisting of rejoined wounded from the Somme battles, put fresh heart into all. The men held themselves well; they drilled well; in spite of the winter weather they looked pictures of ruddy health. Faded and torn khaki and worn boots had been replaced to a great extent, and opportunities had been seized of getting alterations made to tunics and trousers, either by the battalion tailor or, more frequently, by the ladies of Auchel. Buttons and badges glinted in the winter sunlight, and web equipment looked as well as 'Khaki Blanco' and meticulous brushing could make it. In short, we felt ourselves a real fighting force once more. Still below strength, but with the advantage that nearly every man was a veteran of the Somme.

We would, of course, gladly have stayed on for the 'duration', to use the vernacular, but knew this to be impossible and that we would have to go back to the line somewhere very shortly. For all that, we now faced the future with renewed confidence, whatever it might hold for us.

It is interesting to note that among ourselves, and, I believe, the British Expeditionary Force as a whole, we had long since ceased to consider the ethics of what we were supposed to be fighting for. We laughed contemptuously at newspaper accounts of Hun 'atrocities' and the childish attempts to belittle the military

AFTER A CHRISTMAS REST — THE 8TH.BATT. LEICESTERSHIRE REGT. LEAVES
AUCHEL. JAN. 4th 1917.

"A BON TIME!"

qualities of our opponents. We knew better; knew them to be so efficient, so brave, so ingenious and so well equipped, that if we didn't get our man first, he would certainly get us. That was all there was to it, as far as we were concerned.

Therefore, when our marching orders came about the end of the first week in January, and we paraded for the last time in the

238

village street in full kit ready to move off, we felt ready for the next dose of whatever was coming our way—although the knowledge that Nöelle was standing at the *estaminet* door behind us, with Marthe, Louise and Madame, all of them blowing their noses frequently, made it hard to leave Auchel on that cold January morning. For a good many days afterwards—yes, and nights, too—I remembered her fluttering handkerchief and shining eyes as we tramped by down the hill out of Auchel, past the great slag heaps and up the reverse slope to the Doullens–Lillers Road. There we turned to the right, for Lillers, with a snow-laden north-east wind in our faces.

AUCHEL
Dec.23rd.1916.

CHAPTER 13

COLD INTERLUDE

WE entrained in a siding at Lillers in the snow-laden dusk of a leaden January afternoon, our mode of transport the customary freight cars. Although ours appeared crammed to capacity, we found it difficult to keep the chill from creeping into our bones. Soon after, we were on the move north, for a destination unknown to us, and it started to snow hard. Heaps of powdered snow indicated the chinks in the sliding doors as we rattled along through the night.

Some stars were shining when at length we clambered down into the deep snow beside the train, after much shunting and jolting. An icy blast met us, and although the snow had ceased, as we fell in finely powdered snow blew into our faces and stung them into numbness.

We were thankful to march off, and as we did so we saw that the station was Proven—a railhead for the Ypres Salient. That we were in Belgium again did not exactly cheer us. We slogged on and actually marched until daylight, during which time we seemed to cover much of Flanders.

A grey winter dawn revealed flat, snow-covered fields; frozen ponds; black lifeless trees, on the north side of which the snow had frozen. The bitter wind still blew drifts into our faces, and towards the end, when we halted hourly for the customary five-minute 'easy', we all were seized with an overpowering desire to lie down and sleep. Many did, and were awakened only with difficulty when the march was resumed. Indeed, afterwards the story went around that several stragglers from our brigade died from exposure as a result of falling out and going to sleep.

When finally our company halted before a collection of miserable-looking farm buildings, seemingly isolated in a dreary expanse

The Barn.
Winnezeele.
JAN. 4/5/1917.

of white, the men lay down on the road in their ranks upon their packs, and were asleep within seconds. The extreme cold, the rigours of the night march, following hours in the train without sleep—these factors combined to produce this state of affairs. I only managed to keep awake myself because, with Sergeants Chesterton and Kirk, I went with C.Q.M.S. Peach to examine our billet in a barn. When we returned, after an absence of five minutes or so, to get the men in, we awakened them only by prodding, or by literally kicking their packs from under them as they lay there.

Blankets were issued, three apiece, and three of us—Fatty, Jackie and myself—pooled ours to obtain the maximum warmth. We got under them as soon as we could, removing only our boots. Had we known what would happen to them, we would have put them under the blankets also. The straw was deep and clean, and I knew no more until noon that day, when Peach woke us. Kirk, Chesterton and I followed him into the farm-house at his bidding, for the issue of something or other, but not until we had thawed out our boots in the warmth of the blankets, while he chafed at the delay. He had a stove in his room in the farm-house, where he had set up his store, and his bed was in the corner. Although the stove was lit, we thought our barn warmer than his room. I don't suppose the stove had been in action for years, and a full week passed before the chill left that room and poor Peach enjoyed some degree of warmth at his tasks. Compiling daily returns was no joke under such circumstances.

Unfortunately, our company's field cooker was in another farm about half a kilometre along the road, so that most of our meals were getting cold before the dixies reached us, until the cookhouse fatigue party wrapped old blankets round them.

On the night following our arrival, we were to learn another lesson. Bread and other rations were issued in the evening, and I recall that four shared a loaf, each putting his portion in a mess tin to thwart the depredations of rats and mice. In the morning our bread was frozen hard in the tins. I took several pieces to the stove in Peach's room, but it was quite useless. Thereafter, already taking our boots to bed, we took our bread also beneath the blankets.

Shaving and washing presented another real problem. Laboriously, we collected pieces of wood and paper from letters, carrying them to dry them, in order to take the chill off the water in our mess tins before shaving with our cut-throat razors. Many stropped their razors on a leather belt worn about the waist—often a German belt as the war progressed, although it was said that, if taken prisoner, things would go hard with wearers of such trophies!

Winnezeele (Nord) Jan. 1917. [signature]

The nearest village, and therefore the nearest *estaminet*, was at Winnezeele, about a kilometre distant across the fields, but considerably further by road. Our Company H.Q. was there. We were surprised to find ourselves in France again, here.

From our billet we could see another church spire much further off; by name, I believe, Houtkerke. When lucky enough to be off duty, which was rare enough, we used to cross the snow-covered fields to the village, under the stars, our only guides the few pinpoints of light and the dark outline of the church spire as we neared it. Many, however, were the nights on which we had to work, providing fatigue parties for the sidings near Poperinge which, while we were in the area, were bombed almost nightly.

These visitations caused hurried scrambles for cover, generally a shallow ice-bottomed ditch or trench, half-filled with drifted snow. In those days, engine drone became audible appreciably before the great lumbering machine arrived overhead, flying very slowly and very low by modern standards. Moreover, unless the night was cloudy or hazy, the plane was often visible, especially in moonlight. Anti-aircraft fire from improvised guns mounted on lorries tearing along nearby roads, opened up more than once, and bits of shrapnel whizzed among us plentifully, with occasionally the louder, more menacing whirr and thud of a nose-cap. Whether they hit anything I know not, but the intruders' tracks across the night sky were certainly dotted with 'bursts'.

There was so much ammunition of all kinds lying around in camouflaged dumps, apart from the loaded trucks in the sidings that, with the recollection of an exploding dump on the Somme, seen from a considerable distance, we little relished the possible dire effects of a lucky hit. Fortunately, however, we were spared this, and I recall an incident during one such scramble for cover not without its particular twist of stark humour, which afforded us considerable amusement in retrospect.

We had jumped into a shallow trench near the truck of stores we were unloading, when we heard running footsteps and laboured breathing approaching. As they halted momentarily to regain breath, a Scots voice panted between gasps, 'I'll be f. . . if I can run!' and his mate jerked out, 'ye'll be f. . . if ye don't!' Whereat we called to them to get down with us, to do which they needed no second bidding. Breath regained, they were soon laughing, telling us that they were of a working party of, I believe, Royal Scots, from another division. As I have indicated, this incident was recounted among us with relish long afterwards—not always, I might add, by those who had actually been present on the occasion described!

It was said that we had come north as a precautionary measure against a possible attack by the Germans across the Yser Canal, reported to be frozen—which we could well believe—although what truth there was in this I know not. If the canal was anything like the pond beside our billet, it was certainly frozen, hard as iron. This piece of solid ice provided us with a pitch for a species of ice hockey, as football became impossible. At ice hockey I recall scraping the skin from an elbow, an ear and a knee through getting in the way of an opponent's stick, but it was quite good fun.

Came a partial thaw, and we were in real trouble, with sudden seas of mud on the tracks calling themselves roads. Boots leaked, and the entrance to our barn became a morass of half-frozen mud and dirty straw. Everyone became heartily sick of Flanders, when suddenly orders came and we were on the move again.

CHAPTER 14

THE HINDENBURG LINE

WE marched back to Proven, entrained there, and in less than a week were back in the line somewhere near Loos, which we approached by ways already familiar to most of us. Our sector was somewhat to the right of our previous position, and 'C' Company manned the eastern rim of a huge mine crater, reaching it through a long, deep tunnel. At the exit into the crater, a crude and much-battered path above a morass of evil-smelling slime and wire led to our several posts.

As long as we kept quiet, the enemy did likewise. For the least activity on our party, however, such as firing bursts from Lewis guns at suspected wiring parties or patrols, we paid heavily in the shape of snorting rum jars which trundled over a-plenty and could scarcely miss causing damage and casualties if they fell within the crater perimeter. We had no adequate reply to these monsters. Should our own trench mortar sections endeavour to silence them by firing sixty-pound toffee apples or Stokes bombs from positions at our rear, our tormentors always seemed to send over an extra dose of their medicine shortly afterwards. Snipers and grenades were very real additional worries, and, without exaggeration, our crater could be termed a 'death trap'. Our artillery seemed quite powerless to find these great mortars, which no doubt were moved frequently.

When not on duty, men snatched some sleep in excavations at intervals along the tunnel way, where the dim yellow glow of electric lights relieved what otherwise would have been a Stygian blackness. Branch tunnels led down steeply into the bowels of the earth, where teams of our tunnellers were burrowing deep under the German line, literally around the clock. DeCauville rail tracks lay along the floors of these tunnels, up which the excavated soil was hauled on little trucks and put into sandbags. These were removed at nightfall by our fatigue parties, and taken well to the rear, where they were dumped and camouflaged.

It was a strange and unreal world we lived in there, the electric light supplying a certain novelty and somehow a link with the civilization we had left behind. It was a mole-like existence. Save for the unsettling probability that German miners were working beneath us, preparing a nasty surprise, things weren't too bad in the tunnels, but there is no doubt that our morale suffered considerably during our tour of duty there. We came to dread approaching the exit to the crater and paused uncertainly there, blinking to accustom our eyes to daylight and listening for a possible rum jar before threading a way through broken duckboards, timber and wire along to the posts. Indeed, when on duty and the rum jars did come over, it was almost beyond endurance to stand one's ground, more or less, and not run blindly for the tunnel entrance and shelter. We never succeeded in discovering the source of the electric light, as none of the tunnellers seemed to have any information, although it must have helped them tremendously. No doubt it had been the brilliant idea of an engineer-turned-soldier. We concluded that the transmission lines were buried and came either from Sailly-la-Bourse or Annequin. Probably, too, several similar tunnels in the Loos sector were lit in this manner.

We held this crater for upwards of two months, returning to huts near Philosophe between spells. Eventually, relieved by our regiments 1st Battalion of the 6th Division, we went back via Mazingarbe to Béthune.

We were not at all sorry to leave the crater—for good, we hoped fervently—and gave ourselves up to the civilized delights of war-time Béthune for two days, between parades and checks of arms, equipment and clothing, before sober conjecture as to where we were bound for next tempered our relief at being out of it once more. Rumours were plentiful, a strong one, I recall, being that we were taking over the line at the Cambrin 'Brickstacks', which we could see from the support trenches when at the Hohenzollern Redoubt. The trenches there appeared to run through a large but ruined brickworks, a kilometre or so to our

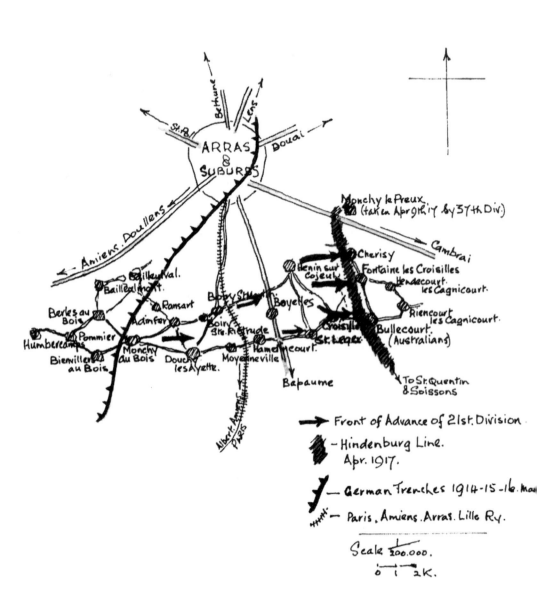

Front of Advance of 21st. Division.

— Hindenburg Line. Apr. 1917.

— German Trenches 1914-15-16. ma...

— Paris, Amiens, Arras, Lille Ry.

Scale $\frac{1}{200.000}$.

0 1 2K.

left, and by the clouds of reddish dust and the sounds of the frequent explosions, we judged it to be a pretty hot spot. I believe that we were correct—they were always at it there!

Another rumour designated Souchez, which by repute had a particularly ominous sound, in view of the enormous French losses there the previous year, in repeated attacks and counter-attacks. In the event, of course, both were wrong, and one morning in March we 'embussed' for the first time, in vehicles of one of the newly formed bus companies of the Army Service Corps, and went south.

The buses were a mixed lot. Some were double-deckers similar to the London buses of the period: indeed, probably they had been part of the London 'General' fleet. Others were single-deckers. All had boarded-up windows and solid tyres, so that on the sadly deteriorated pavé of the French roads the journey was not exactly pleasurable from our point of view. One and all, however, we envied the drivers—for two very good reasons: they didn't have to go into the trenches; and, whereas an infantryman's pay was 1s. 3d. per day (with proficiency pay), theirs was 6s. 0d., with all sorts of extras.

In our bus we could see little or nothing, but apparently our convoy skirted Arras, leaving it well to the east, and the afternoon saw us trundling along once more over roads already familiar to those of us who relieved our French allies at Berles-au-Bois in September 1915—Saulty, Mondicourt, Humbercamps, La Couchie, Gaudiémpre and Pommier.

I believe we 'de-bussed' at Humbercamps, and it was then that we had our first news of a great German retreat hereabouts. We were told that they had evacuated the whole of their trenches from Arras in the north to St. Quentin in the south. Thenceforward, every hour seemed to bring further confirmation of ground and towns recovered and of the terrible damage wrought by the re-treating Germans. At last, we thought, at last they were beaten; and we conjectured, correctly, that our division was about to join in the chase back to Germany.

So the excitement mounted, and our eagerness to get going increased—to participate in what we imagined to be a 'drive' offering innumerable opportunities of seeing what the countryside and the people (especially the women) were like on the other side of those trenches which we had faced for so many months. Little did we know then what lay in store for us there as, on the following morning, in drizzling rain, loaded to the limit with extra rations, ammunition, shovels and bombs, we tramped through Bienvillers and took the shell-torn road to Monchy-au-Bois. Near the village, the wire of our own and of the German trenches had been moved to the side by those preceding us, and the worst holes filled with rubble to enable supply limbers to use it. In the wilderness of ruined buildings there, great concrete redoubts stood out prominently; several, we noticed, on either side of the road to Berles, leading uphill past the mill and our old 97 Trench. Everything looked deserted, sodden and derelict, our impression heightened by the rain, now changed to a driving wet mist. Little had we thought that the 110th Leicestershire Brigade would enter Monchy-au-Bois in this fashion.

We splashed on in silence, enveloped in our dripping groundsheets, our thoughts of other days: of the winter of 1915, and of pals now gone. Ahead lay the dark mass of Adinfer Wood, and beyond, the ruins of Adinfer village, where we halted, looking upon another vista of desolation and noticing that the fruit trees in the gardens had been ringed by having a complete strip of bark removed at the base. They would die. It was a few yards from the road to the well serving a destroyed farm-house. We looked down it, but the appalling stench drove us away—it had been fouled with excreta. I think at these moments we felt more bitter about the enemy than at any time before or after.

Resuming our march, we saw a German signboard on a wall marked 'Nach Boiry', and we reached this village eventually by frequently taking to the fields at the roadside, as the road itself had been made impassable either by blowing up long stretches of the pavé or by felling trees across it. Some distance from Boiry—at, I believe, the ruins of Boiry Ste Rictrude—we crossed a main road which was completely blocked by the felling of trees crisscross fashion. Boiry was Adinfer repeated, and when we halted there we were warned not to wander among the ruins because of the many booby traps. Here we saw that the fruit trees had been sawn through a foot or so above the ground, and that the wells had been disgustingly and systematically fouled.

Beyond Boiry the going worsened considerably, and we began to see dead horses and mules by the roadside. As infantry, we were able to get by somehow, but wheeled transport or artillery had had to take to the sodden fields alongside, where the strain involved in pulling the laden limbers or guns through the soft earth soon told heavily on the overworked and, as we saw, double teams. In most cases it looked as though they had been shot to put an end to further suffering. There was no water for them here, either, as every source seemed to be polluted, and we began to realize that, to all intents and purposes, we were in a desert; that, with every step eastwards, we went further from civilization and the necessaries of life.

So far, the information we had been able to glean as to the extent of the retreat to our immediate front had been meagre in the extreme, but our officers now told us that the enemy was reported to be in the neighbourhood of Croisilles, several miles further on, and that the two other brigades of our division were now driving them. The probability that organized resistance was now being encountered pointed to a limit of the retreat having been reached, at least temporarily. In any case, if we proceeded much further through this devastated countryside, the enemy would be fighting us with great tactical advantages.

In this manner we reached the ruins of Moyenneville and pressed on for a kilometre or so further, where we came upon what had been a double-track railway level crossing. We could trace the deep cutting on our left, and the low embankment to the right, but there were neither rails nor sleepers. A little further on, however, we passed a large pond with rail ends protruding above the surface; while hard by, a large dump of rail lengths removed from the track had been made useless by the explosion of gun cotton charges. Just then, in our lowly positions as infantrymen, we did not realize the importance of this railway to our commanders, but as a matter of fact it was the main line from Paris to Lille via Amiens, Albert and Arras. The enemy had not underestimated its value.

We bivouacked for the night on the outskirts of Hamelincourt, making ourselves shelters from the masses of stone, brickwork and timber lying near to hand. There was a superabundance of firewood—mostly soaking wet, unfortunately, but with patience we found some pieces which had escaped the recent deluges. Our fire was soon spluttering merrily, shaded by our waterproof sheets and my big German groundsheet, which I had always carried since Gueudecourt, as did others. They were far superior to ours in every respect. In this manner we did our best to dry our sodden clothing and warm ourselves, for the evenings at this time of year are invariably chilly, and this was no exception. All ranks were enjoined strictly to keep fires under cover as far as possible, although we had been surprised at the inactivity of the German planes. Perhaps they had been grounded by the bad weather, and this was the explanation at the time. Within a few days, however, we had cause to revise this opinion and attributed their temporary absence to deliberate policy.

In the gathering dusk, following allocation of various duties for the night—of which there were plenty, a large party being required by the engineers for an unnamed task—several of us went scrounging among the debris for more dry wood. Here we found a small house, more or less intact save for doors and windows, and after careful examination of the gaping doorway we went in, gingerly, step by step, fearful of booby traps. Nothing happened, and shortly after our C.S.M. and C.Q.M.S., having heard our news, promptly appropriated it for themselves and their minions, forsaking barely completed shelters. The C.S.M.'s batman was in the act of laying a fire in the grate of one of the two ground-floor rooms when two of us, exploring the cellar with my torch, spotted a cluster of gun cotton slabs in blue cardboard containers, smothered with printed instructions and diagrams in German, hanging from a cord about two feet from the floor. What looked like a slow-burning fuse was wound loosely round the cord, and as we traced it upwards, we heard the batman chopping wood directly above it.

We rushed up the cellar steps and raked out the wood and paper—sure enough, the end of the fuse terminated in a coil under the grate, and we and the surprised batman, now joined by the rest, thanked our lucky stars for a few moments. Spirited argument followed as to the best way of dismantling the arrangement, but such was our abysmal ignorance of explosives at that time, and so healthy was our respect for German ingenuity, that the C.S.M. ordered the immediate vacating of the house, and all concerned returned to their shelters. Some hours later I was told that an R.E. subaltern and his sergeant did what was necessary and moved in with their men, but we never found out what actually would have caused the explosion—the slow-burning fuse, or the burning through of the suspension cord followed by the drop to the floor. Had there been a suitable detonator in the gun cotton, the impact when the mass dropped would have set it off—with all above sitting unconcernedly round the fire above it.

It rained again heavily for part of the night, and by morning, as movement among the bivouacs became general, churned up mud added to our discomfort. In spite of this, numerous checks were made of arms, ammunition and equipment. At dusk, double rations having been distributed, we dumped our packs in tarpaulin-covered heaps and assumed battle order once more; being allowed, I seem to recall, to wear our leather jerkins.

We marched to St. Leger, another ruin, where we took a road to the north. Here we stumbled along in pitch blackness, with frequent halts, as though those in front were either meeting more obstacles or were unsure of the way. Eventually we left the road and started to plod eastward across the glutinous mud of what seemed to us recently ploughed fields.

Now reports of desultory rifle shots and of short bursts of machine and Lewis gun fire about a kilometre to our front indicated that we might be nearing our immediate goal. Away to the north also, perhaps five kilometres distant, we saw at intervals pinpoints and the faint surrounding aura of Verey lights. Daylight found us lining a cart track with a bank on either side, which we promptly designated a 'sunken road'. Half-right, in the approximately direction of Croisilles, firing broke out with considerable intensity, punctuated with the explosions of German shells.

They couldn't have been ours, because at this stage the advancing infantry were far in advance of their artillery, obstructed as they were at nearly every yard of the way. Guns were of no use, either, without shells, and tremendous supply difficulties had yet to be overcome by the already overworked ammunition columns.

As a matter of fact, a 4.5 howitzer battery did get into position near us during that day, while we remained lining the road awaiting events. When first arriving they didn't resemble howitzers at all, so thick was the mud on their coverings, and we could only guess at the future shell supply difficulty.

Very early the following morning we moved up in artillery formation across more fields in a thick mist. We proceeded slowly, therefore, but on reaching a road our officers checked on their maps and, as they appeared satisfied, we crossed it at right-angles, making our way in a clearing mist up a long gradual slope, culminating in a definite ridge. Here we extended and were ordered to get down in the wet grass until our officers, having again checked our position, waved us forward again. Rising to our feet, we saw at the bottom of the long slope of open fields perhaps a thousand yards distant, a dark brown band many yards in depth, threading its way as far as we could see it on either side of the front. Three hundred yards or so in the rear of this, we could see another band of staggering thickness, running approximately parallel with it. We came upon three khaki bodies lying about twenty yards apart. By their appearance they had not been there long, and were lads of the 6th Brigade of our division. They had been caught by an unlucky burst of machine-gun fire.

As we slowly picked our way forward, we made out the brown bands to be belts of rusty wire defences of terrific strength, and hoped fervently that we would not be called upon to surmount these obstacles that morning. Between the belts of wire we could make out the piles of sandbags and turned up earth of a trench system, and we were expecting to be fired on when a single machine-gun opened up, the bullets whistling high over our heads. We lay down under orders, and now advanced in short rushes of fifty yards or so by sections, between whiles eagerly examining the landscape before us, which stretched for several miles up a gentle slope behind the German trenches, dotted here and there with villages untouched as yet by shell fire. We wondered how much nearer that wire we were expected to go, and speculation among us became intense. Then we saw that those in front were dropping into a half-hidden cart track, and within a few seconds we had joined them in a final rush, considerably out of breath, with the machine-gun opposite still firing bursts.

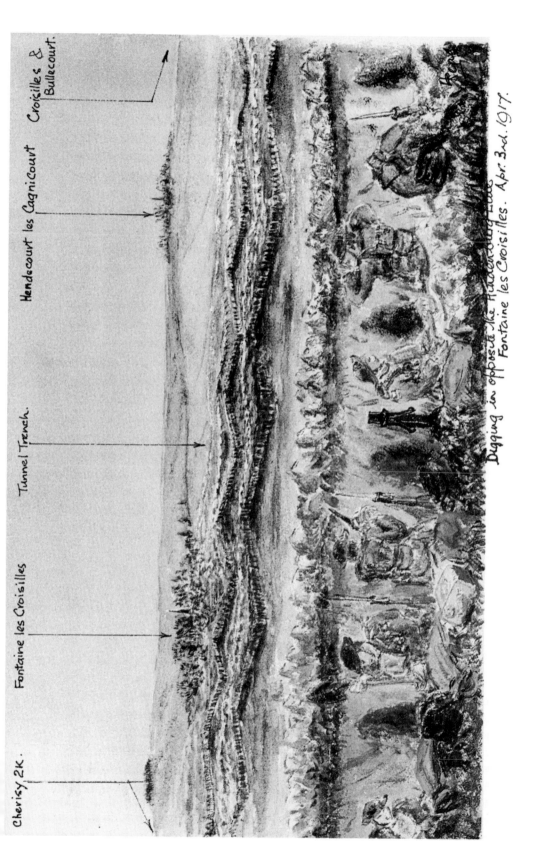

Cherisy. 2K.

Fontaine les Croisilles

Tunnel Trench.

Hendecourt les CagniCourt

Croisilles &
Bullecourt.

Digging in opposite the Hindenburg Line
Fontaine les Croisilles. Apr. 3rd. 1917.

As we crouched there, about 350 yards from the first wire belt, we were told to dig in—and to put our backs into it!

We needed no second bidding, expecting the shells to start dropping at any moment, and wishing that we had brought up twice as many shovels. Still, our entrenching tools were quite useful. Occasionally we would look over the top of our excavations and saw that parties of Germans were working in the approaches to the nearest village behind the reserve trench system. They had a concrete mixing machine and were trundling wheelbarrows of cement to and fro with a will. We wished that we had some of it, and many jokes were made as the lads dug. Through field glasses, it seemed that the Germans were joking also; some certainly appeared to be singing. They were about nine hundred yards away, and we thought of turning a Lewis on them, but just then we were too busy getting our own houses in order. By nightfall we possessed a tolerably deep trench, with funk holes dug into the side, and in the gathering dusk we saw that the Germany party had knocked off for the day, but their wheelbarrows, cement sacks and the various etceteras were still there—about eight or nine hundred yards off, we calculated. Perhaps we would interrupt them in the morning but, truth to tell, we could not escape a real feeling of uneasiness, difficult to define, but sensing the calm before the storm. Although no shells had fallen our way, around Croisilles it sounded as though a full-scale German bombardment was taking place. Indeed, in the half-light, we could see the gun flashes of the German batteries near Riencourt—another village, untouched as yet, on the low ridge half-right behind the Hindenburg system. Many of these shells were heavies, and we hoped that they would not switch in our direction.

We were told that a brigade of our division was in action at Croisilles, and that the Australians were having a go at Bullecourt. Apprehensive of the probable effects of five-nines on our improvised trench, we N.C.O.s inquired urgently for sandbags to build traverses and consolidate the parapet, but were told light-heartedly by two recently joined young subalterns that we wouldn't be there long enough to need them! At this we old 'uns looked at one another significantly, and then at those great rusty belts of barbed wire. With a wry grimace, Sergeant Chesterton ventured to hope that they were right and, breaking off, we attended to the duties of the night.

It turned bitterly cold, and we prevailed on the lads to deepen the trench for two hours or so, if not actually on duty. This kept some of them reasonably warm and occupied by turns until daylight and 'stand to', when it was apparent that the added protection gained had been well worth the effort.

The morning broke fine and clear, but very cold, and the enemy, having of course duly noted our digging efforts, put a field battery on to us, the 'whooshes' coming—one, two, three, four— 'daisy cutter' fashion, the H.E. either blowing our improvised parapets away in showers of clods, or missing by inches and bursting a hundred yards or so behind. We received these attentions at frequent intervals throughout the day, and the company sustained some casualties by shrapnel—one fatal, I recall.

Meanwhile, our own field batteries were getting into position behind us, and in the early evening commenced registering on targets to our front, including the village of Fontaine les Croisilles. The German working parties had ceased work an hour or so previously, although we had enjoyed scattering them once or twice with our Lewis fire. They wouldn't have relished the shrapnel the battery sent over. The F.O.O. observed his fire from our trench and was very pleased with himself when, at his second attempt, he hit the spire of the village church and a cloud of reddish dust rose and obscured the late golden sunlight in which it had been bathed seconds previously.

Throughout the following days we remained in this 'sunken road' trench, while the weather changed for the worse and the shelling increased greatly in intensity. Moreover, the German planes came over frequently, and they seemed to have the edge on ours. Indeed, we saw one of ours shot down directly above us, the blazing machine disintegrating midway to earth and falling in several smoking heaps amid the German wire round Fontaine. We hoped the pilot had died before he fell.

Bitterly cold winds brought showers of sleet and finally snow as darkness fell, and by morning—Easter Monday, 9th April 1917—everything around us as far as we could see was covered with a mantle of white, except the belts of German barbed wire, which stood out in stark relief against the wintry landscape. In our trench we moved with difficulty among pools of muddy snow water, and felt anything but comfortable, especially with no prospect of getting a hot drink.

Snow started to fall again, and a few miles to our left, in the neighbourhood of Arras, a tremendous cannonade commenced, continuing in a fashion reminiscent of the Somme.

Heavy firing was taking place also around Croisilles where, our captain told us, a brigade of our division was attacking the Hindenburg Line and, beyond them, the Australians were again assaulting Bullecourt. He told us that we were going forward as soon as that wire in front had been smashed by our guns and trench mortars, which afforded us some consolation, although privately we considered that they had a terrific task on their hands. Towards mid morning the snow ceased and the cannonades on either side of us became sporadic.

The trench became ankle-deep in snow water and it was still bitterly cold. Moreover, we were shelled methodically by field batteries. As darkness fell and ration parties stumbled to us across the open ground behind us, they were full of rumours of great British gains at Arras; also that the Australians had taken Bullecourt. The firing recommenced in that direction and continued at intervals for most of the night. In the meanwhile we saw that the villages in the rear of the German lines were lit by large fires, the pall of smoke above each thrown into relief by the flames, making an awe-inspiring spectacle. In spite of the miserable conditions and the continual shelling, we were in high spirits at what we took to be signs of a further imminent retreat by the enemy, and we even speculated as to whether morning would find the Hindenburg Line here evacuated by the turning of both flanks. Perhaps the two subalterns had been right after all!

These hopes suffered a severe shock shortly after daybreak, in the form of two registering five-nine howitzer shells upon our miserably inadequate defences, followed about fifteen minutes later by a continual stream of heavy shells which, whenever they found their mark, played havoc among us, especially in 'D' Company, who were lining a slight rise in the track to our right. These howitzer shells were very different propositions from the whizz-bangs of the previous days. Of much heavier calibre, they fell almost perpendicularly, rendering our funk holes practically useless.

We heard that the Australians had been driven out of Bullecourt, but that some of our 110th Brigade and our 62nd Brigade were still in the front Hindenburg trench near Croisilles. This village had been taken some days ago by our 7th Battalion. Heavy reverberations reached us from this neighbourhood where, we were told, our artillery was concentrating to support the advance. It slackened later in the day, but as darkness fell, the sky on either side of us flickered with the frequent explosions of heavy shells.

That evening, too, we moved to another position on the track some hundreds of yards to our right, and dug in feverishly some little distance in front of it, nearer the German wire, which here was as yet quite untouched. It would have been madness to attempt anything in the nature of a frontal attack here without terrific artillery preparation beforehand. This we knew to be impossible, as we had very little artillery behind us. We therefore hung on grimly as best we could, suffering pretty severely from five-nines in doing so. Not to put too fine a point on it, sheer exhaustion was slowly gaining the upper hand with us. Continual shelling, the constant necessity of removing debris, and deepening our miserable defences, coupled with lack of sleep—all these were beginning to tell, and the almost total lack of a hot meal or drink for over a week contributed to our sorry state. 'Tommy's Cookers', precious stores of dry twigs, and even matches had been long exhausted, and the cold water we had from petrol tins reeked with chloride of lime or petrol, or a mixture of both. Some men started to complain of small ulcers in their mouths, and I pooh-poohed these until I developed one of my own, when I hope I exhibited considerably more sympathy. The state of our feet generally was also beginning to give rise to real anxiety among we N.C.O.s. All the warning signals were there of trench foot becoming rife unless we were soon relieved. Cigarettes and tobacco likewise had practically disappeared among us. The precious nob-ends, carried in little tins by cigarette devotees and produced lovingly and inspected for a suitable 'two draws and a spit' after 'stand down' of a morning, were almost non-existent.

For several nights our fatigue parties assisted Royal Engineers to lay Bangalore torpedoes in the German wire, but in each instance the cold light of day showed that little, if any, real impression had been made. We found, too, that this wire was of a particularly stout, springy and venomously barbed type.

Possibly to cheer us, our subalterns told us that our 64th Brigade was astride the front Hindenburg trench at Cherisy, almost two kilometres north of our position, and that they were going to drive down it towards our front. In the event, of course, this proved so much wishful thinking, but the lads fastened on any tale of this kind eagerly, and who could blame them? In truth our little world was bounded by our trench, and we hadn't the slightest idea of what was happening even a few hundred yards to either our right or left.

Day followed day thus, although we were grateful that the enemy heavy shelling had now almost ceased by comparison with what had been handed out previously. We never saw a German now, and it was noticeable that any machine-gun fire came from somewhere in the support trench. No doubt the real peril, from our point of view, lurked in each apex of the German front line wire defences—there would be the crack machine-gun teams if a British attack developed.

So we reasoned in our sorry straits, as we endeavoured to maintain morale, dirty, unshaven, plastered with caked mud from head to foot, and of course, thoroughly louse-ridden. But eventually our prayers must have percolated through to Higher Command. One evening as dusk fell, shadowy figures approached over the top who we mistook for our ration carriers. They were relieving troops of another division, and we couldn't help noticing how their youngsters blanched visibly at close contact with the motley crew of scarecrows we had become. We had next to no trench store to hand over—some of our shovels, even, had been buried in debris—and it took only a few moments to transfer a dozen or so boxes of Mills grenades. Then we clambered up the parados we had made and were away up across the fields. After a few minutes we realized that we couldn't maintain that pace in our condition, and the havoc in our feet became only too apparent. Slowly we stumbled along, and eventually reached the outskirts of St Leger, on the ruins of which heavy German shells were dropping fairly frequently.

First Train on the Relaid Line ALBERT-ARRAS delayed at Hamelincourt evening of Apr. 15th(?) 1917.

Other companies were also drifting into our halting place for the night. In a sheltered cutting our field cookers provided hot soup and tea; we could smell it long before we got there. Our grimy 'old soldier' cooks stood with their ladles and dixies, their grinning, welcoming features lit redly by the glow from the half-open doors of their fires.

So we came back! Full now of hot tea and soup, with the promise of nearly a fortnight's mail when we reached Hamelin-court, those of us who had them wrapped themselves in their German groundsheets, the others content with the British variety. We lay down where we sat. Truthfully, we had achieved nothing, at the cost of a goodly number of our best men: some killed; some, we hoped, by now in Blighty. Sufficient for the day . . . We slept.

During the following day we made our ways back to Hamelin-court by platoons, frankly straggling at times because of the general state of our feet, and because our legs had suffered from disuse. I recall that, mercifully, no Red Tabs were encountered on the way, although our young subalterns were terribly apprehensive of this. In a drizzling rain (an April shower by other standards), we reached Hamelincourt and the shelter of the rail-way embankment, where we bivouacked for the night, cheered immensely, however, by the distribution of accumulated mail and a wash and shave under difficulties. When the weather improved we would try to remove the mud from our clothing.

Near Hamelincourt we found to our surprise that the line had been re-laid. That evening several shells dropped in the vicinity. Curiosity drove us to see a train upon it and we heard that one was due. Sure enough, by the level crossing on the Albert side stood a huge black locomotive with a string of freight vans behind, blowing off clouds of steam into the rain. It could go no further because one of the recent shells had dropped between the rails, right on the crossing, uprooting and twisting two rail lengths grotesquely and making a gaping black hole beneath.

After standing a few minutes thus, the crew backed the train down the line—presumably, and sensibly, away from more dan-ger—and within an hour or so Sappers were busy repairing the damage, which must have taken many hours to make good.

That night we felt none too comfortable in our funk holes by the embankment, as more shells arrived at intervals, aimed at the line. While there were no more direct hits, several fell unpleasantly near. Indeed, we were not at all sorry to fall in and move off early on the following morning, which broke fine and sunny. Showers intervened now and then as we retraced our steps as far as Moyenneville. Here the battalion took a fork to the left, finishing our day's march in the ruins of Douchy les Ayette.

Here we improved the shelters other troops had left and enjoyed the warmth of good fires made from the plentiful rubbish lying around. Regular hot meals again were another godsend. We began to scrape off the mud and recovered our packs and greatcoats, besides having the issue of a blanket. Our spirits rose further at the news of our coming march back to civilization; on the follow-ing day, it was said.

When the remains of the company paraded in readiness to move off, we felt fairly presentable under the circumstances, and that day, in bright sunshine, we marched across our old trench lines to the north of Berles-au-Bois, our route lying through Ad-infer and Ransart to the inhabited village of Bailleulval. Although footsore, great was our delight at getting once more within the 'pale'. The little shop where we could buy candles, biscuits and chocolate; the little *estaminet* dispensing *bière, vin blanc, vin rouge, citron, grenadine*; the sounds of female voices—all these seemed veritable bulwarks of civilization to wearily returning soldiers, sated with vistas of mile upon mile of silent, untended fields dotted with ruined, desolate homesteads.

The Return
Bailleulval
Apr-17

CHAPTER 15

UNEXPECTED NEWS

THERE was almost a holiday atmosphere about our first day at Bailleulval. An important factor in this was the spring sunshine at last. In our barn, lying on the clean, sweet-smelling straw, we listened to the familiar barnyard sounds, well content, until the orderly sergeant threw open the big black double gates and invited two platoons of 'C' Company to 'rise and shine'—which was exactly what we did, as the sunlight poured in. Stripped to the waist, the lads sluiced pump water over themselves, after shaving with cracked mirrors stuck at all angles in chinks on the mud and wattle barn wall; they swilled again and scrubbed themselves dry with soap-caked scourges of towels. Then surely, never was there such a brushing-off of mud, polishing of buttons and badges and greasing of boots, while the smell of bacon fat and rashers cooking drifted in. A leisurely breakfast, following which rifle cleaning and inspection followed, and I recall the young subaltern's freshly shaved chubby features as I attended his circuit of the platoon to look down the barrels. What next . . . ? Foot inspection, as two men had reported for sick parade with foot trouble. This was well worthwhile, as some hot water was produced by the cooks and feet were duly washed in a swill tub borrowed from the farmer. The enormous holes in most socks were my outstanding recollection of this parade, and lists were duly made for submission to C.Q.M.S. Peach. Some men had spare clean pairs which as yet they had not bothered to put on; now they did so.

I recall that all paraded at noon for Captain Warner's inspection, reading of orders, etc., and the rest of the day was pay parade and checking ammunition and stores.

In the late afternoon Jackie and I determined to revisit Berles, only five kilometres or so from our billet. We made good progress.

Beyond Bailleulmont we sat down by the roadside for an 'easy', as it was a beautiful evening and we had only another two kilometres to go. Hearing a lorry rattling up the road towards us we stood up, hoping to obtain a lift to Berles, but to our disgust the A.S.C. driver and his mate took no notice of our shouts and passed us without any slackening of speed. As we were pouring maledictions on the receding lorry and its crew, we noticed that the tailboard was down. We walked on and saw something bulky and whitish jolt over it and fall onto the ground almost as the lorry disappeared round a bend. Increasing our pace, we soon reached the object, which lay at the roadside, and saw to our delight that it was a chilled, linen-wrapped carcase of mutton. We hid our prize carefully in a clump of stunted bushes, taking careful note of the position before resuming our journey, and the sun was still shining quite strongly when we came down the small hill into the long street of Berles.

The tilting weathervane of the damaged church threw back the rays of the setting sun as of yore, and as we went round to look beyond the churchyard wall we saw again the rows of little wooden crosses, now almost hidden by the growth of lush grass and weeds, marking the graves of our mates of 1915/16, and of others who had fallen since in the Berles sector.

Returning to the familiar street, sounds of hammering came to us from a dozen or more houses, while ladders stood reared against shell-spattered walls. Several supported ageing men who were endeavouring to repair the worst ravages of shell fire. We greeted one old man. '*Bon soir*, Father!' shouted Jackie, '*obus fini*, eh?', to which the old peasant, turning on his ladder, replied, '*ah, oui monsieur—les Boches* . . . so!' making such an emphatic sweep with his free arm in an easterly direction that he nearly tumbled from his perch.

There were still some British troops in the village, but of another division. They were walking abroad in caps with buttons and badges bright. The tide of war, having beaten against Berles-au-Bois for more than two years, had suddenly receded leaving the village, not exactly high and dry, but very much a back area.

At our knock Émilienne opened the door to us. She did not know Jackie, as he had not been a Lewis gunner in those early days, but when she saw me after a hard look surprised recognition lit her features and became a smile of pleasure.

'Hullo, Émilienne!'

'*Oh, monsieur*—how it is good, you are come back, *hein*. Maman . . . !'

I don't know exactly why we did so—it seemed quite a natural thing to do at the time—but we kissed in the French fashion and we three entered the house. Jackie and I were among friends here . . . 'Maman! Louise! *Les Lestaires* come back!' I greeted Maman, and Skinny Liz, their father, little Étienne, now grown considerably and hauled out of bed for my benefit. Jackie entered into the spirit of the evening with relish. After we had clinked glasses all round and wished one another '*bonne chance et bonne santé*', Émilienne made us tell her of the Somme and of our mates who used to sit around the stove there on those winter evenings of 1915—now gone. 'Tommee Butler, Horace Phillips, Freddie Smith, *monsieur* Lin-ee-ker, Jack Quincy . . .' She referred to his letter and said she had written to him, but had never heard from him again . . . I told her . . . so we passed perhaps an hour.

Well, we told them, we must be getting back, as we had a good walk in front of us. If we could manage it we could come over again before we left Bailleulval. Émilienne and her mother put on their shawls and walked with us as far as the church, where we bade them *au revoir* and set out at a good step, marvelling that these good folks should have retained such kindly thoughts of us amid such trouble of their own. 'Although,' commented Jackie, 'they must have salted away a tidy bit somewhere, selling coffee and stuff to the troops as they've done for a couple of years!'

The night was fine but dark, and we maintained a steady pace until we neared the spot where we judged we had hidden the carcase. In the event, it proved extremely difficult to locate, but when we had almost given up, and Jackie was muttering that 'some lousy b. . . must have seen us and taken it', he almost fell over it. For the remainder of our journey we carried it between us, but we had considerable difficulty in reaching the cookhouse behind our barn unobserved. At length, having hidden it under some sacking, as doubtless the cooks were in the local *estaminet*, we sat down thankfully on the straw by our kits, tired, but thoroughly pleased with our evening. We had returned in good time, as the 'First Post' bugle had just sounded, followed by the call for orderly sergeants.

Shortly after, our orderly sergeant, hurrying to Battalion H.Q. for orders, shouted my name as he passed the doorway. Seeing me, he exclaimed, 'at last! Sergeant, I've been looking for you most of the evening. They want you at Battalion Orderly Room.' Hurriedly I donned belt and sidearms again, and rubbed the dust from my boots with a wisp of straw as he waited. Together we almost doubled up the village street. When we arrived at Battalion H.Q., he joined the line of orderly sergeants standing outside, while I found my way into a back room lit with half a dozen candles, where two clerks were poring over typewriters. A signaller sat in a corner amid festoons of wires and 'phones. A clerk looked up, and on seeing me his face broadened into a grin. 'Some blokes have all the luck, Sarge, don't they?' Suspecting a leg-pull of sorts, I was trying to counter his sally suitably when he picked up a message from a pile in a tray, and read that I was to report to Divisional H.Q. at Adinfer Wood on the following morning for an interview. He added, 'Captain Warner knows. Tomorrow evening you'll probably be off to Blighty—Commission.'

This was stunning news, and left me almost speechless. Since the previous November, when Captain Warner talked to me at the Hohenzollern Redoubt, I'd scarcely given it a single thought. Now, suddenly, it was upon me with all the attendant doubts and fears. I suppose I thanked him and asked him if he knew whereabouts in Adinfer Wood I would find 21st Division H.Q. The signaller gave me a pretty good direction, over the old trench lines, which, in the event, I took, following the track of newly laid telephone cables.

I made my way back to our barn slowly, as in a kind of dream, having completely forgotten the events of the evening. Jackie must have seen that something had happened, for I caught his naturally curious look of inquiry in those wide eyes of his, as he stared out at me from his blankets. Mechanically, I undressed and rolled myself up beside him, wondering just how I should tell him. Around, in the candlelight just before 'lights out' blew, the lads were discussing the news of the Bolshevik Revolution as they lay there, and possible implications of the total collapse of the Russian war effort.

I heard myself telling Jackie, in a low voice, and in so doing I realized, as I spoke, the first pang of parting from the surviving remnants of those grand mates with whom I had been fortunate enough to soldier so long; felt almost a deserter.

Jackie wished me the best of luck, of course, and before sleep came at length I thought of the sheep's carcase which Jackie had left with the company cooks. What a prize that had seemed but an hour or so previously—and now, by comparison with the jumble of thoughts which tumbled over and over in my brain, centred on England again, how insignificant!

The next morning I was advised by Captain Warner, who wished me the best of luck and stood me a whisky, to take the short cut across the old trench lines to Adinfer Wood, where I had to go to see General Campbell at Divisional H.Q. This I did, and duly found it in a collection of newly erected Nissen huts, some little distance from the road, among the tall trees. While waiting outside the hut in which the General was to interview us, I was joined by two corporals of the 9th Battalion, Hemstock and Shooter by name, and the three of us waited outside General Campbell's sanctum with no little trepidation until such time as our names should be called.

My turn came first. In I went and saluted, as smartly as I could, the swarthy be-ribboned figure sitting back in the chair behind a baize-covered table littered with papers. General Campbell summed me up in a glance as I stood stiffly to attention before him, but at once put me at my ease with a kindly word. Leaning over the table, he examined my papers and asked me several questions, most of which I have now forgotten, concluding by asking me whether I had been with my battalion on the Somme. This last query, I remember, I answered with something like a thrill—confidently, and, as I noticed his appreciative expression, proudly—for somehow that look from him compensated me for any privations I may have endured up to that moment. I believe that he signed my papers, and after a final homily from him I saluted and withdrew.

Shooter passed me on his way in, and I suppose my face must have radiated the same pleasure as his did as I watched him emerge a few minutes later, making way for Hemstock. The following night Shooter, Hemstock and myself slept at a Salvation Army canteen at Mondicourt. We had made our farewells to our companions, and had encountered each other once more on the road back to railhead. The Salvation Army people were very good to us, and I would like to say here that they were out to give of their best to the soldiers who came their way.

The next day we managed to get as far as Abbeville, but a further three days had elapsed before we three weary travellers, after a night in the train coming from London, alighted at the tiny station of Glen Parva, near Leicester, and made our way up the 150 yards or so of village street to the depot of the 17th Regiment. The greater part of three years had elapsed since I had last seen those high red-brick walls, and the familiar barrack gates. They had not changed, yet what metamorphoses three years had wrought in us!

Late on a warm September evening in 1914, four thousand of us, marching in fours in our civvy clothes, had passed out of these same gates *en route* for Wigston station and Aldershot, singing the songs of the moment, athirst for the adventure just begun. Young and old; callow youths such as we had been then, grown men in their prime, old soldiers and sailors, well-to-do men and penniless men of 'no fixed abode'; the good, the bad—all in column of fours on that September evening, singing 'McNamara's Band' . . . and now their bones lay scattered over Flanders and Picardy, save for a fortunate few like we three, home from the wars for a space.

On seeing us, the sentry halted and stood at ease before the guardroom door. No doubt he was curious concerning our shabby khaki and greasy, frayed webbing, our dirty yellow distinguishing squares. We had felt rather proud of ourselves, but on discovering that the sergeant of the guard was a 2nd Battalion man with two wound stripes, we came to the conclusion that we might be overestimating the furore to be occasioned by our appearance. As we walked across to the orderly room with him, asking him what things were like, he replied somewhat cryptically that, 'they weren't so bad if you could get on the right side of the b. . . old fossils in charge.' This turned out to be the case.

CHAPTER 16

ENGLAND, 1917

How right that sergeant was! We three were separated immediately. I was allocated to a company sergeant-major apparently in charge of two barrack blocks, and reported at his office. He was over at the sergeants' mess at breakfast and I waited for him with as much patience as I could command, as I was hungry. I saw Shooter and Hemstock disappear into a dining hall carrying mugs and plates, and reappear subsequently, apparently well filled.

When eventually he hove in sight—a greying, middle-aged man with long, twirled, waxed moustaches, and buttons immaculately bright—he looked me up and down as he approached as though I was something the tide had washed up. Sensing possible trouble, I stood rigidly to attention as I reported myself. Without speaking, he unlocked his office, walked in, hung up his cap, straightened his tunic leisurely and turned. Then, 'we've got yer details, report here 10.15 to see Major . . .' (I've forgotten his name), and he sat down and turned to some documents without another word. I stood there, hesitant, for some moments waiting for him to look up, but he didn't. I broke the silence and asked him if I could get some breakfast as I had been in the train all night. He grunted, scarcely looking up. 'Sergeants' mess and look sharp, or they'll have cleared.' Thanking him, I departed, thinking uncharitably about him. I recalled where the sergeants' mess was in 1914; near the wet canteen, where so many hundreds of us struggled in vain to get a cupful of slops of warm beer. It was still there. The few still sitting there gave me a better welcome. I breakfasted well, read the morning paper, and after a good wash and brush-up I left my rifle and equipment with the mess sergeant, less my belt and sidearms. He told me I'd probably go on leave that day and that they would give me a block to look after when I returned.

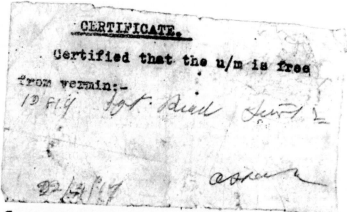

CERTIFICATE.

Certified that the u/m is free
from vermin:-

Certificate produced with PASS, and necessary
before boarding boat for England, issued by
Baths Unit. Boulogne. April 1917.

Near Hurstmonceux. Apr. '17.
On a Country Walk with my Father.

Feeling greatly refreshed, I duly reported at 10.15 to see Major Blank. I entered after a peremptory 'come in!' from the C.S.M. and duly saluted the amiable, stoutish, middle-aged major sitting behind the table in front of me. The C.S.M. took a position behind him. 'Sergeant Read, sir, 8th Battalion for O.T.C., details here, sir,' and he handed the major a sheet of paper. As he read, I thought I saw the major's expression change and stood expectant. 'H'm.' Silence. Then, 'I see, Sergeant, that unfortunately your rank is acting. I'm afraid you will have to take down your stripes and revert to the rank of private after—let's see,' and he looked at the wall calendar, 'er—May the . . .'. I forget the date he mentioned, but it was twenty-eight days after reporting to the depot. 'A pity, pity, but cannot be helped, it seems!'

I felt stunned and momentarily bereft of speech as I heard him; the nearest parallel I can think of is a convicted criminal hearing sentence pronounced. Then I'm afraid my feelings got the better of me and I said, 'but, sir, I should never have come home had I known that this would happen. Can I go back to the battalion?' And I suppose I moved my right arm from the position of attention. 'Stand to attention!' yelled the sergeant-major, and I was sure I saw a distinct smirk cross his features as, hastily, I drew back my hand.

The major looked up at him, plainly surprised and annoyed. Then he turned to me. 'I'm afraid things have gone too far for that now, Sergeant. You might be able to get in touch with your adjutant. In any case, you go on leave today and you won't be here long. I seems a great pity, though.'

I thanked him, saluted and departed with black thoughts of that 'Regular' sergeant-major. Later that day I met Shooter and Hemstock on Leicester Station. They were both in the same boat as I was. We were not a cheerful trio, but were together in the wish to return to our battalions rather than submit to such indignity— the equivalent of being stripped—and in that frame of mind we parted for a fortnight, our first task on reaching home to write to our respective adjutants.

I went to Eastbourne where, of course, my parents were very surprised to see me only five months after my leave the previous December. 'Here I am, Mum,' I remember saying. 'O.T.C. for

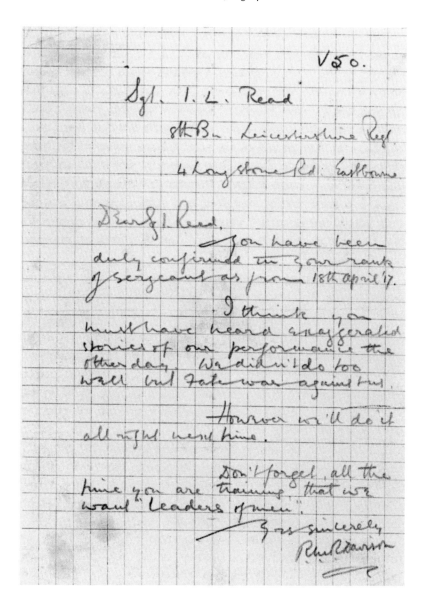

√50.

Sgt. I. L. Read
8th Bn. Leicestershire Regt.
4 Longstone Rd. Eastbourne.

Dear Sgt Read,
You have been
duly confirmed in your rank
of sergeant as from 18th April '17.
I think you
must have heard exaggerated
stories of our performance the
other day. We didn't do too
well but fate was against us.
However we'll do it
all right next time.
Don't forget, all the
time you are training, that we
want "Leaders of men".
Yours sincerely,
Chas R Davison

Commission . . . p'raps!', adding a cautionary note, and thinking of hazards in store.

I duly wrote to Captain Davison, our adjutant, and above you will see his reply, which gladdened my heart as nothing had done since I'd landed in England. Now that darned C.S.M. could jump in the lake as far as I was concerned.

Captain Davison's letter calls for a word or two of explanation. At the depot we had heard rumours of a considerable reverse suffered by the 110th Brigade in a general attack on the Hindenburg Line on 3rd May, and in my letter I ventured to hope that this was not the case. His reply indicates far more plainly than I could explain, the dogged, unbreakable spirit of a British regimental officer at that period of the war. I have treasured his letter ever since; indeed, it was a clear pattern to follow. Many years afterwards, at a 110th Brigade reunion at Leicester in the mid 1930s, I learned that he had died in a subsequent attack at the same place, but in 1964 I ascertained from the Commonwealth War Graves Commission that he had died of wounds at a hospital near London.

After the spell of home leave we remained at the depot for several weeks, now secure in rank, during which my duties there were many, varied and almost unceasing. To my chagrin my C.S.M. tormentor had departed; where, no one appeared to know (but more of him anon), and as yet he had not been replaced.

At this period of the war conscription had been introduced, and the authorities were busily engaged in a man-hunt, described as a 'combing-out' process. This involved, in effect, the screening by local tribunals throughout the country, of every male civilian within very wide age limits. If the tribunal decided that the job a man was doing was not of vital necessity to the war effort, he duly received notice to attend for medical examination and, if passed in either A or B categories, he received calling-up papers. Certain border-line cases were deferred for a few months for reconsideration, or excused service on medical grounds, but the teeth of the comb were very fine, and comparatively few reasonably fit men between the ages of eighteen and forty-five escaped. The result was that the barrack blocks at the depot housed a constantly changing crowd of civilians of widely diverse age groups and all sorts and conditions of men who, often after only a few hours on the barrack square, were issued with clothing and made up into drafts for the training camps of Brockton in Staffordshire, or Catterick Bridge in Yorkshire. I was put in charge of one of these barrack blocks, and took possession of a cubicle at the top of the stairs on the first floor. Corporal Hemstock was my understudy, and he occupied another cubicle on the opposite side of the landing. An elderly Regular sergeant was in charge of the other block, and Corporal Shooter went to assist him.

These two main blocks received intakes of recruits during alternate weeks, each taking them for a week at a time. In this manner, the block actually receiving them direct from their homes filled, while the other block emptied as drafts of the week-old soldiers were made up and sent off either to Brockton or to Catterick Bridge, until by the weekend only 'the lame, the halt and the sick' remained, thus providing accommodation for the following week's intake.

We used to watch with considerable misgiving the drafts march out of the barrack gates in their new, often ill-fitting, khaki and heavy boots, for it was obvious then that many of these men could not sustain for any length of time the rigours of the life we had but recently left behind; quite apart from any damage the enemy might do them. The very thought of military service must have filled the minds of many of the older men with feelings akin to despair, especially if they were married with families, and we could not help sympathizing privately with their lot. It brought home to us also, as nothing else could have done, the terrible toll of the manpower of this nation taken by the war, when replacements with physical disabilities, such as we saw here, were necessary to maintain the strength of the armies.

These 'residues' left behind for various reasons—mostly for foot or eye troubles, but in several instances because of fits—gave us real headaches at times; especially the latter gentry, who threw their fits in the middle of the night, awoke the whole block, and were execrated by recruits and staff alike. In every case but one that came under my notice, these so-called 'fits' were part of an act put on by 'lead-swingers' (to use the argot of the period), in an attempt to get discharged. This was, however, most difficult to prove, but in more than one case the culprits found that their exertions were in vain.

Our other main problem at the depot just then was that of the 'Conscientious Objectors', this description being then a recent addition to the vocabulary of the British nation. I well remember the glorious late spring morning when, on reporting back from

275

leave, I saw a squad of about twenty men in civilian clothes on the barrack square. An old colour sergeant was endeavouring, without success, to form them into two ranks as they stood about, many with hands deep in trouser pockets. They appeared so unusually slovenly that I commented on this to the sergeant of the guard on the main gate. 'Them? Them there? They're a bloody lot of Conchies. Been rounded up in the last few days. Some of us've had a proper holiday, too, bringing 'em in from all over the county. I'd shoot the bloody lot—look at 'em! Look at 'em now!'

I looked, and saw them slouching slowly round the perimeter of the barrack square, with the sergeant and the escort of two men keeping up with them, as they deliberately flouted authority by studied insolence and nonchalance amounting to open defiance. They had all refused to put on uniform.

If hate is the word, I hated these figures of men just then, far more than any German. At least the Germans were worthy of respect as fighters, but when I thought of what my mates might possibly be enduring then, in front of Fontaine les Croisilles, while these long-haired apologies for men skulked at home and went to these extremes to avoid what we deemed to be their clear responsibilities to their country . . . Hemstock, Shooter and I were in complete agreement with the sergeant on the gate. Almost fifty years after, I'm afraid I still feel the same about 99 per cent of them and their kind—an opinion perpetuated, perhaps by experiences of similar conduct in a second world war.

During the six weeks or so that I was at the depot, my duties brought me into contact with a good many of them. I met only one who, in my opinion and that of my colleagues there, genuinely objected to military service on religious grounds, as I shall relate.

We two sergeants in charge used to report every morning to the major, who held office at 09.30 hours. He seemed quite pleased that we had all been duly confirmed in our ranks. There always seemed to be plenty on the agenda, consideration of requests for special leave home taking most of the time. Actually, our additional duties were never-ending and included taking our turns at guard commander, firing parties at funerals, picking up deserters or Conchies. We took the Conchies down to Wormwood Scrubs prison after sentences by courts martial, generally of either 84 or 112 days there, these trips always taking place on Saturdays. I remember taking three there, each occasion being quite an experience.

I suppose I was N.C.O. in charge of the firing party at more than a dozen military funerals, mostly of soldiers dying of wounds at the great base hospital in Leicester, the actual interments taking place at the nearby Welford Road Cemetery. Several times a week, midday saw me parading my party, generally unchanged, running through the reversed arms drill and volley firing before the break for dinner. Then parade again, this time ready to march off. A quick check of uniforms, buttons, boots and webbing, followed by rifle inspection and the issue of three blank cartridges per man (the spent cases of which had to be picked up from the grave side and returned to store) and off we went to the nearby village station where we took train for Leicester, or wherever the funeral was to take place, the buglers and one man carrying a large folded Union Flag bringing up the rear.

We became quite expert at this job; that is to say, conversant with the various burial services, and, with a little practice, able to get the necessary orders executed smartly and volleys which rang out like a single shot, instead of a ragged, imitation of a *feu de joie*. Indeed, until I had mastered the necessary technique, I was always on thorns until the ceremony was over, particularly when a crowd was present, which was frequently the case. A few of the funerals were at country villages in Leicestershire, and I recall that we liked these best because of the refreshments before and after, provided for our benefit by the kindly folk, the relatives and neighbours.

Somehow, however, all this business seemed so unnecessary to us in the light of what we had seen in France, that we made grim jokes about it all in carrying out our parts of the ceremonial. To us it was a form of showmanship, a convention, possibly to satisfy the mourners, but we asked ourselves repeatedly what possible good it did—as though the poor, torn and frequently gangrened soldier within the coffin, to whom the last call had come at length as a merciful release from pain, knew anything about it! As an example of what I mean, I instance the funeral of a Salvationist, whose corps really 'made a day of it', as the saying goes. Flashing silver instruments in the summer afternoon sun, with the crashing, penetrating cacophony of sound of which they are capable . . .

'Blood and Fire!', countless 'Hallelujahs!' . . . and all that sort of thing. Notwithstanding their real grief, and obvious affection for their dead comrade, we could see that they liked this pageantry. Our chaps certainly did not, for it was very hot, and they longed, as I did, to relax and unhook the tight collars of their tunics. Standing at the graveside we caught, amidst the perfume of the many floral offerings, the noxious smell of gangrened flesh. Several of the fellows looked at me significantly, and I could guess their thoughts. Listening to the flood of prayer and oration, I was thinking along the same lines myself: 'get on with it, and leave the poor so-and-so in peace.'

On a somewhat less sombre note, I turn again to the Conchies, and my first visit to Wormwood Scrubs with one. All went well until we changed at Willesden Junction for the electric train to Wood Lane. He was a big, husky type. At Willesden he requested permission to visit the lavatory, which I granted, as it seemed reasonable enough. The two men of the escort and I, having seen him into a W.C. (for which there was about the longest queue I have ever seen), waited outside for him to emerge. Minutes passed and he didn't. We listened, and, on looking under and then over the door, saw that the cubicle was empty. From marks made by his feet on the partition wall, I could see that he had gained the top. By a stroke of luck, as one of the escort assisted me to claw over the top myself, I saw our man disappear into a cubicle several yards up the block. Hastily we changed places, as I told him to go along the top and corner our quarry, the other escort to go along outside in case he came out and ran. The penny-in-the-slot apparatus said 'Engaged' and we couldn't effect an entry by normal means. Already my hands and arms were black with accumulated dust, and it was in no very amiable frame of mind that I went to find someone on the stationmaster's staff to arrange to break in. I was fortunate in finding a foreman almost immediately, who came along with me, but a small crowd of travellers was now gathering, including many servicemen. The foreman and I now resorted to argument with our quarry within, reinforced by the member of the escort kneeling on the filthy top of the partitioning, shaking the worst of the shock-ingly black dust from his hands and uniform as he adjured him to 'stop acting like a bloody fool!'

After a few minutes this seemed to have the desired effect. We heard the bolt shot and our man emerged—a sorry spectacle—to be handcuffed at once to the escort standing ready beside me with the 'bracelets' which we carried for emergencies of this kind.

As our party issued from the lavatory, headed by the foreman, and made for the electric train to Wood Lane, derisive shouts, catcalls and remarks pursued us along the platform from the many servicemen and their women companions, whose sympathies were wholly with the grimy figure in civvies who, no doubt, they took for a deserter. We didn't wait to inform them of the facts, we were late already. On the short journey to Wood Lane we did our best to clean ourselves, keeping silence with difficulty when meeting the eyes of the now-smirking Conchie. No doubt, we thought—and fervently hoped—they would take the smile off his face in the Scrubs; and they certainly did, shortly after we had entered by the main gate and crossed the pleasant garden-like approach to the reception office. After I'd handed over his documents, the warder there made him turn out all his pockets, one after the other, while he made a complete list: a surprising collection lay on the table, including a fair amount of money. He had to sign the list, after checking it, and then he was told he was to have a bath. For the first time he seemed to realize that he was not exactly going to do as he liked any longer, and as we left to get a wash and brush-up, the smirk had been replaced by a half-frightened look. As we towelled and brushed ourselves we heard the metallic clang of a heavy door—a cell door?

We were glad enough to regain the street outside, passing on the way to the gate several prisoners in dark brown denim jackets and trousers, studded plentifully with black broad arrows. In a cubicle near the gate, a prisoner stood talking to a woman visitor through a grille. Altogether a memorable, but at times distinctly unpleasant, Saturday afternoon.

I should have said that both of the escort were, like myself, waiting to go to O.T.C. Although they were privates, they were above average types, one a huge chap from the 6th Battalion born, he told me, in India, which explained his permanent suntan. We got on well together and arranged to meet at Euston on the Sunday evening to return to the depot, as all three of us had weekend leave, having parents or other attractions in or near London.

The two following Saturdays saw us repeat the journey; the first quite without incident, with a pale, colourless-looking youth with long hair, for whom we had a sneaking sympathy as we left him at the reception office, as he had remarked on the 'lovely garden' on the way there from the main gate! On the second occasion, however, our prisoner was an entirely different type: a strongly-built, pleasant-looking, well-spoken fellow of medium height. I should say his age was about twenty-five. We had all seen him for days past in the guardroom after sentence. He was a vegetarian and was allowed to have food brought to him from outside while there, but we just failed to understand at all why such a seemingly good chap should have chosen this course. He was, I recall, the son of a well-to-do manufacturer in the Hinckley district.

As usual, we caught a London-bound train at Nuneaton for Willesden Junction. Having a compartment to ourselves, and partly to while away the hours of the journey, we got into conversation with him and, after a slow start, fired questions at him one after the other, in the end with no reservations on either side. We could not help being impressed by what, for lack of a better description, I would call the common sense sincerity, without a lot of doctrinaire religious trimmings, which permeated his opinions. He just believed it wrong to fight anyone—about anything, any time—and he joined heartily in the general laughter when we told him that, over there, he would be darned lucky if he ever saw someone to fight! Rather the reverse; Jerry's five-nines, or rum jars, or machine-gun bullets, would probably find him first.

As we approached Willesden he said suddenly, 'Look here, Sergeant, I don't suppose I shall see the outside world again for three or four months. What about us all going on to Euston and doing a matinée somewhere? I'll do the necessary. You've been sports, what about it?' . . . and we did: he took us to the old Alhambra. He was the only one who had been there before—a number of times, he told us. We thoroughly enjoyed it, but it was so late when we emerged into Leicester Square that I began to worry about what the Scrubs people were thinking. After all these years, I recall that we eventually alighted at the prison from a taxi, but just where we got in it I cannot say. I remember, though, that the taxi driver thought we were a rum lot!

On arrival we found that they had telephoned to the depot and had been told that we were on the way, but probably had missed a connection. I didn't feel very happy at the prospect of making explanations on the Monday morning. In the event, however, nothing was said. On the other hand, our man had made us think far more seriously about the Conscientious Objector problem than we would have done had he been of the usual kind. We did now see that there were instances of genuine belief among the welter of those hiding under the cloak of religious scruples, who were prepared to suffer much for them. Later on I often wondered how he fared. He was a really brave man.

I recall two other events, now history, which occurred before we left the depot: General Plumer's successful attack and capture of the Messines Ridge near Ypres, and the first mass daylight raid by German planes on London one summer morning, when, among other terrible casualties, those among the children at an East End school remain in the memory. Truly a sinister augury for the future.

At length our orders came: Shooter and I to report to No. 8 Cadet Battalion at Whittington Barracks, Lichfield, and Hemstock to another at Rhyl. On the whole we had enjoyed our stay at Glen Parva, but wondered now what the future held in store for us.

CHAPTER 17

LICHFIELD—NEWHAVEN—CHERBOURG

DURING the afternoon of that day in early July 1917 a steady stream of taxis, either from Tamworth or Lichfield, deposited well over a hundred warrant officers, N.C.O.s and privates at the gates of Whittington Barracks—the depot of the South Staffordshire Regiment, but now appropriated for another purpose. Here a Regular captain of the Northumberland Fusiliers, a Grenadier subaltern and a Regular company sergeant-major of the West Yorkshire Regiment, with four sergeants at his beck and call, swiftly sorted us into four platoons and told us that together we constituted the new 'F' Company of No. 8 Cadet Battalion, the previous 'F' Company having passed out about ten days previously.

In the late afternoon, having been allotted our beds and deposited our kits thereon, we paraded for the first time as a company and were issued with a white hatband bearing a red '8' in the centre. At first sight we were a strange-looking collection—a C.S.M. with the M.C., D.C.M. and M.M. standing in the ranks beside a lance-corporal of the Black Watch—and so on. But at the word of command the parade sprang to attention and the West Yorkshire C.S.M. handed over to our new company commander. He stood us at ease and then gave us a short homily, the substance of which was that if we worked and studied hard, we had nothing to fear, and that he was quite certain we would find the instructors helpful at all times. It was up to us!

We noticed then that he wore a special glove on his left hand and that on his sleeve were two wound stripes. He told us that dinner would be at 7 p.m. and he looked forward to meeting us there. The parade then dismissed. Dixies of tea, slices of bread and butter and pieces of cake were forthcoming at the entrance to the barrack room, for which we produced our own utensils.

After that we settled down on our beds, getting acquainted with our next-bed neighbours, shaving, cleaning our buttons, some writing hurried letters, doubtless to say they had 'arrived'.

Just before seven we filed into the dining hall with some diffidence. Near the entrance stood our company commander and the Grenadier lieutenant in their mess kits, which caused us some needless apprehension at first. They entered into conversations with us, the captain chatting smilingly with the company sergeant-major with the imposing row of decorations. A bell sounded and we all filed in and took our places along either side of four long tables. The captain said a short grace, we sat down, and a mixed force of older soldier waiters and W.A.A.C. waitresses served soup. For many of us this was a new experience. The sight of spotless white napery, shining cutlery (and the usage of same), and the table manners in polite society were our first lessons in the process of becoming 'officers and gentlemen'.

To the best of my recollection no intoxicants were ever served at dinner, but at the close of the meal the captain rose and raised his glass, addressing the Grenadier at the other end of the room, saying, 'Mr Vice . . . the King'. All rose, including the Grenadier who, raising his glass, addressed the company: 'Gentlemen, the King!' And thus we learned to honour the Loyal Toast in the traditional fashion of most British Army messes—a most valuable lesson, showing how matters were conducted 'decently and in order'. Thereafter, by rota, a cadet presided at dinner and another took the role of vice president, and this method was adopted to teach us many things. By turns we were orderly officer, orderly sergeant, guard commander, platoon and company commander; the latter an experience many of us rather dreaded, as it entailed drilling and manoeuvring the company through a whole series of evolutions on the parade ground. In the event it wasn't too bad at all, although in a few cases cadets failed dismally at this hurdle. This, and failure to speak and instruct on various subjects, were the main reasons why a few of us disappeared at intervals, having unfortunately been R.T.U.—Returned to Unit—as unsuitable.

There was no doubt that we received splendid instruction here for undertaking the responsibilities of commissioned rank—principally training for ruthless war as junior leaders. For me it was four months of absolute physical fitness; of striving for all I was worth to attain the end marked out by our instructors. In the possession of healthy bodies and sharpened faculties, we were tuned up to concert pitch, although I will admit that the bugbear of possibly being 'Returned to Unit' as unsuitable worried us at times and acted as an additional spur.

I feel I cannot let this eventful period pass without brief reference to our outfitting as officers while at Lichfield. The regulation then in force provided for an allowance of £50 for this on commissioning, credited by, in most cases, the bankers acting as regimental agents; usually Cox & Co., a branch of Lloyds Bank.

What actually occurred was that, in off parade hours, we were besieged by the oily, if affable, representatives of tailoring houses, apparently only too anxious to provide us with everything on credit (although on taking delivery, I seem to recall that we signed a chit acknowledging our indebtedness). In this manner, by about halfway through our course most of us had been fitted out with subaltern's uniform. This we wore in the evenings, including a 'Sam Browne' belt without the cross strap and, of course, without any badges except the white band and the '8' on our caps. This, in the mess, produced a pleasing uniformity and eliminated the last vestiges of non-commissioned rank from among us.

We were all on the same footing, and, thus arrayed, we formed the habit of dining out once or perhaps twice a week at hotels in Lichfield or Tamworth, depending upon the state of our exchequers. On these, I generally went with Shooter and a next-bed mate: Tutt, a Londoner, or Sanders, a quiet-spoken Scot. Both were considerably older than we were and, as we soon learned, were far more accustomed to so-called 'good living' than we were. From scraps of conversation we gathered that Tutt was an insurance official, while Sanders was of independent means and much travelled. Between them these two were our invaluable mentors in many things, for it should be realized that both Shooter and I had been taken away from normal processes of youth development and thrust for a vital three years into an existence utterly foreign to the usages of an average peace-time, middle-class society—with the inevitable consequences. For instance, the only wines we knew anything about were *vin rouge*, *vin blanc*, malaga, and a cheap champagne, on which I had become horribly drunk. Sanders, particularly, gently initiated us into the mysteries of wine so that, thereafter, while being far from knowledgeable on this subject, we knew enough not to make fools of ourselves in polite company.

So our re-education continued until the end of October, when most of us passed out and one afternoon the stream of taxis appeared again at the gates—this time for a departing crowd of hand-shaking, waving, soon-to-be-possessors of one 'pip'.

We had been asked to state our preference for regiments. As a native of Sussex I had put the Royal Sussex Regiment first, the Leicestershire Regiment next, and in the event, a few days after I had reached home, a long envelope from the War Office arrived, stating that I had been granted a temporary Commission in the Royal Sussex Regiment, with orders to report to the 3rd (Reserve) Battalion at Newhaven. Also enclosed were a lot of forms—for travelling warrant, allowance, etc.; forms for Cox & Co.—which at first sight rather frightened me, but everything worked out and I duly reported as instructed. It was in early November, and I recall that the local church bells were ringing—as I believe they did in many other places—at the news of Byng's 'victory' at Cambrai.

At Newhaven I met several old school friends, like myself newly commissioned, and we were soon irritated beyond measure by the wiles and sarcastic digs of the Regular adjutant—one Keep—who, probably rightly regarded us as a pretty shocking lot. Captain Keep, I will say, never missed a chance of humiliating us, but he observed the rules and, so far as I am aware, never did this in front of either N.C.O.s or men, of whom there were several hundred, the great majority rejoined from hospitals and waiting to be redrafted.

As news of the German counter-attacks at Cambrai trickled through, heads were shaken ominously, and notices of drafts for France started to appear frequently. We young subalterns daily expected our marching orders for France, but they didn't seem in any hurry to arrive and we carried on with our daily duties of drilling, arms handling, open order exercising and, on several occasions, night operations. On the day before the last of these nocturnal excursions in February 1918, one of our number, a

Sussex man of Canadian adoption and latterly of Toronto, rushed into our hut after mid morning parade. He looked almost wild with excitement. 'What d'ya think, fellas . . . What d'ya think? We're all for Egypt!' And so it was. We devoured our names from the noticeboard in the mess ante-room. The relief, at the time, of not being sent back to France cannot be described, and the possible hazards of the Egyptian Expeditionary Force were quite discounted.

We couldn't celebrate that evening for, as I have said, we had a night operation exercise. This took place on the slopes of the Downs, north-west of Newhaven, in the course of which one of our number, Gilbert, freshly gazetted from Eastbourne College O.T.C., fired a Verey light which landed on top of a haystack in the yard of an isolated Downland farm. In a few moments the stack was well alight, and a man dashed off on a bicycle borrowed from the angry farmer and his wife to fetch the Newhaven Fire Brigade while we formed a chain of bucket passers from the kitchen pump. As it was thrown, the water in each bucket went up in a cloud of steam, illuminated by the spreading flames, and the troops waited anxiously for succour from the fire brigade, having moved stock as far as possible and drenched the nearby barn walls as thoroughly as we could.

At length we heard the sound of galloping hooves in the distance, and within a few seconds the Newhaven Fire Brigade made a spectacular appearance in the firelit, smoke-filled scene. On the fire engine, of which we couldn't discern the details, was crowded an array of firemen in enormous, polished brass helmets. They jumped down, one rushing to the heads of the rearing horses, which appeared to be a very fine team of greys. The fire chief was directed to the nearest pond, accompanied by two firemen carrying lengths of hose connected to the fire engine, which we now saw was of the 'manual' type, with handles six feet long on each side. Two more firemen ran out lengths of hose from the engine to the scene of the fire, the second of these, in his enthusiasm, rushing forward beyond the length of his hose, with the result that he was pulled back violently with his brass helmet over his eyes—greatly to the merriment of the watching soldiery.

In a few moments, however, all was ready. There was no lack

of volunteers to man the pump handles, and they set to with a will. Lit up by the flames, a fireman stood impressively holding the nozzle of the hose, directing it at the blaze—but only a miserable trickle emerged from the end, falling at his feet, which provoked a fresh outburst of merriment from the watching troops. The chief, worried, ran towards his man to find the cause of the trouble, and on the way he found it. Several soldiers were unwittingly standing on the hose as it trailed amidst the trampled mass of wet or smouldering straw lying around. The obstruction removed, and pressure thus released, the strength of the sudden jet of water shot the hose almost from the fireman's grasp, and gushed clean over the now-glowing remains of the stack and right into the crowd of watching men on the far side.

Serious as the occasion undoubtedly was, if still dry one just could not help laughing. Music hall sketches based on 'the Village Fire Brigade' were as common laughter-raisers as mother-in-law jokes, and here was the very thing in reality. No doubt at Newhaven they now possess up-to-date appliances, and the old 'manual' and those wonderful polished brass helmets are now museum pieces. They should be!

On the following evening, in Brighton, six of us celebrated receipt of our orders for Egypt. Probably we were a bunch of young fools, but our relief at escaping a draft for France was so great that we must needs find some outlet for our feelings. Just about that time it had been stated that the average life of an infantry subaltern in France was about a month. We had been lucky enough to miss Messines, Passchendaele and Cambrai. Our luck seemed to have held. Therefore, notwithstanding food rationing and war-time restrictions, youth called to youth in Brighton that evening in no uncertain fashion. A dinner at the Old Ship, the forerunner of an hilarious but exceedingly expensive evening; the more especially for four of the party by the inclusion, in the later stages, by a like number of newly found but engaging girl friends. I recall that two of us left them sitting in two taxis somewhere near Rottingdean at about midnight, and the adventures of at least one of them I may relate later.

Pegg and I managed to get through the barbed wire fence into the garrison camp about an hour later, and crept thankfully into our beds in the officers' block as noiselessly as we could, hoping that the others would be equally lucky. In the event, they did manage it—at varying times, and with varying amounts of damage to clothing and hands, one unfortunate leaving his gloves on the wire. They did not require breakfast!

Apropos of this, I should have explained much earlier that at Newhaven the port and garrison were prohibited areas and were fenced in by a thick band of barbed wire entanglements. The port worked round the clock, loading vast quantities of stores in small cargo steamers running a shuttle service to French Channel ports, and the garrison found strong guards for all exits and entrances. Passes were a necessity. Faced with the difficulties of either expired passes or the lack of a pass at all, past members of the garrison (now long departed, alas) had devised two tortuous yet practicable ways through this wire; one on the Brighton side and one on the Seaford side. The first was also useful for walkers from Lewes, while the latter catered for latecomers from the general direction of Eastbourne, and took a deal of finding in the dark. With the added hazard of drifting snow, finding it at all was pure luck—as we did one shocking night when returning from a visit to the Devonshire Park Theatre at Eastbourne, after a call at home to see my brother Selwyn. He was on leave after an arm wound sustained in August at Polygon Wood at the outset of the Passchendaele 'show'. Shortly before leaving Lichfield, I went to London to see him in hospital at Endsleigh Gardens, one week-end. He said then that the weather breaking had made the mud almost impassable there. Now a lieutenant, he was off to Italy with another six-inch howitzer battery. As I was getting back to Euston, there was an air raid on London, with the result that three of us didn't reach Whittington Barracks until 09.00 hours on the Monday morning, owing to dislocation of the train service. Another result—seven days' confined to barracks, no excuses, however legitimate, being entertained. As I was broke, it didn't matter very much.

It was not until 7th March that, following final leave, eight of us gathered at Waterloo to get the boat train to Southampton, the crowded platform smacking of the East already with the topis (pith helmets) everywhere in evidence.

The assembled medley of wives, sweethearts and relations, many pale and red-eyed with weeping, waved wanly as the long train pulled out, and at the sight of them I was glad that no dear one of mine stood among them.

On reporting to the R.T.O. Southampton, we were told that we were not proceeding further that day, with the consequence that we spent a very uncomfortable night on a billiard table at the South Western Hotel. At least, some of us did, for in spite of the tearful farewells at Waterloo but a few hours previously, several of our number had already found feminine consolation of a temporary character; which, I suppose, was one way of forgetting what they were leaving behind them. Four of us achieved Nirvana by other means, invoking the aid of Bacchus—with fairly successful results, to judge by the regrettable fact that the manager came round to our box at the Southampton Hippodrome and requested us to leave unless we could moderate our high spirits. It is too late now, I fear, to apologize for annoying those great stars Talbot O'Farrell and Wilkie Bard, but we must have been rather amusing in our interruption of the latter, the crowded house taking it for a time as part of the act. It wasn't a very clever thing to do, though.

The following morning we received our movement instructions and got our kits trundled by hand cart on to the steamer *St George*. We were ordered to report on board at eight that evening and, with the day on our hands, while away a good deal of the time looking round the docks where, at that time, there was much to interest landsmen like ourselves; including two large cargo carriers in dry dock, with great gaping holes below the waterline where German torpedoes had struck them.

At dusk we went on board and secured berths. Soon after nightfall the steamer slipped away, and once clear of the Needles headed hell for leather across the Channel for Cherbourg—as we found on waking early the following morning, having turned in and slept soundly after a few drinks, leaving the U-boats to do their worst. The sun had just risen and the smooth surface of the magnificent harbour of Cherbourg looked sparklingly lovely as the night mist cleared. Within a few minutes we came alongside and disembarked, and shortly after, with various drafts and details which had constituted the *St George*'s burden, we marched out of the docks *en route* for the rest camp of Tour la Ville, a pleasant spot situated on a height a few kilometres above the town and served from it by a typical French tramway system.

The rime of a white frost covered the countryside, but in the rapidly strengthening rays of the rising sun this vanished, except for occasional shaded patches, while the bracing morning air gave us terrific appetites for the adequate breakfast we hoped was awaiting us. In both this and the camp we were not disappointed, and the morning passed quickly as the camp commandant informed us of the camp rules and gave us a working topography of Cherbourg. He also told us that we had a long train journey ahead, probably on the morrow, and advised us to lay in a good stock of tinned stuff and cookers of the 'Tommy's Cooker' variety, so that at least we could make a cup of tea occasionally. Finally, he told us that the field cashier would attend after lunch—a most welcome piece of news for all. Already the finances of several of our circle were known to be in a parlous state, the ladies of Southampton being in part responsible. Although we had been thrown into the close company of one another for a matter of hours only, it was apparent that the heaviest spenders had the shortest purses. On the frequent occasions when finances were discussed, several of us who were endeavouring to husband our slender resources in view of possible hazards ahead, looked at one another somewhat uneasily, expecting at any moment requests for temporary loans. Indeed, the notice displayed prominently in the camp mess—very much to the point in its request that 'officers would kindly settle their mess accounts before leaving'—seemed to indicate that a shortage of funds at this stage of our journey was no new phenomenon. I forget now whether the mess secretary accepted cheques, but in retrospect I hardly think so. He was courting trouble if he did!

From the field cashier we all drew £5 in francs and caught the tram into Cherbourg. That far-seeing gentleman wouldn't let us have any more!

CHAPTER 18

THE OVERLAND ROUTE

AT the Expeditionary Force canteen our hastily formed purchasing committee, armed with a pool subscribed to by all, secured a good supply of tinned goods, condensed milk, tea and Tommy's Cookers, which filled three infantry valises brought into town for the purpose. Two of us, taking our turn to look after them, were landed with them for most of the afternoon as the others, by pairs, drifted away with promises to return within a few minutes after doing some shopping. Thus Pegg and I, left to ourselves, sat down in the bright sunshine outside the nearest café, at a table where we could relax and watch the world go by, aided by several café cognacs. Here we noted the undoubted attractiveness of many of the female passers-by, possessing, as they did, that indefinable chic which has had such a devastating impact on the male of the species from time immemorial. None of our party put in an appearance, and in view of our observations Pegg and I began to suspect what had happened to them—suspicions that turned to conviction when our elderly waiter, with a knowing grin, offered to tell us where we could find *belles demoiselles*, supplying, with significant gestures, a wealth of detail.

We thanked him, our pique at being left stranded thus rising, but the loads on the ground beside our chairs were a sufficient deterrent just then. To pass the time I went to a nearby booksellers and bought a *Carte Taride* of Europe, which we spread out on the café table and studied together. If, as rumour had it, our destination was Taranto in Southern Italy, we saw that we had a very long journey in front of us.

As we sat thus, four of our party appeared within minutes, looking very smugly one at the other. As they brought chairs from other tables, we caught the whiffs of scent they now carried with

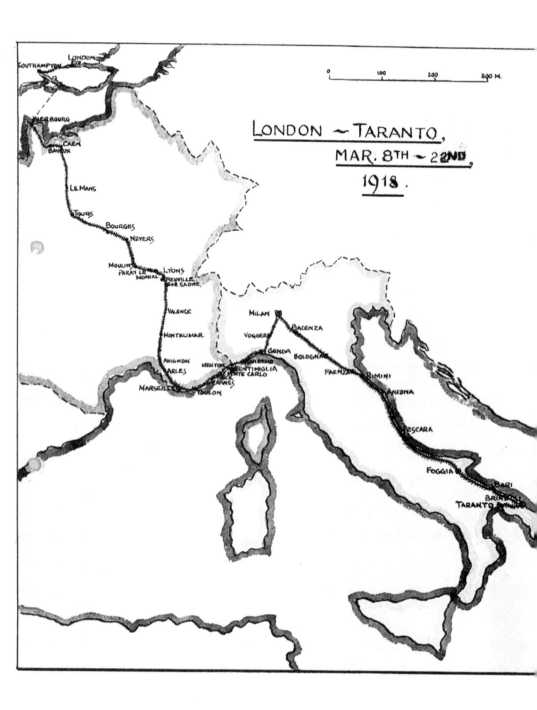

them. They started to apologize for their long absence, but Pegg cut them short with a significant sniff and, 'all right, you lousy so-and-sos—don't tell us, we know already!'

We waited a while for the missing pair, but as they didn't turn up and we wished desperately to know whether we were off on the morrow, we made our way back to Tour la Ville.

At dinner in the camp we encountered them, but for some reason they were reticent about the afternoon, notwithstanding a good deal of leg-pulling on our part. Indeed, I thought, one of them hardly looked himself; but then, that might be the after-effect of seasickness. He had said he was a rotten sailor.

We entrained during the following afternoon at a siding near the docks, and even at first sight the immensely long collection of nondescript shabby green carriages looked shocking examples of what proved to be Italian rolling stock. Four bodies were allocated to each compartment by the R.T.O. and his minions. Our was labelled 'Fumatori' and bore the number FSA 8902. Luckily we made a note of this as we bundled in our kits, which we estimated would be our requirements for the journey, our rolled valises and camp kit having been dumped in one of several freight cars at the rear of the train. After a fruitless journey to extract some more blankets from these, we only managed to find our compartment again from the track by the number on the door.

Thereafter, until the train started, we busied ourselves in blocking up two almost windowless voids in our compartment with portions of boxes scrounged from the rear of the B.E.F. canteen. We had noticed that several freight cars, next to those carrying our heavy baggage at the rear of the train, were loaded with boxes of rations: bully beef, pork and beans, McConochies, biscuit, jam and tinned butter; and, of course, tea.

While drawing our rations for the morrow, we were very lucky to escape the eagle eye of the O.C. Train, appointed by the R.T.O. He was a major returning to Palestine from leave, and just then he was looking for unsuspecting bodies for guards and O.C.s guards on the baggage and rations. From our cracked windows we watched the unfortunate subalterns, N.C.O.s and men detailed from drafts and those returning from leave dragging their kits sorrowfully in the general direction of these vans—of the variety 'Chevaux en long 8, Hommes 40'.

At length doors were slammed, amid much shouting by the French railwaymen. Their high-pitched little horns blew, and with a series of mighty jerks the tremendously long troop train pulled slowly out, drawn by two great locomotives, the driving wheels of which slipped continually until momentum was gained. It would have been about 3 p.m.—or, in the modern idiom, fifteen hundred hours—on a lovely sunny afternoon, with all the promise of spring in the air. We were indeed relieved to be on the move once more, and Pegg struck the right note by inquiring, 'what about a cup o' char, you so-and-sos?' Our supplies and rations were broached: French bread, rolls, tinned butter and jam appeared. A mess tin was filled from our water bottles and the first of our Tommy's Cookers went into action on the carriage floor. Both mess tin and cooker had to be held continuously as we jolted over the seemingly interminable array of points, but there was no lack of volunteers for this job, and the resulting brew was well worth the effort. Greatly refreshed, and having at last left the environs of Cherbourg behind, we were fairly on our way, rattling along through Normandy at twenty-five to thirty miles per hour, but often slowing down to half-speed near stations, or stopping altogether as the westering sun threw long shadows and tinged the well-tilled countryside with pink and gold. Then, entering a cutting, the sun suddenly was gone; a sudden chill draught crept through our patched windows and caused us hurriedly to overhaul our handiwork.

We felt hungry again, and in the gathering twilight took out our mugs, plates and eating irons, lit two candles, and enjoyed a hearty meal of tinned tongue, garnished liberally with pork and beans and washed down with a bottle of St. Émilion. Then it was dark. We removed our boots, wrapped ourselves in our blankets and took up our positions for the night. I was on the floor, and hoped that neither Wallace nor Pegg, now stretched at full length along the seats, would fall on me during the night. The floor wasn't too bad when I became used to the proximity to my head of Bartholomew's socks—with his feet in them!

Before sleep came to me, I thought of those sunlit towns of old Normandy through which we had passed—Carentan, Bayeux,

Caen—names redolent of history and romance, of which we had read in our history books as schoolboys and which, as Sussex boys, we associated with William the Conqueror and Bishop Odo, as with Senlac and Pevensey and Hastings. Nearly fifty years later, men who were, no doubt, the sons and grandsons of some of our trainload traversed the same French ground after D Day 1944, but under bloodier circumstances.

We awoke in broad daylight as the train ground to a standstill in the station of Le Mans. There was a white frost on the roofs and the rolling stock in the sidings, and I was glad to return to the warmth of our carriage after running along to the nearer of the two locomotives for a canvas bucket of hot water. As the sun rose and we shaved and then breakfasted, so our interest in the changing countryside increased as once more we got under way. Slowly, for our train never hurried, we passed through Tours (crowded with Americans), Vierzon, Bourges and Nevers. Bourges I remember particularly for the considerable number of uniformed Russian soldiers working along the railway track and in the sidings.

At some of these stations we managed to obtain bread, rolls, fruit and, once, an omelette, from the buffet. That day we learned that, in order to obtain an omelette, it was of vital importance to be among the first at the counter when the train stopped as, within seconds, it was besieged by a bedlam of shouted orders to the harassed and quite inadequate staff. Therefore when, at dawn on the day following, 12th March, we came to a standstill in a station bearing the name of Paray-le-Monial, which we read with sleepy eyes and between yawns, we were galvanized by the magic word 'buffet' directly opposite our compartment. Slipping on our boots, dishevelled as we were, we rushed across and were among the first dozen to place our orders with the black-bearded Frenchman in charge. Within the next few moments he was almost driven to distraction by successive streams of shouted requests which, it was perfectly obvious, he could not possibly fill unless the train stayed there for most of the day. Nevertheless, we managed to get hold of our own trays of omelette and coffee which looked, and were, first class. It was impossible, however, to eat them in the confines of the buffet owing to the crush, and we struggled to the entrance, pursued by the envious glances and sniffs of our less fortunate comrades and by incomprehensible shouting from the harassed Frenchman, and then to the shelter of our carriage. Our repast finished, we then endeavoured—without success—to get to the counter again and return our trays, and, incidentally, to pay.

At length there was a shrill warning whistle from the locomotive, followed by shouts of '*en voiture, messieurs!*'. Hearing then the terrific tortured jolt travelling the length of the train as it got into motion once more, we joined the rush to get aboard, dropping the trays with a clang upon the platform—a truly despicable exit, but unavoidable. Between gasps for breath, Pegg remarked 'Bad show lads, bad show. Remember, we pay coming back!' As the platform slid by from our ken we laughed wryly and speculated in silence for some minutes as to what our chances were of coming back at all, never mind *that* way, but we soon recovered our spirits amid fresh scenes of interest.

Around midday we stopped at the station of Ste. Germaine au Mont d'Or, a few miles from Lyons. Here we left the train and proceeded to a well-organized rest camp near by, where we stayed the night. That afternoon, having been warned by the camp commandant that Lyons was out of bounds, we four walked to the pretty village of Neuville sur Saône, where we enjoyed a pleasant meal and a sit-down in the sunshine on the forecourt of a little café overlooking the river.

Later that evening, one of us pointed out that the pair who were very late returning from our trip into Cherbourg were again missing. In the general conversation ensuing we gathered from their carriage mates that, notwithstanding the ban, they had gone into Lyons—and for a special reason. Apparently on the second day of our journey, following considerable embarrassment and unpleasantness, one of them had confessed to having contracted a dose of what was then commonly known as 'the clap' from his girl friend of the Brighton celebration. He had been treated privately in London and thought mistakenly that he would be completely fit again by the time we sailed. Fresh trouble had occurred, however, and in Cherbourg he had found a doctor who had treated him. There seemed no doubt that they were on a similar quest today. This news spoiled for us what would otherwise have been a most interesting interlude in an enchanting countryside.

The unfortunate and his friend—who, to his credit, stuck by him through his trouble—had our sincere sympathy, and among us there was a general feeling of relief when at length the pair made their appearance; very tired, but much happier somehow than for days past, having apparently found what they were looking for and gaining relief, however temporary in character. As a matter of fact, our mate seemed to improve steadily from that day onward, and by the time we reached our journey's end no one thought any more about it. Indeed, there were many other matters to occupy our attention then!

The morning following saw us descending the lovely Rhône Valley, alongside the swiftly flowing river. Successively we passed through the historic towns of Montélimar, Valence and Avignon, with its famous and many-arched bridge, coming eventually to a halt of three hours' duration at Arles, and there our train was shunted into a siding. Within minutes we were in the mediaeval town, the sunlit streets of which were gay with the bright red and blue uniforms of French Colonial troops, for which the barracks here appeared to be a depot. Already we seemed to have left the cold weather behind, an impression strengthened by the frequent palms and other semi-tropical trees to be seen along the wide boulevard near the ruins of the great Roman coliseum. At the time, we wished we could have stayed much longer at Arles. The inhabitants seemed welcoming. We liked them and admired especially the women—their black hair, dark velvety complexions and darker eyes flashing beneath long black lashes, surmounted often by the unique and becoming Provençal head-dress.

Leaving Arles with real regret, southward we went, the scenery of the Rhône Valley giving place to wide expanses of flat, uninteresting country, the seemingly sterile ground sparsely covered with scrub and coarse grasses. After passing the junction of Miramas we turned in for the night, and I awoke some hours later to find that we were at a standstill in the yellow light of a solitary station lamp, on the glass of which I deciphered the blue-lettered name 'Toulon'.

To the notes of the shunter's horn and the sound of a spirited conversation beneath our window in rapid and quite unintelligible French, I dozed off again, and the sun was quite high when I raised my head (it was my turn to sleep on the seat) to read 'San

Rafael' and see for the first time the blue of the Mediterranean
Sea, over the smooth sparkling surface of which two seaplanes
from the French station there were skimming to and fro. Thrilled
by the sight of the sea, I shook Pegg and Bartholomew and trod
upon Wallace in endeavours to wake them, but was told sleepily,
and unmistakably, to leave them in peace; so I drank in my first
impressions of the Riviera silently, with no one to whom I could
enthuse and share my excitement. Consequently, also, my comrades had no one to blame but themselves for what occurred
shortly afterwards when our train came to a standstill in the station
of Cannes. Here they roused themselves, awakened by the shouts
of cheerful urchins selling newspapers, fruit and chocolate; also by
the unexpected cadences of pleasant feminine English voices,
which belonged to lady canteen workers of the local British colony
there, busy dispensing hospitality to the troops in the shape of
very welcome cups of hot tea and other light refreshment. All four
of us now sat up in our pyjamas amid the jumbled paraphernalia
of our makeshift couches—by common consent we had undressed
after the first night in the train—but our heaps of clothes didn't
exactly contribute to the tidiness of our compartment.

Heads tousled, rubbing the sleep from our eyes, three of us
shed pyjama jackets and started arm exercises to loosen up. I—the
fourth—having sliced some bread, now wrestled with a tin opener
on some sausages, using a narrow windowsill as the only available
'table' on which to rest the tin.

At this juncture came the shrill whistle of an approaching train,
and within seconds a Paris-bound express had come to a standstill
beside us, blotting out, to my disgust, most of the morning sunlight.
Looking up from the sausages I was horrified to see two fashion-
ably dressed young women, unable to move an inch because of
the crowded state of their train, looking directly in at us from the
corridor window. Their embarrassment was evident. 'Hell!' shouted
Pegg. 'Shut the bedroom door, Read. Pull the curtains!'

Hurriedly, Wallace and I essayed to place some tattered remnants of blind between ourselves and the fair ones but, having
done this, we observed through slits that they were now suppress-
ing their amusement with difficulty into two dainty handkerchiefs.
When a few minutes later their train drew out, we, having

hurriedly put on some clothes, raised the blinds and expressed our undisguised admiration of the fair ones; but they, influenced perhaps by the stony stares of the people on either side of them, tried to look outraged. As their carriage disappeared from our view, however, we caught a last glimpse of two little fluttering white handkerchiefs held in black-gloved hands, waving from the window. After that we returned to our sausages, and I recall that Wallace upset a tin of tomatoes on the floor.

For the whole of that spring-like day we travelled slowly along the length of the French and Italian Rivieras, drinking in our delighted impressions of each succeeding 'pocket Paradise' of sunlit bays and wooded headlands, which sometimes our train skirted but more often pierced, to emerge each time upon a fresh panorama of beauty; save when we came upon the towns, disappointing, shabby and often dirty with the forced neglect of the long years of war. Nice, at any rate, viewed from the railway, looked dirtier than Brighton when seen under similar circumstances—which is saying something!

Further picturesque touches were added to our route by the French Colonial troops who guarded the railway, and in particular the numerous tunnel entrances and exits, where they were much in evidence. We passed the last of these picturebook sentries at the tunnel entrance shortly after leaving Menton, and on emerging at the eastern end saw, by the grey-green uniforms of the sentries, that we were in Italy. Shortly afterwards our train came to a standstill in the station of Ventimiglia, where we halted for an hour or so while Italian railway officialdom did its worst with it. Outside the station we changed our French money into wads of five-lire notes: losing, of course, in the process. The notes were new and they stuck together, so that in purchasing some tinned supplies from a nearby shop I found, when we resumed our journey and we all checked our currency, that I had paid heavily for my few tins of sardines. But it was some consolation to find later that I was not alone in being mulcted thus.

Our first impressions of Italy were mixed. Sunset at Porto Maurizio provided a spectacle of sheer beauty of which we had never seen the equal, lifting us clean out of the train as we looked, entranced, upon the gorgeous sky and the Mediterranean Sea, on which danced the reddish-brown sails of the fishing boats. Around us the warm colourings of roofs and walls of the little town caught the rays of the setting sun. Turning from this to the evidences of poverty, neglect and decay due to the war which could be seen everywhere along the railway, particularly the groups of ragged children imploring us to throw them 'bully bif', and the frenzied rush and scrimmage when a tin was thrown, we wondered somewhat apprehensively at the state of Italy.

Bordighera and San Remo seemed in somewhat better case. some people in both towns appeared well dressed, the hotels and buildings in reasonably good repair, although decorations had suffered, especially the exterior murals with which, at that time, the Italians loved to adorn their stuccoed walls.

For most of that night we slept undisturbed in some goods sidings at Genoa, leaving shortly before daybreak in a drizzle which betokened a change in the weather, and first light revealed a grey sky overcast with hurrying clouds, making the outlook from our carriage window cold and cheerless. The buildings were decrepit, the floral murals on the stucco more faded than ever, the few inhabitants we glimpsed in the dripping countryside more wretched. The Italian police and soldiery, the former conspicuous by reason of their picturesque headgear, stood about on wayside platforms as we passed, chins and necks buried deep in the collars of their capes. They looked the reverse of happy. The one thing that impressed us favourably was the intensive cultivation of the fields. Every scrap of arable ground was being worked.

Towards midday we halted for an hour at Voghera and seized the opportunity offered of having lunch at a restaurant near the station. We voted our first tastes of Italian cooking and wine good, and it was only at the close of our repast that we found that we had been thoroughly enjoying horseflesh. The poor devil of a waiter was at a loss to understand our indignation on soliciting this from him, but we soothed his agitation with a good tip and returned to the train.

That afternoon we halted on the outskirts of a fair-sized town. The cold drizzle still persisted, and on leaning out of the window to see what was happening, we saw on the tracks below an Italian sentry staring up at the train in a listless, dejected attitude, back hunched, carbine slung, so that he could put both hands in his pockets. Raindrops glistened and dropped from his moustache onto his cape. Thinking to ask him the name of the town, I proffered a cigarette and addressed him in vile French. The cigarette he took with a gesture of appreciation and, spitting vigorously, left me bereft of further speech. 'Say, you guys,' he ejaculated, 'this is one goldarned shithouse of a country, ain't it?' All crowded the window to hear this American son of Italy voice his disgust with things in general until such time as the train started again. The town was Piacenza.

The following morning we arrived at Faenza. Here a well-run British rest camp enabled all of us to stretch our legs and obtain a bath, also to replenish depleted stocks of necessaries, including tobacco and cigarettes. We visited the potteries which have been famous for centuries, the ware taking its name from the town. Most of us sent some pieces to friends and relatives at home, but I regret to say that few of these carefully packed parcels reached their destination. It was certainly very interesting to watch several generations of one family sitting around at various tasks—one at the wheel, another painting designs with marvellous dexterity, and so on.

As we four made our way back to the station, the sun was setting and, as is the custom, many of the inhabitants were taking their evening constitutional along the pleasant tree-lined road. Unfortunately they had before their eyes the unedifying spectacle of many of our party issuing from the local brothels and other dubious pleasures, some in a somewhat elevated condition. In uproarious fashion they crowded round a red-haired Scots major, who flourished upon the end of his stick souvenirs in the shape of a lace cap and a pair of ribboned garters. As may be imagined, the locals did not look kindly upon this procession to the station. Although we could not understand what they said, their gestures were eloquent enough.

That night we reached the Adriatic Sea at Rimini, and the port of Ancona, having been warned to show no lights after leaving Faenza as Zeppelins were reported in the vicinity. so we journeyed on from one town to another in a very leisurely fashion along the varied Adriatic shore, never ceasing to marvel, when curves enabled us to see it, at the great length of our train. Particularly

were we interested in the two locomotives now pulling it—old
Midland Railway goods engines—familiar features of the Leicestershire landscape before 1914. Owing to the war, coal was then
almost non-existent in Italy and the tenders were piled high with
the gnarled branches of old olive trees, which the firemen attacked
unceasingly with axes to feed the boiler fires.

One night about ten o'clock, as our train stood in some sidings
at Foggia, the Zeppelin alarm was given, and we lay upon our
improvised couches in the darkness, waiting for something to
happen: either for the train to start, or for the Zepp to arrive. I
suppose we must have dropped off to sleep, but I awoke suddenly
in a kind of perspiration, conscious of a hand passing over my
face. Jumping up with a start I trod upon the unfortunate Wallace,
who smothered an agonised yell (justifiable, in the circumstances),
and staggered to my feet just in time to catch a glimpse of a black
slouch hat and of a hand disappearing over the edge of the
carriage window. In a matter of moments my three comrades had
roused and wanted to know 'what the hell the row was about'. I
opened the carriage door and, with Wallace, gave chase to the
shadowy form of our quarry, which disappeared behind two strings
of freight cars. After stumbling about in the blackness for some
minutes—quite fruitlessly, of course—we returned to the carriage,
completely out of breath and marked by abrasions in several
places.

Apparently these gentry were no novelty; in fact they were a
pest. Both at Ventimiglia and Faenza we had been warned never
to leave our kits unless assured that they were well guarded by
sentries. The reputation of the Italian railways regarding this question of pilfering did not stand very high just then, and the saying
went 'they'll pinch your shoes on these trains and come back for the
laces'. Indeed, it transpired on our arrival at Taranto that two young
subalterns had lost practically everything they possessed to these
jackals somewhere between Brindisi and Taranto.

At about this time, too, we gained our first inkling of the great
German drive on the Western Front against the sector held by
the British 5th Army south of the Somme, which started on 21st
March. We heard with dismay of our enormous losses of territory,
men and guns. While the possibility of a German spring offensive

had been hinted at as we passed through France, we were staggered at the immensity of the German gains, and concluded that very soon, in all probability, we would be sent to the 'right about' to assist in stabilizing the line; that is to say, if it wasn't too late.

Still, however, we trundled on, and came to Brindisi. Here we had time to go down to the harbour and docks, doing our poor best, as directed, to conform to the usages and customs of the country by saluting the many officers of both Italian services we encountered *en route*. Nearly every naval officer we judged to be at least a rear-admiral, so loaded were they all with gold braid, decorations and other insignia of rank, with the result that, by degrees, we almost gave up the saluting business as a bad job and proceeded to inspect from the quay two weird units of the Italian Navy lying alongside. Apparently, judging from the festoons of apparel adorning every rail and wire, it was washing day. We could forgive them that, but on perceiving in the offing our own cruisers *Lowestoft* and *Gloucester*, our interest in the Italian Navy ceased. Perhaps the fact that we were in a foreign country and a long way from home gave us an additional thrill of pride as we viewed the graceful lines and impeccable turnout of these representatives of the British Navy. The flashing brasswork, the long waspish guns, the holy-stoned decks dotted with the white figures of the ships' companies in their white ducks, all working, gave us somehow a new sense of security—a sense badly shaken by the news from France, where disaster seemed to succeed disaster.

Soon after leaving Brindisi our train broke into two halves, the couplings no longer able to stand the strain. This occurred in a stretch of flat open country, so that we had the unusual—and to us, amusing—experience of seeing the rear portion, still moving slowly, recede into the distance. I recall that we continued for quite a few miles thus before the engine drivers discovered that things were not as they should have been, although I believe the alarm signals were pulled long and vigorously throughout the front half. I don't suppose they worked!

CHAPTER 19

EGYPT

THE British rest camp in the base on the outskirts of Taranto, where we bade a fond farewell to our train—and particularly to compartment FSA.8902, our home for eleven days and nights—was a hive of activity. The occupants—mainly fellows like ourselves proceeding as reinforcements to the East, various details of the Egyptian Expeditionary Force who had been either misdirected or completely forgotten by the authorities, officers and men returning from or proceeding on leave—all appeared to be busily employed doing nothing except eat, sleep, scan the noticeboard a dozen times a day, and grouse.

The worst grousers, we soon found, were those who had waited there longest for train or transport to remove them from this spot, reputedly a hot-bed of malaria. As newcomers, however, there seemed much to interest us. The weather was fine and warm. After having our quarters under canvas allotted to us, we forgot for the moment the Western Front and the German offensive, and lost no time in exploring our new surroundings. We saw that the base lay upon a great land-locked arm of the sea, several miles in length and of considerable breadth; a magnificent natural harbour, with a narrow bottle-neck entrance spanned by a swing bridge, on either side of which lay the town of Taranto. Upon its placid waters lay a considerable portion of the Italian Navy at anchor in several imposing lines. Also, judging by the number of craft we saw, Taranto was a considerable base of operations for our own naval forces, the senior officer and his minions being centred aboard the old battleship *Queen*. This relic of Edwardian majesty lay at a quayside just inside the harbour, and thus almost in the town itself.

Between the harbour proper and our camp, a distance of two miles or so, huge constructional works were in progress, comprising additional quays, sidings, store sheds and living accommodation on so extensive a scale that Pegg remarked, 'good Lord, it looks as though they expect the damned war to last another fifty years yet!'

A considerable portion of the labour employed seemed to be furnished by the West India Regiment, almost 100 per cent negroes. As they worked they laughed and sang almost continuously; but, as we watched a gang laying rails, one of them had a difference of opinion with an Italian workman, resulting in an unintelligible argument while tempers flared. Suddenly the negro swung aloft the sledgehammer he held for driving in wedges, waving it above his head in menacing fashion, and advanced upon the Italian who, for a moment or so, appeared petrified with fright. Then, recovering his faculties, he fled with a shrill scream of alarm, pursued by the yelling soldier swinging the sledgehammer about like a toy. When we lost sight of them behind some freight cars a quarter of a mile or so away, the Italian seemed to have increased his lead somewhat. We hoped that he was able to maintain it!

In Taranto we soon had occasion to observe that it was small wonder if malaria was prevalent in the district. In common with other Italian towns we had seen *en route*, Taranto boasted one or two main streets named after Garibaldi—Vittorio Emanuelle and Umberto—with statues of these worthies generally occupying prominent positions thereon. These streets were fairly well surfaced and tolerably clean. Beyond their confines, however, lay hinterlands of appalling filth, the roads themselves of the most elementary character, their principal use as receptacles for all descriptions of rubbish. When it rained the gutters soon became choked with garbage and the road surfaces expanses of great puddles, beneath the surface of which lay everything which should not. After the rain, as the sun dried out the puddles, the mosquitoes danced over the stagnating filth, while the inhabitants sat on their doorsteps or on crazy balconies and gossiped across to their neighbours, and their crowds of children—fine little people, some of them—played around. Every few minutes a fresh shower of household rubbish, or worse, descended into the street, to be ransacked by all the mongrel dogs in the neighbourhood.

I write from memory of an Italy torn by war. Mussolini changed all this, I believe; but then the country had made, and was still making, tremendous sacrifices both in resources and in men. As elsewhere, only the women, the young and the old were left to carry on as best they could. Beggars abounded and were an absolute nuisance. If, in sympathetic moments, we gave them a copper or two, they called down upon us the blessings of all the saints; if we passed unheeding, they poured forth maledictions, the nature of which we could only guess.

Deciding to lunch in the town, we entered the restaurant of one of the largest hotels, saluting those at the tables in conformity with the national custom, and being rewarded by slightly supercilious stares from the few Italian officers seated there. I don't think that at heart they liked the British—in fact, at this stage of the war I believe that they blamed them for most of their troubles. Moreover, the shadow of the Caporetto disaster and its consequences still lay heavy on them. These chaps were no exception, as they sat toying with their food, perfect specimens of the tailor's art, their tunics fitting skin-tight to figures which we could have sworn were corsetted. They had perforce to hold their chins high, their stiff white choker collars beneath their tunics precluding any other position.

However, in our enjoyment of the meal which followed we forgot everything else, for never before had we eaten fish so delicious and so perfectly cooked and served. We told the elderly waiter as much in our enthusiasm. He beamed and bowed his appreciation, returning to our table a few minutes later with two cartes-de-visite upon a salver, which turned out to be the camouflaged business cards of two establishments of dubious character. With much gesticulation and voluble explanation on his part, we gathered that there was dancing and 'amusement'. There certainly was! We emerged from there considerably poorer, and in our poverty visited, with some success, the local Italian agent for Cox & Co., our bankers. He let us have the equivalent of £5 each, but to reach him we surmounted heaps of rotting vegetables to reach the narrow staircase to his office. The refuse lay all around in the road outside the wholesale greengrocer's below, and the stink was appalling.

That night we hired a four-wheeler in the town square to take us back to camp. As soon as our design became manifest, the assembled cab drivers rushed at us in a body, waving whips and shouting 'Me, very good 'orse, *signor* . . . Me der bes' 'orse', and so on, until we mounted a decaying specimen of the coachbuilder's art and were rattled over the cobblestones. Once beyond the town we enjoyed the drive, as the moonlit night was fine and warm.

At the camp entrance we inquired of the driver his fare and he leaned down from his box to me with an ingratiating smile. 'Forty lire, *signor*.' We were prepared for something like this. Before setting out we had read a scale of local cabmen's charges pinned on the mess noticeboard. From memory, I believe that the recognized fare from camp to town and vice versa was sixteen lire, and we were strongly advised not to pay more. Recovering, therefore, from my surprise at his demand, I put twenty lire into his hand to settle once and for all—on the generous side, as we had enjoyed the ride. We were walking off, when I found the notes thrust back into my hand. The cabman, his smile now missing, angrily demanded forty lire. Backed by my friends, I gave him to understand that if he didn't take the twenty lire he could jolly well go without altogether. Impasse, as in the moonlight he glared at us and, with an angry exclamation, again refused. Now thoroughly annoyed, we walked away, I with the fares in my hand, but had only gone a few yards towards the camp entrance when Pegg suddenly turned about and there was a momentary scuffle behind me. I looked round to see Pegg holding the upraised arm of the cabman—in his hand was a knife!

Pegg thrashed the wretched man unmercifully with the heavy silver-knobbed Malacca stick he habitually carried, and told us afterwards, still out of breath with his exertions and indignation, that when he turned the cabman was about to knife me in the back.

On the following day a liner of considerable size steamed slowly across the inner basin and dropped anchor off our camp. Her appearance was the signal for violent outbreaks of speculation among us: 'would we be lucky enough to get on board? . . . had it come to take us back to France?' and so on. Meanwhile the situation on the Western Front appeared more desperate with each succeeding communiqué on the mess noticeboard; but we were in a state of jubilation late that evening when gloomy apprehension disappeared as by magic on reading our names on one of several foolscap-size lists pinned up by an orderly room clerk, who had to struggle at his task amid the excited crowd around him. We were under orders to embark the next morning on the S.S. *Indarra*, and shortly before midday had the satisfaction of treading her decks and of putting at least the water of the inner basin between us and the Western Front.

Our first meals on board the *Indarra* provided some pleasant surprises. She was an Australian boat, not long arrived in the Mediterranean. Perhaps for this reason, she carried an abundance of supplies unobtainable in England owing to the war. Indeed, I have so far omitted from my story the rapidly worsening food situation at home, due to wholesale U-boat sinkings of our merchant shipping. This hit the civilian population to a much greater degree than it did the Services, where food became much plainer but not unduly restricted. Rationing of meat, butter, bread and sugar hit the former hard and, as the months went by, the faces of many reflected the shortages. To maintain morale they were told that the German ration was in far worse case which, in 1918, was probably true, owing to the blockade firmly established by the British Navy since 1914. Here on the *Indarra* there was plenty of sugar—lump sugar, castor sugar, brown sugar, all kinds of sugar—likewise several sorts of fruit cake and many other delicacies not seen in Britain for many months past.

As may be imagined, we revelled in renewing their acquaintance. In addition, the spotless napery and appointments were a welcome change from the cracked cups, tin mugs and plates of the previous fortnight. We had excellent sleeping accommodation, two of us sharing a berth. In this we were very fortunate, and in view of the hardships suffered by many thousands of troops before and since in crossing the 'Med', I should be the first to admit it.

Lingering apprehension regarding a possible last-minute change of plan in our case was not set at rest, however, until the afternoon of our third day on aboard, when we saw that, at length, preparations for departure were being made and our spirits rose accordingly. We didn't mind the showers of smuts from the funnels which descended in the evening air as the engineers raised steam. As the sun set, the *Indarra* weighed anchor and made slowly for the bottle-neck entrance to the great inner basin. On the way we obtained some fine views of the assembled battleships of the Italian Navy. A hoot from the ship's siren and the bridge opened to allow our passage, and the *Indarra* slipped slowly through as we stood at the rails and watched the houses, shops and people glide by. Outside we passed a larger boat than our own, which steamed slowly in through the entrance we had just vacated. She was heavily camouflaged, and we were told she was the P. & O. liner *Kaisr-i-Hind*. We were destined to meet her again.

We anchored for the night in a maze of what were obviously anti-submarine defences. Early on the following morning—having been joined meanwhile by another transport, the old Royal Mail steam packet ship *Tagus* and an escort of British and Japanese destroyers—the convoy weighed amid much fluttering of strings of flag signals and made for the open sea, where a fresh breeze met us. After boat drill, the posting of a rota of lookouts, and other shipboard chores, there was nothing to do but eat, sleep and look at the empty horizons of the blue-green Mediterranean Sea until the morning of the third day out. Then a naval craft appeared towing an observation balloon and two fast patrol boats joined our escort and made frequent wide circles around us.

These, the birds, and a subtle something in the air, betokened our approach to land—and Alexandria. Our voyage had been without incident save for an exciting few minutes around eleven o'clock the previous night. As we expected to dock during the following day, the troops had drunk everything on board, and many bright spirits were considerably brighter than usual. Below decks it was very sultry, partly because of the order that scuttles had to be shut during the hours of darkness. Apparently an Irish subaltern in the cabin next to ours thought differently and opened his in an inebriated attempt to get some fresh air. The result was that, within a minute, a furious ship's officer came tearing along the alley-way and burst into the offending cabin. We heard the scuttle shut with a thud, and a welter of Australian obscenity. When he emerged, sweating and still furious, he told us that the Jap destroyer had threatened to open fire unless the light was instantly extinguished. As can be imagined, this had a very sobering effect upon everyone, and within a few moments all was quiet.

The smell of the East came over the water to us as the *Indarra* approached the entrance to the Alexandria dock system. This approach was littered with the masts and, in one case, the tops of funnels of sunken ships. Among these we were shown those of the ill-fated *Aragon* (headquarters ship of the Dardanelles expedition), and the *Minnetonka*. A large ship had settled down almost directly in the harbour entrance, its red funnel leaning drunkenly sideways and its decks awash.

As tugs nosed about us and we saw the brown throng upon the quayside where we were about to dock I recognized, with pleased surprise, an old friend at the berth ahead; upon her stern I read *City of Dunkirk*. She was coaling from a medley of lighters alongside, an endless procession of singing and jabbering natives—men and women—moved up and down ramps slung across to her deck, each bearing a great wicker basket. To our amazement, the overseers carried whips with long lashes which they used now and then at the least sign of a slowing down, adding their shouts to the din. I recall that we were genuinely surprised to see these gentry, who were tall Nubians of fine physique, wielding them. The lashes being of considerable length, they could pick out the objects of the wrath unerringly at quite a distance. Furthermore, that such seeming barbarity could be tolerated under the British flag shocked us and gave us food for considerable thought. Later on, when we saw more of these labour gangs working at various tasks, we took a considerably modified view of the system; for, had these overseers been other than what they were, they would have been knifed by their gangs within minutes.

We were soon ashore and in the hands of the R.T.O. Our kits were stacked on the dockside awaiting the arrival of the troop train, due to start that evening for Kantara on the Suez Canal. Till then, we were free to have a look at Alexandria—or 'Alex', the name given to it by generations of servicemen.

With the exception of Pegg, who had seen it all before, our first experience of Alex was of surprising interest, although we saw then only the merest fraction of the day-to-day life of this great and ancient city. We were amazed at the cosmopolitan throngs; the babel of tongues; the smells; the vast commerce of Alexandria; and the intermingling of luxury and poverty in busy, often dusty, streets. The tramcars; the great dirty sandal-shod feet and black attire of the poorer Egyptian women, and their plainness, but partially hidden by the yashmak; their red-dyed finger- and toenails; the swarms of flies on the meat displayed for sale, and in the eyes of many little children. On the other hand, the smartness and chic of many of the women seen in the principal shopping and hotel areas intrigued us tremendously. Here we could see all the signs of luxurious living, with no war-time restrictions. It was soon obvious that there were large French, Greek and Italian elements, besides the British forces of the occupying and Egyptian Expeditionary Forces.

There were newspapers in all these languages; also the *Egyptian Mail* in English, and European journals more than a week old, displayed in the numerous kiosks on the sidewalks of the main streets. Most of these also sold cigarettes, cigars and tobaccos in a bewildering and fascinating variety of brands and aromas.

At Groppi's in the Rue Cherif Pasha, we sampled our first multi-tiered and vari-coloured iced confection. After the rigorously rationed British war-time diet they tasted just out of this world! Whilst sitting there, we learned from a subaltern occupant of an adjoining table that Cox & Co., our bankers, was only a short distance away in this very street. This cheered us greatly until our informant, with a wry glance, advised us not to be too hopeful, as they had there all the latest information from U.K! Forthwith, however, we decided to have a shot at raising some badly needed funds and, thanking him, we departed on our quest. Pegg raised our spirits *en route* by pointing out that the Alexandria branch wouldn't yet have particulars of what we had drawn in Taranto! Hopefully, therefore, we approached the portals of Cox & Co. There, presenting our several cheques, we waited while the Egyptian cashier went behind the screen and, with a clerk, perused long lists. At length we were lucky and duly drew £5 each in Egyptian piastres, notes and silver. The silver coins intrigued us greatly, having a mass of Arabic on one side, and what looked like an 'O' in the centre of the reverse. Pegg explained that he hadn't the faintest idea of what it all meant, but in this part of the world, when one spun a coin, the shout was not 'heads or tails?' but 'arseholes or watercress?' He looked at his wristwatch, musing for a few moments with knit brows which dissolved into a slow smile, then, 'there's one thing I'd like you lads to see before we get back to that train—and the desert'. And he led our now rapidly tiring feet to the Rue de Ramleh.

I recall now—dimly, I confess, after such a long interval of time—a street of mediocre shops surmounted by several storeys of what were small hotels, offices and apartments. The whole had somehow a rather dilapidated appearance caused, I believe, almost entirely by the tiers of crazy looking balconies on which hung, here and there, specimens of mattresses and every description of feminine outer and underwear, presumably to dry or to air. It wasn't for this, however, that Pegg had dragged us hither, but for the occupants of the balconies: literally dozens of attractive young women sitting about in filmy *négligés* in the early evening sunlight, taking their ease, either sewing, reading or dozing, or smiling at pedestrians below.

Seeing our interest, Pegg laughed. 'All you want now lads is some leave, a pocketful of money—and lots of luck! You'll need it!' he added, and then told us that these were the most expensive 'ladies of the town'. Brothels for the troops were situated in a quarter called Sister Street. He didn't know what it was like there these days, but there used to be frequent riots, to say the least of it, and on the way back to the train he reminisced at some length—which showed, indeed, that a soldier needed a lot of luck to get clear without losing his wallet and everything of value he possessed, or even suffering some degree of bodily harm.

We were greatly relieved to sit down in a stuffy compartment of the waiting train, which unfortunately retained the heat of the day, gathered as it had stood in a siding at the sun's mercy. It was unbearably hot and we had divested ourselves of most of our clothing when Bartholomew, our Canadian, wondered whether our kits were safely on the train or whether, by now, they were somewhere in Alex. Thoroughly galvanized into action by his remark, with our recollections of Italian railways, Wallace, Bartholomew and I hastily got into our trousers and boots and went along to the baggage cars. Here our fears were set at rest by two sentries and a corporal in charge who, in assuring us that all was safely in the train, groused bitterly at having this guard duty imposed upon them. We condoled with them and dawdled back to our seats.

Suddenly it seemed to be dusk, and incredibly quickly after, it seemed to us, lights appeared here and there and night had descended. The heat had gone, too, and we felt cold. I was glad to indulge in a nip of whisky from a silver hip flask I had been given just before we left England, and was about to hand it round when, to my surprise, I saw that my three companions had taken the same action—their flasks were much bigger than mine!

Shortly after this the train pulled out and we, tired out with the day's events, dozed off into snatches of fitful sleep, punctuated by blurred impressions of brightly-lit stations and occasional stops. In one period of consciousness, for the first time since leaving England a feeling of loneliness overcame me and I was seized with an acute feeling akin to home sickness which I couldn't explain then. In fact I think this was an after-effect of Alex and the realization, as the train rumbled through the Egyptian night, that we were journeying into fateful events as yet hidden in the future, but further . . . and further . . . and further . . . away from home. I must have slept again.

When we awoke it was broad daylight, and we were running alongside the Suez Canal. From the far window of our carriage we could see a long string of heavily laden camels threading its way across the expanse of sand. We passed a few more small stations and then stopped at Kantara West, where we detrained and crossed the canal by the pontoon swing bridge to the great British military camp on the eastern side. Here, in daily expectation of joining our regiment in Palestine—the 4th Battalion Royal Sussex, a unit of the 53rd Division—we passed a month or so, during which time we became acclimatized and used to wearing topi and shorts. The sun beat down daily with increasing intensity, and as the weeks passed our knees and persons generally became as brown as everyone else's, although the beginning of the process was a painful one in my case. In my haste to lose my white knees, which proclaimed the newcomer to all and sundry, I exposed them to the morning sun for half an hour or so—about twenty-five minutes longer than I should have done. Next day, apart from the painful inflammation, my kneecaps were a deep plum colour, while behind the untouched whiteness was emphasised. For some days I was the target for well-merited criticism, but after the skin peeled off, having learned the hard way, matters soon righted themselves.

WORKING PARTY, TURKISH P.O.WS. EL KANTARA APR. 1918.

We were by no means idle at El Kantara. Often for days on end it fell to my lot to take out parties of 150 to 200 Turkish prisoners on various tasks in and around the camp. At 08.30 hours, with the escort of a dozen men and two N.C.O.s, I went through the gates of the barbed wire festooned compound, where I would find my party on parade, ready and awaiting me, in charge of a Turkish sergeant-major. Before moving off, a nominal roll of the party was given me to sign, the total on which, say 180, had to be checked with some care, as difficulties would arise should the count be 179 on returning in the evening. Each prisoner had been issued with rations for his midday meal, to take which work stopped for an hour. The escort was similarly provided, while I drew some sandwiches from the mess after breakfast, generally of Fray Bentos, which generated a midday thirst ill assuaged by swigs of warm water from a service bottle.

Sometimes we would go down to the canal bank, unloading boat-loads of stone blocks from native feluccas. At other times the party would be engaged on road or camp construction works.

Generally the Turk sergeant-major, whose command of English wasn't too good, acted as interpreter. At noon, after asking permission, he would blow his whistle, at which signal his compatriots would cease work, squat down in groups on the nearest sand and start cooking on little fires they could make in next to no time. They had a way, I believe, of utilizing the heat of the sand. Judging by the smell generated, they had onions and/or garlic, but they certainly were issued with, and ate, large amounts of bread. Commenting on this one day to one of the British officers in charge of the compound, I was told their bread ration was fixed by the Geneva convention, and happened just then to be in excess of the British Tommy's; although he was quick to point out that the latter had many other items of food issued which more than compensated for any discrepancy. Naturally, however, our men, hearing various versions of the story, groused.

They groused frequently, also, when comparing the state of their boots with the excellent footwear worn by the Turk prisoners. Certainly, I can vouch for the fact that just then the condition of their boots was disgraceful. Doubtless there were reasons. For instance, at this base for the units up in Palestine, in addition to drafts arriving from England there were many men lately discharged from hospitals, or returning either from leave or from courses of instruction. Until they regained their units, there seemed little prospect of getting any repairs effected.

One day the mud-wing of a passing lorry caught a Turk of our party a glancing blow in the back as he unwittingly stepped sideways out of file for some reason. The lorry was going very slowly indeed, but the Turk fell to the ground. He picked himself up and did not seem at all hurt—nothing serious, at any rate. We expected a few bruises, but at the midday break the sergeant-major came to me and told me that the man said he was going to die. When I laughed, he looked very grave and repeated, indicating the injured Turk, 'him *kaput*', and he shrugged expressively, as much as to say that there was no more to be said. On the way back to the compound that evening we left him at a field hospital, which at that time was dealing with hundreds of the Egyptian Labour Corps, sick with a sort of 'flu caught in the Judean Hills. They were quite unused to wet and cold weather of any sort, having been recruited in the Nile Delta, and then went down wholesale. In many cases they just sat there, wasted away and died. I saw rows of these poor emaciated people on several occasions when I took working parties there on various tasks. On the following day our injured Turk died also. It seemed simply incredible at the time. He had literally willed himself to die!

Apart from his alleged homosexual practices, we liked Johnny Turk. He was a simple chap by and large, but it was easy to see that, if properly equipped, officered and fed, he made a good soldier—as our own lads had found to their cost at Gallipoli. He was fighting well in Palestine, too, by all accounts, but his government had let him down badly there in the matter of supplies and backing. Jerusalem had been occupied by General Allenby's troops after several severe engagements the previous December. Now sporadic fighting was taking place well to the north, but further progress was slow due to difficulties of terrain and weather, and the need to await the clearing out of the Turks east of the Jordan by the Arabs, led by Feisal and Lawrence, who had advanced thus far up the Hejaz railway from Mecca. Actually, at that time, although Lawrence had already become famous, we at Kantara hadn't the faintest inkling of what he was doing, or even of the broad outline of his campaign.

Inevitably, then, although we were waiting to go to the front north of Jericho, our thoughts continually were of how our hard-pressed armies were faring on the Western Front. The news was grave. The Germans had struck again, this time on the Armentières–Kemel sector and our losses, as previously, had been tremendous. Thanks to the timely arrival of Australian and Guards Divisions before Hazebrouck, a new line had been stabilized there and Ypres itself still held, although all the hard-won gains of 1917, culminating in the capture of the Ridge and more, had been lost. Haig had issued an exhortation to the tired and decimated British Division, which went down in history as the 'backs to the wall' order.

Such was the situation when some of us entrained at Kantara-East, the recently completed line to El Arish, well on the way to our goal—our regiment! I have a confused memory of an all-night journey, followed by a long lorry hop to a base camp, arriving dead tired, only to receive orders to get back to Kantara. This, of course, produced much pungent grousing—not to be wondered at, as we had then no inkling of the reasons, made manifest only weeks later. But in the welter of rumour and counter-rumour rife at a regained Kantara, speculation as to our next move soon drove from us all thoughts of El Arish, and beyond. At length we entrained again at the Egyptian State Railway station and, after a tedious journey across the Nile Delta in sizzling heat, found ourselves at the seaside camp of Sidi Bishr on the eastern fringe of Alexandria, to which it was connected by electric tramway from the nearby suburb of Victoria.

At Sidi Bishr the most sinister of the spates of rumour was confirmed. We were there awaiting a convoy for France, and as the days passed and the situation on the Western Front unfolded in all its gravity, we prepared, in the isolation of our own night thoughts, for the worst. In the summer sun we swam and bathed light-heartedly, indulged in donkey races and idled away thus, straining our eyes many times daily, looking over the Mediterranean along the horizon for the smudges of smoke denoting the coming of the convoy which would take us once more to the Western Front.

Under this treatment our skins became the colour of mahogany and, as may be imagined, we all felt exceptionally fit and well. Occasionally we made excursions into Alexandria, but invariably these put a breaking strain upon our severely attenuated exchequers. Just then we had but one trouble in the world—money—or rather, lack of it. Our finances deteriorated to such a low that Cox & Co. in the Rue Cherif Pasha became stone deaf to our impassioned appeals, and we, without exaggeration, were in desperate straits until one of our number, having an uncle in the government service in Cairo, managed to raise a considerable loan from him. After that we pooled our resources and each paid his messing money every morning before departing, either to the seashore or to Alex.

Beyond the presence of the military there were, as far as we could see, few evidences of war apparent in Alexandria. Of its polyglot population, the rich appeared to be getting richer, the well-to-do to be prospering exceedingly, and the poor to be living in their traditional fashion—that is to say, if their children's eyes were full of flies, they didn't appear to be going hungry, while the parents seemed up to every known device and subterfuge to make a few piastres! The shops were crammed with rich and varied merchandise and many kinds of delicacies then practically unobtainable in Europe. Indeed, Egypt appeared to us, comparatively speaking, a land of plenty for those lucky enough to be enjoying Fortune's favours. Therefore, so far as we could in the short time available, we took what Alex had to offer, but it was an expensive business. The races, for instance. We had good fun on several occasions, although warned beforehand that most of the jockeys had been barred from the British or French turf, and I will say that the girls we had met the previous evening gave us some really good tips. But then, they took our winnings from us in the end. Just a repetition of the old, old story, I suppose. We even visited Cairo for a few hours, returning completely done in, in a variety of respects and for a variety of reasons! Then it was a relief to get away from that sort of thing to our camp at Sidi Bishr by the seashore; to wake up at the approach of the paperboy making his morning round of the lines shouting 'Gyppo M-a-i-l—Gyppo M-a-i-l. Very goot news zis morning! Two Brit-eesh ship sunk!' One morning he substituted 'fourteen' for 'two'.

Or again, the Indian laundry man on his round with clean washing, chanting 'Brown, *sahib* . . . Brown, *sahib* . . . Washeeng—I have it!' and, after a short interval without a response, 'no pice give it . . . F. . . it!' With which expletive the unclaimed parcel would be flung back into the basket, and looking suitably disgusted, he would move a few yards before delving again and repeating his cry, often with success.

At length, one morning about three weeks after our arrival, an excited shouting and pointing by one of our number drew our attention to the smoke of the long-awaited convoy. Soon after that we received our marching orders, though not as we had anticipated, for we were to proceed forthwith to Port Said to embark there.

In the late evening we entrained, after a farewell tea at Groppi's in the Rue Cherif Pasha, where we ate so many cream pastries and multi-coloured ice cream panaches that I was practically a dysentery case a few hours later.

In spite of our ultimate destination, everyone seemed in good spirits at the thought of getting on the move again, and as soon

THE CONVOY - OFF ALEXANDRIA.
FROM SIDI BISHR CAMP. MAY 16.

as the train started rugger scrums up and down the corridors were started, with someone's topi for a ball, until at length, exhausted and dishevelled, we stopped play. I regret to add that considerable damage had been done to Egyptian State Railway's property.

As I have said, I was almost a dysentery case by the time we reached Port Said, but managed to stagger on board the liner which was to take us to France, aided by my old school friend

Brown, with whom I shared a cabin with two other second lieutenants of the Royal Sussex. I was pretty well *hors de combat* for two days before I came on deck to get a look at the ship, now busy loading troops, stores and cargo. She was the new Orient liner *Ormonde*—so new that she had never been completed in the accepted sense of the word, and her interior fittings showed that she had been put into service after fitment of bare essentials only. After a maiden voyage out to Indian ports, she had returned thus far via Basra, where she had loaded a considerable cargo of copra. When we arrived this was being unloaded but, to the annoyance of all concerned, it was now being put on board again.

From the boat deck the harbour of Port Said was most interesting, as were the dark-skinned youths who clambered up the ship's side very few minutes from rowing boats and dived for coppers in marvellous fashion. The water, dirty enough on the surface was, from the height at which we viewed it, translucent in the strong sunlight and one could see almost to the bottom, near which, in fact, many of the coins were retrieved by natives whose cheeks bulged to bursting with recovered small change. A little way off several men were diving to the bottom to bring up huge lumps of coal, which by some means or other, fair or foul (and most probably the latter), had found a resting place there. They remained under water for incredibly long periods while they tied one end of a rope, which each took down with him, round the lump, which was then hauled aboard.

Indeed, on that particular late May morning we watched, fascinated, while this was going on, until unmistakable signs that we were about to sail shortly appeared in the form of showers of black smuts which descended from the *Ormonde*'s two funnels (for this was before the days of universal oil firing) as the engineers proceeded to raise steam. It would be about midday, and as we retired to a more sheltered coign of vantage the entire 'black squad' of Lascar firemen downed shovels. We gathered that they had just heard that they were to cross the Mediterranean and, notwithstanding an offer of double wages, they had refused in spite of all the efforts of the captain and his officers who, thereupon, had them clapped in irons. In this condition the melancholy procession trooped ashore, and later on we understood that an urgent request for replacements had been wired to Alexandria. In the meanwhile the engineers asked for volunteers to feed the fires, and there was no lack of these. But once down in that veritable inferno, their sole desire was to leave as soon as possible, and few stuck it for longer then ten minutes or so, as the white heat from the boiler fires was blinding and searing in intensity. On deck again, I recall that a certain sympathy was felt for the mutinous Lascars, and it was a sobering thought to consider the slim chance of escape after a torpedo hit down there.

In due course the replacements arrived by special train, and as they came over the brow they seemed to us to constitute the most nondescript collection of humanity we had ever set eyes upon. Most of them looked as though a puff of wind would blow them away, they were so thin and emaciated.

They disappeared below and shortly after, as night fell, the *Ormonde* appeared to hum, preparatory to departure. At midnight we sailed and steamed slowly by the great statue of Ferdinand de Lesseps, and out into the rippleless surface of the Mediterranean— alone and in brilliant moonlight. A perfect night, with the moon hanging like a giant silver plate in our path, and many were the comments concerning our apparent lack of an escort as we re-hearsed our boat stations and checked rolls. As soldiers, we didn't presume to tell the Royal Navy its business, but in our humble opinion we must have been a sitting target on that moonlit sea, visible for miles from any lurking U-boat that cared to have a go at us. However, after speculating for some time, during which we strained our eyes looking in vain for what never came, we turned in and slept.

I awoke in broad daylight to find Brown pulling me out of my bunk and shouting at me. 'Quick,' he yelled, as I rubbed my eyes, 'look over there,' indicating the open scuttle above. Staggering to my feet, I caught a momentary glimpse of a large steamer about two miles away, apparently settling down by the bows. Clouds of steam were arising from her amidships. That was all I saw as the scene slid by the porthole in a weird manner. Overhead we heard the tramp of many feet, and by the vibration of the ship and by our instability while trying hurriedly to dress, we realized that we were steering a zig-zag course at high speed. We had overslept, too, and were amazed to see by our watches that it was about 10.30 a.m.

JAP DESTROYER "R"

'CANBERRA'

BRITISH DESTROYER 34

P&O. "MALWA"

ANCHOR LINE "CALEDONIA"

P&O. "KAISR I HIND"

'INDARRA'

JAP DESTROYER "V"

JAP DESTROYER "J"

JAP DESTROYER "K"

IMPRESSION OF CONVOY FROM BOAT DECK OF ORIENT LINE "ORMONDE" — APPROACHING STRAITS OF MESSINA. 29th MAY 1918.

As soon as we could we joined the throng on deck, where the constantly changing course had the effect of turning many of us quite giddy, the whole panorama to the horizon sliding by first in one direction, then in another. Moreover, to increase our confusion, we were now in the company of four large liners and several British and Japanese destroyers, all of which were now emitting dense volumes of smoke as they endeavoured to make their best speed. At any given moment, one of these ships would appear to be astern of us; almost immediately after, on our beam, and so on . . . a few seconds, and it would be ahead. There were now boats and rafts around the torpedoed ship and she looked considerably lower in the water, with a destroyer standing by and steaming slowly about.

To landlubbers such as we were it was completely bewildering, as the whole of the convoy was zig-zagging save the destroyers, which raced round the flanks of the convoy at terrific speeds, throwing up sheets of sparkling white spray at the bows and leaving long foam-flecked wakes. Streams of signal flags fluttered every few minutes from the British destroyer leader, replied to by us with an answering string.

One of the ship's officers told us that we were the 'lame dog' of the convoy and had been ordered to 'put a jerk into it'. Whether we were able to respond is doubtful, as we seemed to lag behind. The excitement died down, ending as far as we were concerned, by the dropping of two depth charges by one of the destroyers. The sinking liner now lay far behind us.

It was then that we were told that she was the Union Castle liner *Leasowe Castle*, with several county yeomanry regiments on board, and that it had been torpedoed just as we were joining the convoy which, of course, had sailed from Alexandria. At breakfast the second officer, at whose table we sat, told us that a radio message had been received to the effect that almost everyone had been rescued.

After lunch we had leisure to examine through field glasses the other ships of the convoy, which were all ahead of us in a kind of diamond formation in which the *Ormonde* constituted a laggard tail, although easily the largest and newest of the bunch. The trouble seemed to be that our makeshift and obviously inadequate complement of stokers could only raise enough steam to give the engineers slightly more than half speed. As I have said, we were always behind and through the day appeals were being made to us by the destroyer astern—just then the whipper-in—to 'come on', and we noticed that they took turns at this unenviable task.

Among the other liners it was easy to recognise the *Indarra*. Somehow she had a top-heavy look, although to be sure she must have been crammed to capacity with troops. she seemed short in proportion to the height above the waterline. Then there were the two P & O liners *Kaiser-i-Hind* and *Malwa*, the four-master *Caledonia*, and finally the much smaller *Canberra*.

Throughout the summer day and night we steamed without incident on a blue sea almost devoid of shipping, the two old 'tramps' we did encounter flying the Spanish and Norwegian flags with their names painted in large dirty white letters along their rusty sides. On the following morning we passed a dim smudge, hull-down to the southward, and were told that it was Malta.

Towards midday our peace was again disturbed by the report of a gun which, by the puff of smoke, had been fired from the stern of the *Caledonia*. For some minutes there was suppressed 'wind-up' while everyone stood at boat stations, but eventually things quietened down again. That afternoon, having been joined by half a dozen United States patrol boats and an aerial escort of seaplanes, we passed through the Straits of Messina, and early that night saw the eastern sky illuminated by the island volcano of Stromboli.

The following evening the sun was setting in a copper-and-gold-streaked sky and an almost purple sea, which was practically motionless when, save for the escorting destroyers, the convoy came almost to a standstill. Again, all crowded to the rails to inquire the reason, and again rumour was rife. Rightly or wrongly, we gathered that we were nearing the French coast and awaiting instructions, but in any case we presented, as did the other ships, sitting targets for a U-boat commander. Indeed, it seemed pretty plain to us that those of the *Ormonde*'s officers passing on their business weren't too pleased at the situation. At length, after barely moving thus for half an hour or so, our engines restarted, or increased revolutions, and the *Ormonde*, as did the others, turned slowly about and steamed, as we thought, away from the coast, but darkness soon enveloped us and left us guessing. There being nothing else to do, after drinking the bar dry most of us turned in and awaited the coming of morning.

In anticipation of getting our first glimpse of the coast of Southern France, we were on deck unusually early and saw a wonderful sunrise which betokened another fine day, the sea becoming a marvellous blue. The other ships were now around us and seemed closer than previously. There was, indeed, much to interest us, when a sudden shouting and pointing caused us to turn sharply and look for the source. Afterwards there was endless discussion as to what happened, but it all took place so quickly. Several of us in our group on the boat deck thought we saw a white line of foam which seemed to disappear beneath the ship— an illusion caused by the height above the water at which we were standing. Actually, opinion hardened to the theory that the torpedo, missing us, passed close to our stern, went on and hit the *Kaisr-i-Hind*. There was no doubt that she had been hit, although we heard only a muffled explosion. Later, she took on a pronounced list, but by good fortune reached port without further incident; as, in fact, did we and the remainder of the convoy.

At breakfast we were told that ninety-two had been drowned in the sinking of the *Leasowe Castle*, and in that day's French newspaper read that it was 192. The approaches by sea to the city and docks of Marseilles, dominated as they are by the great statue of the Virgin, Notre Dame de la Garde, are very fine in scenic quality, and we enjoyed every moment of our progress as the *Ormonde* steamed slowly by the Château d'If of Dumas' famous novel *The Count of Monte Cristo*, and other well known landmarks, until the great port came into full view. This was France again, and as we packed our few belongings we wondered what lay in store for us. I remember that Egypt and the Canal Zone, indeed the last three months, seemed already like a dream, and that I had four main recollections only which came to mind, when I harked back in thought to our experiences there. They were, strangely enough, not what one would expect to remain fixed in the memory, but here they are, just as they were that morning as we docked at Marseilles.

First, the old-fashioned Victorian English water cart on its daily
progress down the main camp road at Kantara, and the natives
on their knees behind it, catching the falling spouts of water in
their hands and mouths. Next, a gang of Egyptian Labour Corps
natives moving a shed by passing two stout poles through it and
lifting, with six bodies at each of the four protruding ends. At the
shouted word from the giant Nubian ganger, who flourished and
used to effect his long whip, the shed was raised and moved a few
yards at a time by the sweating, screaming natives—poor devils!
Then the memory of lying on my back sunbathing sleepily on the
surface of the buoyant water of the middle of the Suez Canal; of
something bumping me lightly on the back of my head; of turning
lazily, and of alarm at seeing what the object was—the largest,
longest turd I had ever seen! Lastly, the unexpected meeting
outside the orderly room at Sidi Bishr, among a draft of newly
arrived elderly second lieutenants of our company sergeant-major,
tormentor of Leicestershire Regimental Depot days of 1917—the
blighter who did his best to get we three N.C.O.s from France
stripped of our ranks, as I have narrated. Suffice it to say that the
boot was on the other leg from that evening on, Pegg, in particular
giving him a shocking time. Maybe we overdid it, but four years
of war had induced in us a real dislike of barrack square paragons.
We had no use for them.

As we docked, showers of topis descended into the oily water
at the end of unravelled puggarees, a traditional rite observed by
troops returning from the East, we were told, and after that it
wasn't long before we were lined up on the dockside in readiness
to march off to a rest camp. We bade goodbye with genuine regret
to the *Ormonde* and those of her officers we had met, and wished
we could accompany them on their next trip—to the U.S.A. for
American troops.

Under the hot June sun we marched through a maze of railway
sidings choked with goods wagons, and a series of mean streets,
into the tree-lined boulevard of one of the most important streets
of Marseilles—in many ways a unique city. As at Alexandria, East
and West met, though in different fashion. While Alex seemed the
gateway to Asia, Marseilles was that of Africa. It was said during
the 1920s that it had become the Chicago of Europe, but as far as

we were concerned it was then. Never since have I seen such an ill-favoured cut-throat crowd, flotsam of North African and goodness knows what other ports, as that through which we marched that day. At times in the meanest of the narrow streets of slum-like buildings, blowsy and sometimes horrifying screaming women with tousled hair leaned from upper windows and spat on us contemptuously, or with savage pleasure. It was only with considerable difficulty that three Argyle & Sutherland Highlanders were restrained from leaving the ranks and dashing into one house to exact vengeance on a black-bearded old apparition with one tooth and a shrill, obscene laugh who derided, too obviously, their kilts. On reaching the rest camp of Pont Rouet on high ground in the outer suburbs, we learned the reason for this open show of hostility.

A fresh German offensive on the Chemin des Dames had completely broken through the French and British Divisions, already decimated by hard fighting in previous actions, and the victorious Germans were reported to have reached the Marne at Château-Thierry. This new disaster, following closely the 5th Army collapse near St. Quentin and the considerable losses of ground further north, culminating in the capture of Armentières and Mont Kemmel, caused feeling among many uninformed Frenchmen to run high against the British, who were blamed for this new débâcle.

At the Pont Rouet camp, the provost marshal gave us a pretty straight talk, advising us, should we visit Marseilles, to keep strictly to the tramlines. In other words, if we left the comparative safety of the main streets, he could not be responsible for what might happen to us. Recently, he said, several British officers and men had disappeared completely, without trace, while cases were occurring daily of knifing, drugging, robbery, or a combination of these. With our march through some of these villainous streets still fresh in our memories, we were suitably impressed, and made up our minds to be careful, at any rate, as we caught a tram for the centre of the city the following morning after breakfast.

There the famous Cannebière seemed quite undisturbed by the German drive in the north, and the café tables under the sunlit trees were crowded and gay with uniformed officers of many services and of many nations plus, in nearly every case, their chic and chattering lady friends. An additional touch of gaiety was lent to the scene by the fact that it was a local flag day, and the methods adopted by the fair sellers of flags were extremely entertaining. We had a pretty shrewd suspicion that a goodly number of these girls were members of an age-old sisterhood, but they were most certainly young, vivacious and attractive, with the result that we began to like Marseilles immensely. That evening, having called on the local office of Cox & Co. successfully, we dined at the Hôtel du Louvre et de la Paix, returning to camp in good time, tired out but well satisfied with our experiences.

We stayed four days in Marseilles, and I recall that on the evening preceding our departure, the impact of the provost marshal's homily having lost its impetus somewhat in the gay atmosphere of the city, we joined a party intent on visiting a Madame in a large house just off the main street. All went well until one of our colleagues objected to charges made for a round of drinks. In the ensuing argument, he pushed the steel-shod point of his newly purchased walking stick through the front of the piano, after which things happened very quickly—almost too quickly. By great good fortune my two immediate companions and I managed to reach the foot of the staircase, *en route* for the front door, as the rough-house with two giant African chuckers-out started on the first-floor landing. Our luck nearly ended there, as a shower of contents from several fairly full chamber pots descended from a vantage point above the well over the second-floor staircase, projected by the now-screaming girls up there. As we left by the open front door, the shattered remains of one of the receptacles followed us. Somewhat later, safely in the shelter of a rocking street-car, we brushed ourselves down as well as we could and straightened our ties. It had been quite warm enough while it lasted!

On 4th June we left Marseilles with real regret, in spite of the hostility with which we had been received. Indeed, two of our number only just managed to board the train, having spent three days with two of the fair sex at a cottage in a seaside suburb. Listening to their adventures, and considering our own, as the dirty old troop train rattled over the points and through the outskirts of Marseilles, we all wished we could really have missed that train: for, we thought, in a few days' time, where should we

MORNING ABLUTIONS - JUVISY. NR PARIS JUN 6th 1918.

be? It just would not bear thinking about. We were still packed four to one compartment, and slept as on the outwards journey, as we made our way leisurely north. At every stop the train seemed to shed a few of its load, and as the numbers of 'missing' increased we were forced to the conclusion that in many cases this was by deliberate design! It may be of passing interest, however, to record that the train came to a halt, to our intense surprise, at Paray-le-Monial, and we were nearly left behind through endeavouring to pay for the meal we had consumed on the outwards journey. While we were trying to explain, the shrill note of the guard's horn and shouts of '*en voiture*' cut short our explanations—and, I might add, gesticulations—to the middle-aged lady now behind the counter, who obviously thought us *dérangé* and smiled for the first time as we vanished through the buffet door.

Two mornings later, 6th June, our long train halted outside the station of Juvisy, a busy junction on the outskirts of Paris, just as the city was waking to a lovely summer morning. Obtaining some hot water from the engine, we were washing and shaving from our canvas buckets placed at the side of the tracks, when our ablutions were pleasantly interrupted. A suburban train crammed with working girls, city-bound, stopped alongside. They were cheery souls, in the mass, at any rate, as they crowded to the carriage windows, whatever their individual worries must have been at that trying time, with a victorious German army again threatening Paris. Our semi-nudity sent them into shrieks of delighted banter at our expense, and although we couldn't fully understand much of their chatter, we managed to gather import of some of the more obvious sallies, which were distinctly bawdy in character. Then our general amusement and individual embarrassment sent them into renewed gales of mirth, and made us wish that in certain cases, as we looked up at the sea of faces, we could get to know them better.

Becoming serious of a sudden, however, they told us of the ravages of 'Big Bertha'—the great German gun then firing on Paris from behind their lines, over fifty miles distant. Indeed, even as their train bore them away, waving furiously as we stood there on the tracks, we were practically certain that we heard, very high overhead to the east, the faint chortle of one of those great shells.

A huge American locomotive, complete with cowcatcher, now coupled on to us and drew our train through Versailles and the western suburbs of Paris. By way of Mantes and the Seine Valley, we reached Rouen about mid afternoon, and shortly afterwards were trudging uphill on the same cobbled tram-lined road that several of us with previous service in France knew of yore, that led to the series of great base camps and hospitals above the city. Our particular destination was the Camp de Bruyères, which forest of tents and marquees seemed, at first acquaintance, to house some dozens of subalterns with a good sprinkling of senior officers, all in transit, in addition to many hundreds of drafts newly arrived from England.

The camps had grown enormously since I was last there in December 1915, and a startling change to us was the presence of khaki-clad women everywhere, the first of the W.A.A.C.s we had seen in France. I recall that we thought their long, thick, ankle-length skirts and ugly shoes pretty dreadful; but, as one wag remarked, it probably assisted them to keep their virtue! Apropos of this, one of the first things we were told was that on the former racecourse, now a huge hospital, the equivalent of a division was 'down' with V.D. A pretty staggering thought, and a warning!

As the sun set we started shivering as the chill of the north crept into our bones and overcame the resistance of blood thinned by Eastern temperatures. On our journey up from Marseilles we had learned of the ravages of the Spanish Influenza then rife among the armies and civil populations alike. Our apprehension of being almost certain cases in the immediate future can, therefore, be well imagined. In desperation, but principally to keep warm, we drank whisky on an unprecedented scale; and actually, whether by this means or by luck I know not, we managed to avoid this scourge. For scourge it was: in many cases it produced fatal results, for the virus encountered little resistance from populations weakened by years of stringent rationing and latterly by the almost total absence of nourishing 'extras' in their diets. Indeed, when at length these Spanish 'flu victims, having weathered the worst, rose from their beds under the stress of the war effort, they looked positively ghastly for days, and as though a puff of wind would blow them away.

Although we had escaped the 'flu we had other troubles. In the train, shortly after leaving Marseilles, Brown and I had started to itch around the crotch, and by the time we reached Rouen it had become almost unbearable.

Until after we had showered and cleaned up, we thought that the cramped conditions of the train were responsible, but as there was no improvement we decided to report sick. On the morning following our arrival, therefore, we saw the camp M.O. He examined Brown first, he having been quicker to comply with the order, 'drop your breeches'. The medico appeared interested, and duly pronounced the trouble to be a species of eczema, caused by the hot weather and lack of facilities for undressing, in all probability. He would give him something with which to treat it. Then, turning to me, 'let's look at you'. He looked and could not suppress a broad smile as he said, cheerily, 'crabs, and pretty bad, too!' He went away and returned in a few moments with a sizeable box of blue ointment. I won't describe the drastic pre-treatment necessary before applying the salve, but this caused much hilarity in our tent, as Brown put finishing touches to the job with my razor. A watching Coldstreamer and an Argyll & Sutherland subaltern were convulsed with mirth, and this affair persists in my memory.

I can also recall the discomfort occasioned. This, however, was not so bad as the itch. The M.O. told me that in all probability a W.C. seat in the camp at Marseilles was responsible. To this day I am ignorant of the strictly medical term for this most uncomfortable complaint; only that which I heard used for it by the army. I believe that, louse-ridden as several million British soldiers were for years on the Western Front, 'crabs' was a rarity. It was caused by a certain parasite which bored under the victim's skin and multiplied exceedingly while so doing.

Our tent held four of us, A.V. Brown and myself, the Coldstreamer and the Argyll & Sutherland Highlander, the latter both lieutenants. We were all waiting to go up once more to the line, the Coldstreamer now recovered from an arm wound received near Hazebrouck in April, the Scot coming over in our convoy to rejoin his battalion in France on evacuation from an Egyptian hospital, following a bad bout of malaria and dysentery, which had laid him low somewhere on the Judean Hills.

Thrown together thus, I had, as I have said above, provided hilarious amusement for the three of them by their witnessing the necessary tonsorial preparation practised on the itching parts of my person by A.V. Brown. As his itching trouble had been diagnosed as a type of eczema, his treatment was far gentler in character than mine, though considerably longer in taking effect. Indeed, within two days I was pronounced cured of those boring little devils the 'crabs', and in our tent was 'whiter than the whitewash on the wall'!

Amid such well-intentioned leg-pulling at my temporarily uncomfortable situation, conversation turned inevitably to what is now called 'sex' and, asked for his opinion on a point raised (which I have long forgotten), the Scot, to our utter surprise, stated with a gesture of loathing that he thought the whole business absolutely disgusting. Protest was general and protracted, but he stuck to his guns. The strange upshot was, briefly, that though he hated it, he wasn't a funk at this sort of thing, and he bet us twenty francs apiece that he would go down to Rouen with us as soon as opportunity offered, and accost the first really attractive lady we might indicate to him there. We took him on, and did exactly that. About mid morning of a lovely June day, we indicated a lady as she stood looking into the window of a shoe shop in the Rue des Carmes, not far from the cathedral, on the opposite side of the road. Without the slightest hesitation the Scot set off and, to our surprise—and, indeed, consternation—engaged her in conversation for a few moments, they looking in the shop window together. Then they strolled off, smiling at each other. She was a brunette, well tailored, of medium height and, judging from our distance, around twenty-two or twenty-three years of age. Like many Frenchwomen at that time of day, she carried a large shopping bag, and as they disappeared in the hurrying throng, we noted how jauntily the Highlander's kilt swung from side to side as they walked.

More than impressed, we sat down outside the nearest *brasserie* to speculate, thinking amongst other things of our twenty francs which we could ill afford just then. 'Well, well . . . and the blighter speaks French, too!'

I have long forgotten how we passed the intervening hours that day before returning to camp, considerably before we would have done in different circumstances, appearing before our tent, perspiring and rather weary around 6 p.m. The flap was folded back, but the canvas still held the heat of the June sun. Within the shady depth of the interior, our man lay on his back, reading and apparently not noticing us as we shed most of our clothing before adopting similarly relaxed attitudes on our bed rolls. At length, from one of us, 'any luck, Jock?' Voice from depths of the book: 'disgusting, as I knew it would be.' 'Oh . . . why?' 'Absolutely revolting!' putting the book down, 'really'. And he exhibited the extreme loathing of the previous evening. A silence, broken finally by an urge from our side for details. Yet another facial contortion of distaste. 'She told me that her husband was the stationmaster at a small town on the Dieppe line and that she had come in on the morning train to do some shopping. Certain things back there had become very scarce and *la grippe* the Spanish 'flu, had been very bad. Her husband was still an invalid after it. We went to one of those wretched so-called hotels—the entrance was between two shops, just off the Grosse Horloge street. We were there about half an hour—and it cost me—the room and some horrible wine—the ruddy ear-r-th! Which reminds me—twenty francs each, please!' and he held an outstretched palm aloft. He gave a final 'ugh' as he put the notes in his wallet—there was no doubt he meant it.

The Coldstreamer, counting his depleted resources, ventured 'what about the girl?' The Scot was caught, we thought afterwards, right off his guard, because he said with real feeling, 'och—she would h' stayed there all day!'

Many weeks afterwards on a rain- and mist-laden September evening, I sat with a young colleague on S.A.A. boxes within a badly damaged German pillbox on the shattered slopes of a re-occupied Mont Kemmel, a few kilometres south of Ypres. Just relieved from a day-long spell along a very temporary and thinly held front by two colleagues, we sat sipping Old Bushmills Irish from chipped enamel mugs, watching Captain White (M.C. and Bar) writing reports and returns in a field message book by the light of a guttering candle stuck on an upturned Player's tin. Suddenly putting down his pencil and tearing out the relevant page, he called for the runner on duty. Then, turning to me as he waited, and picking up his mug, he said, 'Richard, you were going to tell us about that impotent stationmaster—where was it—Rouen?' 'On the Dieppe line, sir,' I corrected, as tactfully as

334

I could, as the runner appeared and departed for Battalion H.Q. Then I told them, and we toasted the stationmaster's wife.

We subalterns were rarely without employment while at Rouen, at least during the mornings and afternoons. In June 1918 the British manpower barrel was really being scraped, and drafts were arriving literally in thousands. They were hitherto back-area and Blighty types of Army Service Corps and other regimental depot staffs, who had probably now been replaced by W.A.A.C.s. Generally they had received little or no instruction, either in handling arms or in infantry drill—not, at any rate, for a very long time.

In many instances, several years must have elapsed since the rigours of the parade ground and of warlike exercises had been exchanged for what then was thought to be a safe job in a store or depot office. With the more elderly, one could not but feel a degree of sympathy for them in their predicament at being thus winkled out. Nevertheless, we endeavoured in the short time available to inculcate some basic principles before their drafts left Rouen *en route* for the decimated regiments now holding the newly stabilized lines before Amiens and Hazebrouck.

When not so occupied, we took these drafts for route marches through the wooded countryside behind the camp area, arranging these to be roughly circular. Here, during the hourly halts, the trees afforded generous shade to those whose questionable marching qualities we were trying to improve.

The halts, according to the 'book', should have been of five minutes, but on the first occasion that I essayed one of these marches it must have taken twenty minutes before the various N.C.O.s reported their sections 'present and correct'. The reason? Several gangs of men in various stages of khaki *déshabillé* appeared through the trees at the roadside as by magic as soon as the draft had fallen out. They carried either Crown & Anchor boards or decks of cards, which they proceeded to display in the nearest

335

patch of greensward—with considerable effect, as in next to no time several schools were in full swing. The majority of these men were either Anzacs, Canadians or Jocks. The few obvious English-men that I saw were not very likeable types: in any peace-time society they would exist by their wits!

We were informed on good authority that the Military Police and the camp command knew all about them, and I would say that I never experienced the slightest trouble with them in falling my charges in again on blowing the whistle. Indeed, many emerged from the brambles considerably sadder and wiser, and their stories, retailed when the march was resumed, were pathetically amusing. I don't know whether these deserters lived in the woods or not, or whether they were ever rounded up, but I should be very surprised if they hadn't good friends in the camps and adjacent villages who would advise them in good time of any such attempt. They had plenty of money. It may seem strange that neither I nor my fellow second lieutenants on these marches tried to do this ourselves in order to uphold authority. We didn't for two reason: first, that these de-serters were big, husky types, especially the Anzacs, and our charges were no match for them physically; secondly, we knew that, probably within a few hours, our unfortunates would be marching down to the station for the line, and would have precious little opportunity again for relaxation of this sort.

Which reminds me of the frequent pay parades, for which I was detailed on several occasions, when I would disburse perhaps twenty-five thousand francs at the rate of ten francs for single men and five for married men—poor devils! I recall that, through sheer weariness towards the end, I would place the note mechanically in the tendered brand new paybook and sign it almost without looking at the soldier. When at length the quartermaster sergeant gathered up the remaining notes and the nominal roll before departing, I was reminded irresistibly of that German trench near Flers of 2nd October 1916, when our own remnant was withdrawn there from Gueudecourt. Then, at dusk, we buried many men of the King's Royal rifles whom we found there among the shreds of rusting wire. They had lain there for nearly three weeks—since 15th September, in fact. The majority had new paybooks, with one payment only of ten francs detailed therein. Now I knew where, perhaps, they had received it; and wondered, too, how many more payments these poor fellows would live to get.

We did manage a few half-day periods of relaxation. Then, if the field cashier had called beforehand, we went down to Rouen and sampled the flesh-pots as thoroughly as we could, until funds ran low again. No doubt we were very foolish at times, but in retrospect I have no regrets whatsoever.

On 14th July it was our turn to take the road to the station to join, at long last, the 4th Battalion The Royal Sussex Regiment, now, we gathered, 'Somewhere in France'.

Divisional Sign. 34th Division.

CHAPTER 20

THE XTH ARMY (MANGIN)

NORTHWARD we went, and as the sun was setting on the following day detrained at Mendinghem, west of and near the Ypres railhead.

Times had changed indeed since last I had been in the Nord Département; 'Doughboys' (as the U.S. Army called their soldiers) now marched along its roads and filled the village *estaminets*. Around Mendinghem we saw that there were several field hospital units, red crosses prominent among the marquees, no doubt because of the now-frequent bombing of our communications. For half an hour so before reaching Mendinghem we had been noticing quite a few recently-made bomb holes in the fields at the side of the railway line.

Around here the enemy had retaken Messines, Wytchaete Ridge and Mont Kemmel, Armentières, Bailleul, Merville, Estaires and Vieux Berquin. Méteren had been retaken by the 9th Division on 19th July. Things were bad.

A British three-ton lorry lumbered by outside our camp with the legend painted upon the tailboard 'EAT LESS AND SAVE SHIPPING'. What a great thought, after nearly four years of war! Another passed, bearing the same legend, but a wag had substituted two Ts for the two Ps in the final word, giving us a real laugh!

Soon after nightfall the Nissen hut in the transit camp which we occupied near Mendinghem station had a narrow escape, a bomb dropping nearby which riddled the roof like a sieve, snuffed our candles, and knocked all of us over. Upon the road outside lay two American soldiers, unfortunately past aid. I believe them to have been of the US 30th (New York) Division, of which more later. It was said that a cook had left his campfire uncovered, and that a passing flight of German Gothas *en route* for Calais or Boulogne had reminded us of the fact. If a fire was responsible for making us a target, however, I personally thought that the glowing fire-boxes of the locomotives in the nearby sidings must have been equally visible from above, and hoped secretly that we would get a move on pretty soon. I need not have worried. During the following afternoon the 4th Royal Sussex marched in and we reported ourselves for duty, Brown and I being assigned to 'D' Company.

At the makeshift tented camp on the outskirts of Mendinghem, we soon found that the battalion second-in-command, adjutant, transport officer and several other subaltern officers, including two from 'D' Company, were all on leave, following arrival in France after nearly three years absence at Suvla Bay (Dardanelles) and in Palestine. This was all very right and proper in its way, but the immediate trouble was that it now formed part of a reconstituted 34th Division, composed of similar units withdrawn from divisions in Palestine, one from East Africa, and that the 34th Division had been ordered into action somewhere.

A few hours after we reported, we entrained in the gathering dusk and off we went—in a state of considerable confusion, may it be added. At least, Brown and I were confused but, as new-comers each assigned to a platoon, we obeyed orders to the best of our ability and held our peace, endeavouring, however, to help when we could. Although handicapped by the absence of nearly all the senior officers, the remainder were plainly unused to French railway travel behind the Western Front and appeared to grouse at trifles. I did my best to get to know the N.C.O.s of my platoon and was heartened to hear again the Sussex speech.

We spent the night in the train, and it was hardly daylight when, full of sleep and completely mystified, we detrained at Chantilly, on the outskirts of Paris. Unacclimatized as they were, the men shivered pitifully in the dawn light, and in a drizzle of rain the battalion bivouacked on a considerable open space near the village, where everyone made the best of things. As the morning progressed the rain ceased and the emerging sun warmed the thinned blood of the battalion. There was no doubt that they were good material, but of fighting as we had known it on the Western Front, they just hadn't an idea yet. To be fair, however, they had probably endured considerably more actual privation by hunger, thirst, and the ills common to the East from which they had come: principally dysentery and malaria.

REFERENCE

...ne 17th July	———
...r 18th "	— — —
...orning 20th	••••••••
" 21st	+·+·+·+·
" 23rd.	·—·—·—·
" 24th	+··+··+··
" 27th	—··—··—
" 28th.	—···—····
" 29th	—···—···
" 30th	oooooo
" 31st	××××××
" 2nd. Aug.	++++++
" 3rd. "	—+—+—
End of Battles	— — —

I, Vic
AISNE
162 le Port
Fontenoy
osly Mercia
Permant
SOISSONS
72 la Fosse
Vauxbuin
Belleu
153 Courmelles
1 U.S. Dommiers
Berzy
Sabrmon
XX MOR
Chaudun
Verte Feuille Fm.
Villemantge
2 U.S.
Vierzy
38
Longpont Paes Harte
15
Villers- Corcy
Villes Helou
Cottarets
La Flessie Ga Ro
HX1 5 128
St. Remy
Hulli
ARMY BDY 41
Billy
IX1
33
Noroy
OURCQ Ouku
¼ 4 U.S.
Marizy
Bregy
II
la Ferté 2
Milon
Gatilly
47
Dammard
½ 4 U.S.
Chézy
Hautavesnes
Bonnes
Ba
VII 164
Torcy
CLIGNON
Belleau
Etrepi
167
Bouresches
26 U.S.
1 U.S. le Thiolet.
ARMY BDY
Charly
PARIS
34 m.
MARNE la Ferté
Sous Jouarre
5

AISNE

AISNE

VESLE

Braine

uqyo

Quincy

of

se
ntreuil
Cilly
Housse

Mont N.D.

St.Thiba

Ville
voie

Fismes

Magneux

Breuil

VESLE

Muizon

Canal

Béthen

Joncŕery

Thillois

REIMS

34

Branco
Bruys

Chéry

Arcis le Ponsart

Branscourt
Crugny
oRasnay

Trigelon.

ARDRE

Loupeigne

2 COL.

1 COL.
(from 22nd

venay
neux
ramaille
Saponay
Sevinges

Mareuil

Cohan

Tramery

Chéry

Largery

Bligny

31t.

62 from 2 o till 1 t.

Fère en
Tardenois

Nesles

Ville en Tardenois

Champrecy

120

(till 20th

XXII
(from 20th

villeneuve.

Bois
Meuvieux

Charmery Martau

o Pourcy

51 from 20

Courmonto

Champvon

Passy

Cuisles

Jonquery

Cuchery

14

40. 9

Romery

V

I

uvardes

le Charmel

Chatillon

Reuil

10 Col

7

Jaulgonne

Chartaves

MARNE

Mareuil

Venteuil

Canal

Dormans

Foch

5 & 3 COL.

EPERNAY

THIERRY

Reuilly

Comblizy

77

131

I CAV (till 20th.)

3 U.S.

Crézancy

St.Agnan

20

18

Igny

XIV (after 20th

73

Condé

4

III

VIII

N T

H

F

I

5   10   15 MILES

o Montmort

That evening our acting C.O. had the misfortune to fall heavily from his horse, and our company commander, Captain Weekes, took charge of the battalion, with command of 'D' Company devolving on a lieutenant, one Boniface; a good fellow with a good Sussex name. He now had three subalterns to help him—Jackson, Brown and myself—but within a few hours Jackson departed for Battalion H.Q.

We moved the company into neighbouring barns and our padre found a good billet for the four of us in one of the lodges of the château. By now thoroughly tired, we were just getting off to a good night's rest when an air raid by some Gothas on Paris started in earnest, rendering sleep impossible. We therefore stood at the lodge gates and watched the French mobile anti-aircraft guns tearing up and down the road firing into the night sky, now swept by dozens of interlacing searchlight beams. We couldn't see them but could hear the drone of the motors very plainly, and between the barking of the guns we could also catch, now and then, the dull reverberations of exploding bombs.

Towards midnight things quietened down, and we were preparing to retire once more when a runner from Battalion H.Q. reported to Boniface. A few minutes after the runner's departure we noted in our message books the following: 'Battalion less surplus personnel to embus 5.50 a.m. on Senlis–Chantilly road, where French bus columns will be in readiness. Brigade may be billeted in area Coyolles–Vauciennes . . .' There were many other matters of detail also. Having no maps of the district, the above-mentioned area conveyed little to us, but we had quite enough to do before 5.50 a.m. to worry much about that. Since our company commander's departure for Battalion H.Q., I now had two somewhat under-strength platoons and I had my hands full: briefing N.C.O.s; arranging with C.Q.M.S. for an early breakfast; distribution of extra iron rations and rifle ammunition; checking of Lewis guns and crews; Mills bombs.

Another delicious July summer day dawned and breakfast was up. Then parade, and a final check in the village street before moving off, heavily laden, to the rendezvous, where we met the rest of the battalion on the road, facing a long line of blue-grey French camions, tarpaulin-roofed, Western wagon-fashion.

We were soon aboard, packed like sardines, and I admit to having shared with the men the novelty (for them) of this form of transport. Brown and I were about the last to clamber over the tailboards of our respective camions, observing in passing the grins of our swarthy French drivers and their equally swarthy mates. Choking clouds of road dust and, presumably, overlong hours of driving over roads never designed for this kind of traffic, had reddened their eyes and streaked their faces, bristling with a week's stubble under blue steel helmets. They had discarded their tunics and sat with rolled up shirt sleeves, which reminded me of what my platoon sergeant had told me a few moments previously. He had been talking to an Englishman employed at the famous Chantilly racing stables nearby, and from him learned of a great French 'push' which had started near Villers Cotterets on 18th July. The very fact of going up to the line in these French camions made speculation inevitable as to whether we were booked for this. Once more we deplored our complete lack of maps.

One by one the long convoy got into motion and 'D' Company, filling the camions almost at the rear, passed through the dust clouds churned up by those in front. However, we moved at a cracking pace, considerably faster, in my limited experience, than our British bus columns travelled on similar errands. On the solid rubber tyres, coupled with hard, lorry-type springing, and especially upon the long stretches of unrepaired pavé, we were shaken and thrown about like peas in a colander until, to some extent, we became used to the motion.

At first, men hanging on to the tailboard rope or curtains seemed to find plenty to interest them in the countryside. We soon passed Senlis, noting a number of badly damaged houses which, I believe, marked the limit of the German advance on Paris in September 1914. Beyond Senlis we passed several field defence systems, fronted by rusty barbed wire belts and earthworks stretching away on either side as far as the eye could see. Some work seemed of quite recent construction.

As far as Crépy-en-Valous traffic in both directions was exceedingly heavy, the dust choking and, consequently, as soon as the sun made its presence felt, the combination of dust, heat and petrol fumes, plus the continual shaking, became well nigh unbearable.

NEARING THE VILLERS-COTTERETS FOREST.
JULY 19th 1918.

Crépy presented a sorry spectacle and appeared to have been evacuated, as we did not see a single civilian. There seemed scarcely a whole building in the town, by reason either of long-range shelling or by bombing. Our road through was pocked with many rubble-filled holes, which didn't make our ride any easier.

Some distance beyond, in rolling open country, there was a short halt to answer calls of nature, and soon afterwards the summer heat began to take effect, intensified by our tightly packed condition under the hooped canvas coupled with the ceaseless jolting, inducing a drowsiness which soon became an uneasy slumber as, one by one, the fellows slid down onto the floor in confused heaps. In this manner we must have trundled on for some time, until I roused at a temporary halt, my head resting on a rifle bolt, the impression of which was deep upon my right cheek. Around me men snored in stertorous chorus, many dribbling with open mouths, while other faces (where visible among the tumbled mass along the floor) were streaked with dust and perspiration.

Struggling to the tailboard for a breath of air, I saw that we were about to leave comparatively open country for a thickly wooded area. Indeed, the vista ahead was of unbroken forest above which, on the skyline, hung at intervals several observation balloons—presumably French. At a random guess I estimated them to be about twelve kilometres distant. Most of the men had awakened and were looking around. We noted huge recent shell holes and splintered and up-rooted trees; also, in the distance, the continuous dull rumble of artillery fire. At length, in mid afternoon of 19th July, we were dumped upon the tree-lined roadside on the outskirts of the village of Vauciennes. The battalion fell in and marched away, and I recall the faces of our driver and his mate, their sizzling hot engine now stopped, as they took hefty swigs from their wine flasks. They paused and held them towards us as we passed. Still grinning through their grime and stubble, they wished us *bonne chance* and drank again. Just then I felt that we needed all the luck they wished us, but their gesture raised an answering laugh among our fellows; for they, having by now only lukewarm dregs of chloride-treated water in their bottles, plumped on the spot for the French system of a daily wine ration. They hadn't tasted it, though, I fear!

As our company spread out among shattered houses and barns,

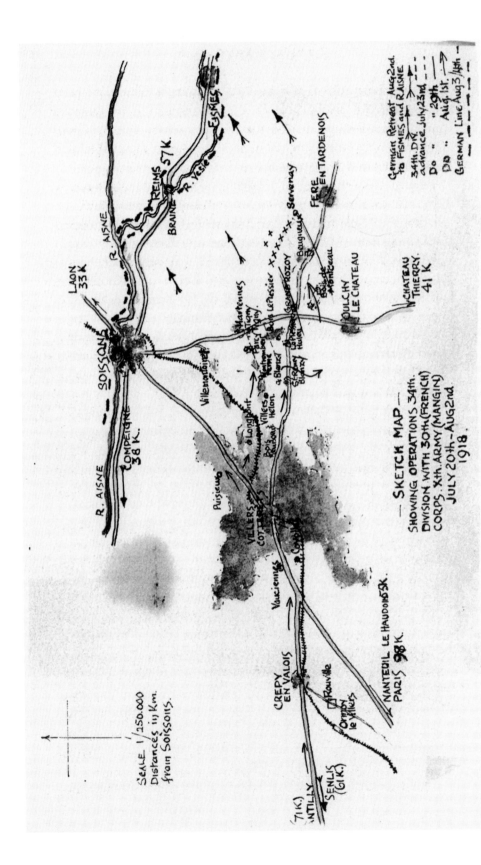

— SKETCH MAP —
SHOWING OPERATIONS 34th.
DIVISION WITH 30th.(FRENCH)
CORPS, Xth.ARMY (MANGIN)
JULY 20th—AUG2nd.
1918.

SCALE 1/250.000
Distances in Km.
from Soissons.

German Retreat Aug.2nd.
to FISMES and RAISNE.
34th.DIV. advance, July 23rd.
Do " "29th.
Do " Aug.1st.
Do " Aug.3/4th.
(GERMAN Line Aug.3./4th.

we saw many evidences of recent occupation by French troops in our search for *eau potable* in order that our cooks could make tea and corned beef stew. Indeed, small parties were continually passing on the road, some lightly wounded. Among them were Turcos, Moroccans and Senegalese. Somewhere in front of us the report of a heavy gun reverberated through the trees at half-hourly intervals, and tiles from roofs, already loosened, cascaded to the ground.

Boniface, who had departed for briefing at a hurriedly impro-vised Battalion H.Q., returned with the news that we were moving off at ten that evening. Pulling out his field message book, he told us to take some notes; which we did, seated on a fallen beam half-buried in brickwork, thus: 'we're part of 30th Corps, 10th French Army, now in action on front Soissons–Villers—Cotter-est—Oulchy-le-Château.' Here Boniface held up a pencilled sketch, which didn't help us much. Sensing this he continued, 'maps and a lot more bumph on how to read them will be issued at our next stop. They're altogether different from ours.' Seeing my consternation, he had to laugh; and so, at length, did we.

He turned to his notes again. 'Make a note of this, chaps—I Infantry, 34th Division. We're part of 101 Brigade! Others—2/4 Queen's and 2nd Loyal North Lancs—got that? Right!—102nd Brigade—4th Cheshires, 1st Herefords and some Somersets. 103rd Brigade—all Jocks and Argyll & Sutherlands and K.O.S.B.s . . . I missed it—I couldn't write fast enough!' he concluded, picking up a mug of tea. We forgave him and went to find our acting company sergeant-major and quartermaster sergeant. The few hours rest had, at any rate, enabled all ranks to wash away the dust of the journey and regain the use of their limbs. Rations for the morrow were issued and the corned beef gyppo consumed. The cooks packed up again.

In the dusk, several French motor ambulances passed by, laden with more wounded Frenchmen, Turcos and Senegalese. On the latter, the white bandages stood out starkly on their black skins.

We paraded at 9.30 that evening, and at this stage Boniface told us that we were in the Villers Cotterets Forest, on the northern arm of a great salient created by the success in June of the German drive to Château Thierry and the Marne crossings. On 15th July a further immense German onslaught around Reims had been

347

successfully repulsed with heavy losses to the attackers, and on the 18th the Xth French Army under General Mangin, advancing from the forest with tanks upon the extended German divisions holding that arm, had made considerable gains. We were here to help them, he added darkly.

Having ascertained this much, we were quite certain that we were for it very soon, and it was with a feeling that I had not experienced since April of the previous year, before the Hindenburg Line, that I paraded my men in the gathering darkness of that summer evening, in readiness to move off. With hourly halts, we marched for the whole of the short night through rides in the forest, in silence save for the tramp of feet and desultory reports of artillery fire, at some distance yet. We noted that some heavy howitzers, positioned in forest clearings, were being moved, the crews working flat out by shaded lights. In our column smoking was taboo and there was much grousing on this account, but with the faint light of dawn fags and pipes were lit. It was hardly full daylight when we came upon the forest village of Puisieux, its château heavily damaged by shell fire and its park already an overgrown jungle of weeds. The lake had a thick covering of green scum.

Here our company fell out and we settled down as well as we could among the ruins. Within a few minutes most of the men were sound asleep, and a short while after, having attended to essential matters, Boniface, Brown and I joined them. Jackson had departed for Battalion H.Q. When I awoke towards midday, rain was falling heavily from a leaden sky, rendering the whole aspect of our surroundings forlorn in the extreme.

From the broken window of the room we had made Company H.Q.—in a lodge at the gates of the château, partially demolished by shell fire—we looked out upon the lake on which floated a derelict punt, almost obscured by scum, water weeds and driving rain. Behind the lake, a misty background of tall and damaged trees completed the picture of destruction and neglect. A long-range shell screamed over and burst among the trees, awakening startled echoes from the nearby forest and causing cascades of water to descend from the dripping foliage around us.

There was not much time for rumination just then, however, as a runner from Battalion H.Q. arrived with a hefty package.

Maps! At Last! Within a few moments we were studying them eagerly and endeavouring to follow the instructions for reading them supplied by 34th Divisional H.Q. At first these seemed to be quite beyond us, but gradually we came to realise that, once having grasped the basic principles, a point could be given a reference on these French maps with considerably greater facility and accuracy than on our own. Moreover, the maps themselves were larger and appeared to show considerably more detail, both of natural features and of trench and artillery positions. At the time, it was comforting to know just where we were and be possessed of means of finding our way about in the future.

By the time we moved off again at four the next morning (22nd July) the weather had improved. The morning was fine, and we soon reached the zone of the French heavy artillery.

We marched still through wooded country, dense in places, but by now the forest was no longer continuous. Clearings became more numerous and progressively much larger, so that at length the belts of trees took the form of isolated islands in comparatively open stretches of undulating countryside carrying ripening corn crops, now sadly downtrodden, partially blackened and burnt, and pocked by many shell holes. The tide of war had ebbed here.

We came upon the ammunition columns and horse lines of the medium and field artillery; those, too, of the infantry in front. Senegalese walking wounded, some heavily bandaged and helped by those with lesser hurts, were still trickling down from the line and stood aside for us to pass; their thoughts, I could not help feeling as they watched us, an enigma! Personally, I could not see then—and cannot see now, after fifty years—why those African soldiers could fight so valiantly for France amid such slaughter, as undoubtedly they did. What possible interest could they really have had in the result? Thus were my thoughts, as several of them smiled broadly at our marching files. I can recall now their white teeth flashing in the morning sunlight.

Moving in artillery formation, with platoons at hundred-yard intervals, we reached the battered village of Villers Helon by mid morning. Here 'D' Company prepared to bivouac on the outskirts in a sadly splintered orchard, until called on to move forward—on what errand we knew not, but the infantry front was now quite

With my old friend and colleague A. V. Brown at Rouen, before joining the 4th Battalion, The Royal Sussex Regiment, July 1918.

close and the frequent bursts of mitrailleuse and rifle fire less than two kilometres distant.

In the early evening, a runner brought operation orders for our attack on the morrow, and we were in the act of jotting down details in our notebooks when a German five-nine battery plastered our orchard viciously for ten minutes with shrapnel and H.E., probably in an effort to reach the nearby road, on which pedestrian traffic was quite heavy at times. We were lucky in escaping casualties, the men scattering into two lengths of shallow trench which was already sprouting summer weeds. Many remained there long after the shelling ceased, and Brown and I scarcely knew whether to be annoyed or grimly amused. When the shelling had started, our Lewis guns and ammunition were being checked and a fresh issue of Mills grenades detonated. In order to 'get on with the war', we hurriedly called on our sergeants to flush their charges from the cover they had taken and check for losses and damage while there was still time.

That these Sussex lads were sturdy fighting material we had no doubt, and personally I never tired of hearing the Sussex talk once more, but we came to the conclusion that Johnny Turk had not thrown heavy stuff at them in Palestine on this scale, and left it at that, as we completed our notes and briefing from Boniface. Unfortunately, they would learn—and all too soon!

More orders arrived, and repetition of these would be wearisome. Briefly, our 34th Division was to relieve the 38th French (African) Division which, having made considerable gains, was now holding two kilometres of front between the village of Parcy Tigny and the wood of Le Plessier-Huleu on the extreme edge of the Villers Cotterets Forest. The French 58th Division would be on our left and the 19th to our right. The relief was to take place that night, so that our division had an attacking front of two brigades, the 101st and 102nd, of which ours (the 101st) would be on the right. The 4th Royal Sussex was detailed as brigade reserve to the 2nd Loyal North Lancashire and the 2/4th Queen's West Surrey, who would attack on a two-battalion front as part of a general advance planned to start at nine the following morning (23rd July).

From the foregoing it will be seen that, so far as our own small 101st Brigade front was concerned, it was necessary for the North Lancs and Queen's to precede us, and we therefore followed them in the dusk, moving up slowly with frequent halts, by platoons in file, at an interval of a hundred metres. We soon left the road for the open fields, Boniface leading the way with a French poilu as a guide, we fervently hoping that he knew where he was going! Had we been taking over a front line position we should have been more anxious on this point than actually we were, but eventually we halted in the half-light of the July night along a cart track at the edge of a field of standing corn. Here, after posting sentries and establishing liaison with those on our flanks and in front, we awaited events. By observing the flares sent up by both sides we were able to gain some idea of the approximate positions, and desultory machine-gun and rifle fire assisted to some extent.

The frequent scream overhead and bursting of shells around the village we had just vacated, and on the back areas beyond, marked for Brown and myself a renewal of the usual nightly experience on the Western Front. By midnight, however, this slackened, to be renewed again at first light.

As we lay beside the corn, relieved French Colonial troops passed us on their way out in single file, like huge shadows, in a silence broken only by the creaking of leather and equipment and the padding of many boots on the soft earth. Each man had his eyes either glued to the ground or upon the back of the man in front. Even in the semi-darkness of the July night, we noticed particularly the French officers and N.C.O.s. When I state that they looked as though fighting was their trade, I do not exaggerate one iota. Many years afterwards I read an account of the great battle for Verdun in 1916 and, with a special thrill, saw that the French division with recaptured the key fortress of Douaumont— of immortal fame—was the 38th (African). Having seen them myself, I could well understand their success.

At daybreak the French artillery of all calibres and the British eighteen-pounders covering 101 Brigade (102 had 75s) opened a furious and sustained bombardment. The enemy's reply was feeble by comparison, although the shrapnel from one of their field batteries caused several casualties, the high explosive bursting several hundred yards to our rear. We endeavoured to see what was taking place in front, but our position in a small fold in the ground completely obscured our view. There was a period of drum fire, and we thought of our lads then going over, and waited.

On the stubble immediately before us lay several dead Turcos, khaki-clad, with two of them still clutching their long Le Bel rifles with bayonets attached. Probably they had been caught by a machine-gun posted on the crest of the rise, as they had risen to advance from the track we were occupying. It was our intention to bury them but, suddenly, orders came for us to move.

Unfortunately, Boniface didn't know precisely what we were expected to do, so we once more followed the other companies, getting into extended order, however, before breasting the rise. On the crest we saw that the ground fell away in more trampled and blackened corn and arable for five hundred metres or so, to rise again gently to a thickly wooded background of tall trees. It was clear that fighting was going on there, as the rattle of machine-gun and rifle fire was almost continuous. To our left front, almost a kilometre distant lay, according to my map, the village of Parcy Tigny.

As I was taking this in, shrapnel started to burst over us, and it seemed clear that the German field batteries had missed the leading companies before getting the range, but now that they had it we were plastered—incredibly, with only a few casualties, although I recall that Brown and I had some difficulty at first in getting our charges to act as a disciplined unit. In achieving this we soon saw that the hard core of N.C.O.s and pre-1914 Territorials were invaluable, and truly of the right stuff. In this manner we reached the comparative shelter of the dead ground afforded by the next rise, and after an irritating halt, during which all efforts to obtain information were unavailing and most of us chewed ripe grains of wheat to while away the waiting time, we were ordered to advance five hundred metres or so half-left, to occupy a cart track on the extended crest of the rise just discernible in the trampled, sodden corn. Occasional bursts of machine-gun fire from several points, fortunately aimed high, seemed to indicate that it was held in strength. We could see nothing whatever of any of our lads between us and that wood, although they must have been there somewhere.

At this stage I recall that, in an effort to make the best of things in a situation where poor Boniface, as acting company commander, was left entirely without orders or information for many hours, A.V. Brown and I compared notes at intervals and seized the first real opportunity offered since we had joined the battalion of getting to knew our men better. Our chats with them and the mutual exchanges established, I hope, the confidence that, in matters of life and death, with which we were shortly to be faced, was so vitally necessary.

That evening at dusk a staff captain from 101 Brigade came our way, and in the dusk we withdrew to the shelter of a shallow but thickly wooded ravine about a kilometre to our rear. This, fortunately, provided good cover, although splinters of timber did some damage when a few shells came our way. The ground between the trees was littered with abandoned German equipment and ammunition, discarded clothing and newspapers only ten days or so old. These latter were all in Gothic type which, together with the language difficulty, conveyed little or nothing to us with the exception, readily recognizable by shaded torchlight, of many columns of soldiers' obituary notices inserted by mourning relatives. I would add that much of the ground had been fouled and that the overall stink was abominable, but in the darkness there was little we could do about it. In this atmosphere the rations—biscuits, corned beef, pork and beans, cheese—came up in sandbags; also well-chlorinated water in petrol tins which, however, wasn't too bad. Owing both to the persistent drizzle and the danger of showing lights of any sort, it was not possible to make a hot drink. Therefore, after sentries were posted and duties for the night arranged, all who could covered themselves as best they might with their groundsheets and dozed uneasily until daylight.

Here we stayed for another day, in total ignorance of what was happening around us, speculating helplessly as successive periods of heavy firing in front were followed by sporadic machine-gun bursts, and then almost total silence. The weather improved and we attempted to clear up and bury the worst of the disgusting mess around us.

From a runner who brought Boniface orders for an imminent move we gathered, for what it was worth, that the French divisions on our flanks had been held up, and that the attack had been only partially successful. This only confirmed our own surmises, but now Boniface told us that the whole division was being withdrawn and the French would extend on either side to fill the gap. French guides would report to him and lead us to a new position that night. This they did, and we marched at their direction some kilometres to the south-east, mostly through forest, and rejoined the remainder of the battalion in a clearing in a considerable wood, which our own guide told us was the Bois du Boeuf.

All around, the wood bristled with huge French howitzers, together with piles of shells and baulks of timber used in their service. Their intermittent detonations made the remainder of the night and the following day just hideous.

Another morning of slight drizzling rain didn't improve matters, but in the afternoon the weather improved and we received operation orders for the morrow. This time the 4th Royal Sussex, with the 2/4th Queen's, was to be in the forefront of a general attack by 101 and 102 Brigades a few kilometres to the south of our previous effort. The battalion's final objective was a ridge of high ground beyond the villages of Beugneux and Grand Rozoy which, if we managed to reach and hold it, would represent an advance of over two miles.

Our 34th Division was now attached to the 23rd French, troops of which we were relieving. The 19th French Division would be on our right and the 58th on our left. In the dusk we moved off by companies in artillery formation and marched by a misty moonlight, obscured momentarily by shreds of hurrying cloud, through the shattered villages of St. Remy and Blanzy. Beyond Blanzy we met parties of French Senegalese soldiers coming away from the line, and at the Ferme Montrambert we picked up our guide, a swarthy French Colonial poilu. He took to the fields and in silence our company proceeded in single file, our slow progress interrupted only by the sullen searching fire of the German five-nines, one shell in particular causing casualties and some delay as we neared our goal. Hereabouts the frequent wobbly whistle and 'plop' of gas shells hindered us also, but mercifully not enough to have to don our respirators. We passed a shattered railway embankment (that of the narrow-gauge line running from Soissons to Château Thierry), and after trailing across a cornfield for a further five hundred metres or so we were challenged in French. A minute later 'D' Company were taking over our section of about 250 metres of front along a fairly deep cart track, the bank of which might afford some small protection. The French Senegalese soldiers stood silent as statues, ready to move off, but their two officers

THE RELIEF.
NIGHT, JULY 28th
1918.
4th R. SUSSEX TAKE
OVER FROM FRENCH
AFRICAN REGT. NR.
ST. REMY-BLANZY 4 Read

greeted us cordially and, after pointing out our first objective, a wood dimly discernible in the misty moonlight seven or eight hundred metres in front, wished us good luck and, in gruff undertones, ordered their men to march. One of them, as he passed, gave me a pillbox containing a dozen or so small white tablets, saying, '*bon pour le gaz!*' I thanked him, and subsequent events were to render me immeasurably grateful to him. It would have been about 2 a.m. and we were to go over at 4.15 a.m.

Left to ourselves, we first made contact with the company of the Queen's on our left who were going over, and then arranged our own order of going forward, detailing a leading wave of two platoons, to be followed by the other two at an interval of about 150 yards.

In any case, in view of the shelling, we were far too crowded in that cart track just then, and the two leading platoons were filing out under my direction when Boniface told Brown to report to 'A' Company. We thought we were getting along fairly well, until he had to leave us because a single five-nine had burst right in the track further along and had killed, among others, the acting C.O. (Captain Weekes), the padre and the regimental sergeant-major. It appeared, also that several other officers were already casualties and that Captain Peskett of 'A' Company was now in charge of the battalion. There being no alternative, Boniface asked me to take over the two leading platoons. I hadn't the faintest idea where the barrage would fall that was to precede our advance, and to be on the safe side I went forward about eighty yards and extended them there, telling them to dig like hell before daylight. They needed no second bidding, as they now knew what was happening along that crowded track, and felt safe—for the moment—out there. We had French guns behind us and they would start the creeping barrage just before 4.15 a.m.

At 4 a.m. I went along my line with Sergeant Clark and issued the lads with a good rum ration, which we had brought up neat in some wine bottles. This done, I was walking back to the track to Boniface for a last word with him when, of a sudden, all hell seemed let loose upon us. In the shattering flame and smoke of salvoes of 75s I caught a glimpse of Boniface as he staggered and clapped a hand to his side. The guns had started their creeping barrage about 150 metres short, right on the cart track which, unfortunately, was sheltering two of our platoons. Those of the poor fellows still able to do so started to run about wildly, while the wounded called piteously for aid. I could do little but collect the remnants with the help of N.C.O.s as the barrage lifted, fortunately, about fifty metres beyond my two platoons in front. The whole business had been so sudden and so terrible that I had to strive desperately to collect my own faculties. We had not started; and here I, a second lieutenant, was left with a company at least 25 per cent of which was already out of action. The barrage now started to lengthen again and it was highly important to keep up well behind it. Therefore, placing the remnants of the two platoons in charge of a sergeant, and directing him to follow me up and not lose touch in the mist and smoke of the first light of dawn, I hurried to the leading platoons, which I was greatly cheered to see were—as by a miracle—almost intact. They rose at my call, and as we went forward in orderly fashion I had the satisfaction of seeing shadowy figures on our flanks moving forward in line with us through the haze. Here I cannot help recording how I took fresh heart when I saw how genuinely pleased these good lads were to see me, and how they went forward.

In a few minutes, moving as though through a thickish fog, we came (as my map foretold) upon a hastily dug line of trenches, with no wire whatever in front. The men gave a great shout on seeing several Germans coming towards us with their hands up, those lads nearest rushing forward with their fixed bayonets and causing the wretched prisoners to cower, fearing the worst. We didn't waste time, and in the meanwhile collecting about half a dozen more, sent them to the rear.

Now with map and compass on the ground in the gathering light, as the haze was lifting, I tried to get my exact position and saw the corner of the wood pointed out to me by the French lieutenant. This, the map told me, was the Bois de Montceau and, if so, we should soon come upon the Paris Line system of trenches. Having ascertained this I indicated to all, as well as I could, the direction to take and what they were looking for. We then went forward again, with the haze now clearing and the light growing stronger every minutes. The Paris Line, now easily distinguishable, we found quite unoccupied, after taking the precaution of approaching it in short rushes. The lads were now in the best of spirits, the taking of a few prisoners having had a wonderful effect on them, and I was glad to see that Sergeant Clark, with the rear platoons, had kept well up. The German counter-barrage so far had not amounted to much, but on the next stage of our advance over open fields to the Grand Rozoy–Beugneux road, shrapnel bothered us considerably, and a number of men in our own and flanking companies were hit. I noticed blood on the back of my left hand; the result of two small abrasions caused, I supposed, by fine shell splinters. A few moments later my head sang from a crack on the rim of my tin hat, probably from a flying stone, but what was much more serious now was the whine and smack of machine-gun bullets from the rising ground beyond the road— another wood, in fact, which, we afterwards found, half-surrounded the village of Beugneux.

We reached the road and the cover of the banking at the double, including my two rear platoons, and here I let everyone have a good breather while I studied the map again. We had to advance up to and through the wooded slope in front, to a point well beyond the crest, before digging in. I established contact with the Queen's on my left who were well up, and our own companies to our right who, just then I recall, were doing a lot of shouting. Thus reassured, I prepared to take the leading platoons across the hundred or so metres of open ground from the road and into the Bois de Beugneux in one rush, as machine-guns, while quiet for the moment, were there. Scrambling to the top of the banking, we were scarcely on our feet when a machine-gun spat from the edge of the wood, laying low a dozen or so of us in a few seconds. I had a narrow shave myself, and, back behind the bank once more, saw that we must try other means. But by this time our blood was up, and the thought of our poor fellows just fallen out there, and the sight of others who had dragged themselves back somehow, spurred me on. Doubling down the road for fifty yards or so, I found what I sought—a small depression like a dry ditch running towards the wood and marking the boundaries of two fields. Returning, I told Sergeant Clark what I intended to do. Followed by one Funnell, my hurriedly designated batman-runner since Parcy Tigny, and two men from our left platoon, we four crawled along the ditch on our stomachs and reached the cover of the wood without difficulty. Once there I saw that, with any luck, we were now in a position to bag two of our tormentors; but I decided first to settle the gentry who had first hindered us so tragically. It was an easy matter to locate them through the undergrowth, as they were firing short bursts at the road every few seconds, and we just went towards the sound.

Thus we emerged on the flank and slightly to the rear of our quarry. The two Germans sat, one crouched over the sights of the heavy machine-gun, the other at the ammunition belts, quite unaware of our presence. With a heart now thumping wildly, I watched them for an instant at their work, oddly fascinated, as I saw, too, the spouts of earth shoot up from the top of the road banking, and the huddled forms of our fallen boys. Then, I suppose, I let out a yell and shot the gunner through the head at point-blank range. Funnel shot his mate as, startled, he turned. It was, in retrospect, a horrible thing to do, and in quieter moments over the years I have never ceased to regret it. On the other hand, had they spotted us and turned the gun quickly, we wouldn't have stood an earthly chance.

Now flushed with success, I ran to the edge of the wood and yelled to the lads to come, and, seeing me, they needed no second bidding. As we made our way up the slope among the trees, I noticed that the other machine-gun was now silent. Puzzled, we heard Scottish voices and sounds of men thrashing through the undergrowth to our right, and then a subaltern of the King's Own Scottish Borderers, revolver in hand, came across to me, followed by a corporal and half a dozen men—pretty wild-looking types just then, I thought, but damned good lads in a fix like this. Their leader seemed very annoyed with me, and it appeared that we were extremely lucky not to have been fired on by his men. Emerging from the trees on the hilltop together, I managed to convince him that he, and not I, had lost direction, and he and his men departed along the edge of the trees towards Beugneux village. I did not see him again. I was, however, fearful about the fate of our other companies, and about Brown, who should have been where we encountered the Scots.

We now found ourselves on almost the highest point of a spur, consisting wholly of either standing corn or stubble, which fell away gently to our front and half-left for a kilometre or more, to rise slowly again to another ridge, beyond which we could see only the sky.

In the midst of the rolling expanse of damaged corn, again

half-left and almost a kilometre distant, stood a copse of tall trees, like an island, which I judged would be either in the path of the Queen's or of the French troops to their left. I could see both in thin lines amid the corn, the blue of the French now well to the east of the shattered village of Grand Rozoy. In that direction I could see for several kilometres, and was cheered to note that the Queen's were well up on my left flank. Grand Rozoy was being heavily shelled, and the clouds of reddish dust reflected the morning sunshine.

I had put down my map and compass again to get my exact position, when Funnell drew my attention to a group of dark figures issuing from the copse in our direction, carrying heavy loads. Quickly, I called for a Lewis gun—and here came the first bitter realization of how completely I had forgotten to ensure that, notwithstanding our heavy casualties, somehow our precious Lewis guns and ammunition drums were brought up. Now I feared that most of them were lying by our route—casualties! I raved helplessly as several more parties, with their burdens, issued from the copse and disappeared into the ample cover afforded by the corn. I tried to concentrate rapid rifle fire on the Germans, but without any visible effect at that range.

After what seemed an age, Sergeant Clark, carrying two buckets of Lewis drums, appeared with a lance-corporal carrying a Lewis and staggering under a slung load of another two buckets. The lad was wounded in an arm and a leg; not seriously, but he needed attention. He said that his Number Two and the rest of his team had been laid out by a five-nine between the Paris Line and the road. I thanked him as he put down his burden and told him to get back as quickly as he could, although, gallantly, he assured me he was 'all right'. When I turned to the task in hand, the enemy had disappeared completely. This slip, admittedly in the face of many difficulties, was to cost us dear, and too late I ordered Sergeant Clark to check how many Lewis guns and ammunition pans we had. I should have had four, at least, instead of one.

We now noticed frequent explosions among the Queen's and French, which puzzled us, and almost as we saw first the French and then the Queen's waver and then start to fall back, we heard the first whistle of an approaching trench mortar shell followed by a terrific crash in the trees a few yards to our rear. Within a minute there were several more, and chaos followed as several men were hit and one killed outright. In a temporary lull I managed to get order again. Had the advance continued I would have gone forward, but as things were I couldn't risk being left in the air; and at the next lull, with regret and bitter disappointment, and carrying on assisting our wounded as best we could, we withdrew slowly down the hill to the road again.

The German trench mortar batteries were now reinforced by their artillery who, by their comparative silence during the last half-hour, had pretty obviously been on the point of packing up and moving to new positions further back. Together, the rain of projectiles for the last hundred yards through the trees made an inferno I shall never forget, hampered as we were by getting our wounded over fallen trees and torn undergrowth. I had found several lads who knew the Lewis, and bravely they covered our rear, but under the hail I called them in, as the enemy would scarcely come forward until it ceased.

Back on the road and the slight shelter of the bank, I saw that towards Grand Rozoy it was lined already by Queen's and by Royal Sussex under an officer who was urging his men to dig in. Going to him, I was staggered and overjoyed when he turned and I saw that it was, indeed, Brown, scarcely recognizable. He had been hit in the arm and leg by shrapnel and it was only too apparent that he had lost much blood. Only his terrific energy and drive were keeping him going. I urged him to get to the rear, but he refused point blank saying that, as far as he knew, there were only two officers besides the two of us in the whole battalion, apart from Peskett at H.Q. (wherever that was), Lieutenant Fortescue, and Marks, one of our draft who joined with us at Proven. As he was hurriedly saying that they had been held up for some time by machine-gun nests between the Paris Line and the road, and hadn't been able to get up through the wood, a great dirty black five-nine shrapnel burst in the air just behind us. He started and held his shoulder, hit again, and there and then I prevailed upon him to go. Frankly, I was relieved when he tottered off, although I hardly expected I would have the luck to see him again. Although I didn't know it at the time, it was the most serious of his injuries, and I believe he carried the shrapnel ball somewhere around his heart until he died in June 1967, mourned by his family and very many friends, one of the most successful and respected citizens of Eastbourne.

Turning to the wretched situation in which we now found ourselves, I made a hurried attempt to sort out the men by companies with the help of the remaining N.C.O.s and managed to get a quick word with Fortescue, who I liked from the start—a first-class chap. Briefly I told him where we had been and what I was now trying to do. He seemed genuinely pleased, and this encouragement, even under these conditions, was the first I had received from an officer of the 4th Royal Sussex. Fortescue, too, hadn't the faintest idea where Peskett and Battalion H.Q. was.

The men were digging cubby holes in the bank, and I had organized a hunt for Lewis guns and pans, with the result that in the remnants of the battalion along the road we managed to account for eight, together with a captured German heavy machine-gun. Greatly reassured, and feeling confident that we could stem an infantry attack, in spite of the mortaring and now-sporadic shelling, my attention was drawn first to the French and then to the Queen's. The French were now the wrong side of Grand Rozoy again, and the Queen's were withdrawing from the road to the trenches forming the Paris Line. Within the next ten minutes our left flank was in the air. In desperation, we sent two men to find Battalion H.Q., or even Brigade H.Q., at all costs, with messages calling urgently for reinforcements and for artillery support.

More enfilading machine-gun fire now came from just beyond where the Queen's had been, and we were being assailed from three distinct directions. With bitter feelings, Fortescue and I saw only too plainly that, under the circumstances, we could only consolidate on the line being taken by our neighbours. It appeared also that to our right the North Lancs and the Scottish Borderers of 103 were in similar difficulties around Beugneux village. Therefore, a company at a time—each now resembling a platoon—we withdrew in extended order across the fields to the Paris Line and the Bois de Montceau, harassed by five-nines and long-distance machine-gun fire for the whole of the way. A new menace was the 'plop' of numerous gas shells, sent over by a now-reassured

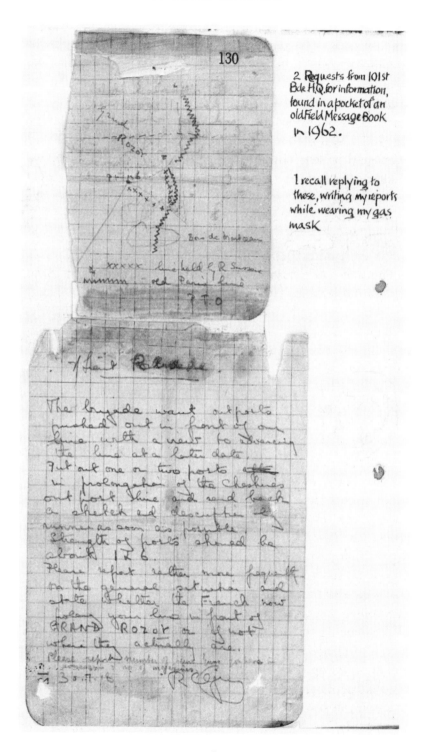

enemy artillery. Once we arrived we again strove to make what order we could of chaos: got the N.C.O.s together, briefed them on essential matters, posted sentries established liaison with both flanks, and did what we could to get the wounded away.

Meeting again, Fortescue and I sat down in the crumbling trench, both dead beat, and deeply resentful of the way in which things had been bungled. It was obvious that communications had completely broken down—if ever they had existed, which we doubted. This applied particularly to the artillery and to our own Battalion H.Q. Comparisons and recriminations were useless; but where, I asked myself, would the old 21st Division have been by now had they been allotted this job? About three miles beyond that ridge, I told myself and Fortescue, bitterly. For in the early stages there had been no real opposition. If only we could have kept up that advance the other side of the ridge. 'Where,' we asked each other, 'where in heaven's name was that reserve brigade?'

As we argued thus we observed through the trees what was probably this brigade on the move, advancing across the fields in our direction a kilometre or so to our rear, doing what they should have been doing a couple of hours previously. Apparently this move was countermanded, however, before they reached us and it now seemed pretty obvious that we should get no further that day.

In this state of depression at the fortune of war, my good Funnell came between us with two mugs of tea. I'm sure he could see how grateful we were, and here I pay my small tribute to a sturdy Sussex lad with a good-humoured, rosy-cheeked countenance, tanned by long exposure to Eastern suns. Already he had proved an 'ever present help in time of trouble', and he was to do more sterling work before, unfortunately, he had to leave us. I hope he still adorns a farm-house somewhere in West Sussex, three score and ten, with the roses still in his cheeks.

Smelling almost like Cherry Blossom shoe polish with a touch of geranium, gas shells continued to worry us and we endured several prolonged spells in our respirators, during which I was having to do all sorts of jobs, including the writing of a mass of returns and reports, now called for by a Battalion H.Q. who had, at length, discovered us. I have saved two such requests signed, presumably, by an officer, unknown either to me or, surprisingly, to Fortescue. The runner told us that Captain Peskett had given him the messages and that he was to wait for a reply.

Fed up with having to write these, peering through the eye-pieces of my gas mask, I tested for gas as per the drill book but foolishly took the opportunity of shouting to some men some yards down the trench to douse the dense smoke of a particularly undesirable fire. Due, I suppose, to the quick intake of breath occasioned by this effort, I must have swallowed some pretty concentrated gas, and was seized with a fit of coughing and near suffocation. Hastily I re-adjusted the mask, in which I struggled for breath and thought my head would burst. The while, Fortescue and Funnell banged my back, loosened my collar and shirt and made me lie down. In desperation, I remembered the tablets given me by the French lieutenant. Somehow I managed to cram two of these under my tongue and tried to lie still. Whether it was the psychological effect or not I'll never know, but gradually I could breathe more easily. Some minutes later Fortescue tested again, as a westerly evening breeze had arisen. He pronounced all clear and masks were removed for the time being. I had been badly shaken, and felt it! We were deluged with gas shells that day and the next.

Shortly before the 1939 war my wife and I became air raid wardens, and attended lectures, including several about poison gases. I was most interested to hear at one of these that the effect of a gas (whose official name I now forget) was first a violent fit of coughing, followed by a temporary improvement. Collapse some hours subsequently was expected to occur. Whether this gas was the one I swallowed I will never know, but my 'bellows' have been my weak spot ever since that day.* Over the years I have told two doctors of my experience, and although they listened indulgently, it was clear to me that they didn't believe my story. It doesn't matter, anyhow. It was so long ago. But of one fact I am absolutely certain, without those white tablets I should not have been able to carry on.

Before darkness fell, Funnell and Fortescue's batman between them served up hot pork and beans, welsh rarebit made from issue

---

* I. L. R. died of chronic bronchitis, aged 76.

366

cheese (with sandbag hairs adhering), and mysteriously softened biscuit, served in their mess tin lids and followed by strong cups of char, the meal doing much to restore our equilibrium. That evening, with another man for company in case of mishap *en route*, I sent back the runner to Peskett, giving the battalion strength as two officers and 210 other ranks. For this we could show an advance of about a kilometre, having been driven off the major portion of our gains by a few intelligent Germans who knew how to handle artillery, machine-guns and trench mortars.

During the night we were greatly troubled again by gas shells, and had to wear our respirators almost continuously, but early the next morning (30th July) during a clear spell when the sun was rising above the ridge and Bois de Beugneux, and outlining them sharply, we noticed in amazed surprise the blue-clad figures were moving about in the ruins of, and beyond, Grand Rozoy. Yesterday we hadn't been too impressed with our ally's performance, but this sight made us feel pretty small. The French had walked out; now they had simply walked back again, without any fuss. Watching them, we wondered whether we could have done the same and re-occupied Beugneux Wood.

All that day and the next our position was saturated with gas, causing us practically to live in our respirators, and I recall coming almost to the last of my white tablets. Whether they did any real good, I couldn't honestly say, but at the time I was sure they helped. In those two and a half days we lost around a dozen more men, either gassed or casualties of shell fire, and on the evening of 31st July the expected orders came to regain what we had lost—and a bit more. By this time, however, Fortescue and I had become resigned to the inevitability of this task. Should there be any real opposition, we didn't rate our chances of surviving very highly. My throat and mouth felt lousy; maybe it was the gas, but perhaps I had been talking too much! I coughed almost continuously.

We briefed our N.C.O.s and men, carried out checks of essentials, and issued rations in the last of the light. At midnight we moved off in dead silence and worked our men down to the road again for the best possible jumping-off point, having ascertained that the barrage would come down on the edge of the wood and go forward at 4.45 a.m. I remember that both of us had watches,

Top of the Wood~BEUGNEUX . 5 A.M. AUG 1st 1918 .
(POINT 189)

but with a variation of about ten minutes. No one came up to synchronise them, and so we made the best of it and split the difference. It was pretty quiet, apart from the 'plop' of gas shells.

We arranged to go over in two waves and, as senior, 'Forty' took the rear of these when we moved off from the Paris Line. To make for easier travelling, and to ensure direction, we risked it without respirators. Unfortunately, he must have inhaled a nasty whiff of gas, I suppose from a recently dropped shell. When I found him, after positioning my fellows, he was in a bad way, but Sergeant Constable and another sergeant (whose name I forget) had prevailed on him to remain lying down. Gradually he coughed less and his breathing became somewhat easier. When he felt he could walk, between us we got him to the road banking as he insisted that he was feeling better, but I wanted him to get away out of it.

Now, having done everything possible, we waited in the chilly dawn for the barrage to commence. It was quiet, and borne on the morning breeze came sounds from the rear, behind the French, that I had not heard for almost two years—tanks! This cheered us a lot,

The shattered Trees now regrown.
50 YEARS AFTER

BOIS DE BEUGNEUX – from GRAND ROZOY- BEUGNEUX ROAD.
Here, on July 29th. 1918, the advancing 4th R. Sussex sustained serious casualties from machine guns sited near edge of the wood.
X Here, too. A.V. Brown was hit by S.Q shrapnel, his third and most serious wound.

as our orders stated that the 4th Cheshires would support us and, when on our objective, that a French division would come through.

At 4.45 a.m., after the short but intensive barrage on the wood moved forward, we rose to our feet with a feeling, in my own case, actually of relief, and struggled up through the wood again, through the haze and acrid smoke, with little opposition apart from rifle shots, our Lewis teams firing short bursts from the hip. Luckily a heavy machine-gun in our path, with its crew, had been knocked out by the barrage. Nearing the crest, however, but still among the now torn and splintered trees, we were met of a sudden by a hail of machine-gun fire which laid a number of my poor fellows low in the instant, and created chaos among them. For some moments I was hard put to it, before the habit of discipline asserted itself. I yelled for Lewis guns and crawled along to the two nearest. Shoving the muzzle of one over the trunk of a fallen tree, and clamping down a new pan on the post, I pulled back the cocking handle. Calling on the corporal holding the other gun to do likewise, we fired two whole drums low, in the general direction of our tormentors. Then, getting up, I called on the lads to 'come on!' We had only thirty yards or so to go before we saw the two machine-guns about the same distance in front, and the half-dozen or so steel helmets of the crews looking over the edge of two shallow pits. They had taken cover from our fire and were caught off balance. I fired my revolver several times and we were upon them. I must have hit the heavy machine-gunner in the chest, as he slumped over the gun. Funnell shot and bayonetted his mate, and the others, with a light gun, met with a similar fate from a number of our men who had seen that several of the enemy were wearing Red Cross armlets.

The result of all this was that, on emerging from the trees into the expanse of corn in front, I lost direction and bore away somewhat to the left of what should have been my true line of advance.

We kept on until again held up by two machine-guns hidden in the corn. Men started to drop, including my good Funnell who, standing beside me, was hit in the leg, near the knee. Crawling now, and helping Funnell, I yelled and signed to the fifty or so men left, in widely extended order, to get into any shell hole handy for cover. So it was that the majority just went to ground in the corn, and in the haze and drifting smoke of the barrage I could only see the steel helmets of the dozen or so immediately around.

It was most unfortunate, as Fortescue and the rear wave must have been only a hundred yards or so behind. It was then that I saw that the corn was burning fiercely in several nearby places. I asked Funnell if he could get himself between two flaming masses to the rear, and out of it. He wanted me to stay with him, and I had to act in brute fashion to get him to start on his painful

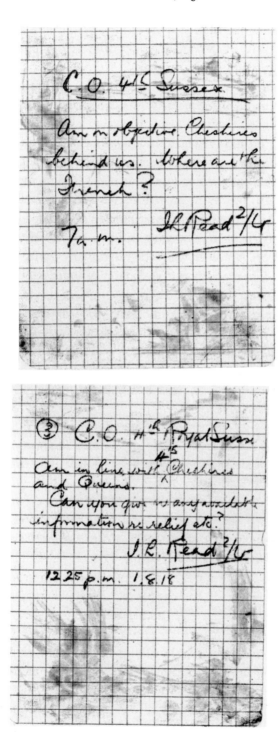

journey back, telling him that there were plenty of our lads there who would assist him. He was a great loss to me, but I was told afterwards that he got away safely.

The burning corn added a fresh horror to war. Subsequently I listened to several theories as to how it was started—perhaps by a retreating enemy. There were, I believe, a number of instances where badly wounded men were either burned or suffocated, but I got those of my men that I could muster to go forward and around a fresh outbreak to our front and, in doing so, must have gone somewhat further to my left. As we went we fired Lewis and rifles from the hip, and had the satisfaction of settling several more of the enemy, who were stealing away. I continued to lose men to these snipers, however, and when eventually I judged it best to halt, found I had about thirty smoke-blackened men, of whom four were Queen's.

I could hear shouting to my right and hoped that this was Fortescue, but had the uneasy feeling that my left was in the air. I therefore decided that, as I must have been approximately upon our objective line, it would be best to await the 4th Cheshires, who were to support us, before the French 18th Division came through finally.

In order to let Peskett, Fortescue and O.C. Cheshires know where I was, I sent several men off with messages to this effect, and asking for information. They were all shot at as they crawled off but, I believe got away.

Shortly afterwards I heard again the roaring of engines and was delighted to see the tops of a dozen or so French Whippet tanks making their way through the corn about 150 metres to my left. Unfortunately, instead of coming my way, they continued straight on and made for the small oasis-like wood in the corn from which the German trench mortar teams had issued on 29th July. I was sniped at in trying to attract their attention.

If only I could have mustered one Lewis gun and a couple of full pans just then to spray that corn in front, I felt sure I could have dealt with our tormentors. My lads were using their rifles as well as they could, but, in exposing themselves, I could see they were inviting immediate retaliation, at which they were at a terrible disadvantage. Bitterly, I cursed my lack of foresight in allowing the Lewis teams—or what was left of them—including the vital guns, to slip from my control for the second time within four days.

Thus were my thoughts as I sat in that shell hole, dejected and fuming, temporarily cornered. Getting desperate, I took the risk and peered cautiously over the edge of the hole to the rear. Then I actually saw, first a blue steel helmet, next the grinning young face of the poilu beneath it as his head emerged at the blackened and still-smoking edge of a great burnt patch of corn, about twenty-five yards directly behind me. Throwing discretion to the winds in my elation, I shouted and waved to him and the lads around me saw him, too. Two cracks, and spouts of dirt flung into my face by near misses brought me down to earth, but after a moment or two I must needs have another look. He was now standing almost in the open and I signalled urgently to him to keep down as he started to run towards me—but it was too late. A sharp double cr-r-ack and he fell into the shell hole on top of me. They had got him, and it was a nasty one, the bullet entering around his left collarbone and coming out under the shoulder blade as he crouched. Now, with each struggle for breath there was a kind of whistle from his punctured lung, which sickened me as I unbuckled his pack and equipment, hastily cut his coat and shirt open, and plugged the holes with my emergency bandages. It was then that I saw that the entire contents of his pack were filled 'segments' of machine-gun ammunition, similar to those used in the Hotchkiss gun. The bullet had come to rest in one of these segments, and had bent it. I propped him up as well as I could and saw that all colour was now drained from his face, beads of sweat standing out on his forehead. I wetted my handkerchief from my water bottle and dabbed it on his face, and this seemed to revive him somewhat. He indicated my bottle, which he took, and drank the contents with a ravenous thirst. I dissuaded him from emptying his own bottle of ration wine. Then he told me that his own sergeant, with a mitrailleuse section, was just behind him. Scarcely understanding him aright, I again peered over to my rear and saw them coming into view amid the trampled corn, heavily burdened and led in Indian file by the sergeant, who carried a long stout stick; the sight reminded me irresistibly of a shepherd leading his flock, the French way.

He saw my urgent signal to keep low, and at his command they wriggled forward on their stomachs. As they neared us the German snipers started on them, whereupon, sensibly, they either scattered into the nearest shell holes or lay flat; but they were equal to the occasion. A few moments later I saw the muzzle of their gun thrust over the edge of a shell hole, and almost immediately after a hail of lead went into the corn, low over our heads, too close to be pleasant. Then all stood up, one by one as they heard the shouting, including about thirty of my filthily blackened Royal Sussex, with a few of the Queen's. They and the French rushed forward into the corn, there was a shout, and a poilu emerged, driving three young Germans before him, with their hands up. One could only raise one arm, having been hit in the other, but they all three now looked very frightened—as well they might, seeing how they had tormented us. I was standing with the French sergeant above our shell hole, explaining about his wounded comrade, now trying wanly to smile his relief. The sergeant shook my hand and gave me to understand that I was too far to my left, pointing to his right where we could see khaki figures moving about some four hundred metres away, but in line with us. I recall that a temporary stretcher was made by stuffing the sergeant's staff and a rifle through the sleeves of two of the Germans' tunics. As carefully as they could, they laid their now semi-conscious comrade on it, and the prisoners, now stretcher-bearers, started off to the rear with a poilu as escort. Then, with a hurried salutation, the sergeant rejoined his men, thrashing through the corn towards the copse, now about five hundred metres distant at half-left, where we could see more snake-like formations of French troops advancing.

Collecting my men—including, I was glad to see, three Lewis guns, but only eight buckets of ammunition—I made my way over to the right, being joined by several stragglers and lightly wounded men *en route*. The sight of several blackened bodies of our poor fellows sickened and embittered us. They must have suffered horrible deaths as they lay wounded in that burning corn.

We came upon the advancing Cheshires, who directed me to where they thought our Battalion H.Q. was, if any still existed. I came upon it about ten minutes later, consisting of Captain Peskett and a few signallers and runners. They had just moved up. He saw me coming and looked at me queerly, as though he had seen a ghost. We had never met before. He wore glasses and peered into my face, then said, 'it *is* Read, isn't it?' I essayed a salute and introduced myself, whereon he thumped me on the back, saying 'good work!' He then told me that he had received my message, sent at 7 a.m., about three hours later; that Fortescue, with what was left, were about two hundred yards in front of the corn; and that he had been told I had 'gone west' when the corn caught fire. I didn't realize what a scarecrow I looked just then, but what he said was great encouragement, as certainly he must have had his own troubles that day.

Finally he warned me that 'poor old Forty' was in a bad way with after-gas effects, but refused to give in, and so I hastened to rejoin him. Collecting my remnant, now joined by a dozen more stragglers, and telling them Captain Peskett congratulated them on having done well, we made our way to Fortescue. It was fine to see him again, although he looked very ill and was racked with coughing and efforts to get his breath. As we shook hands he asked me whether I'd seen myself in a looking-glass lately. I forget what I said but, as he handed me a small piece of cracked mirror from his haversack, I was pretty shocked at my appearance and could well understand Peskett's hesitation. The least said about stubble and grime on it the better, but what really worried me was my singed eyebrows and eyelashes—they were virtually missing. It was then, too, that I realised that my tunic collar was scorched at the neck and that I had a blister there which was already becoming painful. Forty tore up one of his bandages and poulticed my neck with it—the Frenchman had had mine.

As we were talking, a runner from Peskett brought orders that we were to advance a further six hundred metres or so, to bring us into line with the Cheshires and French: news which filled me with a dismay which I could ill disguise, for I had had enough, and the reaction was setting in rapidly. Still, there was nothing for it. Putting on the best manner I could assume, I helped Forty to marshal the few score remaining men of the 4th Royal Sussex, and ten minutes later set out through the corn, determined this time to make the best possible use of our Lewis guns if the need arose.

To our intense relief, however, we were only bothered by one machine-gun and a few trench mortar shells which, fortunately, overshot us. The Cheshires settled the machine-gun, and shortly before reaching our objective—the extreme eastern edge of the cornland down the reverse slope of the Beugneux ridge—we espied a group of the enemy making off as hard as their burdens would allow them. They were about two hundred yards distant, but my lads were too quick for them and two Lewis gunners got on to the target almost immediately. I believe that only one got away.

Arriving without further incident upon our objective, from which we could see Servenay, I could see that practically every man was dead beat, although elated at our success. I could realise how they must feel after the day's exertions and, in many cases, the loss of old mates. More than a week's stubble bristled on their streaked and blackened faces; their eyes, red and sore from gas, were now scorched by fire. The condition of their clothing and boots was, in many cases, pitiable. Nevertheless, I prevailed on them to dig in, after a fashion, before posting sentries and letting the remainder either sleep or make some tea with their iron rations if they could, but we were now short of water and had no means of obtaining any. Fortescue joined us, but I could see that he was now weak with constant coughing. After the particularly bad bout occasioned by this last move, I finally prevailed upon him to go back and get attention, pointing out that we had now done our bit and were due for relief very soon. His batman went with him. I never saw or heard of him again, but trust that with care he recovered and that the years have dealt kindly with him. He was a great colleague and I missed him sadly in the days to come.

In the dusk I went out with a corporal and had a look at the Germans we had caught with our Lewis guns—an officer and five men, with all the paraphernalia of a trench mortar outfit. Tired though we were, we derived a kind of fierce satisfaction at the thought of having caught, at long last, a few of our tormentors of the Beugneux Wood. I was particularly interested in a magnifying periscope made by Zeiss–Jena, like two horns each about eighteen inches long, branching upright from a box through which the viewer looked at an angle of about twenty degrees. This I annexed, together with a Mauser automatic and the officer's map—by far the best of north-western France that I have ever seen, with every hamlet and feature named and marked. German thoroughness, if you like, but very real. Again, the periscope showed in startling fashion how the Germans were able to pick our men out in the corn without exposing themselves. I had seen several of these grey-green painted pieces of equipment lying about. Now we knew the deadly use to which they had been put.

That night a strange and eerie peace seemed to descend over these trampled cornfields. The artillery of both sides was silent, save for the reverberations of long-range shells and the dull rumble of the battle away to the north, around Soissons. At our Battalion H.Q. the ration party of Somersets told us that the rumour was that a general German retreat from the salient was imminent and that French troops were coming through us at dawn. We could see the blue of the French poilus in Servenay to our right.

The Somersets brought us some water, which was truly a godsend, and there were rations enough for double our number. Dog tired, we cared little how we passed the night, in spite of a persistent drizzle. The remnants of the 4th Royal Sussex sat in their shallow holes in the damp earth and smoked their fag-ends, too tired to sleep except in fitful snatches, but how cheerful at the success attained, and by the news of our imminent relief.

Sitting there in the drizzle, I recalled that many of these Sussex men were on Gallipoli in 1915, had been taken thence to Palestine, and then back to Flanders—comparatively speaking, to within a stone's throw of home after three years of it. Now many of them, to whom the long journey across the Mediterranean and France from Palestine had spelled at least 'leave' and Arundel, Old Shoreham, Worthing or Littlehampton again, were lying in obscure spinneys and cornfields on the edge of the Villers Cotterets Forest. Now it seemed a long way indeed from those West Sussex towns and villages, of which they had spoken with such affection. Thus I ruminated and waited until the dawn of 2nd August.

At daybreak of a misty, damp morning, a vedette of French cavalry rode up through the corn. Their lieutenant greeted me, telling me that the Boches were in full retreat, and illustrating this with a wave of his arm. A quick salute and he went off at a trot

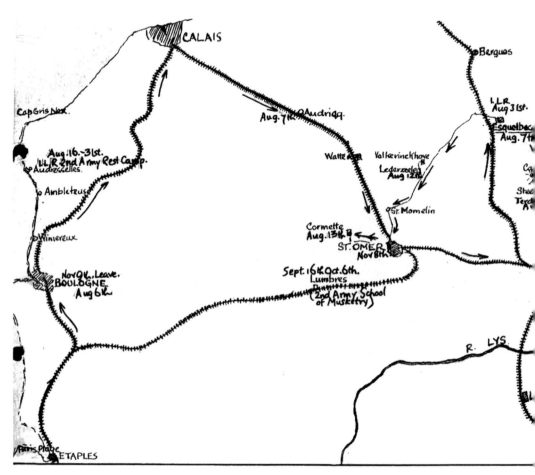

SKETCH MAP SHOWING MOVEMENTS OF THE 4TH BATT. ROYAL SUS
AUGUST 4TH — NOV. 11TH 1918, WITH ADDITIONAL PLACES ME

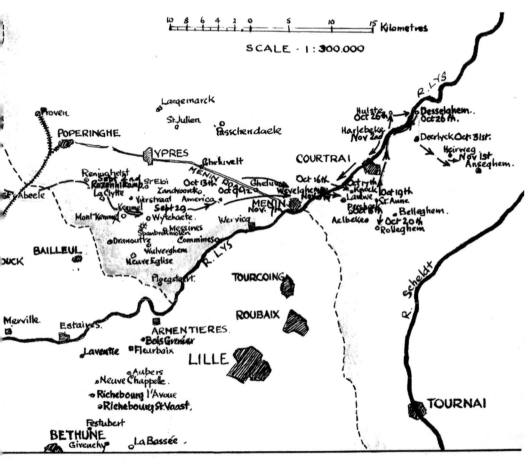

SCALE · 1 : 300,000

GT. 34TH DIVISION. (NICHOLSON), X CORPS. (STEPHENS), 2ND ARMY. (PLUMER)
ED IN THIS NARRATIVE AND APPROXIMATE DATES APPENDED.

to his men. In a few minutes, as we watched their progress, we saw them disappear over the horizon of the far ridge.

Some minutes afterwards, a French infantry regiment passed through us along a track to our right in column of route, and from them came snatches of song. Watching them, it all seemed like a dream; but there lay the German trench mortar team, and all around us the trampled, blackened and shell-pocked corn to testify to what had happened but ten hours or so previously. And so we rested that day, burying our dead and getting away some seriously wounded lads, the while watching the advancing tide of a French Army corps pass by—regiment after regiment of blue-coated infantry alternating with those in khaki: Frenchmen, Senegalese, Turcos, Moroccans, Zouaves; battery after battery of field artillery, *les Soixante-Quinze*; medical corps—observation balloons hovering low over the motor trucks towing them. Towards evening heavy guns and howitzers and supply columns in a never-ending stream, the celerity and completeness of the advance leaving us wondering with admiration at the organizing ability of the French Command.

That night, what firing there was to our front was literally miles away, and we were now in a back area.

The cooks arrived from the transport lines and all enjoyed hot tea, bacon and fried bread. The weather improved and there was a new light-heartedness apparent. I remember how proud I felt of that little band of Sussex man and how, as I walked among them, I felt that I had established a bond between us. I ceased to compare them with my old comrades of the Leicestershires, for flesh and blood could not have done more in the previous fortnight than these lads had achieved.

I managed to get shaved and my face washed—true, a mess-tin affair, but marvellously refreshing, nevertheless. My clothing was another matter, but there was nothing I could do about that until I could get at my kit again. The blister on my neck worried me.

During the following morning we moved back to open ground above the ruins of Beugneux, where Captain Peskett introduced me to a bevy of officers now rejoined from leave in England, including the senior major, Constable, who kindly intimated that in the morning we were going back in lorries and that, as soon as we had settled at the other end (wherever that was), he would like to have a chat with me. In the meanwhile, we endeavoured to form companies again from our remnant, now increased by various rejoined details, transport and the small cadre left at the rear when we went into action, to a total of nearly two hundred men with ten officers, including Major Constable, who now assumed temporary command.

At 10 a.m. on 4th August the battalion embussed in French Army camions at a convenient spot a kilometre north west of Grand Rozoy, and there we caught a glimpse of the French commander who had juggled with us for the previous three weeks—General Mangin. He was with our 34th Divisional general, I believe—Nicholson. We had seen neither previously, of course, but I will say this of General Mangin, he looked a real soldier, and a pretty tough one at that, in spite of his impeccable turnout, his swarthy features tanned by years of exposure to African and Asian suns. We were told that he had come to thank and bid farewell to the British divisions about to leave his command, and it was then that we learned that the 15th (Scottish) Division had been fighting next to U.S. troops near Soissons and had done splendid work there, capturing Buzancy, which village had defied all American efforts to take it.

We didn't mind the shaking up that the camions gave us this time, and as I sat beside the driver of ours I couldn't help wondering what General Mangin's assessment of the 34th Division really was. From my own point of view, things had gone wrong from the word go, particularly in the case of the 4th Royal Sussex, called upon to get into a critical battle minus many of its senior officers and N.C.O.s. A shell had knocked out all but one of the others, Peskett only remaining. I have described how several newly joined second lieutenants and Fortescue fared. There had been a complete and disastrous breakdown of communications and therefore lack of accurate information at Battalion, Brigade and Divisional H.Q. levels. Had there been real opposition of the Somme variety, our own unit would have been wiped out on 29th July.

I could only conclude that the Germans were weakening—really, this time, and not by wishful thinking—a fond hope nurtured to keep the war effort going since 1914, nearly four years.

I shook off these thoughts as we passed through Crépy-en-Val-ous, although the driver indicated that I had been asleep for 'one, two *heures!*' We left the Nampteuil-le-Haudouin—Paris road beyond Crépy, and came to rest at the little village of Rouville. Here, I recall, Clevely, our battalion signalling officer and just rejoined from leave, found me a good billet in a farm-house. Hastily I assigned myself a new batman in place of poor Funnell who, by that time, should have been in Blighty, and his first jobs were to rescue my kit from our transport limber, take it into my room, and then find someone to cut my hair.

The house formed one side of a square, completed by the barns and stabling, the whole enclosing a spacious yard which included the midden. Entrance and exit was through a great archway dividing the barns, provided with black double gates of formidable proportions on the semi-fortified plan common in Flanders and northern France. That it to say, it formed a compact, self-contained entity which could be defended in emergency.

I sat upon an old oil drum on a roughly bricked path in front of the farm-house, relaxed and enjoying the warmth of the late afternoon sunshine after our journey. The farmer, his wife, father-in-law, a boy of about fifteen and a girl of thirteen were all out in the fields, getting in the harvest. The men did not return until it was quite dark, but Maman came back with her daughter and half a dozen cows for milking as I sat there. I remember standing up and greeting them. They looked very tired, as Maman went into the house to more chores there, her daughter to the milking. Dusk was turning into night when I sat there again, smoking a last pipe before turning in on that warm August evening. Now carrying a hurricane lamp in one hand and her stick in the other, the daughter took the cows back to a near-by pasture, assisted by the old farm dog, who knew his business. No doubt she tethered them there again on fresh patches, as was the custom. As they passed me, chewing and pausing anon to whisk away a few flies from the midden, I thought how good the warm cow smell was. The little girl brought up the rear, adjuring them with occasion prods with her stick.

To my awkward '*bonsoir, m'selle*', she held up her lamp and I saw her tired smile. '*M'sieu . . .*' But I digress, in trying to paint a little word picture of rural France after four years of war—a France left to the very young and the old, sometimes the very old.

Our mail arrived with my new batman, one Evans, together with our company quartermaster sergeant and his assistant, between them carrying my valise. Our C.Q.M.S.—Slaughter, by name—became our company sergeant-major in the re-organization of the battalion soon to follow. This was my first real introduction to him, and he was to prove a valued friend in the months that followed. Now he told his assistant to do his best with my hair and took his leave, saying that should I want anything, just let him know. 'Here's the paper, sir, if you'd like it.' It was *The Times*, about a week old.

My barber now tucked a very grubby towel into the top of my shirt and tested his clippers. My little pile of letters and a parcel lay at my feet, while I dived into *The Times* assuming, I hoped, a correct position for him. He proceeded, and I was surprised indeed to feel his clippers travel swiftly up the back of my scalp and beyond, and the harvest tumble over my eyes into the open newspaper. I protested, and although his did his best thereafter to follow my directions tonsorially, it was too late to undo most of the damage he had done, and weeks elapsed before the passing of time mercifully erased the road he had made, fore and aft! I thanked him and he departed; as he said, he had a lot of hair to cut, and I could well believe him. The next day I saw some of the results of his handiwork, and Slaughter and I enjoyed some quiet laughs. Then I showed him my own mop.

I picked up my letters and soon was immersed in them. There were three from my parents and one each from two of my brothers, both serving. Selwyn was now second-in-command of a six-inch howitzer battery on the Italian Piave Front—he had been wounded at Polygon Wood in September of the previous year (the Passchendaele 'show'). Alfred wrote from Bushey, where he was training with the Inns of Court O.T.C. and was hoping to obtain a commission in the Welsh Guards. I was just opening my parcel, stained with water and addressed to me with the Egyptian Expeditionary Force, when, hearing a footstep behind me, I turned to see Major Constable. Hurriedly, I rose and apologised for my undressed state but, with a genial smile on his rubicund countenance and a wave of his stick, he put me at my ease at once. He indicated the house. 'Let's go inside. Have they made you comfortable, Read? Hm . . . hm . . . not too bad, eh?' We sat down and he offered me a cigarette and I asked him if he minded if I smoked my pipe. 'Certainly, my boy,' and seeing me forage in my valise and produce a quarter-pound tin of Dunhill mixture, 'Ha! That fellow Dunhill must be making a fortune out of you chaps, Read. That toilet paper packet in every tin is a winner and no mistake!' Chuckling thus he started his chat, and first he wanted a short account of our adventures since leaving Proven. When I had finished he lit another cigarette. 'Now, Read, you were there. I have to recommend an officer for a Military Cross, a D.C.M. and two Military Medals—what can you tell me?' I recommended A.V. Brown at once and gave several good reasons for doing so. For the D.C.M. I told him about Sergeant Constable (his namesake), and two men for the M.M.s.

He rose and, standing there in the setting sunlight, tapped his boot with his stick. 'Well, Read—thanks very much indeed—we shall see. Now, must be going, feeding time. We'll get a battalion mess going in a few days if it's possible. Good night.' I watched him to the gate, suddenly struck with a new train of thought. No doubt he would question a good many men including, of course, Peskett. What about poor old Fortescue? Perhaps he would think I'd recommended Brown because he was a friend and had joined the battalion with me.

Cogitating thus, I suddenly felt hungry and went and found Evans, who had made himself at home in the kitchen with a bowl of coffee supplied by the farmer's wife. After the usual salutations I conferred with Evans, who told me that Madame had been asking *him* about a meal for me. Tired and overworked as she was, she gathered the import of our conversation and straight away suggested 'an omelette, perhaps?' She assured me that she had plenty of eggs. Suffice it to say that within half an hour Evans brought in on a tray an omelette with fixings fit for the gods. Not since Rouen had I sampled anything approaching the delicious taste of this, of the salade, and of the long thick slices of home-made bread loaded with country butter—what a change from army tinned stuff! I have never enjoyed a meal more, and after drinking my bowl of coffee I went and told her so. Then, into the farmyard again and the cool of the evening with my pipe, as nearly at peace with the world and everyone in it as it was possible to be. It was then that little Marie brought out the cows after milking, as I have described.

I sat there until it was quite dark, alone with many thoughts, interrupted at length by Slaughter, who brought a message from Battalion H.Q. In the morning at 7.30 the battalion would parade, march off at 7.45 to entrain at Ormoy le Villers at 8.45. We smoked another pipe together before turning in. Then, on the chester of drawers, I saw my still unopened parcel—a Valet safety razor. What a prize! I could hardly wait for the morning. My mother had sent it off to me in April and it had reached me, at length, after a journey back across the Mediterranean, torpedoed, probably, on the way!

Six o'clock on a bright August morning. I was awakened by men's voices in the courtyard below, and I jumped from my bed and thrust the window wider to drink in the air and see what they were doing.

To wash—yes—and to shave with my new Valet autostrop razor. I just couldn't wait, and unwound the leather strop. It had a loop on one end to secure it and, with the razor in the other hand, I soon saw the idea and fixed it round a brass knob on the end of the bedstead. Gingerly I inserted the other end into the razor and started stropping. Wonderfully simple and practical! Then the voices below grew louder, concentrated beneath my window. I ceased stropping and leaned out, razor in hand, to be met with several *bonjour m'sieus* from the men looking up at my window. It was the strange sound of the stropping which had attracted their notice! I demonstrated. I hadn't met them on the previous evening, as I had turned in before they came home from the harvest field, but I heard the horses and the gruff words to them as they were stabled; the snorting and the occasional stamp of iron-shod hooves on the cobbled flooring, before sleep intervened.

Telling the farmer that we were moving off very shortly, I thanked him as they stood there with their horses, ready for another day's toil. His wife came out with their wrapped *casse croûte* and they passed out through the big double gates. I went back to my new razor—a new experience after years of the old cut-throat which, after that day, I don't remember ever using again.

Quick thanks and salutations to Madame and little Marie—delighted with two partially squashed bars of Fry's chocolate cream I'd found in my valise. I seized a quick mug of tea and a bacon sandwich with Slaughter, and we were on parade for the short march to the wayside station of Ormoy-le-Villers to entrain for where . . . and what? There, we were told that on the front we had left, the Germans had retreated to the line of the River Vesle, a tributary of the Aisne, at Fismes.

CHAPTER 21

FLANDERS AGAIN

SKIRTING the suburbs of Paris, we journeyed north by way of Pontoise, Gisors and Amiens. I recall that we stopped a few kilometres north of Pontoise at a small station called Chars. There, to the amusement and then amazement of everyone, old soldiers pushing urns of tea appeared on the platform—most welcome refreshment. No doubt they were on temporary duty there.

That evening we passed slowly through the suburbs and successive mazes of points and sidings around Amiens, and were shocked to see the dozens of damaged locomotives of many types, probably victims of the now-frequent enemy bombing of communications. They stood in long rows, forlorn and already rusting. One depot in particular resembled a huge scrapyard.

During the following morning we arrived at Esquelbecq, in French Flanders, midway between St. Omer and Dunkirk—a pleasant village, and both officers and men had good billets. The weather in the main was fine, and with the arrival of numerous small drafts the battalion began to take shape. Jackson, who left us before the Beugneux attack, had apparently been doing the adjutant's job (the latter having been on leave), and he now returned and took over the company. I regretted the loss of responsibility, but this was tempered to a great extent by the arrival in 'D' Company of two subalterns from the 13th Battalion, Dobbie and Newman. Both were seasoned officers; Dobbie in particular, having commanded a company for nearly three weeks after St. Julien (the Passchendaele 'show') in 1917. Newman was an Irishman, bubbling over with Irish humour.

In the April battles south of Ypres, the 39th Division, of which the 11th, 12th and 13th Royal Sussex formed a brigade, was almost destroyed.

SUNG AROUND LT. DOBBIE'S GRAMOPHONE IN HIS BILLET— ESQUELBECQ, NORD. MID AUGUST 1918.

Dobbie and Newman mentioned many officers I heard A.V. Brown talk about, and I liked both of them from the outset. Somehow, we spoke the same language and, off duty, we were much together. Dobbie brought with him a Decca gramophone, with a number of well worn records of current London hits. His favourite was 'Any old Night is a Wonderful Night if You're out with a Wonderful Girl'. There was, for a week, a chronic shortage of needles, but that tune continued to grind out its course as best it could until a letter brought a fresh supply. We had, too, what Dobbie termed 'better nights' in our billets, when the tunes on the gramophone and the contents of bottles assisted us to sing lustily songs from *The Maid of the Mountains*, *Chu Chin Chow*, *Tonight's the Night*, *The Byng Boys*, and so on. Newman introduced me to Irish whiskey, 'the cratur'!

On Sunday 11th August I took a party from the battalion to attend a church parade at Terdinghem, at which King George V was present, being then on one of his visits to the armies in the field. On 8th August—described by General Ludendorff as Germany's 'Black Day'—the British, Australian and Canadian troops had scored a great victory east of Amiens and were still advancing. The gains were spectacular in ground recovered, in prisoners and captured guns. For these reasons there was a new spirit manifest among us all, and it was a well turned-out body of men with shining buttons, blancoed belts and well brushed khaki that boarded the lorries sent to fetch us to Terdinghem. Just before leaving Esquelbecq, I was informed that I was to take charge of similar parties from other units of the 34th Division, which we were to pick up *en route*. I felt somewhat fed up at this news, but duly collected them. It was a lovely Sunday morning, however, and as we passed through the villages, where church bells tolled and the country folk in their black clothes walked to and fro to Mass, I recovered my good spirits.

Approaching Steenvoorde, what must have been a long-range high velocity shell whistled over and burst in a cornfield about a quarter of a mile away, making us wonder whether the enemy knew of King George's presence in the neighbourhood.

However, in our three lorries we trundled through Steenvoorde—a large village well known to habitués of the Ypres Salient as a Second

Army rest area—and arrived at Terdinghem without further incident. There we found that the service was to be held in a large marquee erected for the purpose, into which we were duly marshalled.

Officers in charge of parties were directed to some rows of chairs in the front, and three of us made ourselves at home in the second of these. For some minutes we were the sole occupants; then, to our consternation, a veritable avalanche of Brass Hats, stiff with the highly polished, creaking brown leather which encased large portions of their persons, descended upon the chairs all around us. Whenever one of these Olympians deigned to notice us, he appeared to radiate superiority. Overcome and dazzled by the rows of medal ribbons in view, the three of us looked furtively around, seeking desperately some means of escape to the rear . . . but it was too late. We were engulfed in a fresh flood, this time of nursing sisters, starched and also creaking at many points. There was nothing for it but to resume our seats.

We had scarcely done this when the whole parade rose, to familiar strains played by a regimental band in attendance, and stood rigidly to attention. King George, followed by a galaxy of army commanders whose turnout and medal ribbons put that of our immediate neighbours completely in the shade, made his way down the centre aisle between the chairs. There followed a few seconds' creaking silence, during which the king placed his cap and gloves under the chair in front of me, under the scrutiny of a hundred pairs of eyes, and the service commenced. Standing immediately behind him, I have never been so close to a king—or a queen, for that matter—since!

My recollections of that service itself are chiefly limited to what happened during the sermon, when a cat stalked slowly up the aisle and made its way under the king's chair. With bated breath, we watched pussy step delicately in and out of the royal hat, and the consternation portrayed on the august faces of some of the Brass Hats would have gladdened the heart of any cartoonist. Happily for the blood pressure of all concerned, the innocent cause of all these suffused cheeks and stertorous breathings stalked slowly away and, to much creaking of gear, the tension relaxed. The king, of course, was quite unaware of what had happened and was following the sermon with keen attention.

The final hymn after this was 'Fight the Good Fight', in the singing of which the king joined lustily. I remember that he was of under average height, and his hair was pretty thin on the top, but I was interested chiefly in the thousands of tiny little dark crimson veinings covering his purplish cheeks and part of his neck. His beard concealed the rest of his features.

After the service there was a march-past of the troops attending, the king taking the salute on a raised dais at the road side. I remember deriving a considerable thrill of pleasure when giving my 34th Division party 'eyes left' and receiving an acknowledgement of my salute from His Majesty.

These few summer days of a seemingly idyllic existence in a Flanders back area were drawing to a close. Before we left Esquelbecq I attended a brigade parade at which French decorations were distributed by one of their generals after the recent fighting with their command near Soissons. General Nicholson was there, also. At this parade I received the Croix de Guerre with Star, and Sergeant Constable the Medaille Militaire, this last being about the highest honour a French soldier could win. I was informed by Battalion Orderly Room that A.V. Brown had won the Military Cross, and I was very pleased. I hoped he was recovering: unfortunately, I had heard nothing since he tottered off.

Then one morning we took the road again in full kit, our faces towards St. Omer. As we marched the strengthening sunlight of a perfect August day fell, slantwise as yet, upon the flat landscape of ripe and partially cut cornfields which stretched away on either side of the road, unrelieved save for occasional spinneys, often acting as windbreaks for the scattered farm-houses. Here and there, too, the village church spires broke the level horizon. Across the corn the breeze rippled at intervals like a faint shadow, leaving in its wake a waving sea of alternating browns and golds—of hidden riches into which wind and sun had combined to pry. As the battalion breasted a barely perceptible rise I, bringing up the rear of 'D' Company, was struck by its still pitifully shrunken appearance in column of route. Behind me stretched the transport limbers and smoking field cookers, in a train of normal dimensions which emphasized the paucity of our numbers.

But this was our sole battle scar, for everyone seemed in good spirits and in fine fettle. Khaki, if the worse for wear, had been well brushed; badges and buttons glinted brightly as the sun caught them. 'Blanco' and 'Soldiers' Friend' had been exploited to the limit. The transport mules looked sleek and Solomon-wise, harness well oiled and metal portions scoured to perfection, vying with the buttons of the drivers for brightness.

A fine morning, indeed!

At the first halt, Dobbie and I sat ourselves down upon a heap of stones by the road side and munched wheat grains from the ear, plucked from the encroaching harvest. The men, rid of their packs for a few moments, lit pipes or cigarettes and sat about contentedly along the grass verge, the pink of their shaven countenances now deepened to warmer hues by reason of their exertions. I remember looking from one to another of them, and pointing out to Dobbie and Newman a few of their individual characteristics. Dobbie, of course, couldn't help comparing them with the lads of his cherished 13th Battalion, and I with the old 8th Leicesters. Was it merely an illusion on our part to agree that, though these 4th men looked healthy enough, their average height was several inches less than that of the infantrymen of two years ago? As we prepared to resume the march we concluded, somewhat sadly, that physique had deteriorated. Either that, or else tall chaps stood a greater chance of being knocked out than the short ones.

However, before our next halt our topic of conversation changed. Dobbie announced that the countryside hereabouts was familiar to him and that, unless he was very much mistaken, we would soon be passing the village of Volkeringckhove. Apparently his old 13th Battalion had trained around there for the St. Julien attack in July of the previous year, and as we progressed he became certain, recounting incidents recalled by various landmarks. Indeed, as we neared the by-road leading to the village, his anecdotes became increasingly animated; and, as I had surmised, there was a lady in the background somewhere. I therefore derived considerable quiet amusement at his expense when we marched by the signpost for Volkeringckhove, keeping to the main road. Dobbie looked at the distant village longingly; what a fine billet it had been! He relapsed into temporary silence, his thoughts no doubt of his girl friend there. Then, catching my eye, Newman joined in. Together they told me of their colleagues before St. Julien—old so-and-so, and so-and-so—some since immortalized by Edmund Blunden in his saga of the South Down Brigade of the Royal Sussex Regiment, *Undertones of War*.

To Dobbie's joy, however, we halted for the day at the next village, Lederzeele, and no sooner was the company billeted and fed than we were off to Volkeringckhove. Unfortunately, Newman was on duty.

Sure of his way, he led me to a large farm-house on the outskirts of the village, surrounded by tall trees. In the yard the watchdog growled and then rushed at us threateningly; but Dobbie called him by name, greeting him as an old friend. The old dog pulled up short and, after a moment's suspicion, wagged his tail and ran round and round, getting between Dobbie's legs as we made our way towards the house where, attracted by the barking no doubt, a girl appeared in the shady doorway.

She looked hard at us, and then, recognizing Dobbie, she ran to him with outstretched hands, beaming with pleasure. Dobbie, his face alight, introduced me, and I could have sworn I saw damp in his eyes. Not that I couldn't well understand his emotion, for I had experienced the same lump in the throat at seeing Émilienne and her family again after several great battles and long absence. He had not exaggerated the good points of Louise, either. She wasn't exactly pretty, but hers was a face of character—striking, in fact, as she led the way through the farm-house kitchen on the way to a sitting room. I call it 'sitting room' for lack of the correct term to use, but the furniture was huge and dark, and the walls were thickly studded with ancestral likenesses and various heirlooms. Her mother came in as we were sitting down, and she, too, was genuinely pleased to see Dobbie. She hurried away; perhaps to the cellar, as she returned with a bottle of wine and four glasses upon a tray. Louise was very like her mother, I thought.

I endeavoured to make conversation with Maman while Dobbie and Louise reminisced. She asked me about the fates of several officers whom she remembered as visiting Dobbie while he was billeted there, but of course, I had to refer to him. The answers he gave were, I recall, mostly '*blessé*', '*tué*', or '*kaput*'. The woman looked genuinely grieved. Apparently Maman's husband was now, like all farmers, endeavouring to get the harvest in with very little help: old men, boys and girls. She must go back to them. We rose as she handed round the glasses of wine and drank, wishing them *bonne chance!* The refreshment occasioned more reminiscences, and so the pleasant afternoon passed, till in the early evening we made our way slowly back to Lederzeele. I had gone ahead and did not see Dobbie take his final leave of Louise, but when he rejoined me I could see that a sombre mood had settled upon him, and we walked mostly in silence, each wrapped in his own thoughts. I could realize what he felt. When we spoke, both of us seemed affected with a kind of gnawing loneliness: a longing, so difficult to describe, for days that were past; for the sight of faces and the sounds of voices that, alas, were gone. Inevitably, this frame of mind produced a vague feeling of hopelessness in facing the future, and of intense regret that things could never be the same again. To both of us, our everyday lives of three years, two years, even one year ago had now taken on the atmosphere of romance; our dead comrades the mythical stature of heroes. In spite of the pressure of events, this mood persisted for days.

The battalion marched early the next morning, entering St. Omer by way of St. Mommelin and halting finally at a tented camp near the hamlet of Courmette, situated on higher ground a few kilometres west of the city. Here we received considerable drafts, totalling around two hundred N.C.O.s and men and about a dozen officers. Many were veterans of the South Down Brigade of the regiment, now disbanded. Practically all the officers were known to either Dobbie or Newman, and both were overjoyed to see them. As opportunity offered they introduced me, and I could see that they were all good fellows; moreover, the manner of their coming warmed me towards them. It so happened that I was battalion orderly officer on the day that they arrived at the camp entrance, hot, dirty and hungry. As it was the men's dinner time, I was going the rounds of the messes with the orderly sergeant and, in doing so, saw them. Surprised, and considerably annoyed because I had not been apprised of the draft's arrival, I hastened across, wondering on the way how on earth I was going to arrange accommodation and about two hundred extra dinners at such short notice.

The major in charge came towards me, and as I saluted I saw, somewhat wide-eyed, that he wore the ribbons of the D.S.O. and M.C. and Bar. It goes without saying that to describe him as 'soldierly looking' would be a blatant understatement. Such was my introduction to Major Rothschild, and at that moment he was looking pretty wild about something! Curtly ordering his charges to fall out, he requested me to take him to the Battalion Orderly Room, as he wished to see the adjutant at once—which, as may be imagined, I did.

Gently pulling back the flap of the Orderly Room tent, and entering foremost, I saluted the adjutant, Captain Middleton, as he sat at his table. He looked up, appearing to resent my somewhat abrupt entry, but I duly reported both the arrival of the draft and that the officer in charge was outside and would like to see him at once.

Now the adjutant—presumably one of the original pre-war officers of the 4th (Territorial) Battalion, Royal Sussex Regiment, and therefore 'county' in his outlook—had, since rejoining from home leave after the Soissons fighting, treated all newcomers like myself with an air of tolerant, though unmistakeable, superiority which, in my youthful ignorance of the ways of the world, I couldn't help resenting. In retrospect, in all probability my progress would have been smoother had I stifled this more effectively at the time. However, on this occasion, doubtless thinking to himself that some more 'outsiders' had arrived, and at the same time that it was a good opportunity to snub me, he smiled in a bored fashion, lit a cigarette and remarked languidly, as he lay back in his chair blowing smoke rings, that he would be along in a few minutes.

We were both unaware that Major Rothschild had both seen and heard this, but he had. Smacking his riding boot furiously with his cane, he thrust me to one side and faced the now-bewildered Middleton, to whom he gave the nastiest and completest dressing down it was ever my lot to witness in the service—so devastating, in fact, that the recipient was literally speechless.

The upshot of all this was that, that evening, the battalion mess divided into two distinct 'camps': those who comprised the old 4th Royal Sussex, and 'the others', consisting of Major Rothschild and the officers he had brought with him, plus Dobbie, Newman and the few who came with them.

As orderly officer, and on duty, I thankfully escaped the difficult decision of taking sides—especially difficult in my case as, of the 'originals' I liked Major Constable, Captain Peskett and another captain now become major, one Warren.

I dreaded the morrow, however, as I heard about this and that the two groups were not on speaking terms in the mess. But I need not have worried, as that night I was told I had been selected for a fortnight's rest at the Second Army rest camp at Audresselles, on the Channel coast near Cap Gris Nez. Secretly very glad to escape, I departed early the next morning in the mess cart for St. Omer station. Later, as the train rattled towards Calais, it occurred to me that Captain Middleton had seized a heaven-sent opportunity of getting me out of the way before I could spread the story of his discomfiture at the hands of Major Rothschild. For a few moments, until anticipatory thoughts of pleasures to come intervened, I became apprehensive as to whether I had made an enemy of the adjutant by being a witness, however, unwilling. Still, I thought, 'sufficient unto the day . . .'.

I didn't particularly require a fortnight's rest, but I reached Audresselles with others I met on the same errand, determined to make the most of it. Indeed, it was a wonderful break, my only moments of any feeling akin to depression when, almost daily, from the cliffs near Cap Gris Nez, we used to watch the leave boat to England clear Boulogne and follow its progress until it was only a smudge of smoke on the horizon. On clear days, too, we could see plainly the line of white cliffs near Dover. Then it seemed hard lines, after doing the round trip to Egypt and almost back, to be marooned upon the wrong side of the Channel, within a few miles of home.

Most afternoons and not a few evenings found us in the company of nurses from the great field hospital nearby at Wimereux, now occupying what, in happier days, had been the casino and its extensive grounds, the latter packed with additional hutted wards and staff quarters.

They were jolly girls from the various voluntary nursing services— St John, British Red Cross or V.A.D.—generally with either a

MONT KEMMEL
Sept. 2nd. 1918,
"Coy. H.Q."

brother, a fiancé, or even a husband, serving somewhere. We never mentioned the war; they talked mostly of home, of what they did before 1914, or of what they, and we, planned to do when it was all over—if ever! A very pleasant change for youthful sub-alterns, and perhaps for the girls, to sit on the dunes or the cliffs in the warm afternoon sunshine and chat thus. For them, too, it must have been a few hours relaxation away from the shattered forms and the gangrene within the hospital. I recall that on more than one occasion a girl asked if we minded if she removed—temporarily, of course—her high white starched collar. They hated them in hot weather. We raised no objection, but the afternoon came when a collar, lightly discarded, was caught by the sea breeze and travelled quite a distance before, breathless, we retrieved it; the owner, between gasps, telling us that she daren't return without it!

Then there was afternoon tea and, on two occasions, a mixed foursome at dinner in Wimereux. but, like all good things, the fortnight at Audresselles came to an end, and two drizzling morn-ings later, having missed the battalion as directed as Esquelbecq,

I reached the little station of Abeille, then a railhead for the Ypres Salient. Here the R.T.O. informed me that they were holding the line near Mont Kemmel.

I managed to get a lift on a lorry as far as the brigade transport lines at Rozenhill Camp. The feeling of well-being with which I had left Audresselles, already blunted, was now destroyed completely by the forlorn and tortured appearance of the country as we neared Reninghelst in that drizzling rain from an overcast sky. Once more the scream of high velocity shells and the hollow staccato reports from our own guns, carried across the Flanders plain by a chill autumn wind, brought me back to grim reality. They echoed and re-echoed across that dreary expanse of derelict camps and abandoned dumps; relics of one-time horse lines and battery positions; heaps of shot-torn, rusty corrugated iron; ragged, dripping remnants of what were once spinneys; piles of rubble that were once hamlets; the whole dominated by the frowning mass of Mont Kemmel, seen in the misty distance through the now-driving rain and now in enemy hands—a veritable 'abomination of desolation'.

When I arrived at the brigade transport lines—a miserable, semi-camouflaged huddle of tents, with a few patched-up huts—I learned from our battalion quartermaster that, during the previous night, the enemy had evacuated most of Mont Kemmel and our brigade was now feeling its way forward. Late that night I rejoined my company and, by candlelight in an evil-smelling German pillbox on the slopes of a partially re-occupied Mont Kemmel, met my new Commander, Captain White, M.C. and two Bars, and his Number One, Lieutenant Fenton, M.C. Dobbie had been transferred to 'A' Company; Newman and a new arrival—one Chalk, but lately commissioned—were up with the men in a line of outposts, but at the moment the 4th Royal Sussex were in reserve.

I took to 'Skipper' White and Fenton from the very beginning, making a good start by unearthing two bottles, one of Black & White, the other of Old Bushmills in deference to Newman's preference. Mugs were produced at once, and as I hung my haversack on a nail left by an obliging enemy it felt considerably lighter, containing now only my shaving kit and toothbrush wrapped in a somewhat soiled towel, spare socks and some tobacco. They charged their mugs and Captain White raised his, holding it in both hands as he sat on a box of small arms ammunition. For a moment or two he appeared to be thinking deeply and sniffed lightly—not nastily, or ill-manneredly; just, as it were, to make for clear thinking. (I soon discovered that he always did when pondering a decision, or before breaking a silence.) Then: 'cheer ho, Richard! Hope your stay with us will be a pleasant one!' Raising his mug, he looked across at Fenton, and by the guttering candle stuck on a jam tin I saw the twinkle in his grey eyes as the latter added significantly, as he lifted his tot, '. . . and a long one, too!'

In that German pillbox on Mont Kemmel that evening, notwithstanding the running wet walls and the foetid atmosphere, I felt that I had come among friends. Our trials and tribulations to come were to be many, but I became then one of a happy family under White paterfamilias—fortunately right to the end, and beyond!

Captain White told me to get my head down if I could, as he was awaiting orders and the indications were that we should move to the front line on the morrow. Pleasantly warmed by the whisky, I lay down on some Mills bomb boxes and pulled my trench coat as tightly as I could around myself. I seemed to see, in a last few moments of wakefulness, Fenton buckle on his revolver and fix his respirator before leaving for a round of the company posts. On my sleepy inquiry, he said that Major Rothschild had only stayed about two days with the battalion after I'd left for Audresselles, and he added, as he disappeared into the darkness without, 'he's a *real* soldier!'

CHAPTER 22

THE FINAL ADVANCE

In the chill dawn at 'stand to' I emerged from the pillbox entrance to see, in its grim reality, the horror of Mont Kemmel. A few yards away, half-buried by overturned earth and uprooted trees, lay the smashed remains of two French 75s and their crews, the tattered and saturated remnants of uniforms and steel helmets still faintly blue. A little further away lay what was left of several mouldering horses. Unused shells, complete with cased charges, lay scattered amongst this ruin. Fenton, a regular soldier commissioned from the ranks, stood beside me and pulled me out of my thoughts. 'Come on, Richard, not very nice that, is it? I'll show you where the lads are'; and as we stumbled over the torn ground he remarked, 'these poor devils of Frenchmen never had a chance to clear up. They are all over the shop around here.' They were.

It looked as though the French Alpine Division, put into the struggle as a last effort in those April days to plug the British line and to hold Mont Kemmel before the onslaught of the German Jaeger *Sturmtruppen*, had been annihilated by an avalanche of huge shells which had produced the effect of an earthquake. With the prospect of nuclear Armageddon in the offing, many are the learned (but more often journalistic) views expressed to the effect that this will prove far more terrible than the two previous wars. Probably it will be, as the civilian population will be involved equally with the armed forces, and therefore casualties will be far greater. So far, however, as far as the actual manner of dying or mutilation is concerned, I have yet to be convinced that there is much difference between being blown to pieces or gassed by a shell which the victims have heard coming, or death by radiation. In any case, it is difficult to see 'progress' in the latter. But I am getting out of my depth. To those who were there, Mont Kemmel could not have lagged far behind Hiroshima.

It was good to see Newman again. We shook hands, and his reaction when I told him, in a quick aside, that we had some Old Bushmills in stock at Company H.Q. was typically and lovably Irish. Indicating his unwashed, sprouting chin, his mud-plastered trench coat and boots, he said that, without doubt, I'd saved his life!

A little further on, with debris and mud much greater hindrance than the enemy just then, we came upon a lanky figure in a newish but filthily muddied trench coat, sitting on the trunk of a fallen tree and looking fixedly to his front. I saw that he wore pince-nez, secured by a fine chain which disappeared behind one ear. What hair I could see under his tin hat, his untrimmed, untidy moustache and the unshaven growth beneath were all sandy—almost ginger—and his features still bore traces of boyish freckles. It was Chalk. He, too, was glad to see us and introductions by Fenton were followed by a short chat and a report on the night's events, principally concerning 'bloody great rats'! They departed for Company H.Q. intending to pick up Newman *en route*, and I was left in charge, in a drizzling rain.

I had just learned that a former C.O. of the 4th Battalion in Palestine had rejoined while I had been away at Audresselles. His name was Sir William Campion, and reputedly M.P. for the Lewes Division of Sussex. For the record, this was 3rd September, and I didn't see him, nor was spoken to by him, until 15th December. Then, I hadn't the slightest idea who he was, as I shall try to relate.

I found plenty to do, if only in meeting again well tried N.C.O.s and men, and also the newcomers in the drafts arriving at Esquelbecq and Courmette: mostly youngsters, but with a sprinkling of old hands from various other battalions of the Royal Sussex. The rain glistened on their tin hats and the rubberised groundsheets around their shoulders. At least I provided a temporary diversion for them in these miserable surroundings.

With the trench map White had given me, and my compass, I endeavoured to get my bearings accurately and study the terrain. To our right and almost to our front, the view was blocked by the mass of Mont Kemmel, topped by gaunt, broken skeletons of trees, half-hidden in the mist. Artillery and machine-gun fire beyond was fairly continuous, but not at all heavy.

I could see more to my left front, including some ruins of Kemmel village; but beyond, rain and mist obscured the tortured landscape towards Wytchaete. Fenton came up at midday with news that the advance was proceeding slowly and that we were moving up through Kemmel that evening and getting into position for a push forwards towards Wytchaete–Messines at nine the following morning. U.S. troops would be going over on our left. I produced my map, which we studied for a few moments while Fenton explained the general idea. Our jumping-off position was roughly between the so-called strong points of Forts Saskatchewan and Regina, relics of old Canadian trenches of, I believe, 1917.

That evening at dusk we concentrated near Kemmel village, and, as we moved off again, passed an American regiment coming out. We were mildly surprised to see how they had so quickly assumed the same hunched shoulders and stumbling walk under heavy burdens; the same resigned, fixed look, half forward, half groundward, as British troops inured to trench life.

We descended into a shambles of a communication trench near the eastern end of Kemmel village and made slow progress with frequent halts which, for a time, gave us considerable cause for anxiety. I found afterwards that this trench ran roughly along the side of the Kemmel–Wytcheate road, and that evening the German artillery were giving it an evening 'hate' of five-nines. No wonder it went by the name of Suicide Road.

A shell from one salvo fell—fortunately, I suppose—on the trench side in a small gap between two platoons, narrowly missing Chalk. There were, however, several casualties, one instantly fatal. Chalk was temporarily dazed, as were half a dozen others. As movement forward had ceased, I hastened along past my lads to find the reason. As well as I could, I organized first aid to the wounded and sent the walking cases off to the rear. Two obvious stretcher cases remained, and I hoped that the message for bearers transmitted to the rear by word of mouth would soon bring them along. In the meanwhile, we managed to get the file moving again, while I stood with my back to the dead man and urged the men forward past this and the stretcher cases as quickly as I could.

I'm afraid that, at this stage of the war, the training of stretcher-bearers had become sketchy in the extreme. All of the 'originals' had disappeared long since—one way or the other—and men were detailed to carry the complement of stretchers and first aid boxes. Few had specialized knowledge. On the other hand, most men with battle experience had done bandaging of comrades and were conversant with elementary procedure; and believe me, this was invaluable that evening.

As the men stumbled by the acridly stinking shambles in the last of the daylight I saw that some of the youngsters were frightened, while the old hands grunted unintelligibly after a sidelong glance and pressed on. Once more the procession halted and all ducked into the trench bottom as another salvo burst nearby, and, as soon as the clatter of skyward-thrown earth and iron had descended, moved on again. Here were the stretcher-bearers—at last! I hoped fervently that there was morphine in their box.

With Newman bringing up the rear, and having done what I could, we were eventually challenged by a sentry at what proved to be our new Company H.Q. White's batman, Pearson, C.S.M. Slaughter and two runners had lit candles in what I saw to be a miserable shanty which wouldn't have stopped a whizz-bang. White stood looking at them, thinking, and as he saw me he sniffed. I reported the casualties and action taken. Then: 'this is Parrain Farm, Richard. There isn't any of it left, but there's a dead mule here,' and he showed me the approximate positions of both the farm and the mule. True enough, the map read 'Parrain Farm', and it was just north of the Kemmel–Wytchaete (Suicide) road. He continued, 'old who-is-it—the Q.M.S.—is going to have a holiday tomorrow night, coming up here along the road with the rations on mules. By the way, look for booby traps up there,' and, taking me aside, he showed me several messages from Battalion H.Q., one warning about these. 'You've been with this lot longer than I have. Would you say this was the adjutant's [Middleton's] signature?' I looked in the uncertain light of the smoking candle. It seemed an illegible scrawl, unlike any signature of his I'd ever seen. I said so. 'That's what I thought, Richard. I fancy I've a bone to pick with Captain Middleton!' and he put them back in his pocket. 'When you get up there, ask Fenton to come down as soon as he's satisfied things are O.K. and we are on the right starting line. Try to contact the Yanks on our left unless Fenton has managed it already.'

As soon as Fenton had established our position in line, along a labyrinth of odd pieces of old trench, I arranged with him to take Lance-Corporal Shiere and two men and endeavour to make contact with the Americans on our left flank. Waiting until a falling German Verey light lit the scene fitfully for a few seconds, so that we could get some idea of the ground and a general direction, we set out, halting every few yards to listen for sounds of human occupation—enemy or otherwise. Our progress was necessarily slow, and I was beginning to wonder whether we were on the right track, when one of the men called my attention to a faint and intermittent glimmer of light almost directly behind us. Cautiously, therefore, we made our way towards this (hampered, I recall, by old wire), and a few moments later we were challenged—and shot at—simultaneously. Our allies could be pardoned for being some-what trigger-happy under the circumstances, but we managed to establish our identity with a 'lootenant' who, to our surprise, was addressed by men of his patrol as 'Gus'. Apparently he had been ordered to find us!

We crouched in the slit trench bottom while we indicated our relative positions on his map. From this, their right flank company appeared to be about two hundred yards to our left and about a hundred behind, straddling a track leading to Wytchaete from the Kemmel–Vierstratt–Ypres road. He confirmed that they, too, were going over at 9 a.m. when the barrage lifted. We parted with swigs of liquor for good luck, I had my first taste of bourbon from a large hip flask he carried; which, as I gasped, caused great amuse-ment to all. Gus took a really generous drink of neat rum from my water bottle, but we were on our way back before we could see the, probably delayed, effect on him. I remember that the lads were tickled pink with our excursion, especially after a nip out of my bottle just before we reached the company again. Thereafter I was to hear Gus discussed on many occasions: and on one, indeed, how I had choked.

With the coming of daylight and 'stand to' we were all busy checking equipment, rations and our dispositions for the advance.

Captain White came along and assured us that, to the best of his knowledge, after inquiries at Battalion H.Q., we were behind the initial barrage line, due at 8.55 a.m., and we synchronized our watches with his. Fenton had already told him of my American contact, and my conclusion that they were well behind their correct starting line. He smiled, but made no comment.

The barrage was short in duration and pretty accurate. As soon as it lifted we were up and over, threading our way as best we could through the maze of rusty wire and corrugated iron in front. To our right we could see our other companies going forward in like fashion, but to our left there appeared to be no movement as yet by the Americans. In the meanwhile, showers of SOS rockets were rising from the German positions—which to us seemed to be at least six hundred yards distant—and we looked anxious for shelter from the counter-barrage we knew would follow. The result was that, when it came within a minute, it caused our lads to duck into the first bit of old trench they came to and, while it lasted, cohesion was quite lost. A machine-gun, firing unpleasant bursts as we subalterns and N.C.O.s showed ourselves in running here and there to re-establish the advance, didn't help matters, but by the late afternoon we had progressed about seven hundred yards. Here, I should have said that, for reasons best known to themselves, the Americans chose to go over just as the German counter-barrage descended, but, from what little we saw of them, they didn't suffer from 'wind-up' and advanced resolutely even though quite a few were dropping.

We had reached a line along a track with a bank about four feet high, running parallel with our front, my left flank resting about one hundred yards beyond what, by my trench map, went by the name of Alberta Dugouts. In getting there we had been bogged down in another ruined camp shown as Beaver Huts, by a machine-gun firing apparently from a mass of rusty wire and smashed huts on a perceptible rise, three to four hundred yards distant. The map showed that we were approaching the line of great mine craters blown on the Messines Ridge at the outset of the successful British attack in June of the previous year. Those in our immediate neighbourhood were, from our left to our right (i.e. from north to south), called Warsaw, Peckham and Spanbrok Molen, the first-named being nearest us just then.

It had been a very tiring day, although it had been obvious from the start that the enemy were not holding their positions in strength and were fighting a rearguard action. I can assure anyone without a similar experience, however, that the sensation of picking a way over and through a maze of man-made obstacles such as I have described, in momentary expectation of encountering a blizzard of machine-gun bullets from a well-hidden enemy biding his time, is the reverse of pleasant! Indeed, many times this occurred, and escapes verged on the miraculous, especially during the fairly frequent hurricane crashes of five-nine defensive fire. I believe we only sustained four casualties that day, none, as far as I recollect, of a really serious nature. Believe me, in those days the prospect of getting out of the mud and shell fire, and back to England, gave many a wounded man strength to bear his hurt and smile as well, if he could smoke a fag.

By nightfall, as it became clear that the enemy did not intend to fall back further just then, we did our best to consolidate our positions and mark them accurately on our maps, to find our posts in the dark; also to get rations and water to them. Acting on instructions, I had given orders that any dugouts found were to be left severely alone pending investigation for booby traps. This applied, really, both to Alberta Dugouts and to several other shelters of former British and Canadian construction found along the track; but I couldn't be in two places at once, and I found that sections had occupied several of the latter, fortunately without incident. I recall my annoyance at the time, but a sergeant pointed out that these places couldn't be called 'dugouts'; they were just a few rotting sandbags over sheets of corrugated iron. I had to agree, and at least they afforded refuge from the drizzling rain and a temporary respite for those men not actually on sentry duty.

Captain White came along with Fenton in the last of the light. He had decided to leave Company H.Q. at Parrain Farm until our next move forward, unless Alberta Dugouts (or what Battalion H.Q. called 'Siege Farm') nearby proved to be habitable after investigation. I pointed out that the flimsy shelters on the track might be Siege Farm, but there certainly was not a vestige of any previous building there. White smiled kindly, then said, 'what have you been leaning against, Richard?' He and Fenton pulled tufts of rough wet grass from the bank and rubbed the haversack, strapped pack-fashion on my back, for some moments. Throwing the grass over the bank in front, bomb-fashion, with the remark 'that's a bit better, Richard!' they departed. Several weeks elapsed before a chance sally made over a dugout meal prompted me to ask White what he and Fenton had rubbed off my back that evening. Once or twice, at odd moments, I had wondered, concluding that it must have been excreta or something equally unpleasant, picked up during the day's adventures, which wouldn't have surprised me at all. Now, however, they looked at each other queerly, and then Fenton, always John Blunt, said laconically, 'brains'.

It was some moments before, with a horrible sensation of nausea, I remember how I'd stood, back against the damaged trench side and in front of the mangled remains on the previous evening, going in near Kemmel village, while I urged the lads to hurry on past before the next salvo arrived. In Germany, months afterwards, Fenton was recounting this incident late one night in our mess, at my expense, telling them how shocked I'd looked. Apparently, Beaumont Hamel and St. Julien had given him similar experiences, which I could well believe.

I only recall this, now, as one fact of war—waged by the now so-called 'conventional weapons'.

After 'stand down' that evening, Fenton told Chalk and me to get back to Company H.Q. and get some sleep, arranging to be awakened in good time to relieve him and Newman at midnight. In the drizzle we set off, aided by the occasional German Verey light, but had it not been for the tell-tale stink of the mule we should have been much longer finding our goal. As we arrived we heard the padding of approaching hooves and low voices. Sure enough, we made out in due course our C.Q.M.S., Mitchell, M.M., an 11th Battalion N.C.O. with his assistant and two grooms from the transport section, leading two heavily laden mules 'Solomon' and 'David'.

Across their blanket-padded backs they carried, pannier-fashion, sandbags of rations, tins of water, the mail, and a box of S.A.A. balanced by two boxes of Mills grenades. All helped to unload the precious burdens and get them behind the shelter of the dugout curtain. Freed of their loads, the mules shook themselves. They wanted to look for grass, and in the fitful light spread for a few moments by a German rocket, the steam rising from their bodies from their recent exertions showed white. They stood quite still. Then C.S.M. Slaughter emerged from the shelter with something in each hand, which he held to them. 'This is what they like, sir!' They did, too, and munched contentedly on a packet of Woodbines apiece, as the little procession started back for the transport lines.

We remained here for a week, working our line a few yards forward daily—or rather, nightly, as we found that the enemy moved back at dusk as a rule—but we were considerably hampered by the vile weather. Before we were relieved, we reached the rim of the mine crater known as 'Peckham', but were glad when the support company took our places, and we went back a few hundred yards to the rear. When we returned to the front line it was to the right of our previous position, and approximately on the western edge of Spanbrock Molen crater. White's H.Q. was near two cross tracks called Pall Mall.

The Germans were very nervous just then, and, at the most unexpected moments of the day or night, up would go their SOS signal, followed almost immediately by half a dozen more further behind their line. Then down would crash two distinct lines of five-nine barrage fire, very unpleasant while it lasted, one for our front line, the other intended to stop our supports. We were very lucky to escape sustaining more casualties than we actually did.

While here another captain—one Lewis by name, and originally a 6th Battalion man—joined us, under a cloud. Apparently, on reporting for duty with the battalion a few weeks previously, he had taken over command of a company but had soon fallen foul of the H.Q. people—and, more particularly, the adjutant, Middleton. This, of course, we could quite understand! To crown his misfortune, however, in the early morning after he had taken his company back to support positions following relief from the front line, our C.O., decided to make a tour at 'stand to', accompanied by Middleton. Lewis and his second-in-command were found fast asleep and under the influence of rum, while the men were either asleep or taking things very easily, at a time when they should have been cleaning their rifles and getting themselves ship-shape generally. At the approach of the C.O. and Middleton, a quaking batman, who barely realized the identity of the visitors, attempted to wake a resentful Lewis and was duly consigned to perdition. Middleton prodded Lewis with his stick and received another broadside for his pains—in the hearing of the C.O. The upshot was as I have recorded. We considered him fortunate in escaping more severe punishment; nevertheless, save for his one apparent weakness—rum—we found Lewis to be a stout fellow who really pulled his weight, and he soon settled down with us.

During these trying days, too, Captain White displayed on many occasions qualities of tactful yet firm leadership which first attached and then endeared him to us. Invariably quietly spoken, with him, however, an order was an order. There was no nonsense about him, as all ranks soon found. Of medium height, with the build and shoulders of an athlete (he played centre forward for a well known North London amateur side in happier days), his rosy cheeks and toothbrush moustache accentuated his somewhat youthful appearance, but in his grey eyes and the set of his jaw one saw the soldier. On the breast of his faded and leather-elbowed tunic, the soiled blue and white M.C. ribbon with its two bars lay like a hall-mark. He possessed, moreover, that precious quality which many otherwise good officers lacked, a real sense of humour, having the happy knack of being able to move a crowd of grousing men and disgruntled N.C.O.s to gales of laughter by a sally at a grouser's expense—in which the latter generally joined, if somewhat sheepishly. Then the whole spirit of the men would seem changed in the instant, and White would laugh, too, pleasantly and without malice. What a difference this made when working parties, patrols and advanced posts had constantly to be found from the ranks of these over-worked and, in many cases, overwrought youngsters who now comprised 75 per cent of our effectives.

Luckily, as I have said, in spite of the miserable weather and the terrible state of the waterlogged ground, we suffered remark-ably few casualties. Moreover, reports coming in from time to time of the advances our armies were making to the south contributed much to the maintenance of a reasonable standard of cheerfulness. Apropos of this, a nocturnal incident which put the whole com-pany in good humour for a day was the escapade of Lewis in the great mine crater of Spanbrok Molen.

We had reached the western lip at the summit of a short, steepish slope, where our advance was held up by two cunningly placed machine-guns on the far edge, about 150 yards distant. These, in daylight, sniped any silhouette of ours appearing even momentarily above the tangle of split bags and rusty wire forming the lip. Lewis volunteered to take a patrol out that night to see if he could find a way round or across, intending to wait until one of the machine-guns fired, and then to stalk it by the flashes. Fenton and I, from our post near the crater edge, wished him luck as he and his small party disappeared into the total blackness, listening thereafter intently and, truth to tell, somewhat anxiously. For moments, not a sound—then scuffling and muttered curses, becoming of a sudden louder and, somehow, from below. Quick to grasp the situation, Fenton took his runner and disappeared in the direction of the noise, with the terse comment, 'Lewis—for a quid!' A few minutes later—the commotion, meanwhile, continuing unabated—Fenton's runner re-appeared and reported to me that Captain Lewis had fallen down the side of the crater and was entangled in the barbed wire there. Fenton and the patrol had made a chain and were trying to get him out.

Just then the nearer machine-gun opened up, but mercifully the bullets went over high, followed by several flares and what I was fearing—an SOS rocket, answered quickly by others in the German artillery zone which, in a few moments, was firing hard. Mercifully, everything dropped well behind us: for once, Jerry was wide of the mark. After ten minutes or so the shelling slackened and then ceased, enabling our still-singing ears to catch once more the mutterings and cursings of the unfortunate Lewis. Eventually— and, as we afterwards realized, almost miraculously—rescuers and rescued materialized from the pitch blackness, unrelieved just then by even the fitful glimmer of a distant Verey light, and the little procession stumbled back on its way to Company H.Q. As Fenton passed he informed me in a fierce whisper that they were 'all covered in shit and cut to b. . .y!' Lewis, now assisted by two of the men, appeared to be incoherent, and I did not see him until after 'stand down' the next morning. Then, relieved by Newman, I made my way to Company H.Q. in the half-light for a few hours sleep, and I was shocked, as White and others had been, at the sight of Lewis, still sleeping off his hangover, wrapped in a blanket above which his face showed as a mass of scratches with mud and dried blood mixed with two days' stubble around his lower jaw. His jacket, torn in a dozen places, with the lining protruding from the elbow of one sleeve, seemed to be pretty well a write-off as it lay muddily across a box of S.A.A.

Fenton was shaving, while his batman strove to remove the worst of the mud from his jacket. In the background White, writing his report by the light of two candle-ends stuck in Players' tins, looked up to confide in a low voice, and with a significant sniff, that he hoped to God the C.O. and Middleton, the adjutant, wouldn't put in an appearance that morning!

They didn't, and for once luck favoured poor Lewis. After some breakfast I got down on the floor beside him and slept until midday, when I awoke to see a still dazed and bedraggled Lewis, sitting up and examining ruefully the tears in his breeches.

That evening, in another attempt to reconnoitre Spanbrok Molen and, if possible, get at the enemy holding us up, we lost one of the best N.C.O.s in the company—Corporal Durrant. We were working our way around the left side when a burst from an alerted machine-gun got him in the neck and he died within moments. At 'stand down' the next morning we buried him near Company H.Q. dugout, and I recall how depressed at this everyone was, from White downwards. (Durrant is now buried in Messines Military Cemetery, where I visited his grave in 1964.) By that time sudden death among us was, indeed, a commonplace; but, maybe because—luckily—we had escaped casualties for a few days previously, and because, too, of the hilarity engendered by the escapade of Lewis, the corporal's untimely end affected us with an additional emphasis.

There came a day when White showed us a chit from Battalion H.Q. He was to send one officer to attend a course at the Second Army School of Musketry at Lumbres, near St. Omer. None of us wished to go, as each felt he would be letting down the rest; whereon White called on his batman, Pearson, to bring a pack of cards, with which we cut for it. Mine was the lowest—a deuce— and I was ordered to remove myself forthwith and not dare to come back without some genuine Scotch. I was away for nearly three weeks, thereby missing the great Allied drive of the British Second and Belgian Armies of 29th September, which took them beyond the high watermark of the Passchendaele Offensive of the previous year. On that occasion our battalion was in reserve and followed up the advance through Wytchaete village and Oosterverne.

I rejoined them on the night of 9th October, by way of Zand-voorde, and found our company holding a line of shallow trench immediately south of, and at right-angles to, the Ypres–Menin road on the outskirts of the village of Gheluwe. White's H.Q. was a pillbox built into the back of a partially demolished farm-house some three hundred yards back, the route to it from the front line pretty well across the open. Movement, therefore, was severely restricted during daylight hours, but the morning mists usual at that time of the year provided much welcome cover. I was very glad to see them all again, and they to see me, as I had managed to scrounge several precious bottles at Lumbres and St. Omer. Naturally, I went on duty immediately, White telling me, with a grin, that I'd had a jolly good rest and could now expect some real hard work. My efforts to convince him that the course at Lumbres had been equally exhausting raised a characteristic sniff—almost a snort—as I departed.

Daylight showed me our position and, fascinated, I studied the landscape as revealed by a slowly clearing morning mist. For no longer did I see the customary dreary expanse of mud and ruin, but an interesting countryside, with shell holes here and there almost the sole reminder of the enemy. Half-left and only about half a kilometre distant, lay the red-tiled roofs and gardens of Gheluwe, almost intact; while directly to our front, three hundred yards away, lay half a dozen railway trucks on what obviously was a German military siding; behind them, orchards and the still-dark foliage of standing trees.

Across the expanse of low-lying fields to the right, I made out in the far distance two tapering church spires, marking villages in the valley of the river Lys—Wervicq and Commines. My map showed, too, that the Lys marked the Franco–Belgian boundary there.

Although shells still fell, and the familiar rat-tat-tat of the German machine-guns was audible every few minutes, the war had become—of a sudden, it seemed—intensely interesting. Even our shallow trench was virgin soil; clean-cut, narrow and as yet unsullied either by shell fire or by heavy rain. In the sharp morning air the men busied themselves cleaning Lewis guns or rifles, washing their mess tins and even shaving. They seemed in good fettle.

While I was looking about thus, a low-flying German plane came over. Hastily I ordered everyone to lie as flat as they could, anticipating several bursts of enfilade fire along the trench from his machine-gun; and, indeed, he appeared to be getting into position for such a run in. To our amazement, however, the pilot, whose goggled features we could see very plainly as he examined us, did not fire but went along further down the line on a leisurely tour of inspection until lost to view. The least we expected was a good shelling but, strange to say, it was not forthcoming just then.

Lewis and I were required at Company H.Q. at noon on the following day, and together, after relief, made our way across the fields, sniped at for most of the way as we dodged about, making a considerable detour to avoid disclosing our rendezvous with White, who we found somewhat preoccupied. Pearson served lunch almost at once, and not until we sat with enamelled mugs of Scotch and water afterwards did White unburden himself. Then, producing two air photographs, he informed us that Corps H.Q. required identification of the German regiment opposite us, and that Lewis and myself were to do the needful that evening.

After a few moments' pause for Lewis and I to digest this not exactly pleasant piece of news, Captain White turned to the air photographs. These showed the ground around and behind the railway trucks, the latter showing up very plainly and enabling us to get our bearings at once. About a hundred yards behind the trucks, and running parallel with them, showed what appeared to be a hedge bordering an orchard or garden, and along this hedge White point out a small square of a light colour, while about thirty yards to one side two small smudges showed. The light square was a pillbox, partially camouflaged, and the two smudges pits, which our airmen reported were probably manned at night by at least part of the pillbox garrison. The arrangement was that our gunners would put down a box barrage on this small area for five minutes before nine o'clock, after which Lewis and myself, each taking an N.C.O. and six men, would rush in and see what we could find; Lewis to the pillbox, me to the two pits.

That seemed to be all, and after a further few minutes' discussion of details we dodged and crawled our way back to our trench, sniped at most unpleasantly for the last hundred yards. Once we got back we set about getting our parties together and, somewhat to our surprise, there was no lack of volunteers—in fact, *l'embarras des richesses*. Perhaps the dramatic change of the terrain to open country, and leaving the old trench lines, had produced this new eagerness: anyhow, it was there.

Arriving at Company H.Q. in the last of the light, the men dumped their personal belongings, had a good meal and a sleep, with an extra tot to follow on awakening. Meanwhile, Lewis and I, with our two corporals, went out in the darkness and reconnoitred the ground, picking our way under the trucks to within about twenty yards of where we judged the pillbox to lie, but we could neither see nor hear anything, no convenient Verey light assisting us just then. We did, however, stumble into, and note carefully the position of, an almost dry ditch immediately on the far side of the trucks, which might afford us valuable cover while waiting on the box barrage. Then we returned to our trench and thence to Company H.Q. and White, who dined and wined us to the best of his ability, although we could see how he hated the whole business.

As we sat over our cigarettes and pipe after the meal, the mail arrived with the rations. Glancing at it lying on his makeshift table, White suddenly picked a greenish-looking envelope from the pile and threw it to me with a grimace. On it I read in angular handwriting 'Le Lieutenant Read C. of E. 4th R. Sussex, B.E.F.' The postmark was St. Omer. Completely mystified and taken aback, but realizing that I was being watched, I slit the envelope as carelessly as I could and withdrew a single folded sheet of notepaper, from which dropped a small crushed flower. The note was short, but somehow, as I read it, a load of anxiety as to the success or otherwise of our night's work seemed to be suddenly lifted from my mind. Forgetfully, I looked up, elated, to see the inquiring faces of White, Lewis and Newman, with Pearson, the batman, and two signallers in the background.

A barrage of good-natured chaff followed, in spite of repeated calls to 'shurr-up!' I denied giving the girl my address. 'C. of E., eh, Richard?' goaded White. 'Come, come, tut-tut!' and so on. Whereon, in desperation, I picked up the note and, translating as best I could, read it to them. As I did so, the solution suddenly dawned on me. She had obtained my name and regiment from my silver identity wristlet, as I admitted to them subsequently, while I was asleep.

The note, as I have said, was short. She said that no doubt it would come as a surprise for me; that she didn't suppose she would ever see me again, but she sent it to wish me 'good luck'. These last two words she had written laboriously in English.

I looked up from it to see that all three had stopped laughing, for they, too, were now impressed by this amazing coincidence. There it was, just when I needed all the luck that was going it had come out of the blue. It certainly augured well for the success of our errand, and I told them if we managed things all right I would, when my turn came for leave, get off the train at St. Omer and thank her. We toasted her then, in some of the whisky I scrounged at Lumbres, and then it was time to go. Carefully we synchronized our watches, went to our waiting men, and departed.

A few minutes before nine we lay in the wet grass of the 'dry' ditch, waiting for the gunners to start. Fenton and Chalk had wished us 'all the best' as we left our trench, having previously taken one last precaution of getting our lads to discard their bayonet sheaths and entrenching tool handles which, from experience, always rattled on one another at every movement of the wearer.

We noted that a small fire had started in the eastern outskirts of Gheluwe, in the faint and intermittent illumination it afforded we peered to our front in an endeavour to see our goal. As we peered, fancy played the usual tricks with us, and, eerily, we saw things that were not, in fact, there. Then the guns started and a shell seemed to drop about every twenty seconds, as we judged, beyond the target, although clods of earth and iron smacked against the trucks behind us, and we were glad of the small cover the ditch afforded. Then an SOS rocket rose from our front. Tension rose, as I hoped fervently that the shelling would stop, fearing that it had now robbed us of the precious element of surprise. Suddenly I couldn't wait any long and, with a yell, we rushed forward blindly towards our objectives.

I remember a machine-gun spitting out as from the ground—firing, mercifully, at an angle—as we stumbled forward. As I ran I emptied my revolver at the flashes. It stopped, and almost as it did so I saw two upraised arms and a German steel helmet, but was too late to avoid falling into the pit on top of the owner. Scrambling to our feet, the German raised his arms again shouting '*kamerad*' and something about '*muder und kinder*'. He was thoroughly frightened, as half a dozen bayonets were now pointed at him. Suddenly I thought of the gun, and scrambled out of the pit to see a running figure carrying something heavy in the greenish light of an ascending rocket. I yelled to the men, who fired as hard as they could, but the quarry escaped into the darkness beyond.

We were disappointed at this, but soon recovered our good spirits when eyeing our prisoners. Then we heard two bombs explode and, as I was hacking off one shoulder tab from the German's greatcoat, the shouts of Lewis, who shortly afterwards joined us, calling, 'any luck there? The pillbox was empty!' He was overjoyed to see our man, patting him on the back and telling the poor devil that he was a 'lucky little fellow'. Then one of the men started to sing 'Good-bye-ee', and, elated, in a confused atmosphere of song and shelling and noise, punctuated by outbursts of laughter, we escorted our quarry back to our trench, completely oblivious, we were told afterwards, of the commotion we had caused.

White had come up and was waiting for us, with Fenton. They were laughing—with relief, and at our totally unorthodox method of returning notwithstanding, as they pointed out to us, that the German artillery was dropping stuff all over the place and that ours was now busy replying. Half an hour later, however, the guns were quiet and we were all back in White's pillbox answering questions, with *carte blanche* as far as the whisky and rum were concerned, while an escort was on its way to Brigade H.Q. with our prisoner of the 122nd Regiment, who I have omitted to describe. He was of medium height, apparently much married, about thirty-five, normally clean shaven but with the curious pinched, sallow complexion on which the chin stubble stood out darkly—so common to his kind in 1918. This was put down to the effect of continual shell fire, trench conditions, and so on, but we soon found that, primarily, it was due to under-nourishment.

I have mentioned the small fire in the Gheluwe village. This developed rapidly into a conflagration of considerable proportions, doubtless fed by the retreating enemy. Although accustomed to sights like this, nevertheless we were impressed by the grandeur of the leaping flames, which threw into savage relief billowing clouds of smoke hanging in the night sky. These events occurred on 10th October, and on the evening of the 12th we were relieved and made our way up the Menin road to some shell holes near Zandvoorde which our maps, for some reason, designated as 'America'. Here, I recall sitting under a sheet of corrugated iron and writing to my well-wisher, telling her that her letter had brought me luck and that I would certainly call and see her when I was granted leave. Very sentimental, perhaps, but I plead youth, and the feelings of youth.

We stayed here two days, and on 15th October we moved up through the northern outskirts of Gheluwe, which had been taken by another brigade of our division. Here we marched north in artillery formation for several kilometres, halting for a few hours in a collection of battered houses. In the kitchen garden of one, I remember finding a dead lieutenant and two men of, I think, the Cheshires; no doubt sniped as they were advancing, and, by the look of them, within the previous twenty-four hours. At dusk we moved east across country, using at times several muddy cart tracks, and by nightfall I hadn't the faintest idea where we were: not even White now possessed an adequate map, as we had moved beyond the area of those previously issued. He, with Fenton, was somewhere in front while Newman, Chalk and I brought up the rear platoons and whipped up the few stragglers. The main thing was to maintain contact and this, fortunately, we were able to do.

Occasional long-range enemy shells shattered the night, while from far to the south came the sustained rumble of a heavy cannonade. It seemed as though there was a moon rising some-where to the east. It was misty and cloudy, yet there was enough light to see a few yards as we stumbled on. Eventually we started

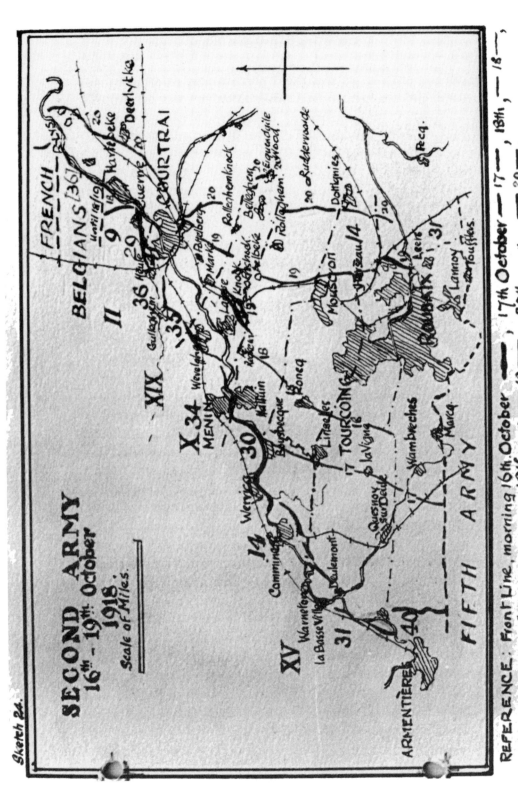

Sketch 24.

SECOND ARMY
16th – 19th October
1918.
Scale of Miles.

REFERENCE: Front Line, morning 16th October ——; 17th October —— 17 ——, 18th , —— 18 ——
19th , —— 19 —— ; 20th , —— 20 —— .

to mount a pronounced rise, slipping and slithering in the mud churned up by those in front, and on reaching the crest the word was passed back to halt, then, 'fall out, absolute quiet, no smoking!' In the uncertain light I saw that we were on a level stretch, on the left of which, about 150 yards away and silhouetted against the lighter horizon, a fine and apparently undamaged windmill. All were very glad of a chance to rest, and each man subsided pretty well where he stood.

After such an interval of time it is hard to describe the suppressed excitement and pleasure of the men as they discovered they were in the middle of a turnip field. Jack knives were out in a trice, and I remember Chalk, his mouth full of succulent turnip mixed with mud, speculating in a loud whisper whether the miller and his lovely daughter were about! Indeed, we had been wondering what was happening the civilian population as we advanced, although so far it appeared that the retreating Germans were driving them before them.

Fenton appeared, and our ruminations in the turnip field were cut short by the order to fall in. In the now-clearing moonlight we were keyed up with expectation of further good things to come as we passed shapes of farm buildings scarcely touched by shell fire, moving perceptibly down hill for a kilometre or so, looking, as it seemed on a plain still bathed in misty moonlight.

Then the outline of farm buildings amid trees materialized, and voices. Fenton stood by a gateway and, as he motioned to the men to file in, called me to one side. White appeared with a subaltern of another regiment of our division, who then led his men out and back the way we had come. White spoke to me for the first time for some hours. 'What do you think of this for a billet, Richard?' and, indicating the departing platoon, 'they only got here this afternoon!' adding, 'they did very well, I believe.' I inquired hastily whether we were in the front line. 'Not exactly,' replied White. 'The Queen's and North Lancs are in front somewhere between here and the River Lys—we're in Brigade reserve, but probably we're moving up in the morning.'

We were grateful for this information, anyhow, and turned thankfully to look over our lodging for the night. I went round with Fenton and inquired what we were doing about sentries, to hear that Chalk's platoon were doing the needful. 'Come and have a look at 'em,' he added, and we found the sentries in pits, beyond the edge of the kitchen garden. After being challenged, we had a look at them. One lot had set up a Dutch clock with pendulum and weights complete, inherited from their predecessors, and altogether the men were like a lot of schoolboys on holiday. The platoons not on duty within the barns were also in hilarious spirits, and several had dressed up in women's clothing—one even in a white poke bonnet with great flaps and long strings. Others had found cabbages, potatoes, carrots and turnips.

I told Fenton that, for once, it was difficult to take the war seriously, especially as it was comparatively quiet: only odd rifle shots and short bursts of machine-gun fire, with a shell now and again a fair distance away, breaking the silence.

'I don't know about that, Richard. Have you seen this lot down the lane?' So saying, he led the way down the track beyond the gate, and within a hundred yards or so we came upon the wreckage of a four-gun German 77mm field battery. According to Fenton, they were limbering up when they were caught in the act by our advancing troops with their Lewis guns and rifle fire as they came over the brow of the hill. Neither men nor horses had escaped. The latter, probably hit and panicking, had bolted, thereby overturning several of the limbers. The moonlight softened, to some degree, the stark details of this gruesome sight, but these were horrific enough and we turned away from it, returning slowly to the farm-house, each immersed in his own thoughts.

At the door a shout from the interior greeted us—actually from Newman—'don't forget to wipe your feet as you come in!' Captain White's batman-cum-groom, Pearson, normally a stolid enough but thoroughly trustworthy individual, hurried by the entrance towards the kitchen with his arms full of crockery, and his excitement may be judged by his voluntary incursion into the realms of speech: 'look, sir . . . real plates and cups an' saucers . . . an 'ole service!'

Within, we found White, Newman and Chalk seated round a fine mahogany table on which several candles guttered in the draught from the open door. They were drinking whisky from enamelled mugs, which looked strangely out of place on the still-polished surface; and their obvious good spirits, too, were eloquent of the change which seemed to have taken place in all of us since sitting down in the turnip field two hours or so previously. Indeed, we felt as the Israelites of old must have felt when they entered the Promised Land, and it was then, for the first time, I believe, that it was borne upon us—me, at any rate—that we might be really winning the war at last. For us all, emerging from the dreary soul-destroying expanses of churned-up mud, water and rusty iron which girdled the Ypres Salient, these evidences of a return to civilization counted for much more than any newspaper victory of ten thousand prisoners and a hundred guns.

In the morning some maps arrived, and with them we soon obtained a pretty good idea of what was happening. Our company was in battalion reserve, while the other companies were now in the line and feeling their way forward towards the River Lys and the outskirts of the considerable village of Wevelghem, itself almost a suburb of the ancient city of Courtrai.

Late that afternoon, however, we moved up in artillery formation and entered Wevelghem in the dusk; slowly and circumspectly, for occasional shots were still echoing from the far side, while occasional shells also fell quite near. I was leading, and had understood from White that the other companies had gone forward on either side with the object of trapping any of the enemy still in the village.

From the little we could see, it had been systematically pillaged by the retreating enemy. We were not molested, however, as we picked our way over fallen brickwork, broken glass and tangles of telegraph wires, and I well recall seeing, lying on the roadside outside one of the first houses, the body of a German soldier. He had been strangled with a piece of cord. Here was a mystery which, in happier times, would have made headline news, but just then we hadn't time to investigate, I'm afraid.

We arrived at a level crossing without seeing any trace of the enemy, but we did encounter something that might have hindered us considerably—an obvious booby trap, consisting of a bunch of half a dozen big shells, replacing the balance weight of the familiar long, painted arm which barred our way. Fortunately, we spotted this and made a detour, getting through a fence about fifty yards to one side. The R.E.s who removed this cleverly-made arrangement told us the next morning that, had we raised the arm, we would have been dead meat. As ordered by Captain White, we crossed the Menin–Courtrai road which constituted the main street, and took possession of a large, unoccupied farm-house towards the eastern edge, quite near the River Lys, from which it was separated by a series of water meadows. In the house were plenty of reminders of recent German occupation, including some peeled potatoes in a saucepan of water upon a stove in which the now-dead fire still gave the top a distinct warmth. We suspected another booby trap but, after inspecting it from all angles, including the interior of the stove, Sergeant Clark removed the potatoes without incident and the N.C.O.s soon had a healthy fire going. We were very comfortable, and now possessed an oil lamp which the Germans, or the Belgian farmer-folk, had left actually burning low. Again we were mistaken in suspecting a trap. We found some oil in one of the outbuildings—by a piece of luck, as it was hidden under straw and only exposed when the men moved it to improve their 'beds'. All unnecessary movement in daylight outside the farm buildings was forbidden on White's orders, and for very good reasons.

Late that evening we were ordered to make rafts to effect a crossing of the Lys. The following morning, in bright sunshine, I went with Fenton and two of our runners to reconnoitre the approaches to the Lys, and we chose a way by the lane leading to a farm marked on the map 'Groot Vollander'. On reaching it we found that Major Warren of our 'C' Company had made his H.Q. there, on the Courtrai side. He, too, had forbidden all movement of his men in daylight, and told us, as nicely as he could, that a whizz-bang battery behind the railway embankment on the far side of the river would snipe at us if we showed ourselves on the river bank. We discussed our chances, and after Fenton had explained that 'D' Company had orders to get over somehow that night, we decided to take a chance. Perhaps, Fenton suggested, there might be a boat, or boats, but Major Warren warned him that he had been half a mile along the river bank across the front of Wevelghem village the previous evening in the dusk and had found nothing. That morning they had tried again and had been whizz-banged so badly that they were very lucky to escape with whole skins. 'Well,' Fenton said, 'we'd better have a try, anyhow!' and so we saluted and set out.

All went well for some minutes, although, as Warren had said, there wasn't a sign of a boat. We therefore retraced our steps to the farm and went down the lane which led direct to the river bank, about four hundred yards distant. There was scarcely any cover, unfortunately, and we realized that the track was completely dominated by the higher ground on the opposite bank. However, we moved forward as best we could, and, just as we had gained an actual sight of the water, and what appeared to be the remains of a waterlogged bridge of boats, bullets started to spit and sing by us with alarming suddenness and rapidity. As we breathlessly flattened ourselves into the long grass, we judged that our tormentors were firing from a large tile works high on the opposite bank. Then a machine-gun started as well, the bullets whipping up splashes of mud and water along the path—much too hot a spot to remain in. Each minute seemed like an hour. Then, as the machine-gun stopped for some reason, Fenton darted across the track and through the long grass. We followed, practically on our stomachs, and found ourselves with our boots full of water, standing in a stagnant ditch full of weed and slime, but fortunately under some sort of cover. Here one of the runners showed us his bullet-punctured water bottle, the contents having well-dampened his right leg.

Once more in comparative peace, we lit cigarettes and pipes and indulged in the luxury of a smoke and a laugh or two at our plight and, on comparing notes, agreed that there existed some means of crossing at the end of the path, probably put out of action, but which we hadn't the chance of examining. On looking at the very inadequate map which Fenton had, we decided to work along this ditch, roughly parallel with the river, and progressed thus for some distance, but when we came in sight of the Lys again we couldn't see the waterlogged boats, as a bend of the river now hid them.

Here I remember spending a few minutes making a sketch plan, taking bearings, and so on. Then, as no one appeared to take any notice of us, we proceeded cautiously along the riverside at a respectful distance from the bank, in the direction of the

Wevelghem–Lauwe bridge which, we had been told, the Germans had rendered useless. The sun shone brightly, and behind us, some hundreds of yards away across the boggy water meadows and fields of roots, lay the back gardens of the low row of houses marking the main street of Wevelghem. From across the river came the lusty sound of a cock crowing, and Fenton had just said how he'd like to put it in the pot when there were four sharp bangs, and simultaneously the arriving shells, well before we could flatten ourselves—for the second time that morning. Clods of wet earth and mud spattered down all around us. They had fallen around fifty yards short. Fenton spat and swore and we doubled half-right for a cart shed about two hundred yards away, but almost as we reached it a second salvo removed the roof and one wall. It was good shooting, and as we lay behind the far wall, panting, we realized that the German battery was firing at us over open sights from the railway embankment on the other side of the river—a range of less than a thousand yards.

Another lot came over, and now, almost deafened, with our mouths full of fumes and brick dust, we realised that if we didn't clear out it was only a question of time . . . ! Fenton decided to make a bolt for it, and I shall never forget our breathless, ludicrous, zig-zag bid for safety across those meadows. It will always remain a mystery to me how we got away unscathed. Shrapnel sang by our ears ever few seconds, and fountains of earth and dirty water shot up all around us as we ran. I have a particularly vivid recollection of jumping a ditch I wouldn't have deemed myself capable of tackling under normal circumstances. To the accompaniment of tinkling glass and cascading tiles, we dashed wildly through a back garden and into a house; thence into a cellar, where we lay for some moments incapable of speech. Then, the shelling having ceased, and with our breath regained, we could see the humorous side of our flight and the manner in which we had gone to ground, as fags and pipes were lit again.

In the village street we looked at one another to see several little gouts of dried blood on our hands and cheeks, where tiny specks had hit. It had been a pretty narrow shave for us, and an experience we would not care to repeat in a hurry. The morning's events had shown us one thing very clearly—that within the last few days life had become doubly sweet and precious to us, and we told Captain White so during lunch following our return. Thinking thus, and watching our fellows making rafts of stitched-up canvas bags stuffed with straw and roped to planks, under the direction of R.E. instructors, I remember feeling pretty uncomfortable at the prospect of crossing the Lys that night by this questionable means.

At dusk we moved off, with orders to occupy the railway embankment on the far side. Our progress was slow because of the rafts. Darkness was complete in the October evening as we reached Groot Vollander Farm, when Captain White sent me with my platoon down the path to the riverside to reconnoitre and find whether a crossing by the semi-submerged boats was practicable. Nearing the bank, we heard footsteps approaching and listened expectantly as I ordered complete silence. When the footsteps were almost upon us I challenged, to see, very dimly, an elderly Belgian civilian and his wife, who, unfortunately, spoke pretty unintelligible Flemish.

I recall that just then the darkness was lightened somewhat by the reflection in the night sky of a fire in the direction of Courtrai, which assisted me immeasurably in questioning the Belgians as to how they had crossed. While I was thus engaged our men challenged some newcomers: more than a dozen appeared, including two women who spoke French. They told me all at once, in a flood, pitiful stories of the hardships they had endured through being evacuated from their homes by the Germans, and it was somewhat difficult to establish the vital fact that they had crossed by the boats. I gathered that what I understood to be planks had been laid on them by some of the party, who had waited all day, hidden in some bushes near a cottage underneath the railway embankment.

This was great news. I sent a runner back to Captain White to tell him that I was going to try to cross immediately, and for him to send the rest of the company along; also that I would let him know if I encountered any difficulties.

Thanking the civilians—who, I saw, were all either young boys or elderly men and women, haggard, worn, ill-clad and hungry—I called on the lads for a real effort, and they responded in no

4th Royal Sussex crossing the River LYS near Potelberg, COURTRAI.
Night of Oct.17th,1918.

uncertain fashion, keyed up as we all were. When we arrived at
the bank we saw, faintly, the half-submerged barges and several
planks. Just then a machine-gun opened up from the tile works—
the Tuileries de Potelberg—but, mercifully, the bullets went high

426

overhead, and without more ado we went forward. The actual crossing was easy.

I was in mid stream there, and stepping gingerly along a semi-floating plank, when our artillery opened a sustained and heavy bombardment in the direction of Courtrai, and the gun and shell flashes, coupled with the glare of what had now become a huge conflagration there, made the rest of the journey much easier.

Notwithstanding the bursts from the Potelburg machine-gun, which were still going over high, my platoon was soon across and, under Sergeant Clark, fanning out; but as I stood assisting the heavily loaded men in their last jump from the barge nearest the bank, I noticed that this moved away an inch or two as each man made his leap. The sluggish flow of the river assisted this, and just then I would have given a good deal for a length of stout rope and a screw picket. I therefore told two lads to shove a plank into the river and against the side of the barge, and to hold on to it. This had the desired effect, until about six men only of the company remained to cross. Then again the cumulative effort of a hundred men jumping proved too much for the 'holding' party, and the stern of the barge moved slowly away, leaving a nasty gap of two feet or so. Captain White now hove in sight and came through the men with a 'hallo, Richard—good work!'

Newman and Chalk were already on top of the railway embankment with their men, and he went to have a word with them, followed by his runner. I could see the near-by cottage, and, as he departed, suggested it might make a good Company H.Q. Then the last men started to jump, and unfortunately they were a Lewis gun section with all their buckets of drums and etceteras. I'm afraid I was in the water above my knees before the last man made the effort, over a gap which had now widened to a good four feet. When he jumped he landed well and truly in the water, and in a futile attempt to tide him over I got much wetter. Nevertheless, we were all in such high spirits that it would have taken much more than a ducking just then to dampen them. We had crossed without a casualty, and kidded ourselves that we were 'first over the Lys'—an honour much disputed subsequently, I'm afraid!

On White's instructions I now led my platoon to the top of the railway embankment on the right of our line up a path past the cottage, where I found an elderly Belgian couple still in occupation. I also disturbed a hen-roost in knocking them up and persuading them to emerge from the cellar, assuring them that the Boches had *partis*.

As we reached our position and I set my sentries, the moon rose in a cloudy sky, so that it was quite easy to see a few hundred yards to our front and to our flanks. Captain White came along and told me he had reported the crossing accomplished; also that the signallers had put out a line from the cottage and that he had requested help via Battalion H.Q. from the R.E. to secure our 'bridge'.

A few minutes after he left, three huge Gotha biplanes droned very low overhead, silhouetted against the moonlit clouds, and dropped their load of bombs upon Wevelghem. The huge detonations made us feel thankful to be where we were. With certain reservations, the front line seemed a safer place than some of the rear areas at this stage of the war.

Recalled by Captain White to the cottage (I have called it that, but I suppose it was really a small farm-house, as there were a few outbuildings), I found Chalk, in his new capacity of mess president bargaining with the old Belgian, by signs and by much waving of arms, for a stringy-looking hen, while the 'Skipper' was poring over the only map of the neighbourhood we possessed, with the aid of a smoking and foul-smelling oil lamp. Just what the civilian population used for lamp oil in these parts at that time I'll never know, but with all the windows shuttered, the air was indescribably close and foetid. White, seeing my sniffing around, agreed with an expressive grin that there was certainly a good fug on, but that one became used to it, and no doubt the old couple would be having a bath when the war was over! He then told me to take my platoon and reconnoitre, and occupy, if possible, the railway station at Lauwe-Knocke and the village of Knocke which, by his map, lay about half a kilometre east of the station, with houses lining the road all the way.

I found that Sergeant-Major Slaughter had assembled my lads when I returned to them. As quickly as I could I briefed them, and Slaughter said he'd love to come with us, but I said he'd better not, as good sergeants-major were scarcer than subalterns.

He laughed and wished us luck as we started to pick our way along the grass-grown track towards our first objective, the station, and clearing two farm-houses on the way. They were both occupied by greatly surprised elderly Belgians, and there were no Germans in either.

By the light of the now fiercely burning fires in the western suburbs of Courtrai which, Captain White had told us, were being assaulted by the 29th Division, we could see for some distance ahead, and advanced cautiously along the grass-grown tracks, investigating on the way a windmill on a rise half-left, and two farm-houses. In neither of these could we discern a sign of life.

Half an hour of this brought us within two hundred yards or so of Lauwe station, around which we noted a considerable cluster of houses. Taking every precaution and maintaining (beyond necessary whispers at intervals) absolute silence, we crept forward, ready for instant action, but we failed to flush out a single enemy. Our sole bag was a very old Belgian couple sitting on either side of a dying fire in the nearest house. We couldn't get a word of sense out of them and therefore pressed on, mystified as to the fate of the other inhabitants.

Beyond the silent station buildings we made out, by the moonlight, a level crossing with more houses, including a shuttered *estaminet*, grouped around it, and I recognized from my sketch the Wevelghem–Lauwe–Knocke–Aelbeke road. Reaching it, we noted with interest the two lowered arms of the crossing—and, more particularly, the balance weight hanging on each, consisting of a cluster of large shells, as at Wevelghem. Needless to say, we gave them a wide berth.

All was quiet, and, as the mist had cleared somewhat, I decided to investigate the adjoining village of Knocke, uphill on the Aelbeke road, and we therefore continued our cautious advance in that direction. The houses were almost continuous, and in the moonlight the silent street produced eerie feelings as we progressed slowly in two single files, one on each side, close to the houses, which were quite undamaged. In many cases the shutters had not been closed, and we surmised that there must have been a hurried evacuation only a few hours before we arrived.

In this fashion, listening intently and prepared for instant action, we reached the furthermost buildings in the village. On one side there was a large brewery, and on the other, practically opposite, a row of terraced houses ended abruptly. Beyond this point open fields stretched away eastward into the soft hazy moonlight.

Here I posted two sentry groups, and as soon as these were established to my satisfaction I sent two runners back to Captain White with a message reporting my position; also that there was no sign, either of the enemy, or of the local inhabitants. This done, I determined, with Sergeant Clark's help, to investigate the inside of the last house. With his entrenching tool he broke first the ground-floor shutters and then the window behind, making, it seemed to me at the time, far too much noise in doing it, although no doubt this was unavoidable. Soon we were inside, and by my shaded torch we saw what might easily have been an English artisan's front room, the clock ticking away happily on the mantelpiece serving only to whet our curiosity still further. The kitchen was distinctly warm, and in the darkness a glimmer of dull red indicated the still-hot ashes in the stove; but the mystery of the inhabitants certainly deepened as, one by one, we examined a goodly number of tins in the larder, which all bore the marks of either Spanish or Swiss relief organizations. Regaining our broken window and the night air, we were met by the corporal in charge of the brewery post who, after reporting all quiet, inquired whether his lads could have a few chairs to sit on when not actually on sentry-go, as the grass was very wet—a request which took me somewhat aback, although had he made it a few minutes previously I should not have hesitated in giving him an immediate go-ahead. I did this now with a certain reluctance, and saw, in rapid succession, the front room suite, including the table, moved across the road to the position on the grass under the lee of the brewery wall. News of this kind travelled very quickly among the lads, and within ten minutes the kitchen furniture suffered a similar fate at the hands of the other post a hundred yards or so away up a rough track leading off half-left from the main road; unmarked, as far as I could see, on the sketch I'd made from Captain White's map.

This sort of thing was all very well as a morale booster, and the lads had certainly done well, but I was now concerned as to what daylight would bring, for instance, in the way of whizz-bangs, from a retreating enemy battery in a position to fire at us over open sights, and my recent experience of this was very fresh in my mind. I therefore began to consider seriously the question of cover, and determined to investigate the brewery cellars without delay, as I figured there were bound to be some. In the meanwhile, I ordered all those not actually on sentry-go to start digging where they stood—or, rather, where some of them now sat—and to keep at it, giving them the reason why as an additional stimulant to action. They fell to with a will with their entrenching tools, and it kept them warm, at any rate.

The great double gates of the brewery were ajar and there was no difficulty in getting inside the yard, where many barrels were stacked. To the right of the entrance I saw a ramp, leading, no doubt, to the cellars. Before descending I called to Sergeant Clark to find me one of the lads, as I'd no idea what I should find below and thought it well to be prepared. Thus reinforced, we made our way slowly down the steps between the ramp surfaces until we came to the bottom, which led into a passage lined with barrels, at the end of which my torch showed what appeared to be a closed steel door. As I extinguished my torch I noticed the merest glimmer of light from under this door, and at the same time both of us became aware of a sudden warmth and a pretty unpleasant smell. We prepared for instant action as we crept, step by step, towards the door, listening intently, and I was then certain that I could faintly hear low voices on the other side. In a hurry to make sure of this by taking the last two steps to put my ear to the door, I blundered over a plank. There was no time to take cover behind the nearest barrel as the door opened slowly before I could regain my feet. Dazzled and blinking in the sudden light, yellow and thickened with smoke as it was, we could only make out a sea of faces and huge shadows behind, as two candles in front of the huddled mass of humanity guttered and spluttered in the draught on an upturned barrel standing against one of the main pillars by the opened door.

As we passed over the threshold and our eyes became accustomed to the light we made out, propped against the pillar, two women suckling babies; another was milking a goat. The young

Cellar of the 'Brouerie Frik", KNOCKE - LAAWE-AELBEKE RD. Oct.17/18th.1918.

woman who had opened the door came from behind it. She looked white-faced and frightened as she clutched a black shawl about her head and shoulders. Till then we hadn't thought of lowering our weapons, and now did so hurriedly as I noticed women crossing themselves and one or two kneeling in prayer. The men, either elderly or young boys, looked first at us and then one to the other, in indecision. Then one of them shouted 'Englander!', and then '*les Anglais!*' and in a moment pandemonium broke out in that cellar. I recall that the lad with me was seized, kissed and hugged by the young woman as he stood behind me, while I was submerged in a bout of hand-shaking and being hugged and kissed on both cheeks—the later experience, from more than one elderly moustachioed and unshaven man, being rather overpowering! Looking back on this scene nearly fifty years after, I'll admit that we thoroughly enjoyed our fleeting roles of liberators of the villagers of Knocke and Lauwe, who endeavoured to show their gratitude by offering to cook us some *pommes de terre frites* and an apologia for

432

coffee, while the lady who had milked the goat brought me a basin full of milk and insisted that I drank some. She indicated that there were several more goats in the depths of the cellar at the back, which may have accounted in part for the smell down there. Every few moments, folks of both sexes unashamedly dissolved into both tears and laughter, and indeed, we could well understand how, set free after over four years of the German jackboot, their emotions could not be withheld and, welling up in them, over-flowed like a flood. In all there must have been several hundred people in the cellars of that brewery, and I had to advise them to stay where they were until we were sure that they were safe from enemy shelling; also that our troops, coming up within the hour, in all probability, might mistake them for enemies in the darkness. Nevertheless many, especially men, crept off on the pretext of fetching something or other of vital importance, and only in a very few cases did they return. I hoped uneasily that the occupants of the end house were among those staying, and thought of the broken window, and their chairs.

The appearance of Sergeant Clark in the doorway brought me down to earth sharply. He had been looking for me when he heard the noise of the celebrations within the brewery and, not knowing the cause, came to rescue me. *Le Sergent* received a great welcome as a newcomer and an invitation to savour goat's milk and chips, already on a paraffin stove of sorts, which smoked and stank abominably, making it difficult for the smell of the frying chips to rise up the ramp. It did so, however, and when I went with Clark to have a look at the state of affairs at our posts on the road, the boys on the post by the brewery wall were literally drooling at the aroma, while at the same time mystified by it. I explained matters and found from Sergeant Clark that I had forty-one men with me, including himself. I returned to the ladies in the cellar with my news, which didn't seem to dismay them one little bit. Certainly, they seemed to have the best part of a sack of potatoes down there, and I arranged for the chips to be sent up in relays. I had just sat down on a barrel specially arranged by willing helpers, to enjoy my own *repas*, when I heard a familiar voice and then a chuckle, as Captain White appeared in the doorway with my two runners. With a broad grin, he told me to consider myself under arrest for making a misleading report. 'Why,' with an eye on my sizzling plate of *pommes frites*, 'haven't I been informed of this?' He was damned hungry, anyway, and Chalk, back at H.Q., had only just succeeded in buying that stringy old hen and it would be hours before Pearson could have it ready to eat.

To do the honours properly I called for silence, and the buzz of conversation ceased as I introduced *le Capitaine* White to the throng. Actually, I think he was pleased, but he gave me a quick dirty look as they pressed to shake his hand. Through them came the lady with another plate of chips for him, holding them high. He sat on my barrel and we discussed matters of moment between mouthfuls. I think we could well have eaten some more when White rose, telling me to remain where I was for the time being and giving me a map, for which I blessed him; also that the 41st Division on our right would be advancing diagonally across our front at 08.00 hours, and that this would take in Aelbeke. After he went back, taking one of my runners, we were left to ourselves until the first streaks of dawn were appearing, during which time I snatched a little sleep and afterwards studied the map.

A thick early morning mist lay heavily over the fields and the Aelbeke road before us, limiting visibility to a few yards. For aught I knew, the enemy outposts might be a hundred yards away or two kilometres, and so we listened intently for the slightest sounds ahead. Therefore, great was the excitement when we heard approaching footsteps on the road, and then saw what appeared to be a blackish shadow. Two sentries stepped on to the road at the ready and challenged: 'halt! Who are you?' The answer was a woman's shriek and then excited jabbering. I went forward, to be clasped around the legs by a poor soul, now so frightened that she had gone upon her knees and was crossing herself as she looked up at me.

When I had calmed her to some extent, I gathered from her, with some difficulty, that the Germans were certainly in Aelbeke—where she had now come from—and that their outposts were at Preshoek, a hamlet shown on the map as about three-quarters of a kilometre along the road towards Aelbeke from where we standing. This was quite helpful, and after obtaining this piece of information I handed her over to the good folk in the cellars. While down there,

I again warned them to stay where they were, as I expected some shelling before long and I had noticed quite considerable movement to and from their homes with the coming of daylight.

I had just regained the road when two cyclist scouts—attached, they told me, to the Queen's Westminsters, of the division advancing across our front that morning—informed me that they had been detailed to make a quick reconnaissance as far as Preshoek to find whether it was being held. I gave them the information I'd obtained but they still wished to go, and, curious to see myself, I offered to join them. They seemed very pleased, as they stood their bikes against the brewery wall in the charge of my fellows and I told Sergeant Clark of my intention. I lightened myself as much as possible, also giving Clark the care of my personal possessions, as one never knew.

We three then set off in the still-thick mist along the shallow ditch which ran alongside the road. Heavy beads of moisture hung from every blade of the long grass through which we threaded our way for ten minutes, and we were soon pretty wet, but we found this stalking business exciting and exhilarating. At length the ditch ended abruptly and we came upon a pavé path leading to a farm-house on our left, faintly visible through the mist. We listened intently for a minute or so but couldn't hear a sound within. Leaving one of my cyclist friends on guard upon the road, two of us approached the house cautiously and carefully lifted the latch of an iron gate; unfortunately, it creaked hideously, causing a dog somewhere at the rear of the premises to bark furiously. Hastily we took cover by crouching close under the windows, while the dog roused several more of his kind. This, in a way, was useful to us, as it told us that there were a number of houses fairly close by in the mist. For all that, we cursed the dog heartily, and waited for what seemed an age—about five minutes, really—until the noise had subsided. The farm-house appeared to be unoccupied, but as we raised ourselves and peered into the front room we saw, to our amazement, a very old man, asleep in a battered armchair, while at his feet played a little girl with fair curly hair, aged between two and three years. She was extremely dirty and looked somehow 'vacant' when, by signs, we endeavoured, without success, to get her to wake the old man. The front door was undone

Reconaissance. Oct 18th
PRESHOEK. 1918

and we therefore tiptoed in, on the watch for the dog who, fortunately for us, must have been in one of the outhouses.

We managed to rouse the poor old man but he was, as far as we were concerned, quite incoherent. He was so old, too, that British and Germans must have seemed alike to him; as, evidently, they were to the poor mite on the floor. As we left, my companion gave her a bar of rather soiled chocolate he happened to have in his pocket, but it was obvious that she had never seen anything

436

like that before and somehow wasn't interested. Leaving as quietly as we could, I remember feeling as we did so that, somehow, here was real tragedy and that they had been left to their fate. However, on joining our companion upon the road, other pressing matters occupied us, and in like fashion we investigated three more small farm-houses without finding a sign either of the enemy or of the occupants.

At length we judged ourselves to be well into the hamlet of Preshoek, for through the now-lifting mist we could make out the outline of a block of small terraced houses. The light was also getting much better. I therefore decided to complete our reconnaissance as soon as possible and return before the mist finally dispersed. At the first of the cottages I left my companions at the front gate of the small garden and, after a look into the lower windows, I tried the door, which was locked. I then threw some gravel at the upper-floor window, and almost immediately I heard sounds from the bedroom above, raising my revolver as the window opened noisily and a nightcapped head peered our sleepily, then, querulously, down at me. By frantic signs I endeavoured to get him to talk quietly, but it was useless. As soon as he realized I was English, he shouted to his wife and disappeared, obviously preparatory to descending the stairs. In the same instant the sharp crack of a rifle behind me caused me to turn hurriedly, to see my two companions kneeling and starting rapid fire at a dozen or so Germans just leaving the end cottage, dressing as they ran and dragging their kits as they disappeared into the mist. Several were hit, one obviously in the leg, and I was making up my mind whether to make the most of our advantage when, from somewhere down the street, a light machine-gun sent a long burst very close to us, followed by another.

That decided me. We had the information we wanted and ducked down, therefore, into the dry ditch, making our way back to the brewery without further incident. There the cyclists thanked me for my company, retrieved their bikes and left after I'd shaken hands with them and wished them luck. I remember thinking at the time that they seemed to be in a great hurry, and turned to see two gorgeously accoutred red-tabbed staff officers approaching, only a few yards distant. I forget their names after such a long time, but they were from the 41st Division who were making the advance across our front that morning. They were quite affable, but the major ticked me off in a nice way for setting a bad example to my men by walking about minus my box respirator. I was explaining matters when a salvo of whizz-bangs streaked over and burst on the roofs of the houses just behind us. As the tiles and brickwork clattered around, Brass Hat Major hurriedly consulted his wristwatch and told Brass Hat Captain that they 'must be gettin' along' and they departed, the next salvo helping them to speed on their way, much to my lads' amusement—and, incidentally, my own.

Hurriedly I sat down and wrote a message notifying Captain White of my patrol, and sent back the two runners with it, also inquiring for news. As I rose to my feet I noticed a stream of civilians coming back to the brewery cellars. They had soon learned, but we heard subsequently that several civilians had been wounded by the last salvo. The advance of troops across our front that morning cleared Preshoek and occupied Aelbeke. After that the village was left in peace, and all emerged to resume, as far as circumstances and damage permitted, their normal lives. Early that evening we were withdrawn and moved about two kilometres north, the whole 34th Division pivoting on us, as it were, preparatory to a new general advance eastward, and taking up a position between us and Courtrai. To their left lay the 36th (Ulster) Division which had relieved the 29th around Courtrai.

Our move forward that night entailed occupying a stretch of the Courtrai–Aelbeke road and the hamlet of Klarenhoek. White made temporary Company H.Q. in an isolated farm-house on the line of our advance and briefed us by the yellow light of a reeking oil lamp in the kitchen, provided by the bewildered Belgian couple and their two daughters. He was just concluding when a salvo of whizz-bangs fell unpleasantly close, causing them to dive for cover into the cellars, and it was then that we saw that a near-by outbuilding was on fire. Within a few moments this spread to the farm-house itself, and the German gunners welcomed the target in no uncertain fashion, but then desisted, enabling the unfortunate Belgians to remove masses of supplies and goods hidden in the cellars. They were still doing this when Chalk and I left to rejoin our men. I had the furthest to go in the darkness that had descended as the flames in the farm-house subsided and glowed dull red. I remember feeling just about lost when, by the merest stroke of luck—if one could call it that—a lad who should have known better struck a match between cupped hands to get a few draws on a fag-end. I saw the faint light, about thirty yards distant and getting nearer, heard Sergeant Clark growling, 'what the bloody hell d'you think you're doing?' I was home and dry, and as there was no time to waste made immediate preparations for our advance, with particular attention to liaison with Chalk and Newman on my right.

The moon had started to rise and shone mistily through low clouds as we picked our way over the silent fields in formation of 'snakes' with intervals of fifty yards or so between them. There was enough light to enable us to keep direction and discern, after ten minutes or so, the low ridge marking the course of the Courtrai–Aelbeke road. Getting nearer, we made out the shapes of houses marking the southern end of Klarenhoek. All was quiet and we stood at length without incident upon the pavé of that main road, somewhat wary, and started investigating. As soon as possible I posted sentry groups along the road, with the dry ditch on the eastern side for cover, and, with a runner, went to find Chalk and Newman. On the way some of my lads met me with two young Belgian youths whom they had found beneath the straw in a near-by barn. Apparently they had been too frightened to answer when challenged by our men poking about with bayonet points in the straw, and had nearly paid the penalty. From them I gathered that the German rearguards had left only half an hour or so previously and were now at St. Anna, to the east. I made them understand that they had better stay with us for the time being, although they wished to get to France, near the coast.

Coming to some crossroads—that going eastwards the road to St Anne—we noticed a shuttered *estaminet* with yard and outbuildings behind it and then, to my amazement, distinct strains of music. My runner, Palanza (a good lad, by the way) ventured the opinion that Mr Chalk was in there. Somewhat taken aback, we went into the yard, which was full of Chalk's platoon. The music, louder now, was 'Alexander's Rag-time Band', reinforced by

Chalk plays selections from "The Bing Boys" to his men. (ourtrai-Aelbeke Rd. Oct. 19th 1918.

hearty singing! With thoughts of the job on hand, I pushed my way inside in a pretty wrathful frame of mind at Chalk's apparent neglect of elementary precautions. Several guttering candles lit the room, and there sat Chalk, playing with feeling, with men all round him singing, while the Belgian and his wife leaned over the back of the piano in high spirits at their liberation.

I hesitated as 'Alexander's Rag-time Band' gave place to selections from *The Byng Boys on Broadway*, and he was halfway through that simple, yet immortal song to English ears, 'If You were the Only Girl in the World' when a terrific crash outside stopped the proceedings. A big shell had landed on the furthest of the outbuildings, and by a mercy none of those outside the kitchen door in the yard were casualties. They had now scattered for cover, and I was getting some sort of order with his sergeant when Chalk appeared, and together we posted sentry groups along the road. We then returned to the *estaminet*, where I wrote a note to White—using the piano lid as a desk—reporting objective occupied. Palanza took it. I told Chalk I didn't know he was a musician, and at my request he played tunes from *The Maid of the Mountains*, inducing, somehow, an almost overwhelming nostalgia for England and home. He had not finished when another shell fell, nearer than the first, and the ceiling plaster descended on us in chunks and a cloud of dust. However, we were fortunate in that we again escaped casualties. Madame seemed to take the damage in her stride and suggested some ersatz coffee. We voted that a good idea, but when it arrived and we sipped it we gained an inkling of what these poor people had suffered for the previous four years. This may have been ground acorns. Anyhow, it was warm.

The *estaminet* and the outbuilding had suffered badly, and what puzzled us quite a lot in the meanwhile was the heavy calibre of the guns and the way the shells arrived among us.

Dawn was just breaking and I was snatching a fitful forty winks on a borrowed groundsheet in a near-by dry ditch at the roadside, when Captain White and two gunner officers arrived with their telephonists. One of them, it transpired, was from a sixty-pounder battery and he apologized profusely for two of his shells falling short, before departing a few minutes later. We were very relieved at this, as we didn't relish being strafed by heavy artillery at that stage of the war.

The other gunner, White told me, would give me eighteen-pounder support for the next move forward at ten that morning, my personal objective being the group of large buildings on the next low ridge, about three parts of a kilometre due east, which we could now see, and which White's map designated as the 'Institute St. Anne'. I was most interested to see the location and names of the villages on the other side of that ridge while the opportunity offered. The Skipper then wished me luck and went along to see Chalk, and the young gunner and I got together. He said he had two guns, and at this news I was very pleased. We were discussing how he could best assist me when a salvo of whizz-bangs rudely interrupted our conversation, falling about a hundred yards to our rear and throwing up fountains of earth. They seemed to come directly from the buildings, and the subaltern, on scanning them through his field glasses, reckoned the German battery was firing from the gardens surrounding them. He suggested having a go at them there and then, but I proposed that he waited until nearer 'zero' at 10 a.m., thus utilizing the element of surprise. It might make any lurking German machine-gunners keep their heads down, but he thought that, if he could get the range just beforehand, it was worth trying.

We therefore kept constant watch on this considerable range of buildings through our field glasses, and although we concluded that it must be a school or college of sorts, we couldn't discern a single sign of movement there. Doubtless, we thought, it had been evacuated by order of the retreating enemy. Meanwhile the telephonist laid out his line to the guns in a small depression, eight hundred yards or so to our rear, actually near our jumping-off line of the previous evening. I was busy with Chalk and Newman, preparing for the move forward and briefing them about the artillery. It was then I found that Newman and Fenton, between them, had similar support laid on. At around five minutes to ten my new friend gave the range to his guns and, following the usual preliminaries, the order to fire brought the projectiles sailing over our heads: one of H.E. and one of shrapnel. We were loud in our praises as one corner of the main building was hidden in a cloud of reddish dust, while shrapnel appeared to burst right over the garden.

Two more followed, and then I thought we'd better get on with it and make the most of the cover afforded. The lads needed no second bidding, and we set off with additional confidence across the fields, as our barrage whizzed over our heads. As we neared the buildings the range lengthened and we saw that the area of the ridge immediately behind was being liberally sprayed with shrapnel. The long high garden wall now faced us; I didn't like the look of things at all, and hurriedly arranged with Chalk, by signs, that he should take his men round to the right while I veered left to the near-by road, which led past where we judged the entrance to be. Reaching it, we proceeded along the dry ditch at the side with considerable caution for the first hundred yards or so, and our amazement can only be imagined at then hearing children's shrill voices, followed by the sudden appearance, through a great gate, of several elderly nuns and a horde of little children, mostly girls. Excitedly they crowded round us while, over a sea of faces, I inquired of the nuns, *'les Allemands?'*

I gathered from them that, indeed, the German battery had been positioned in the considerable vegetable garden enclosure, and that they had pulled out at first light. Leaving Sergeant Clark to deal with our front for a few moments, I followed one of the nuns into the grounds and then realized the havoc that our guns had wrought. Glasshouses and frames had been smashed so that scarce a panel seemed intact; while, along the elevation of the great building, gaping reddish holes showed here and there and shrapnel had pockmarked the brickwork only too thoroughly. Piles of empty shell cases and stacks of unused shells marked the German gun positions, and I reflected somewhat ruefully that, had I adopted the gunner lieutenant's suggestion of firing directly he arrived, we might have caught some of them. Hastily I inquired of the nun whether they had suffered any casualties, but she reassured me on this point, indicating that everyone had taken refuge in the cellars immediately the Germans opened fire.

She smiled when, in bad French, I told her that for them the war was over and that many of our friends would soon arrive. Saluting, I left her, as there was much to be done, and on the way back to my men I met the nuns and the children in the drive, returning to the buildings and, I hoped, to some degree of normality—but I didn't feel exactly proud of what we had done just then.

On rejoining my lads, Sergeant Clark told us that the last German machine-gun post had retired only a few minutes before our arrival. He had been investigating the hamlet around the institute, as far as the crossroads running at right-angles across our front along the ridge toward the villages of Rolelghem, Knocke and Belleghem. On taking some men along it in that direction, I met Chalk with some of his men, looking for me. As we stood

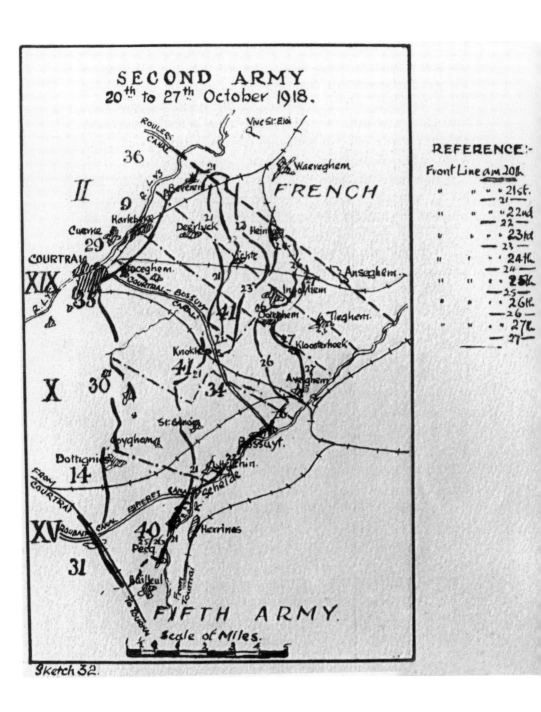

SECOND ARMY
20th to 27th October 1918.

REFERENCE:-
Front Line am 20th

Sketch 32.

talking and studying the country in front of us, which fell away for nearly a kilometre, two machine-guns opened up on us in most unpleasant fashion from a spinney about six hundred yards to our front. We couldn't locate them exactly, but shortly after, as we were searching with our field glasses from cover in the long grass of the road bank, we both saw movement beyond the spinney to the right—a German four-gun battery, in fact. Hastily, I sent back two men with a message urging my gunner friend to come up to me, as there was a wonderful target awaiting him. We watched, with growing impatience, the German gunners prepare to fire in our direction over open sights. After the first salvo had arrived, I collected three Lewis guns and sprayed both the spinney and the battery—apparently to some purpose as, a few minutes later, after a second salvo, the horse teams arrived to limber up the guns and pull out.

Although we might have done some execution by renewed firing with all we had, the while I fumed helplessly, we didn't succeed in preventing all four guns galloping away behind the spinney, probably to the shelter of another dark woodland. The range—about a thousand yards, at least—was far too great for accurate fire. Some minutes afterwards Captain White arrived with the gunner, but it was too late, of course, for the latter to get into action, especially as he was then moving his guns forward. White had moved his company H.Q. to a cottage opposite the institute. Walking there with him for a flying visit, we saw the two guns arrive at the gallop, while some of the nuns and children watched wide-eyed from the great doorway of the institute.

Shortly after midday we again went forward across fields of roots towards Belleghem, where we could see a Belgian flag bravely flying in the breeze from the top of the church spire; but we were held up temporarily by machine-gun and mortar fire, also by isolated snipers among the roots. I had a narrow escape from one of these gentry hidden in some high kale, and only just managed to dodge into an empty, but very filthy, pig-sty. Here I was forced to remain for some minutes, but my lads knew the value of Lewis gun fire in cases like this, and after a few bursts into the greenery this pest made good his escape—if he wasn't hit. My lads were very amused at my predicament, I remember,

445

BELLEGHEM. Oct. 20th.1918.

and held their noses, while I was annoyed myself by the smell that I carried about with me for what seemed like days afterwards.

While working our way downhill through the roots across the remaining fields towards the outskirts of Belleghem, we were amazed to hear distant strains of martial music coming from our right, and within a few minutes observed, to our surprise, a battalion coming along a road leading towards the village, in column of fours. I—and doubtless my colleagues, also—were wondering how we could warn them that the enemy were still in the village, when several mortar shells sailed over and dropped about fifty yards short of the leading files. Hurriedly the leading company took cover in the ditches on either side of the road, and I recall that, in so doing, the band personnel presented an irresistibly comic sight, the big drummer nearly rolling over the top of his drum in his efforts to get down as a further salvo arrived, fortunately dropping on each side of the road. Apparently they had been misled by the Belgian flag.

Shortly after, however, there was a silence and we saw Belgian civilians walking about among the houses, indicating that the German rearguard had packed up.

We were preparing to go forward when Captain White ap-

446

peared, telling us that the battalion to our right (of another division) was advancing across our front. After a wait among the roots, our company withdrew to the welcome shelter of houses and barns in the nearby village of Roleghem Knocke, where we spent the night. Early next morning the battalion concentrated and marched by way of secondary roads in the direction of Courtrai, through which, at length, we duly passed, at times picking our way past heaps of rubble. The suburbs had been badly mauled, but the centre seemed to have escaped major damage, and the few inhabitants we saw in the streets appeared to be in better case than we had anticipated. No doubt, however, appearances were deceptive and they had many problems just then. We marched north-east and at dusk were billeted in and around Harelbeke, resting there until 25th October.

This break was very welcome and, indeed, somewhat overdue as, with few exceptions, we hadn't washed properly or bathed in the usual sense of that term for weeks. It was here, too, that Captain White decided to have his horse up from the transport lines, and Pearson duly appeared riding Digger, obviously proud of his glossy black coat and impeccably polished saddlery. Quarters had been prepared in the stables facing one side of the farm courtyard, with the willing assistance of the Belgian farmer, and an admiring throng of all ranks watched the Skipper mount and, bending low over Digger's ears, disappear through the archway gate to a lunch invitation from Captain Peskett of 'A' Company, whose Number One was my old friend Dobbie. He returned about three that afternoon, and seeing me, asked as he dismounted whether I could ride. I thought it best to admit that I couldn't, whereat he said that it was time I started and that tomorrow I would show him what I could do!

As the following morning passed I began to hope that he had forgotten, but as Pearson was handing round mugs of tea after lunch he called, 'Pearson, is Digger ready for Mr Read?' Digger apparently *was* ready. Captain White and the rest rose and adjourned to the farmyard, while I dashed to get my cap and gloves—in a considerable state of trepidation, let me add. As I appeared I was greeted with, 'come on, Richard, show us what you can do!' from the Skipper. I approached Digger with what I

447

considered a show of nonchalance, catching a slight grin passing across Pearson's otherwise deadpan features as I took the reins in what I judged to be correct cavalry fashion. I turned the stirrup iron—luckily, correctly—and mounted. So far, so good, as from my elevated position I took in the sea of faces around. 'All right?' queried Captain White. I signified in the affirmative with a salute, and Pearson relinquished his hold at Digger's head whereat the latter, without any direction from me, turned abruptly and faced the archway exit from the yard. With a terrific whinny he set off at a brisk trot—so brisk that I only escaped collision with the keystone of the arch by bending low over his ears in the nick of time.

Outside, Digger smelled the grass and plunged towards an open field gate opposite, so that we were all but run down by a three-ton lorry towing an observation balloon, which hovered low overhead and which, obviously, Digger didn't like. With another terrific whinny he reared and set off at a gallop. Round that field we went, twice, while I endeavoured to gain control, at least to some degree—but in vain. Another joyous snort at the feel of the grass under his feet, and Digger was off on the third circuit. In despair I tugged at everything, with the result that, halfway round, he pulled up dead, at right-angles to the roadside hedge. I went clean over his head and the hedge, and fell sprawling on the thick muddy verge about twenty yards in front of an advancing eighteen-pounder field battery. Hurriedly, the leading Indian drivers held high their whip-stocks and halted in a clatter of hooves on the pavé, while the battery sergeant-major galloped alongside to discover the cause. I returned his salute ruefully as I picked myself up and detached the largest pieces of muddy turf from my breeches and elbows. I must have presented a truly comical sight but, to their credit, the faces of both the Indian drivers and the sergeant-major remained inscrutable, as the battery moved on again while I dragged myself, with aching shoulder and knee, the few hundred yards back along the road to the crowd at the archway, which included White, Fenton, Newman and Chalk. To my amazement, they said that I'd stuck on longer than ever they thought I would, and White said he'd lost twenty francs in bets to Chalk and Newman. He promised me another ride as soon as an opportunity offered, but in the meanwhile we were moving up to the front again and Digger would have to return to the transport lines. It was then I inquired about Digger and discovered that Pearson had just about winded himself in trying to catch him, and had not as yet succeeded. The following morning we moved up and halted for some hours at Hulste before again moving forward to Desselghem.

On that day we saw the first French Army camions and poilus—forerunners of the French Army corps about to take over on our left. That night, occupying as we did some German hutments, we were bombed three times, fortunately without casualties. On the following evening we moved up beyond Desselghem, making contact with the retreating enemy after dark beyond the hamlet of Englehoek. Here we found ourselves the left flank company of the British Army, our neighbours being some genial Chasseurs Alpins of that famous French corps. Their nearest H.Q. was in the village of Hierwieg, whither, on Captain White's orders, I accompanied two French lieutenants prior to co-operating with them in a considerable advance in the small hours of the morning, this to occupy two farm-houses some seven hundred metres to our front. I returned to the Skipper with a French sergeant and ten of his men—all of them, incidentally completely dwarfing our fellows in size—and in due course they went forward with us. We occupied our farm with scarcely any opposition, the few of the German rearguard there making good their escape eastwards, according to the farmer, when they sensed our approach. He and his wife welcomed us in no uncertain fashion, producing a profusion of wine and glasses from their cellar. With the coming of daylight on that late October morning, we were sniped at from a farm-house and surrounding buildings and copse about five hundred metres to our front, and when going along our extended line of lads during the 'stand to' hour, I was lucky in surviving several unpleasantly near misses.

As soon as I returned to the farm-house and to our Allies, who had duly reported their objectives reached, the sergeant and several of his men foraged around and, within an hour or so, had produced a *potage* with a truly marvellous aroma. They lent me a mess tin lid, and I can testify that I have never tasted better. The poilu in the role of chef told me that he had worked at the Savoy Hotel in London, and also in Swiss hotels, before 1914.

The unpleasant sniping continued, but we noticed that the farmer and his family could move about quite freely—their cows, also—without molestation. Determined to deal with our tormentors if possible, we went into the loft of the highest of the outbuildings and partially dislodged a couple of tiles from the roof, from which we surveyed the neighbouring farm and environs through a powerful pair of French field glasses, much stronger and clearer than mine. Within a few minutes the French sergeant noticed the muzzle of a rifle protrude from a small hole in the farm-house roof, and then a slight whitish puff, followed by a dull report as it was fired, apparently at a blue French steel helmet lying in a conspicuous position on top of a wall almost below us, with the watery morning sunlight upon it. Precisely who or where the owner was just then I'll never know. Probably he was in the farm kitchen, but it was lucky for him that he wasn't near his headgear as it was a shot in a thousand, the bullet, as we found subsequently, hitting and chipping the brickwork a few inches below it—but we couldn't see that, just then.

The French sergeant, however, called loudly—as far as I was concerned, unintelligibly—and within a few moments two of his men appeared manhandling a light machine-gun. I crouched aside while the sergeant achieved a most uncomfortable firing position without pushing the muzzle outside the tiles. He then fired several bursts at the sources of the bullet which, in the confined space in the loft, made our ears sing. Then, hastily pushing the weapon to one side, he looked through his binoculars for results and, as he handed them to me, he looked pleased as he quipped with his men. He had certainly chipped some tiles, but at that range accuracy was impossible, as with our Lewis, and the tendency was to make a pattern dipping off the target. In any case, our tormentor must have decided he had been spotted, as the sniping ceased around midday and we were all prepared—indeed, eager—to go forward and take possession, but Fenton came up with orders for us to leave our French friends and concentrate as a company. This I did with regret, but it was good to be together again and we marched to the village of Harelbeke for the night where, in

450

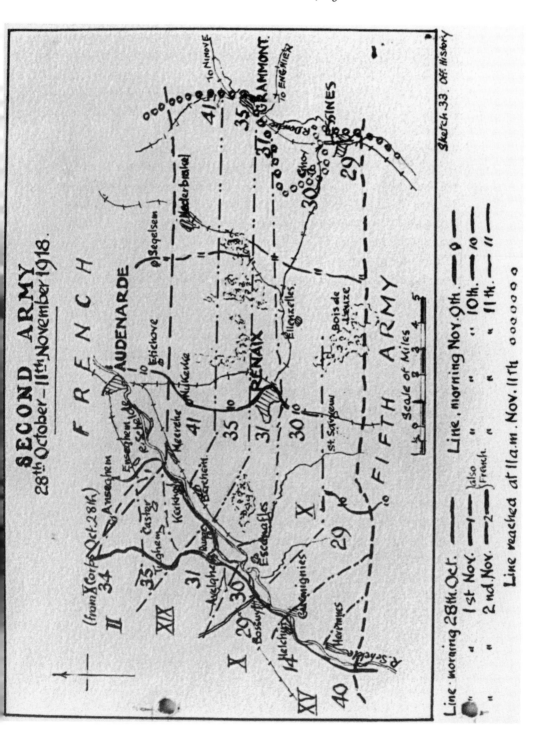

SECOND ARMY
28th October – 11th November 1918.

Sketch 33. Off. History.

Line, morning Nov. 9th. ○
" " " 10th. 10
" " " 11th. 11

Line, morning 28th Oct.
" " 1st Nov.
" " 2nd Nov.

also
French.

Line reached at 11 a.m. Nov. 11th ○○○○○○○○

Scale of Miles

some ex-German hutments, we were again bombed. Our rubber of bridge was rudely interrupted and our candles snuffed by the blast but, again, we were lucky.

On the following day I was detailed, with a subaltern of another company, to reconnoitre the ground on the limit of our division's advance. We each took a runner and, mounted on orderly room bicycles, spent a most interesting day around Anseghem, occupied by the division's Scottish Brigade, then advancing to the nearby River Scheldt. We were told, days afterwards, that the Jocks suffered heavy casualties in an endeavour to establish a bridgehead on the further bank, but on our tour they were progressing through the villages between Anseghem and the river.

I should emphasize the fact that we knew very little indeed of what was happening to our left and right. Whenever rations came up—and, latterly, when in the company of Chasseurs Alpins friends—we endeavoured to ascertain an accurate account of the tremendous gains the Allied armies were making along the entire Western Front. Rumour, however, was rife, and no one knew just what to believe. Any newspapers we had were a week old, at least, and for some reason we had seen precious few of these. Perhaps it was because the recent rapid movements of our own and, indeed, every active unit of the advancing British Army had outrun the postal organization. Certain confirmation we had, however, that to the south we were far east of Lille, Roubaix and Turcoing, while to the north the French were nearing Ghent. However, when we returned to our units that evening of 1st November, we found that the battalion had moved back to Deerlijk and didn't in the least realize that, for the 4th Royal Sussex, their fighting career in Flanders—in that war, at least—had come to an end.

Orders came to move to the rear by easy stages, and that night we slept in some ex-German hutments at Harelbeke. From there we marched back to Wevelghem via Courtrai, billeting in the much-damaged village where, however, some inhabitants had already re-appeared.

NOTES TAKEN FROM
OFFICIAL HISTORY OF THE WAR
`MILITARY OPERATIONS
FRANCE AND BELGIUM 1918´, VOL. 5
26TH SEPTEMBER–11TH NOVEMBER 1918
`THE ADVANCE TO VICTORY´

Action of Tieghem, 28–29th October. 34th Division (Nicholson) transferred from X Corps to II Corps. An International Liaison Company from 8th Scottish Rifles was sent to join similar company from French VII Corps, at junction of the two corps on extreme British left. In the advance a half-company of the Scottish Rifles, with a section of tanks, was held up by heavy mortar gun and machine-gun fire from a village north west of Anseghem, and a gap developed between the French and British (p. 447).
' "A" Company from 101st Brigade (Brig. Gen. W.J. Woodstock) was sent to get in touch with the International Liaison Force and fill the gap between the British left and the French right, which was done' (p. 449).

[This was 'D' Company, 4th Royal Sussex (my company).]
'At 9 a.m. on November 1st the troops of the 31st and 34th Divisions were then withdrawn and the whole II Corps went into Reserve, its 9th Division being in a rear area. At 6 p.m. Corps boundaries were readjusted' (p. 450).

CHAPTER 23

ARMISTICE

We revelled in our rest and rather thought that a new advance was in store for us, although, by the newspapers now arriving, we knew that great events were afoot, and there was a certain air of expectancy around.

Therefore it was with no little excitement that I learned at the Battalion Orderly Room on 8th November that my leave warrant was coming through that night. It did, and great were the celebrations in our company mess that evening—one bottle of Canadian 'rye' among five us, after a meal of pork and beans, corned beef hash, and tinned apricots with sweet Nestlé's condensed milk poured over them. Captain White adjured me to go to Harrods, mention his name to the manager of the wine department, and not to dare come back without at least four good bottles. I promised, but that rash promise haunted me throughout my leave. Late that night I caught a lorry on the main street going into Menin, assisted by good wishes from my cheering colleagues who had stood upon the road and stopped it.

The station at Menin could hardly be called that, but there was an R.T.O. hut—the rails had been re-laid—and the leave train stood there. Still, the slowly gathering throng of all ranks going on leave from divisions in the Second Army soon livened things up. Everyone was in holiday mood: fags and tobacco were exchanged; swigs from flasks and water bottles offered; and with the first streaks of daylight we were allowed into the train. To the mass singing of 'Good-bye-ee' and a series of great jerks, it got into motion—the first to make the journey from Menin to Boulogne. Within an hour or so, the slow-moving train had carried us across the wastes over which, a few weeks previously, we had crept forward yard by yard. Against the grey sky, the gaunt tree stumps of Mont Kemmel stood out in vivid relief, bounding, in that direction, a landscape of unutterable misery. Then followed the rubble heaps, abandoned and wrecked huts, that were Armentières and Bailleul. Then Hazebrouck, badly battered, but seeming that morning a veritable outpost of civilization.

Ruminating during the halt there, I recall turning over in my mind the events of the eight months that had passed since I had last seen England: Egypt and beyond; the return to France; Soissons and the aftermath; Flanders again, and the advance. At this point in my mental journey I thought of the raid near Gheluwe and the letter wishing me luck from the girl at St. Omer. A sudden excitement surged over me. Had I not promised to call and thank her when next I passed that way? Our next stop, in all probability, would be St. Omer. Should I?

The train re-started. Wrapped in my own thoughts, I took little part in the general light conversation of the carriage and when, at length the great tower of St. Omer came into view, I rose and surprised my fellow travellers by removing my pack from the luggage rack and announcing that I was dropping off there to see an old friend. The train stopped, panting. I wished them all a good leave, and, alighting, went along to the R.T.O.'s office. Here I left my pack and ascertained that I could get a train that afternoon at least as far as Calais. I would lose a day in England, however.

With a light heart then, but at the same time wondering whether I'd been a fool, I made my way through the town, still full of English soldiery, and out along the Rue de Longuevile. Near the end of the houses, where the countryside took over from the town, I found the line of small dwellings and managed to knock at the right one. An old lady opened the street door and seemed alarmed, looking up and down the road as if to see whether any neighbours were looking, as I inquired for Mlle Cornélie. At the name she looked really scared, but I managed to gather from her that the girl was very ill with *la grippe*—the Spanish 'flu which had killed many thousands that year. She urged me not to go nearer, but somehow then I just would not be denied, and I stepped inside past her, urged on by faint sounds coming from above. In spite of the old lady's protests I ran up the stairs and knocked on a door I saw ajar on the dim landing. From within came sounds resembling long-drawn-out sighs, and at this I didn't mince matters any more.

I am not adept at describing an incredibly stuffy, yet cold, darkened room, and how a very sick, emaciated and practically starving young woman looked on that raw grey November afternoon. Suffice it to say that she remembered me and made a faint attempt at a greeting, while obviously embarrassed at being seen thus. She was, or had been, very ill, she held my hand and told me, in almost a whisper, as I stood by the bedside. Now, she hoped, she was recovering. Both of us fell silent, looking at one another, I wondering what I could do to help. What she was thinking I'll never know, but as she lay there I fancied I saw some slight colour in her cheek, and to verify this I went across to the window and drew the heavy curtains. She took my hand again and I sat down on the bed—there seemed no need for words, somehow—but then I realized that precious time was passing. I stood up and told her I would go into St. Omer and get some delicacies for her, to help make her better. At this distance in time I forget exactly what I did buy, and what I did may seem silly and naive in the extreme, but I returned with as much as I could carry. Included was certainly a bottle of champagne, oranges and a large bottle of Bovril, and I remember how pleased Cornélie was to see these. After making, at my suggestion, the first cup of Bovril for her, the old lady joined us, and I learned then that Cornélie was a clerk in the local Food Office.

I had to go to get my train, and I'll confess that the parting wasn't pleasant. Indeed, somewhat wildly, I played with the idea of staying on in St. Omer for another day or so, and then thought better of it. As dusk descended, I made my way once more to the station, having promised to call in on my return from leave, if that was possible.

Friends have sometimes told me, on occasion, that I tend to give way to emotional stresses under conditions such as the one I have described, and I record that for many hours afterwards the thought of Cornélie lying there ill and alone in that cold, darkened room was ever present, as the train rattled on towards Boulogne. On the mid morning following, that image persisted as the leave boat ploughed across the bright water of the Channel and the 'white cliffs of old England' came once more into full view—a glorious sight for any returning exile.

Here I feel I must record some incidents in no way connected with what I have described above. At Boulogne, General Townshend, defender of Kut el Amara, and lately released by the Turks under the terms of an armistice, came aboard the leave boat and at Folkestone was met by Admiral Sir Roger Keyes and a lady, presumably the general's wife. We thought he looked pretty well after his incarceration, as we rushed from the boat to get the few available seats in the Pullman, where experienced travellers of the period knew they could get lunch. In this, several of us, including four Canadians and two Americans, were lucky; but we noticed on entering the plush interior that the turbaned Indian orderly was jealously guarding the seats reserved for the general and his wife, immediately adjoining the entrance door. Lady Townshend had been talking to Sir Roger on the platform, but they took their seats as the guard started to blow his whistle, and we all heard the general, in saying his farewells through the open window as the train pulled out, assure the gallant admiral that he was 'ready to have another smack at 'em'. At this the light-hearted conversation among our party ceased abruptly, as the unanimous feeling amongst us was that we had had just about enough, and *sotto voce* murmurs broke the temporary silence. At Sandling Junction on the main line, where the big engines hooked on, the Indian orderly came along and, without speaking, closed all the large open windows of our Pullman. We British were surprised, but this was too much for our Canadian pals and some Anzacs at the far end. Promptly the windows were let down again, and a very awkward situation was only averted when a British colonel tactfully pointed out that the general's blood was unusually thin because of his long imprisonment by the Turks. One by one the windows were *almost* closed, the Canadians stating, however, that they were only deferring to the lady.

On reaching Charing Cross I walked along the Mall once more and booked a room at a hotel I'd been told about in Buckingham Palace Road, the name of which now escapes me completely, but I recall that the bed folded up into the wall at the rear of the head when not in use. I hadn't seen one of these before and couldn't resist trying it up and down several times before descending to the street. There, footloose and thoroughly exhilarated by the atmosphere of London, I made my way out to Ranelagh where (as I had discovered from a letter received at Wevelghem the day before I set out) my brother Alfred, commissioned in the Welsh Guards from the Inns of Court O.T.C. was stationed. I could have saved my legs, perhaps, had I 'phoned first, as on inquiry there I found that he was orderly officer and, of course, would be on duty that evening. However, it was very good to see him, if only for a minute or two, and, indeed, I felt rather awed at his ramrod-like back and impeccable turn-out, completed by the Guards' downward look from under the close-fitting, eye-shading, patent leather cap peak with its wide edge of gold braid. I felt somewhat jumpy, too, at having to acknowledge salutes from Guardsmen passing at distances of anything up to a hundred yards, and concluded that Ranelagh just then was no place for a poor infantry-of-the-line subaltern, back from the wars for a spell. We arranged to meet in town on the following evening, and I departed to make more calls, including a promising one at Harrods and another, in Vere Street, on dear old Horace Phillip's sister Winnie, who gave me tea.

At just after eleven o'clock the next morning, 11th November, I emerged from the Piccadilly tube exit on the corner of Shaftesbury to be wrapped in a very large and dilapidated Union Jack by a rather large and very excited lady with a face reddened by her exertions, and became one of an enormous milling and cheering throng which completely filled Piccadilly Circus. In vain a taxi, loaded with Australians inside and out, endeavoured to make a way through, but came to a halt just where I stood at the pavement edge, disentangling myself from the flag. This I then gave to the 'outside' party, one of whom promptly stood upright on the taxi roof with it, to the delight of the crowd around them. Bottles were being thrown into the mass of people from the upper floors of various buildings around the Circus. Whether they were full or empty, or whether they injured anyone, I'll never know, but, swaying happily to and fro, folks had just gone mad with relief, 'Armistice' or 'it's finished' on everyone's lips.

Standing there, suddenly I wanted to get away out of that crowd, as I wondered whether the news had reached Wevelghem and my friends there—and St. Omer. I remember forcing my way against the press of people and into a side street not far 'from Trafalgar Square. Here I had the good fortune to seek some lunch and a drink in a well known pub, where I got on the right side of a fine piece of steak and trimmings, for which no one would allow me to pay; but I rather think that occurrences of this sort were fairly general that day. Indeed, staffs of pubs and restaurants seemed to have one idea only—to get to the street doors themselves to see what was going on. Who could blame them?

My recollections of the remainder of that memorable Armistice Day, 11th November 1918, are considerably confused. In Trafalgar Square I joined forces with a V.A.D.—at least, she wore a nurse's blue uniform, and I recall that the two small red crosses on either side of the white band on her headgear didn't exactly detract from her appearance! She was carrying a large plaited fish-basket full of brussels sprouts, and with these we managed to board an east-bound bus near Charing Cross station. Mounting to the open upper deck (the tops weren't roofed in those days) we amused ourselves vastly in throwing these at suitable targets all along the Strand, as far as Ludgate Circus—principally at passengers on passing buses going west. Most of these were also well supplied with ammunition of various kinds, some, I regret to say, of a wet or rotting nature, with which we were pelted liberally. All very good fun just then, if rather childish in retrospect. We parted after a cup of tea in a café near St Paul's.

I duly met my brother Alfred, respondent in his long blue-grey greatcoat and gold peaked cap, and later that evening remember the Assistant Provost Marshal, London District, aided by his minions, requesting some of us to cease dancing in the Holborn Restaurant—we were standing on the tables, encouraged by the applause of many exuberant spectators.

The remainder of my leave I spent at home at Eastbourne in the bosom of my family; but before my leave expired I kept thinking of my colleagues and Captain White and 'D' Company. I was quite ready to go back and find them. A successful visit to

Harrods for a pack full of Scotch whisky, followed by an unusual night in the Hotel Russell Turkish bath, and once more I joined the early morning leave train for Folkestone at Victoria.

On inquiry at Boulogne, the R.T.O. office told me to get the next train to Lille—that evening, in fact—and inquire again of the R.T.O. at the St. André station there. I was pondering on this when, unexpectedly, luck came my way. Half-way along a long line of parked vehicles I spotted an ambulance-type van sporting the 34th Division chequerboard sign on the side. As I approached I saw that the driver was about to move off, and, hastening as well as I might with my considerable load, yelled to him somewhat breathless, 'any chance of a lift, driver, if you're going 34th Division way?' Seeing my chequerboard shoulder badges he hurriedly saluted and grinned, 'near Tournai, sir.' 'Good lad.' I hopped up beside him forthwith. He seemed genuinely glad to have my company, the more so as he wasn't too sure of the way out of Boulogne and beyond, explaining that he had brought down a major to catch the leave boat and had collected some urgently required medical stores sent specially from England. He had a thumbed and tattered map, of sorts, which I noted stopped short near Lille.

Sensing that we might have a somewhat arduous and lengthy journey before us, I asked him whether his tank was full. It wasn't, and our first task was to find the nearest A.S.C. petrol point and replenish this; also the half-dozen two-gallon cans he carried. Then we really set out and made quite good progress, pulling up in a much-battered Béthune for a plate each of fried eggs and *frites*. Thereafter, I recall that we avoided Lille and suburbs, making a detour after reaching La Bassée. Here, in sight of the well-remembered slag heaps of Vermelles and Hulluch, I would have liked to linger awhile, but we had to press on. The repaired roads were very bad and there always seemed a danger that, if we stopped upon the wet central pavé, we might slip to one side, off the camber into the muddy morass at the sides.

Dusk on that winter day descended early, and we had driven by our acetylene headlights for some miles when at length we reached Tournai. My driver then struck north, finally dropping me at a village where I thumbed a lift with a convoy of A.S.C.

lorries going west. Like us, they were afraid to stop for fear of sliding sideways on the camber of the pavé, and when we met traffic going the other way a very tricky situation invariably developed; indeed, two three-tonners became immovably stranded before we reached Lessines, where I'd been told the 4th Royal Sussex were now to be found. I 'debussed' in the town square without stopping the lorry and searched in the darkness for some minutes before a group of Royal Sussex, issuing from an *estaminet*, told me that 'D' Company were at a village about three kilometres distant. There being nothing for it, I set out and, very weary, at length reached the hamlet of Triburiau. Within a few minutes I was with Captain White and Fenton, Newman and Chalk, producing my pack of four bottles of Black & White with considerable pride, amid loud cheers. Thus my home-coming was celebrated. They found me a billet—a good one.

Moments before I slept, turning over in my mind the many happenings and journeyings of that long day, I realized with a start that I hadn't given a thought to St. Omer—and, truth to tell, I wasn't exactly proud of my omission. My good intentions had indeed gone the way of many others, and at the time I regretted sincerely that I had, in effect, like the Pharisee in the parable, 'passed by on the other side'.

I slept heavily, nevertheless, and Palanza woke me about 8 a.m. with a well-made cup of gunfire. They had let me sleep on. Drinking my tea, I watched him polishing my buttons, questioning him now and then about events happening while I had been away. Suddenly I decided it was good to be back. Stepping outside my farm-house billet, I noticed a fading white-painted German notice on the wall reading 'Typhus', which perturbed me somewhat until I found that the majority of the buildings in the hamlet carried the same legend. The farmyard pump at Captain White's billet, which was also Company H.Q. and our mess, carried the notice 'Wasser für der Sturmtruppen', and was the subject of many jokes during our sojourn there.

That morning, after parades, Captain White led the way across to the field opposite, where some low jumps had been erected and my face must have fallen as, with his customary sniff and twinkle, he invited me to try my luck over them on the waiting Digger.

Seeing that there was no escape, I mounted and managed to keep on Digger's back, at any rate, although he walked through two of the jumps. I found that I hadn't done so badly, and thereafter determined to persevere whenever an opportunity presented itself. In this way I managed to get a daily ten minutes or so while we were there.

My other outstanding recollection of this village is of our endeavours to feed a few-days-old baby at Chalk's billet. Here I would emphasize the really desperate straits of the Belgian civilians hereabouts. Nearly all their livestock had gone, their potatoes, vegetables and roots pillaged by the retreating Germans. Indeed, I soon found that they seemed almost entirely dependent upon us for food to keep going. In this case the mother was quite unable to feed the infant, and we spent literally hours devising variants of a piece of clean rag—'four-by-two' at one stage—dipped in 'Ideal' milk and slightly sweetened, with which we tempted the unhappy youngster who, to our surprise, at length seemed to look forward to this treatment. The spectacle of Fenton—tough, thickset Regular that he was—crooning to the little bundle he held with one hand while the milky rag dripped all over its face, incongruous as it was even in these circumstances, brought home to us some of the facts of life which, in our youthful ignorance, we had hitherto ignored. It was then that we found that somewhere in England he had a wife, and a little daughter, I believe. That was the only time we ever heard him mention them. There were several more under-nourished young children in that hamlet, among them two at least the shape of whose heads, even at that tender age, proclaimed their fathers to be of the recently departed race.

On the third morning after I rejoined from leave the battalion received marching orders, and I was sent ahead, with subalterns from each of the other companies, billeting. Our next halt would be at Soignies, twenty-three kilometres eastwards, and thither we made our way on bicycles—an extremely bumpy and muddy ride over the pavé to that ancient town—where we reported to the newly appointed town major for directions. Then we soon got busy and, with luck on my side, I had no real difficulty in fixing up the company strength of about 130, together with Company

H.Q., officers' and men's messes, and five officers' billets, well concentrated along one of the main streets.

Company H.Q., Captain White's billet and our mess were in a house next door to a millinery and haberdashery shop, the owner a lady with two daughters who ran the emporium and lived over it. As a temporary measure, her house having been taken over by the military, she had gone to live with them. Here, on going to ask the lady a few questions relating to the accommodation I had appropriated, I was introduced to the two daughters, who promptly invited me to take coffee with them. I needed no second bidding, and we all trooped upstairs to a very pleasant sitting room above the shop. I recall that I was thinking how well I was getting on with the younger daughter over the coffee, when the shop bell sounded and the elder girl descended forthwith. She reappeared almost immediately saying that an *officier Anglais* wished to see me. Smothering my annoyance as best I could, I excused myself, promising to return as soon as I could.

In the shop I was confronted by our battalion padre, who announced that, on the adjutant's orders, he had been attached to 'D' Company for messing and billeting for a month. As I digested this most unwelcome piece of news I saw, through the big plate-glass shop window, over the top of the millinery stands, my fellow billeting colleagues on the pavement opposite, laughing their heads off at my expense. It was then that I recalled a remark of White's to Fenton, saying how he 'had staved off the evil day for the time being, but that as 'C' Company had put up with the padre for a month, we were bound to take our turn shortly'.

Now apparently our turn *had* come; therefore, putting the best face I could upon things, I asked him to wait in our new Company H.Q. while I found him a billet. Now this padre, rightly or wrongly, was most unpopular. A little man, he possessed an enormous appetite, and many had been the wry anecdotes passed along by the other companies who had been host to him. In addition, his wants were many, and that day proved no exception. He wanted a billet with a room where he could talk privately with any man seeking his counsel; further, he wanted a suitable building for a service.

Hurriedly thinking things over, I decided to offer him my own billet, possessed suddenly by a wild brainwave. He appeared satisfied with that and, thankfully, I left him there while I hastened back to my coffee. Over a second cup I explained as well as I could what had happened; also that I must go and find myself another billet before my company arrived. The ladies conferred earnestly and volubly for a few moments, with the result that I was conducted to an attic room reached by some narrow stairs, with the assurance that they would make it 'verree good', according to Madame. They were more than kind, and I hastened to thank them as I dumped the few personal belongings I had brought with me, telling them as well as I could that I would be quite content to sleep on the floor in that house, although my valise would arrive with the battalion.

Considerably lighter in heart, therefore, I rejoined my colleagues and together we made our way to the approach road to Soignies from Lessines, to await the arrival of the battalion. In due course we heard, faintly at first, the strains of the lively 'quick march' of the old 35th Regiment, always played on return to camp or barracks or, as in this case, at the end of a day's journey. Then we saw them, marching now to attention, and indeed they made a fine show, headed by the colonel and senior major and the adjutant, mounted. The long column we observed was faultlessly in step, and we were struck by the uniformity of the 'slopes', as far as we could see. As windows became crowded with heads, and old and young appeared on the pavements, we fell silent with pride, and with our thoughts, at a sight that all too many British lads such as these had enlisted to see in 1914 and had fallen by the way—their regiment marching into Germany!

Captain White thought I'd done very well as, having seen the company bedded down to his satisfaction, and the meal of corned beef hash and tea progressing well in the field cooker, he strode into his Company H.Q. Following close behind him, I had no chance to explain before he saw the padre sitting in the front room. Thereafter, I hadn't done so well! But he impressed upon a subsequent hurried gathering of his officers that there was to be no rudeness from us, and all resolved to stomach this cuckoo in the nest as best we could.

That evening we sat down to our evening meal with a spotless white tablecloth, lit by candles in real candlesticks instead of Player's tins! Pearson, assisted by Palanza, served the soup which, we could not help noticing, the padre sipped noisily, smacking his lips. Whereat Fenton facetiously, by way of conversation, inquired whether he knew any German. Receiving a negative answer, he remarked that we were all learning phrases, for instance, *Wasser für der Sturmtruppen*, and invited the padre to repeat it. With his mouth full of soup, the unfortunate cleric did his best and nearly choked, while our spontaneous mirth was silenced by an ominous frown from White. Conversation languished as Palanza removed the soup plates—souvenirs, by the way, from that first undamaged farm-house we had encountered before Wevelghem.

A grinning Pearson appeared, relieving the tension, and bearing a huge borrowed dish of corned beef slices, following by a bristling-moustached Palanza with its fellow, brimming over with an amazing salad, the sight of which literally held us speechless as he deposited it between the candlesticks. There it lay in its pristine glory of hard-boiled egg slices peeping around mounds of fresh green leaves of chicory, endive, and maybe young cabbage (I don't think it could have been lettuce). 'Pearson,' inquired White, 'are you responsible for this?'

'No, sir,' replied the lad with becoming modesty. 'Madame and the young ladies.' A spirited discussion then ensued among us as to just how they had managed to produce this wonder in the near-starvation conditions prevailing among the Belgian civil population; and a proposition that Pearson fetch them forthwith, in order that we could express our warm appreciation, received considerable support. Captain White ruled, however, that we ask them to join us after the meal, which now proceeded. With a gesture of politeness, he invited the padre to help himself to the salad. He did, and a thunderstruck Chalk, sitting opposite to him at the table, leaned over and adjusted his pince-nez helplessly as we all watched slices of hard-boiled egg fished, in meticulous succession, from out of the greenery and on to the clerical plate. White broke the stunned silence by asking the padre if he would mind passing the salad, if he had finished with it, and, at the lower end of the table, I prayed that one slice of egg would be left when my turn came. In this both Newman and I were unlucky.

There followed a savoury of tinned sardine on toast and finally bread with ration cheese and tinned butter, during which course a now thoroughly exasperated Chalk leaned over and inquired facetiously of the padre, who had all the elements lying around him, if he had a mortgage on the butter. This certainly had the desired effect. Somewhat startled out of his complacent munching, our guest stopped eating. Glancing around at our empty plates and, doubtless, at our expressions, he hurriedly passed the butter and cheese to Captain White.

The memory of that meal at Soignies has remained with me over the years, including its conclusion with the appearance of our hostess and her two vivacious daughters; virtually our first opportunity of brushing up our party manners. The padre, excusing himself on account of a call he had to make at Battalion H.Q., was soon forgotten, and the remainder of the evening thoroughly enjoyed by everyone. We certainly needed some such pleasant interlude of relaxation and re-adjustment after those months of rough living so recently left behind in Flanders trenches and shell-pocked fields, and, as can be imagined, we were sorry when, after a three-day halt, the battalion took the road east from Soignies.

Again Captain White sent me ahead billeting, this time with Palanza and our C.Q.M.S., to the large mining village of Houdeng Ameries on the edge of the extensive Belgian coalfield, which, I recall, went by the name of the Borinage, its centre the great industrial city of Charleroi. Pit heads and slag heaps abounded and, indeed, from Houdeng Ameries eastwards the houses were practically continuous to the town of La Louvière a few kilometres further on. Amid these drab surroundings, differing vastly from those lately left behind us, poverty, under-nourishment and the result of five years of war were only too evident, and to a much greater extent than had shown on the surface hitherto. Along the rubbish-strewn sides of the interminable and pot-holed pavé of the village street, and fronting the rows of miners' cottages, lay masses of abandoned German lorries and horsed transport vehicles, stripped by now of everything of value: a truly depressing spectacle.

I remember raising a laugh, of a sort, among my somewhat disgruntled colleagues on the same errand by wondering how I was going to find a billet that would satisfy the padre, and in that fashion we found the town major and settled down to our work.

Within a few minutes we found how deceptive appearances could be. These miners and their wives, in spite of their privations, could not have been kinder. Moreover, their cottages were real homes into which they were only too anxious to welcome our men. In many ways I was reminded of Auchel, and of our memorable Christmas of 1916 there.

It was truly amazing how soon and how easily the necessary accommodation was found, extending as it did along the road almost to the neighbouring town of La Louvière, amid the littered, chaotic debris of a retreating army. Evidences of hard times, squalor and semi-starvation were only too plain to see in the houses of these unfortunate miners and their families, but even then their welcome was warm and genuine. My memory serves me ill, I fear, as to how I fixed up Captain White, our Company H.Q. and my colleagues, but the men went in two to a house: and I recall my own spartan accommodation in a small first-floor bedroom facing the street; redolent of damp, with peeling flowered wallpaper, my campbed on the bare plank floor, the only other furniture a battered wash-stand containing a cracked and discoloured chamberpot and, hanging on the door, a chipped white enamelled female douche complete with an enema. When I was visited by colleagues this latter was the subject of numerous jokes which did, however, serve the purpose of enabling me to ponder on its usefulness in more normal times!

I recall, also, a distinct shortage of rations of the normal kind, which was to persist for weeks; until, in fact, we were established on the bridgehead around Cologne—or Köln, as we were already calling it. There was neither fresh bread nor fresh meat, and we subsisted on corned beef, McConochies, biscuit, tinned jam and cheese. Much of this, I know, was shared with our erstwhile hosts and their starving families. We had, in fact, out-marched our supplies—or so it seemed.

The night before we left Houdeng Ameries, a party of us went to the theatre in La Louvière to see a gala performance of a patriotic revue, *Sous Épaulette*, which expressed in song, spectacle, and ridicule of their late enemy, the joy and the relief of the Belgians at their liberation. I well recall the procession of the by no means unattractive chorus with the flags of the Allies (the Union Jack a travesty, but no matter), evoking thunderous applause from the packed house. Our colonel was pointed out to me, in the stalls.

Early the following morning, 16th December, my billeting colleagues and I mounted our bicycles once more and headed for our next halt, Roux les Charleroi which, as the name suggests, is practically a suburb of this considerable industrial city. Here I put up with the local schoolmaster and his wife, who, incidentally, appeared to be in better case than the majority of the inhabitants, possessing also a comfortable home, some of the rooms lined with bookshelves. There were a number of such houses in Roux, doubtless occupied by colliery and factory executives and professional men, and for this reason officer and H.Q. accommodation was not hard to find. Neither, for that matter, were billets for the company, who were, again, made very welcome.

Personally, I remember Roux and the *Professeur* René Dumont, because of the conversation we had that evening by his fireside. Although he had few words of English and I few of French, he made me understand that great changes in Europe were imminent, especially in Russia. In doing so, he introduced me to the writings of Karl Marx and his book *Das Kapital*, a French translation of which he produced from a locked drawer in his study desk. He told me that it would not have been pleasant for him if the German occupation troops had found the book in his house by any chance. Now, everyone was free, and very expressive he was in signifying this, throwing up his arms several times.

The October Revolution was just over a year old, and information concerning it was scanty and untrustworthy in the extreme. In retrospect, I don't think that we soldiery bothered very much about it after the first impact following the separate peace made with the Germans, which enabled them to transfer many divisions and masses of artillery from the Eastern to the Western Front for their tremendous offensives earlier in the year. I therefore listened to his prognostications with interest, and with considerable incredulity, but there is no doubt that, in the long term, the schoolmaster was dead right.

We marched again the following morning, and from then on Newman took over the billeting job from me. We passed through Charleroi to the eastern suburb of Montignies sur Sambre, still in the coal-mining area. We halted only for the night, and, after we were clear of duties, four of us went into Charleroi by tram to a wrestling programme, the like of which we had never seen before, and which shocked us at the time. Indeed, as we took our seats at the ringside, one of the contestants in the bout in progress landed a mighty kick on his opponent's jaw and followed up with a butt in the chest which sent him clean through the ropes and to the floor at our feet. Indeed, he grabbed our knees in getting upright again and returning to the ring, apparently quite unhurt. Now, this type of wrestling is, of course, a commonplace, but I'm sure it wasn't so in the England of those days. Indeed, we just could *not* stomach the kicking business, and talked about it for days.

On the following morning, 18th December, we took to the road again. We left the coal mines, and shortly after midday reached the small town of Fosses. Here, Newman had found me a room over a baker's shop in the main street, from which vantage point I had time to become interested both in the passers-by and the customers. It is strange to have to record that we all sensed a change in the attitude of the inhabitants towards us, and during the day I found that the baker and his family had several framed photographs of German soldiers on the mantelpiece of their sitting room behind the shop. On comparing notes with men of my platoon and my colleagues, I found that this was common in Fosses. With this fact in mind, we had no difficulty in determining the obvious parentage of some of the younger children around, with their close-cropped fair hair and square heads. While the people were not actively hostile towards us, we were not at all sorry to march on the next morning and leave them to their own devices.

During the morning it rained, but, having been told that we were on the last stage of our journey for the time being, all were in high spirits when at length we marched through the arched gates into the quadrangle of the considerable monastic college of

Malonne, which lay under the shadow of the fort of the same name, forming one of a circle of fortifications around the key city of Namur, at the confluence of the rivers Sambre and Meuse, only about 3½ kilometres distant. Unlike the similar ring of forts around Liège, which held up the entire northern wing of the invading German Army in 1914, these surrendered by comparison without a struggle, when the French troops retired from the line of the Meuse after the Germans had forced the crossing at Dinant.

Just then, however, we were not bothered about this. It was good to have a clean little room—almost a cell—of one's own, and to know that the whole battalion was comfortably housed. All that was lacking, as we found at our first meal here, was bread, fresh meat and fresh vegetables. Several reasons for these shortages were current. One, not without some foundation in fact, was that our supply trains from the base were being robbed, whenever they stopped, by the starving Belgian civilian population. The battalion had to send a platoon for guards on these trains, but it was realized that first priority for food and all supplies must be the troops already on the bridgehead perimeter, east of the Rhine on a radius of twenty miles around Cologne. Messes on a battalion scale were started for officers, W.O.s, sergeants and corporals. This was, we thought, a good idea as it gave all concerned a real opportunity of meeting their fellows at last; hitherto quite an impossibility, except on a very limited scale.

Day followed day thus, and Christmas 1918 was upon us. On 22nd December I was detailed to take two water carts into Namur and fetch the Christmas beer from a brewery there, for which task I was lent Captain White's horse Digger, with his groom Pearson on a mount from the transport lines as an invaluable aide. Two transport section drivers handled the water carts; and, in view of the importance of our errand, the transport sergeant came too. We were therefore quite a little procession, and had no difficulty on entering Namur in finding the brewery, as there was no lack of laughing Belgians of both sexes to direct us. Digger behaved himself well under the watchful eye of Pearson, and only shied once, when an A.S.C. lorry driver blew his horn to find a way along a busy street. I nearly came off, but, fortunately, not quite. However, the experience made me yearn for the opportunity to learn to ride properly. All eyes were on the beer as it was put into the carts and, frankly, I was considerably embarrassed by the scathing glances and the suppressed remarks made by my personnel, at which the brewery people appeared quite scared, and I considered it desirable to get going on our way back to Malonne without more ado. Indeed, this beer was light yellow-looking stuff, and I shall never forget riding alongside the carts and listening to it slopping about inside whenever we encountered a rough patch in the road—a frequent occurrence, as all were in a truly shocking state after years of neglect. On arrival within the courtyard at the college, I was hard put to it in evading the many questions various officers put to me regarding the quality of the beer, and was glad when the carts departed to the nether regions. Indeed, it looked as though there would be little else to drink, as supplies of whisky, gin, etc., had just about dried up.

Christmas Day dawned cold and cloudy but not frosty, with the tolling bell near by waking everyone, although it was hardly light. I hadn't risen when my door opened and Dobbie, British Warm over pyjamas, stood by me holding out a flask and saying, 'Merry Christmas'. After a pause he added, with the ghost of a smile, 'what a hope!' He shivered in the cold morning air and pulled his British Warm closer around him as I took a generous swig from the proffered flask. He sat down on my bed as I spluttered, 'hey, Dobbie, thanks, same to you, but where did you get this stuff?'

Dobbie grinned and I saw a distinct twinkle in his eyes, although it wasn't properly light. In an acquaintance now of several months' standing, this was invariably the prelude to a description of an encounter with an attractive girl. Already I had listened to several such, the last concerning one of the actresses in the show we saw at La Louvière.

There was no doubt at all that he had a winning way with the fair sex. Indeed, I was envying him this facility when he began, 'd'you remember passing a decent hotel on the right-hand side when you went into Namur for the beer?' I thought, and I did—several. He described one in particular, and said that on the previous afternoon he had called there to see what it was like. He found the café cognac he ordered very expensive, but . . . and he was with his thoughts as I waited . . . 'She's marvellous. I just can't believe it. She's a countess, or her mother's a countess or something—lives in a damn great mansion on the hill on the right going into Namur . . . meeting her tomorrow evening . . .' He fixed his gaze on the floor, overcome for the moment, then, 'seriously, Read old boy, I've never met anyone like her before!' and I should have heard much more, but Fenton and Newman looked in and greeted us. They had towels round their necks and were *en route* for the ablutions. First Fenton and then Newman sniffed the air. 'What's going on? Hey?' Dobbie tried to get away, but failed, and the flask suffered accordingly. He didn't look too worried, though, and I deduced that his girl friend had obtained it for him. I was right, too. I went along to the ablutions.

At breakfast there was certainly a good blazing fire. Our colonel, Sir William Campion, Bart, M.P. and Major Constable came in together, beaming goodwill, and struck a Christmas note with their greetings, the latter saying that there was a considerable consignment of sloe gin and other stuff on its way to him. He expressed the fervent hope—which we echoed—that the Belgians hadn't pushed the cases off the train somewhere back along the line. I recall that we had bacon fried in some sort of batter, ration biscuits, tinned butter and marmalade.

In traditional fashion we waited on the men at dinner that Christmas Day—very enjoyable, too—but there was only corned beef stew enriched with McConochies, and some pretty shady potatoes which, we understood, the quartermaster had obtained at enormous expense. Plum duff followed. Most of it was mashed biscuit, by the taste. Still, there was plenty of beer, and, whatever its composition, it made the lads sing with a will. The harmony was good to hear, especially 'Sussex by the Sea'.

Then followed visits to the sergeants' and corporals' messes; hilarious affairs, where their hospitality was imbibed in bowls of the yellowish beer dispensed from great jugs borrowed from the college kitchens, so that we subalterns were content to get our heads down and sleep off the effects. Indeed, I remember little more of Christmas Day 1918 at Malonne except part of the evening concert and sing-song in the big lecture hall, where a talented lad from 'A' Company, just returned from leave, brought the packed house down with his rendering of what, to all of us then, was a new song, but soon to be famous: 'The Bells are Ringing for Me and My Gal'. There were so many encores that everyone soon had both refrain and words by heart, and, truth to tell, on that Christmas night they must have conjured up in the minds of many of those Sussex lads, far from their own firesides, pictures of home; of a return to civvy street; and of rose-tinted delights which the future might hold in store, now that the war was over and won. The now-bitter cold outside, the bully beef, the hard tack and their worn-out boots and socks were forgotten in the warm fug and the roaring choruses, where bells were ringing, for the nonce.

Came a morning when Newman and I, off duty, took a lift in the mess cart, across a landscape covered with a light mantle of powdery snow, into Namur where, we heard, the ordnance department had opened an officers' clothing depot; most opportunely, as both of us urgently required replacements for breeches, tunics and boots, all very much the worse for wear by reason of months of campaigning. Our underwear, moreover, was almost in rags. Incidentally, there had been a trickle of supplies of this nature for the men, and more were expected daily, but here again the rumour circulated that the Belgians were robbing the supply trains.

Our quest for this depot took us into several of the main streets, and in one of these we stopped of a sudden to look into the shop window of what was apparently, in more settled times, a good class men's outfitters. Now there was practically nothing on show, and we could see the interior of the shop itself—and, more particularly, the attractive girl, busily arranging the contents of a glass counter showcase. Seeing us, she rose to her full height, primly endeavouring to stifle a smile; but what intrigued both of us the more, was the sight of the little black bundle perched on her shoulder—the tiniest dog we had ever seen. Above the shop we read the legend 'Le Magasin Anglais'.

We looked at each other and the urge was irresistible. Into the shop we went. I emerged with a pair of braces, Newman with some studs. In my case, I took also from the Magasin Anglais, and back to Malonne, the mind-picture of a dark-haired girl with the tiny griffon, Mimi, on her shoulder. Notwithstanding the excitement of purchasing new breeches, jacket, boots, and so on, and blueing a month's pay in half an hour at the clothing depot later that morning, they were never far from my thoughts, either then or during the busy days that followed. This was something of a new experience, in my case, as they obtruded themselves upon a state of mind full of conjecture as to what the future might hold.

What I have written until now is a narrative of my infinitesimal part in the war; where actual hostilities had ceased, but where the victorious Allies now stood in armed might over a beaten and starving Germany. Nothing had been settled. There was no *peace*. As yet, only the meetings of the Armistice Commission were taking place weekly, we heard, at Spa, near the Belgian frontier. Indeed, Lieutenant Wilkins of 'A' Company had been sent with a sergeant's party to do guard duties on the train taking the German delegates, including Ebert and Rathenau, between Spa and Berlin. (Both were subsequently assassinated, I believe.)

Among the 'victors', however, the majority of all ranks of the British troops (unless they were Regulars, like Fenton) had but one thought in mind and one only—to get home and back to jobs in the promised 'land fit for heroes to live in', as Lloyd George described it. We didn't class ourselves in that category, but already we had heard of several cases, both of officers and men, who had gone on leave and had not returned. Apparently they had gone to the War Office with letters from their former employers asking for their immediate release. Obviously these had produced the desired result—demobilization—and it will not be difficult to realize the unsettling effect these stories had on all ranks generally. After Christmas and with the approach of the New Year, moreover, there was a tense feeling of speculation as to where, in our case the battalion was going next, and rumour was rife. It was in this atmosphere that Captain White went on leave. He didn't say much as he shook hands with us, but I recall that his eyes and ours were strangely bright. Instinctively we sensed that we were losing our Skipper, as he stepped up into the mess cart for Namur and England.

That evening, New Year's Eve, with the mail came a letter from the firm of engineers where I'd been an apprentice in 1914, with good wishes for Christmas and the New Year, and also inquiring about my intentions on return to civilian life, and so on. Particularly after Captain White's departure, this letter brought me down to earth, and the first serious thinking about what I proposed to do, if and when demobilization came. The firm's letter mentioned that the works was very busy, but carrying on under difficulties. They would be very pleased to see me at Leicester, as there would be openings for overseas representatives in their plans for post-war expansion.

That night in the mess turned out to be a memorable one. Major Constable's sloe gin and other supplies of spirits had arrived and were speedily put into circulation, effectively stifling, for the time being, all speculation as to my role in civil life. After dinner everyone had to sing a song, which I recall I only managed when my turn came (after remembering some lines at the last moment) in a cracked voice; but it seemed to go down rather well with the company. I never knew the name of it. I suppose it was from a war-time London revue. It went:

> When one has one—
> One wants one little one more
> One has one—one has two
> One has three or four!
> What did Gladstone say in 1884?
> When one has one little one—
> One wants a little one more!

Without the sloe gin, I doubt whether I'd have managed it at all.

As midnight approached, by happy invitation of Sir William Campion the mess was invaded by the college staff of monks in their dark brown cassocks, tonsures and girdles complete, who were regaled immediately with generous portions of Major Constable's rum punch. This successfully broke down any barriers to conversation, such as language, and inhibitions prescribed by the order, so that when the colonel called for 'Auld Lang Syne' at midnight, our guests joined hands among us with alacrity; although I'm afraid they were hardly prepared for the somewhat over-enthusiastic 'advancing' and 'receding' which followed for some minutes—a riot of whirling habits and cordage, flying sandals and red, perspiring faces. However, there was no doubt at all that they enjoyed it all enormously, and many were the expressions of mutual goodwill when they took their leaves, and one by one we departed to our own 'cells'.

On New Year's Day 1919 I was sent for at mid morning and told that the colonel wished to see me. Putting myself straight as well as I could, I duly presented myself (via the Battalion Orderly Room) outside the great man's sanctum, but was somewhat taken aback when the door opened and Dobbie emerged. When he saw me his surprised features slipped into the ghost of a smile and he muttered 'knock' as he passed me; which I did, and was told to come in.

Briefly the colonel put me at my ease at once, and after a short chat inquired whether I would be interested in trying for a permanent commission in the post-war army—more specifically, the Royal Sussex Regiment—and if so, he would be pleased to recommend me to boards, and so on. He was kind enough to say that since Soissons he had watched my progress, also that of several others, and that all reports he had received indicated that I had the making of a good Regular officer. While I tried to digest all this he said, 'by the way, Read, you remember that Boche you jumped on near Gheluwe? Did you know that between Division and Corps the so-and-so escort lost him? We never heard whether they found him,' he added, whimsically. Then, 'what d'you think?'

It was then, as I stood there facing him as he sat back in his chair, that I realized with stunning suddenness that he, and his kind, and I lived in two almost completely different worlds. As in a dream I heard him say that the 2nd Battalion was probably going to Bermuda, while I was thinking of the letter I'd just received from the firm. I had no private means, which were considered necessary for peace-time soldiering as an officer; neither had I, on the other hand, the ghost of an idea of what salary or wage I could command in civilian life. For a moment or two I played with the idea of accepting the colonel's offer to sponsor me and carry on soldiering somehow—and to blazes with all the snags!

Then the cold facts of life took charge and I heard myself thanking Sir William, but that with great regret I must try to make my career with my firm and couldn't therefore take advantage of

the opportunity he had offered me. At a complete loss for further
words I stopped, to hear him say kindly, 'well, Read, of course
you know best, but I'm sorry,' and with that I saluted and withdrew, feeling anything but pleased with myself.

Outside the Battalion Orderly Room Dobbie buttonholed me—
how had I got on? He conjectured, rightly, that our interviews
were for the same purpose. I said that I couldn't afford peace-time
soldiering, and it was then that he told me he had other ideas,
too, which were going to make his fortune within a few years. An
uncle of his was a banker who, apparently, had found the secret
of quick money-making.

Months afterwards I learned from Dobbie that his uncle's name
was Farrow. One day in 1920, as I wrestled with export bills of
lading, our typist brought in an evening paper: the front-page
headlines ran 'Bank Crash—Farrows Suspend Payment'. Farrow's
Bank did crash, and, indeed, presaged the bursting of the short
post-war prosperity bubble in Britain. A general panic set in during
which, within a matter of days, practically the whole of my firm's
overseas machinery orders were cancelled. Two hundred men
were either sacked or put on short time. I was lucky to have a
job at all, and visions of being the company's representative in
South America vanished into limbo. It was then, at odd moments,
that I wondered how the 2nd Battalion of the Royal Sussex
Regiment was faring in Bermuda . . . but I digress!

As we walked away together, Dobbie dismissed the subject of
our futures for one of more immediate import; to wit, that he had
a date with his new girl friend for that afternoon and evening in
Namur, but couldn't go because he was remaining 'in' for Captain
Peskett, who would be dining out. Would I go into Namur and
make apologies and explain to her? So that I would identify her
in the hotel foyer, he described her yet again. As it was obvious
that he was treating the solution of his problem as a matter of the
utmost urgency, I undertook the task with some diffidence, as I
recalled acting in a similar capacity at the instance of my old
colleague Archie Brown at Rouen—with unexpected results! However, on reflection I was intrigued at the opportunity thus offered
of appraising Dobbie's new conquest, and therefore it was with
considerable interest that I entered the hotel that afternoon and

somewhat hurriedly took stock of the half-dozen or so occupants of the various chairs in the foyer.

I need not have worried. She stood up, obviously at the approach of a British uniform, but the flush of welcome paled into apprehension as I went towards her. Over the years I have forgotten her name, but I greeted her in very bad French—so bad, indeed, that in explaining how terribly sorry he was, I gave her the impression that at least an accident had befallen him. However, her concern served to accentuate her attractiveness, and mentally I conceded that Dobbie had indeed picked a winner, as I made renewed efforts to straighten things out. Having assured her that he would be there at the same time the following afternoon, we laughed at our bad English and French over drinks for half an hour or so, when I judged that it was time for me to make my exit as gracefully as I could, having about reached the limit of questions and answers of general conversation. Moreover, I didn't think it fair to Dobbie to encroach, although the temptation was great and the company of this striking, golden-haired girl more than congenial.

Outside again, with my thoughts a jumble of conflicting queries, my steps carried me towards the shopping centre without any definite object: and here I found myself, whereas really I should have been making my way back to Malonne. Already the winter daylight was fading, and lights appeared here and there in the windows along the busy street. I came to the crossroads, and there, almost on the corner, I saw again the brightly lit window of the Magasin Anglais. Probably it was the heady influence of the afternoon's events, but I crossed the road with a well defined intent. Sure enough, there she was, standing behind the showcase counter. As she looked up I saw that the little dog was not on her shoulder. She looked in my direction, hard; then, hurriedly, past me into the now-darkening street, and I knew that she remembered. I went in, completely at a loss for something to buy, and inquired where her little dog was . . .

At eight on that clear and frosty evening I saw her come from the door at the side of the shop. While waiting for her I'd eaten an omelette of sorts at the nearest hotel—at a fearful price, but no matter. We walked up the long winding road, uphill to the famous Citadelle, and from the ramparts looked down on the sea of lights of Namur below, which picked out, also, the bridge and the banks of the united rivers Sambre and Meuse, on which the clear light of a now-rising moon danced and sparkled.

Her name was Julie. She lived with her uncle and aunt, as both her parents had died during the war, and her home had been at a village near Dinant, the name of which I have forgotten. This she told me on the way back to her house, and I sensed the faltering in her voice at a recollection doubtless of extreme poignancy. I did not pursue the subject further then, as even by the moonlight I could see her tears. We walked on, silent for some moments, and when next she spoke we found ourselves almost beside the shop. Then, taking my hand, she invited me to come in and meet her uncle and aunt, so naturally and with such a sweet smile that it seemed downright churlish to demur, although my surprise was great.

The tiny dog rushed to greet Julie and was gathered, whimpering joyfully, into her arms as I followed her through the dimly lit passage, or hall, at the side of the shop, into the warm and brightly lit quarters at the rear. Her uncle and aunt, both obviously relieved at her return, rose and greeted me cordially in what was, however, a mutual summing-up, continued as we were seated around the big stove, while Julie, having removed her heavy coat and her headscarf, shook the mane of her dark hair free and bustled about intent on serving some refreshment. Now and again our eyes met happily as I endeavoured, in atrocious French, to make conversation with the good folks—a very worthy couple, in their middle fifties, as far as I could judge. They told me that they had no children and that their niece had lived with them since soon after the Germans came in 1914. I think, perhaps, that they would have told me more, but at a quick glance at each other, and then at Julie, they changed the subject.

Thus we sat and talked, and I drank their health in the wine which Julie served. It may seem a strange statement to make, but there was no doubt about it: in those last few minutes I had stumbled upon what was, for me, a totally new experience—a feeling of having found something precious and worthwhile; a contentment, or an exceptional happiness that I had not previously known.

Making my way back to Malonne by the Vicinale tramway, which ran along the roadside, standing on the rear platform of one of the string of war-worn bumping and swaying cars, I'm certain that I couldn't think clearly—until I remembered, with some apprehension, that I hadn't signed the mess book as 'dining out' that evening, and I was expecting a ticking off when I entered the mess ante-room. It was, however, a worried-looking Newman who rose and assailed me with 'where the blazes have you been? We've all been hunting for you ever since tea. Dobbie told us you'd gone to Namur. Have you seen him? He's going frantic—looks in here every few minutes to see if you've come back. Did you see his girl friend?'

I told him that I had, whereupon he suspected the worst of me. We sat down and I told him the rest, concluding that, as I thought I'd be orderly officer on the morrow, I'd told Julie I couldn't see her in the evening. Newman laughed. 'A good job you didn't—come and look at orders!' We did, and I read that I was to take two lorry-loads of men to Brussels at eight the next morning on three days' leave; whereat I made Newman promise he'd go into Namur and tell Julie, and then borrowed nearly all the money he'd got.

Dobbie appeared and, having put his mind at rest, I borrowed the equivalent of five pounds from him, telling him he'd get it back sometime! Then we three had a nightcap, and so to bed.

Our first call after moving off the next morning was Brigade H.Q., where we joined four more waiting lorries, two each from the Queen's and the Loyal North Lancashires. A staff captain appeared and, detailing me to take charge of the convoy of six, handed me a typed time schedule for the trip. I saluted and did my best to disguise my disgust at landing this responsibility. By the way, there were two officers from each regiment, and before we moved off I delegated some of it to them.

We went via Gembloux and Wavre—names which I had last seen when reading at school about the battle of Waterloo—and before midday parked as directed in the square in front of the Gare du Nord which, in those days, was opposite the entrance to the Rue Neuve and at right-angles to the Palace Hôtel block.

Before turning the lads loose on the town, I paraded them and briefed them as lucidly as I could, putting them on their honour to behave themselves, remember always who they were, and, above all, to turn up on time for the return. And here I recall raising a real laugh among them as I looked hard at the Army Service Corps drivers, who joined in. As I dismissed them I thought how smart these rosy-cheeked lads looked, most of them no older than nineteen. They didn't let me down, either; I didn't get any complaints, and every man turned up on time for the return journey.

Meanwhile, Brussels beckoned! The six of us looked across at the Palace Hôtel and made our way there, with subalterns' thirsts.

Here I am very conscious of recounting occurrences that, in themselves, may seem unutterably boring in an endeavour to paint a picture typical of the experiences of the many thousands of young men then serving who had the good luck to reach 11th November 1918 still on their own two feet, and more or less sound in wind and limb. The point I would make is that the majority had lived for several years monkish, unnatural lives at a critical period—the youth to manhood stage.

Now both they, and also the civilian populations of Belgium and north-eastern France, who had suffered cruelly under the German occupation, felt a great bursting of the bonds, and the Brussels scene after the Armistice provided a typical example. After the first jubilant days following liberation, a great hate of everything German, and particularly of anyone suspected of having collaborated with them, developed. We had heard of many cases of villages making public examples of women who had slept with German soldiers, by cutting off their hair. One had been pointed out to me. For this reason we were somewhat startled at our first sight of what was going on at the Palace Hôtel and, as we were to see, at many other 'hot spots'.

Doubtless accounts exist of this period and of experiences such as mine, some of which certainly, in retrospect, had their amusing overtones, but I have never come across them. I hope I may be forgiven, therefore, if I presume to write for the record here.

Young Morris of 'B' Company, my own colleague from the battalion on this trip, insisted on setting up the first round of drinks, and took the lead as we entered by an enormously long, mirrored foyer, to our surprise crowded with red-tabbed Canadian and British Brass Hats, including, we thought, a corps commander, a major-general and several brigadiers. Either circulating or seated among them we discerned a more than generous sprinkling of smartly dressed lady friends. The nearest of them summed us up with a few expert professional glances as we managed to seat ourselves at a table. Obviously they decided we were not worth bothering about, for they concentrated anew on their Canadian majors who, although the day was quite young, were having an uproarious time and spending freely—how freely we were soon to discover. We considered ourselves to be fairly broad-minded, but realized with a faint sense of disapproval that, in the oldest profession in the world, there was no discrimination. Doubtless, only a few weeks since they had been quite as busy with German officers.

For some minutes, as no waiter appeared, we were quite content to watch the scene, especially as one girl, wearing a brigadier's hat, was now stroking his balding cranium from her perch on his lap. It was then that I raised the question of where we were going to stay and, getting to my feet, picked my way through the throng, closely followed by Morris, to the reception desk. Here we managed to book what we were told were the last two single rooms, on the fifth or sixth floor, at a pretty stiff price—but, at any rate, we felt that we had secured a base near the lorries. Returning to the table, we found the others arguing with a cadaverous-looking waiter about the astronomical prices being charged for the few miserable varieties of drinks they were offering. We were beginning to attract attention, and therefore, when a move was suggested, we all trooped out thankfully, hoping that prices elsewhere were very, very much lower. As we made our way across the square we calculated that the Canadians were paying at least the equivalent of £6 for a round of four drinks. From scraps of conversation overheard, we gathered that they were on leave from the perimeter of the Cologne bridgehead, twenty miles east of that city. We didn't know just then, of course, that the 34th Division was about to relieve them there, but I thought of them when the Canadian unit we relieved handed over to us their schedule of on-the-spot fines levied on the inhabitants for evading the curfew then in force, or for diverse other offences. These varied from fifty to one hundred marks, and a mark then was worth a shilling, although it plummeted very shortly afterwards. This had proved a real bonanza for them, and we carried on with the system joyfully for a week or so. Fenton (in temporary command of our company, as Captain White had not returned from leave) started a fund with the proceeds to purchase extras for the men. Then a Rhine Army order put a stop to the system and substituted trial by military courts at Unit H.Q.s—a real time-wasting procedure, both for us and for the victims, who generally lost a day's work in attending.

It may be of interest to recall, also, that the wealthier German civilians complained bitterly that Canadian officers had 'borrowed' their cars for trips either to Paris or Brussels. These had disappeared without trace. We didn't waste much sympathy on the owners just then, as generally both they and their wives looked grossly fat and well fed, while the ordinary folk were really starving.

But we were crossing the square in front of the Gare du Nord, actually to the Hôtel Cécil on the further side.

Here our four friends, following our example, booked rooms and, to be frank, Morris and I wished at the time that we had waited, for this hotel was not on such a pretentious scale as the Palace, yet more than adequate for our needs. Our drinks, though terribly expensive, were about half the Palace price, and we actually saw a British captain sitting at a nearby table eating what we were pretty certain was intended to be bacon and eggs—a cheering sight. The upshot of all this was that while in Brussels we had all our meals here, albeit at ruinous cost.

We found that our lorry park was Place Rogier, the approach road Boulevard de Jardin Botanique. On the corner of this and the much narrower Rue Neuve stood a department store, Au Bon Marché. A little further on, debouching also into the Boulevard opposite the far corner of Place Rogier, was another wide thorough-fare: the newly named Boulevard Adolphe Max, after the famous burgomaster of Brussels who had gained worldwide renown for his efforts to alleviate the pressure of the German jackboot on the inhabitants of the city—and, indeed, of all Belgium. Both streets led into the heart of the old city and invited our inspection. This we proceeded with, first purchasing a pre-1914 street map and guide at a bookseller's at the head of Adolphe Max. In this manner we made a first acquaintance with many historic buildings and centres of Belgian life, on the way finding many shops, hotels, cafés and 'spots', which now might well be termed 'joints' and which I recall with a certain nostalgia—Le Chatham, Le Merry Grill, Le Bristol, etc. For sheer gaiety, blazing lights and women in the mass, Café Madrid, four or five floors, each with a band dispensing ragtime and *le danse* well into the small hours. In the maze of side streets and alleys around it, seamy 'hotels' catered for the steady stream of soldiers and others led to them by the girls who had picked them up in the Madrid or elsewhere. Generally accommodation for half an hour only was required.

Certainly the atmosphere for a soldier on leave in that part of Brussels was somewhat infectious, especially as many estab-lishments already were employing touts to distribute handbills or cartes-de-visite advertising their specialities, the better to partici-pate in what promised to be a bumper harvest after the lean war years. On this note, catching the mood, we parted with our friends for the nonce with a cheery 'see you at breakfast!'

Left to ourselves, Morris and I explored anew, and in many

instances enthused, but sightseeing was very tiring, and thankfully we sat down in an unpretentious looking café featuring *le thé Anglais*. Here, over our tea, we learned something of each other. Morris told me that he was a master at a West Country boys' school and that he meant to get married to a Bristol girl when next he went on leave. I noted mentally that he seemed to know where he was going, whereas I just hadn't an idea as yet, and I spread my street map over the teacups to forget the vexed and nagging question of my own future in trying to locate the house of some Belgian refugee friends of my family at Eastbourne. This presented no difficulty, as the Avenue de la Reine was a main road leading toward the Royal Park at Laeken from near the Gare du Nord. I wished to find number 126, and we decided to look for it on the following morning, in daylight, as we noted that already dusk was descending on Brussels and that lights were appearing everywhere as we made our leisurely way back to the Cécil, very hungry. On the way we took in a quick look at the Café Madrid, finding it most amusing. However, I found myself measuring this sort of thing against my new-found yardstick— Julie—and suddenly ached for her company. Apparently Morris's reaction was somewhat similar when assailed by commercially minded young womanhood in the mass. His thoughts must have been of Bristol.

Over our dinner—a steak which probably originated in a British Army horse, though Morris assured me it was a mule—we yarned a while with the two Queen's boys who also had returned. We all agreed that we couldn't stand the financial strain for more than another day and night so, feeling really tired and apprehensive of spending yet more money that day, we decided to retire to our respective couches.

Passing through the Palace Hôtel foyer once more, we noted the complete absence of Brass Hats and an influx of lowlier ranks—two or three pips, with a few crowns. Getting our keys from reception, we stood waiting by the near-by gate for the elevator to appear. When it did, two laughing and attractive girls stepped from it. Seeing us, they engaged us in conversation very much to the point, the import being that they were quite prepared to venture aloft again with us under certain conditions; but we just didn't feel that way, neither could we afford their company, and with a *'peut-être demain, cherie!'* we parted on a friendly note. Doubtless they were soon paired off again in the foyer.

With morning light I was roused by Morris with 'sorry, old man, but they brought me two lots of coffee and rolls. Care to come along and help me out with it?' I went with him and I did, but on returning to my own room, quite refreshed, I found that two *cafés complêts* had been put on the bedside table. Evidently the maid had seen me, for as I was getting back into bed she knocked and entered with a cheery *'bonjour'* as she crossed the room and drew the curtains. Then, turning and looking surprisedly across the now-lighted bed, she inquired after Madame, whether she had *'bien dormi'*, and bustled out about her round with a knowing yet friendly smile—whereupon I went and routed out Morris, who had gone to sleep again.

Subsequently, over breakfast with the others at the Cécil, he quoted, aptly, I thought, the old saying that one might as well be hung for a sheep as a lamb, for when we recounted our experience it was quite obvious that they didn't believe us for one moment, especially as one pair definitely had sampled the fleshpots—and looked it.

A visit to the lorries and a word with the Red Cap patrol there, and we made our way down the busy Rue d'Aerschot at the side of the Gare du Nord and soon found the crossing with Avenue de la Reine, where the house I was seeking was situated. After checking numbers we made our way towards the Royal Park of Laeken and, after passing the Consulate of a South American republic, found our quarry, which was undamaged and occupied. In fact, it appeared to be in quite good condition, and having seen this I determined to write to our Belgian friends at home to this effect. This I did, from the Palace Hôtel, while Morris watched the world go by. What I didn't know at the time was that Mima and Guilbert's father was a high-ranking Belgian general who, incidentally, commanded a division on the combined Allied offensive of 29th September with the Second British Army in Flanders, under King Albert. I believe that General Wambersy's men captured the village of West Roosbeek, among others, north-east of Ypres in these operations. He was much decorated; by the British with a C.M.G., having gained previously a D.S.O. My letter home brought a most kind invitation to visit him at Düsseldorf, where he was then commanding the Belgian garrison on the Rhine bridgehead there. I thought he was a fine man, exceptional in every sense of the word, and it was obvious that he had suffered much since 1914, including the loss of his wife, then a refugee in Northern France, in 1917. To a 'wart' of a second lieutenant he was kindness itself—but I am getting off course, I fear.

Apart from finding the house in Avenue de la Reine, only two other incidents remain in my memory as occurring that day—or, indeed, of our stay in Brussels. First, the very nasty explosion of a delayed German booby trap at the old Midi station; second of entering a crowded café restaurant and, while looking for a table, coming face to face with our colonel in an alcove at the far end, with a girl sitting on his knee. She was stroking his thinning gingery hair, and I don't know which of us registered the greater surprise or embarrassment at a most difficult situation. In retrospect, however, I think he extricated himself extremely well by remarking, as unhurriedly as circumstances permitted, 'I've told this lady several times that I'm married, Read, but she seems to like me all the better!' At this we all shared in the general amusement caused by this remark; including the girl, who kissed the balding patch on his head delightedly. However, we begged his pardon for intruding and withdrew on what we considered quite a friendly note, but on reaching the busy street outside agreed to 'forget' the incident completely. This we did.

On the morning of our return to Malonne, I have said that every man turned up at the lorries—well before time, in fact—and before we started I thanked them. *En route*, however, I confirmed what we subalterns had suspected: that their plight was identical with ours in that 'all our money was spent', as the old song has it, and that the majority were actually very relieved to get into the lorries again. One memory only I retain of the actual journey— our convoy passing the signpost 'Quatre-Bras', where I recalled that Wellington held up the advancing French under Napoleon's Marshal Ney on 16th June 1815, two days before Waterloo. As we jolted over the pavé, sadly needing repair in many places, I thought of the many generations of British soldiers who had tramped these Flanders roads in years gone by: of Marlborough's men; of the first Battle Honour on the Colours of my old (Leicestershire) regiment, the 17th of Foot—'Namur 1695'. Should we be, I wondered, the last of them.

So the days quickly passed. I saw Julie frequently, and betimes in the house talked a great deal with her uncle and aunt while her tiny griffon, Mimi, sat on my shoulder and, at Julie's command, licked my ears, to everyone's amusement. There was a great dearth of goods to sell in the shop, especially of a reliable type. They showed me that what they had was mainly of German ersatz material of some kind, actually the fore-runners of man-made fibres, devised under the stress of war shortage by an ingenious and resourceful enemy. I discussed with her uncle the possibility of getting goods from England, in which I should have been only too pleased to assist if I could have been of any use. Indeed, I had written already to several Leicester friends on the matter, but the one reply I'd received to date advised me that stringent regulations had been put into operation which rendered any scheme such as I had in mind quite impracticable. Incidentally, while doing this I realized again my lack of a solid business background common to so many of the men of my current acquaintance, and thoughts of this kind, especially when I looked at Julie and saw how capable she was, induced a sense of depression hard to shake off.

And then orders came for our division to move to Germany and the Army of the Rhine. I heard about this on returning from a mounted 'paper chase' across the local countryside, organized by the colonel and the transport officer, doubtless for the entertainment of senior officers of our own and neighbouring regiments. In this diversion we subalterns were mounted on mules, with blankets for saddles. I suppose I was very fortunate in having Solomon, veteran of our company transport, for my nag; moreover, I had the real assistance of a second lieutenant newly posted to our company—one Dawkins—a swarthy thickset lad with the legs, hands and 'seat' of a born rider. We chummed up on this occasion—actually, we lost the main field, but it would be wrong, perhaps, to say that we did this deliberately. We lagged behind in the first instance as he showed me how to approach a gate, open it, pass through and then secure it again without dismounting.

Indeed, he taught me much, and I was grateful for his help. Solomon didn't move very fast, but, as a reward for not bucking and throwing me over his head, I gave him a packet of Woodbines which I borrowed from Pearson, and which he ate, packet and all, with relish. Dawkins, I recall, was very amused, and I told him how, when Solomon had delivered the rations at bullet- and shrapnel-swept Parrain Farm four months previously, I had seen Sergeant-Major Slaughter give him some. I showed him, also, Solomon's two wound scars received on active service. He was a dear old mule, and should now be enjoying their Valhalla, if there is one!

With the news of our imminent move, all was bustle, clearing up and preparation. A considerable draft arrived and was apportioned to companies: a mixed lot, but mostly young soldiers. We soon learned that many of the older men considered they had been unfairly treated in being sent overseas again, as they thought the war was over and looked surprised when we suggested that there might be a lot to do yet. But perhaps they had a point.

Dobbie and I managed to get into Namur late one afternoon to bid our girl friends what we hoped were temporary adieux, and on the way there discussed the possibilities of getting leave from the Rhine. Dobbie thought it would rank as local leave and thus would not prejudice our home leave prospects. In the event, I will admit that I was considerably shaken, and returned to Malonne with many conflicting thoughts which produced an effect of acute depression, difficult to dispel. However, when I encountered Dobbie in the mess late that night I saw at once by his manner that he was a very worried man indeed, his explanation almost driving Julie from my mind in the consideration of his problem which, at first, I didn't take seriously. Apparently his 'countess' had told of her fixed intention of coming to Germany with him, and that she could get a special permit to enter that country. Until, however, he stressed that she intended to come on *our* train, I was inclined to treat the matter lightly; but, should the girl be serious in her intention, Dobbie would find himself in real trouble. What, he asked, should he do? He slept badly, if at all, and looked it when we met over breakfast; a somewhat hurried meal, as there was much to do, and during the morning we learned that we were entraining at Namur on the following evening.

Outside it was now bitterly cold, the wide landscape under a deep mantle of frozen whiteness except in the college quadrangle, where the many comings and goings prior to our departure had hard-packed the snow into a dirty brown, half-cleared tracks criss-crossing it. That night we gave a farewell dinner in the mess for our clerical hosts, a very enjoyable affair which ended with 'Auld Lang Syne' again. They had been very good to us there.

By nine that next frost-bound night, the battalion had filled to overflowing the long troop train standing beside a platform of planking constructed and conveniently left by our recent enemies, whose expertise at moving troops was well known to us. This was situated, as I recall, about 250 yards from, and to the rear of, the main Namur station—in the goods sidings, in fact (or, in Second War parlance, the marshalling yard).

Silence reigned almost the length of the train in a darkness complete save for the reflection of the glow in the sky from the lights of Namur, and no one seemed to know when we were going to move. Following the departure from Malonne, the march to the siding and the actual entraining, everyone (with perhaps one exception, as I shall try to relate) had two objects in view: a little warmth and then precious sleep, if at all possible.

However, on the staging outside our compartment, five of us—Newman, Dawkins, Hagger, Reddaway and myself—stood alternately stamping our feet and flailing our arms in an endeavour to hold off the bitter cold that was chilling us through to the marrow. Within our compartment was Dobbie—with his countess! Between our stampings and flailings we blessed them heartily, and it seemed that the cold was now so intense that we could hear distinctly the cracking of the frost; but, beyond crowding into the kit-laden corridor, already overburdened, what else could we do for the nonce? The others were hoping that the farewells would be brief, but I kept my fears to myself in view of Dobbie's confidences.

For, having seen our men bedded, as it were, for the night, the six of us had settled down in our compartment with a comfortable sense of duty done. Dobbie seemed quite relaxed but, like us, very tired. I had just snuggled down into the far corner facing away from the engine and was already dozing when it happened. First one crack and then another in quick succession, as stones hit the frosted window near my head. Others followed, and instinctively I rose and let down the window, cursed by my colleagues for letting in the icy blast as I peered out—and there, dimly, right below, I saw her face looking up at me.

What else could I do? What else, indeed, could Dobbie do? together we hauled up the half-frozen and now weeping girl—a pitiful sight—as Newman produced and shone his torch to assist us. Her good looks and attractiveness had forsaken her completely. As she buried her head in Dobbie's greatcoat he self-consciously strove to comfort her, removing her gloves, wet now with thawed snow through groping for the stones, and chafing her frozen hands with his own the while. We looked at one another, and without speaking stole quietly away one by one, leaving them alone. Just how she had found her way to where I saw her, after locating Dobbie, I'll never know.

A Belgian railwayman appeared, with one of those great lamps with a huge circular glass front that his kind used to carry, and I asked him if he knew when we were due to start. Indicating the head of the train with his lamp held aloft, about fifty yards distant, I saw that, as yet, we had no locomotive. Then he looked at his watch and shrugged characteristically. I gathered that the engine might appear shortly before midnight. Still a long wait in store for we poor unfortunates! I communicated my news to them. Then, listening to the groans which followed, I had an idea. Telling the four that I was going to see a friend in Namur (Newman soon told them who the friend was), I hared off at the double along the tracks, across, to and through the station, and out into the street, which was practically empty. After a breather I doubled again, and at least my exertions had restarted my

circulation and warmed my arms and legs. Another breather—
when I concluded that I must have been slightly mad to attempt
what I was then doing—another long double, and I was knocking
at the side door of the Magasin Anglais.

It was thus that I saw Julie again for a precious, bitter-sweet
ten minutes; but I had to go, and kissed her uncle and aunt French
fashion. I lifted up little Mimi and put her on Julie's shoulder.
And then I saw her tears. I couldn't stop my own, either. I held
her close once more and dashed into the street, pulling the door
shut behind me. Then I ran, so emotionally upset, however, that
I had to slow down to calm myself as I approached the station
again, by now apprehensive of the certainty of a court martial if,
by any chance, the train had gone without me. I now had to be
quite careful, too, in getting through the station without attracting
too much attention, as I observed several Military Police on the
brightly lit platforms and around the R.T.O.'s office. Perhaps a
leave train from Boulogne was expected.

By making quite a detour, however, I managed to reach the
goods sidings unobserved, but to some extent lost my bearings
owing to the semi-darkness and the fact that one line of freight
cars looked like any other. Because of this, I thought for some
moments that the worst had happened, but to my great relief I
almost stumbled on the end staging of the platform beside the
train which was still there—and silent. I recall sitting down on a
snow-covered pile of sleepers to collect my wits and calm down;
also, of a sudden, wondering whether Dobbie's girl friend was still
there. I had forgotten them completely (and, indeed, nearly everything else, I discovered) for about three-quarters of an hour.

With breath regained, I decided to avoid the platform and made
my way slowly on the far side of the train, to where I heard voices,
concluding that they were those of my colleagues. At the next gap
between two carriages, in spite of the corridor connection I almost
decided to try a short cut by dodging underneath, but thought
better of it, luckily. About fifty yards further on I came to the
head of the train, where I found two railwaymen standing with
lanterns by the buffers. They were somewhat surprised at my
appearance, but that was all, and I greeted them as cheerfully as
I could. Then one of the men raised his lantern aloft and waved

it into the distance ahead. After a minute or so I heard the noise of escaping steam and then, gradually, the huge bulk of two locomotives came into view, coupled and partly thrown into relief by the glow from the fire-boxes. Ever since I was a little boy the coupling up of engines to trains had had a peculiar fascination for me: I think because of the man who stood between the buffers. Would he get squashed, I used to wonder. I thought about this again as I stood there and watched the tender of the nearest engine loom larger and larger until contact and coupling were made. I suppose that a certain reaction following my recent experience had set in, but I went first to the cab of the nearest locomotive and then to the second, distributing cigarettes, which the firemen stuck behind their ears while they shovelled. The drivers wiped their hands on waste and lit up, while I filled my pipe and stood on the footplate of the leading engine getting well warmed. The two railmen came up, too, for a warm, and we had quite a chat in shocking French and funny English—but very amusing and friendly. Troubles forgotten, and catching the faint scent of Julie's perfume on my coat sleeve, as I descended I wished them good luck and made my way back along the platform; encountering, to my surprise, Major Warren, Captains Peskett and Bridger, and a major (presumably the R.T.O.), in a group. My colleagues weren't there, but my explanation of watching the coupling up satisfied them. Had I appeared from between the carriages, though, it would not have done so.

I gathered that we expected to start in about ten minutes' time and at that I quickened my steps. More by luck than judgement, I opened a second door to find Newman and the rest in our compartment, in deep conversation with Dobbie, who sat with his girl friend beside him, silent, but looking by the light of our torches much better, and now quite composed. She smiled at me as I appeared and told them that we were starting in ten minutes. Dobbie turned and repeated this to her. To the amazement of all of us, she suddenly stood up and told him, and then us, 'soon, I come to Germany! Now . . .'. She was at a loss for English words, but we gathered she was returning to her home that evening. She put on her gloves and pulled her fur stole tightly about her shoulders. Bidding us a collective '*à bientôt*', and with a really

493

wonderful smile, she waited for Dobbie to open the carriage door—the same one by which she had been hauled up. He seemed for the moment deep in thought, however, so I did the needful, but was pretty concerned at what I dimly saw outside. I had a hurried word with Dobbie, who by now had told us that he was taking his girl as far as the station. It was obvious to us all that his relief at this solution of his problem, however temporary, was great, although he tried his hardest not to show it. When I told him that about a quarter of the battalion were relieving themselves along the freight cars opposite, before we got started, he just said he would risk it and trust to the darkness. With that he stepped down onto the tracks and stood waiting to help her as I handed her out. As she passed me she kissed me lightly on the cheek, and a moment later they were gone.

Left to ourselves, we sat and speculated as to whether Dobbie would return before the train started, the tension increasing sharply as, with a tremendous jolt, followed by others, the long train moved. As it did we faintly saw Dobbie's face on the outside of the frost-covered window. He was hanging on, and two of rushed to help him and haul him in—quite a business, in fact, as he had to be manoeuvred through the lowered carriage window after we had removed his British Warm.

When he had blown on his hands for a few moments and recovered his breath, his face now smeared with a sooty mess picked up from the door or window, I ventured the question, 'all right?' just as our train, having at last cleared the maze of points, halted, panting, for a few moments by a brightly lit signal box before getting on to the main line. He was silent for some moments, and then his face slipped into the semblance of his old grin—as it had not done for days past—when he said quietly, 'Read, old chap, you'd never guess where I left her'.

I told him that after tonight I'd no longer be surprised at anything. 'Where?' 'Outside the "*Dames*"—in the station.' He was silent again, deep in thought, then, 'd'you know, I really think *that* was her trouble at the finish. She saw suddenly that her idea wouldn't work—I mean—of sticking on the train with us.' Newman now interposed, 'what was she going to do for clothes? She hadn't any luggage—a bag, or anything, not even a toothbrush.' This was true, but Dobbie hadn't thought of it. Neither had I, but just then the train started again and really got going. Somehow we all found that we couldn't argue the point any longer, and sleep just overtook us, Dobbie first of all—he was all in.

I awoke and rubbed sleep-filled eyes. We had stopped at a station. There were voices—strange—and I rubbed the condensation from the window near my had with a piece of newspaper that had contained sandwiches. The voices came from portly figures in smart blue peaked caps and buttoned greatcoats of the same hue.

It was getting light, and as I watched I saw that it was a large station, brightly lit and somehow raised above the houses around, which, in spite of the snow, had an air of ordered neatness.

The train restarted very slowly, and as the station platforms and buildings glided by, I read the legend 'Aachen'.

We were in Germany, and I dozed off again as fresh snowflakes melted on the windows. When next I woke the January sun was piercing ever so faintly a leaden snow-laden sky, and the north-easterly wind was blowing the powdery snow into drifts as the long troop train carrying the 4th Battalion of the Royal Sussex Regiment rolled slowly over the great Hohenzollern Brücke river crossing at Cologne to its next duty—*die Wacht am Rhein*.

APPENDIX I

IN 1914 I was an apprentice at the old established engineering firm of Gimson & Co. (Leicester) Ltd., ironfounders; makers of steam engines and boilers and, latterly, makers of boot- and shoe-making machinery. The head of the firm was Mr Josiah Gimson and his brothers were also directors. When, as a schoolboy of fifteen, I resisted the sound advice, both of my parents and head of my school, to stay on and get an honours pass in what was then known as the 'Cambridge Senior' examination (as a prelude, perhaps, to a career in a local bank, or one of the lower divisions of the Civil Service), my mother, to whom I'd expressed my determination to be an engineer, wrote to Mr Gimson, an old friend of her father's. The answer came, 'send him along', and I went in the spring of 1911.

The Secretaries of the Leicester and Eastbourne Y.M.C.A.s found me lodgings in a house near the London Road station, invariably full of the lower strata of the theatrical profession who moved weekly, generally on Sunday mornings, but on occasions late on Saturday nights, after the second house. Both here and at the works, the sheltered life I'd lived at Eastbourne received some very severe shocks, although in retrospect these experiences no doubt helped me to cope with problems and trials which lay ahead. However, I did wonder at odd times whether the Leicester Y.M.C.A. had vetted my lodging, and whether the Secretary of the Eastbourne Y.M.C.A. had any idea of the seamy, sleazy, alcoholic 'Heartbreak House' in which his good offices had deposited me.

At the works my fellow apprentices, and, I fear, a good many of the men, thought me quite mad to have left a good home in a posh seaside resort like Eastbourne for the dingy cobbled streets of red-brick terraced houses, with similarly uninspiring shopping areas, constituting industrial Leicester. Actually, there were many times during those first months when, privately, I agreed with them, but, having made my bed, I could do little else but lie on it and put as cheerful a face on things as I could.

I had been assigned by Mr Gimson to the fast-growing department making shoe machinery, but, as far as I know, my slender link with him did not result in any preferential treatment. Indeed, he never spoke to me again after my initial five-minute interview.

Occasionally, however, he would walk slowly along the workshop floors, peering right and left over gold pincenez secured by a thin gold chain fix, in turn—we thought—to an ear. He was a definite character. His piercing glances—accentuated by his grizzled side-burns, drooping moustache, and ruddy features beneath a black bowler hat—were complemented by a longish dark tailcoat with poacher pockets from which the tip of a red silk handkerchief often peeped, a waistcoat crossed by a gold watch chain, white wing collar and stock, and trousers of a distinctly Victorian cut—without turnups, of course. On one occasion I seem to recall having seen spats; but, in any case, these were general wear for men in winter weather at that time.

Regularly his carriage, with cockaded coachman, would set him down at the works at 08.30 hours, and took him home at 12.30, but in 1914 a chauffeur-driven French 'Metallurgique' car took the place of this.

Mr Gimson lived at Stoneygate House, in that residential district around the London Road situated on much higher ground, beyond the Victoria Park, from which could be seen below the host of belching chimneys of the factories making shoes, hosiery and machinery of many kinds. The motive power in most was steam, and Gimsons had made the engines and boilers. In the remainder, noisy gas engines did the needful.

My wage on starting was 5s. per week, which by 1914 had risen to 9s., my parents supplementing by a weekly postal order to enable me to pay for my lodging and allow me around a shilling for spending money. A bonus system was started on the jobs we had to do, which generally entailed working considerable overtime beyond the basic week of fifty-two hours which, of course, included

Saturday mornings. The ultimate rewards, in the case of we apprentices, were miserably small—12s. or 15s. after, perhaps, three months' work—but the overtime became so continuous that at length the trade union, then the Amalgamated Society of Engineers, called a special meeting at a nearby pub, as a result of which all apprentices were called on to join the union. This we did at another special meeting, under threat of a strike by the members unless . . . ! As the membership in Leicester was very strong, we apprentices paid our 2d. per week and, certainly, after that we only worked overtime on two or three nights a week, and not for so long. In what spare time I had, I attended evening classes in three subjects at the Leicester Technical college, and often was hard put to it to remain awake as 9.30 p.m. approached; moreover, we started work at 6.30 the next morning.

Under the Lloyd George Insurance Act the engineering industry was one of those chosen initially both for National Health and Unemployment Insurance Benefit contributions. We apprentices regarded this as a nuisance; as did my harassed parents, who had to augment my weekly postal order, I'm afraid. One day, however, I scraped and burned my hand rather badly on a high-speed grinding wheel. My foreman, having patched me up from the first aid box, told me I'd better go to my doctor. Seeing my hesitation he said, 'you've got a doctor, haven't yer?' I had put down my landlady's doctor on the form we'd had to complete some months previously, but I'd clean forgotten his name and where he lived. However, one of the landlady's sons, who worked on the floor below, put me right on this and I set off, knocking on the doctor's door at about three o'clock on a summer afternoon.

An elderly housekeeper, obviously roused from a nap, ushered me into a darkened hall and, seeing my bandaged hand, said she'd 'see'. She crossed the hall to a door opposite, knocked twice, listened, and, receiving no reply, entered. From where I stood I saw the doctor, head on hands over the table, fast asleep. Gently, she roused him and, seeing me without, he straightened up and I went in. Seeing my bandage, he did his best to become professional and bade me remove it. My hand looked rather a mess. He cleaned it and anointed it with something that made me jump around for some moments. Then he replaced the bandage and, sitting down somewhat wearily at his table, pulled a pad in front of him. As he stared at it, I thought that he could do with a few more hours sleep to recover from the effects of what he had imbibed at lunch time. Then he wrote at some length and, tearing off the sheet, told me to take it to a chemist and 'that should put you right, lad'. I departed somewhat mystified, as he, doubtless, resumed his siesta.

The chemist near our works, in a street of small dingy shops, was a middle-aged bachelor, reputed to be a miser and worth a considerable fortune. He seemed to sell nearly everything and was always busy. Taking the form I proffered, he looked over his spectacles at my bandage and then at me, keenly. Then, with a shrug, he disappeared to the nether regions of the shop. There were two women waiting when he re-appeared with, to my surprise, both arms full. Depositing his burden on the counter, he produced antiseptic ointment and bandages of various widths, which he put into a bag. Giving me the lot, and eyeing the form, he said, 'that's what it says here', as I departed, loaded, followed by the curious stares of several women.

My landlady was very surprised to see me at that time of day, especially with my burden, but when I told her what had happened she sat down and laughed helplessly. It was some minutes before she inquired about my hand, and I remember how very kind and thorough she was in 'doing me up' with samples of the new medicaments, which sufficed for the treatment of cut fingers, festerings and boils for the whole household until I enlisted in September 1914. At the works my leg was pulled unmercifully for a few days, and my experience regarded as a huge joke, particularly as the old doctor and his proclivities were well known locally.

Early in 1914 Gimsons secured a large order for lasting machinery used in the manufacture of welted footwear, for what was then reputed to be the largest shoe factory in the world, in St Petersburg, and our several experts returned from a preliminary visit sporting Russian astrakhan caps and jackets. Our section worked flat out until a few weeks before the outbreak of war to get these machines finished and shipped. I had great difficulty in attending my evening classes and sitting for three City & Guilds examinations in May in Machine Drawing, Applied Mechanics, and Steam. I never did get to know the result of these. Great events complete overshadowed their importance, I fear.

The growing shoe machinery division of the firm was managed by Mr Josiah's son, Kingsley Gimson, who, on leaving Charterhouse, had served his time with the famous Baldwin Locomotive Works of Philadelphia, and at the time of which I write he was almost constantly abroad. On one of his journeys he had fixed up an agency with a well known German manufacturer of shoe machinery, Schöen of Pirmasens, to handle certain of their products in England. By June 1914 our representatives had sold around 140 of one type to English manufacturers, and the first batches were arriving at our works for the small modifications, testing and so on deemed necessary before despatch. The German son of the principal of that firm came over on several occasions, and during the last of these I was with him quite a lot, as I was put on this work. I recall several rather serious conversations with him concerning the trouble between Austria-Hungary and Serbia soon after our papers had reported the assassination at Sarajevo of the Archduke Ferdinand and his wife—of whom most British people had never heard, previously. He was a pleasant, good looking young fellow and had talked freely with many of us, but, as the war clouds gathered on the Continent, he seemed somewhat preoccupied at times, although there was no reason for us to speculate as to the cause. He returned to Germany during the last week of July, telling us that he would probably return during August. We didn't give him another thought, as the works was about to shut down for the annual Bank Holiday week—without pay—and I was looking forward very much to going home to Eastbourne; also to receiving the additional sum on my weekly postal order to cover my train fare. Later we were told that the German was a reserve officer in the German Field Artillery: whether this was so or not, we saw him no more. Twelve months hence I wondered, at odd times, whether he might be directing the battery whose whizzbangs were plastering us. Idle speculation!

I duly arrived home, very tired and dirty, via two sardine-packed trains, repeatedly delayed by troop movements and further crowded by scores of Army and Navy reservists rejoining their units. All of this served to bring home to me at last the grim possibility of war, perhaps with Germany.

A mile and a half off Eastbourne front lay the grey, four-funnelled cruiser *Hampshire* (later to be lost off the Orkneys *en route* for Russia, with Lord Kitchener on board). Along the front, and marching to the station with full packs and equipment, stepped two battalions of London Territorials with bands playing martial music, which thrilled the crowds of holiday-makers. They had hurriedly broken annual camp under the lee of Beachy Head. This was mobilization. Spectators called 'good luck' to them, I remember; and, in the event, they needed it, for many of those laughing, joking lads now lie all around what came to be called the Ypres Salient.

Towards the end of my week's holiday, with the nations declaring war on one another daily, my brother Selwyn arrived home, pretty grimy and dirty after two days in the train. He had been in camp with Eastbourne College O.T.C. and other public school O.T.C.s at Rugeley in Staffordshire. He was in khaki and webbing equipment and had a rifle, with which he instructed me in elementary arms drill, to the consternation of my mother. She went to the station with me for the London train, and her parting words to me were 'now, my boy, don't do anything silly!'

I reached Leicester on the Sunday night to find that the works would not be re-opening on the Monday morning, and that we were to register at the local Labour Exchange for Unemployment Insurance Benefit. Thus, in my case, the British declaration of war simply added confusion to a situation already chaotic in many respects. We had to report daily, our waiting queue gawped at by crowds of onlookers, for Unemployment Insurance related only to workers in engineering, ship-building and coal-mining. At the end of the week we apprentices drew, I think 6s. apiece benefit.

At the end of the second week we were told to report for work on the Monday morning, and for a fortnight worked hard to complete machines needed for the manufacture of army boots. Life proceeded thus until one morning we read that Von Kluck—already famous—had reached the outskirts of Paris. It so happened that the engineer with whom I was working was the son of a well known Leicester builder of hosiery machinery named Spiers. Ernie

Spiers was always quarrelling with his father, this was one reason why he was working at Gimsons and not at his parent's works, which was subsequently taken over by the Ford Motor Co. He told me that, six months previously, after one of these rows, he enlisted in the 10th Hussars and found himself in barracks at Scarborough. Three months later his father bought him out at considerable expense, but the rows had started anew and he was ready to enlist again: 'What about it?'

The result was that Ernie and three of us apprentices—Taylor, Wade and myself—joined the lunch-time queue at the recruiting office in Humberstone Gate, and after a considerable wait found ourselves before two doctors and a colour sergeant. In the event, and to our great surprise, I was the only one passed as fit for service: Spiers was rejected for an ear discharge, Wade for a hammer toe, or something similar, and Taylor for some trouble with his privates. At this I protested, and told everyone that I wasn't going by myself. After a moment's conversation, the doctors had another look at Taylor and passed him fit. Spiers and Wade returned with us to the works, where we told our foreman that we were going and had to be sworn in at three o'clock that afternoon. He called us 'a pair of silly buggers' as he vigorously expectorated bits of chewing tobacco around the surrounding floor. Then, softening a shade, he said that if we came back Gimsons might have a job for us. Taylor and I left hurriedly, as we had to explain matters at our digs, and we feared to be late.

We were sworn in with some pretty drunk reservists, trying to hold a corner of a tattered prayer book, drew the King's shilling and 2s. 9d. ration allowance, and made our way to Glen Parva Barracks via the Aylestone tram. Here we told them that we wished to join the Royal Engineers and got the assurance from a harassed sergeant, who indicated the Orderly Room and told us, 'don't worry, lads, they'll see to you in there'. They did, and in spite of our vehement protests—and, incidentally, those of many others—a few days later we found our names on the list of recruits for the Leicestershire Regiment, Infantry of the Line. My number was 12819, and I was now faced with the problem of informing my parents of events, and also that my landlady, out of the goodness of her heart, was packing up my few effects and sending them home. Looking back, there was no doubt that she was pretty marvellous about this; but then, she had fine sons of her own.

APPENDIX II

A note on the formation in August and September 1914 of the four Service Battalions—6th, 7th, 8th and 9th—of the Leicestershire Regiment, comprising the 110th Infantry Brigade (Brigadier Hessey), 37th Division (Major-General Lord Edward Gleichen), and movements in England prior to joining the B.E.F. in France during July 1915.

The 6th and 7th Battalions were formed of recruits from Leicester and Leicestershire sent to the Regimental Depot, Glen Parva Barracks, Leicester during August 1914. When they left for Aldershot in early September the 8th and 9th were similarly formed. These were mostly from the county, including several hundred miners, and from Loughborough came as many engineering and other students. There were also a few men from Nottinghamshire.

Before the 6th and 7th moved to Badajoz and Salamanca Barracks, Aldershot, the Depot was terribly overcrowded, men sleeping on the parade ground by the hundred without a single blanket between them. The sanitary and catering arrangements were quite inadequate and soon became chaotic, with the result that, for a fortnight or so, we of the 8th and 9th were billeted in the Wigstons before leaving for Bourley Camp, Aldershot, midway on the road to Fleet. As I recall events, nine hundred or so of us in the 8th were commanded by a volunteer captain of the Singapore Artillery, who happened to be on U.K. leave, with two

504

reservist corporals to assist him. The corporals set us a wonderful example and a high standard, and Corporal Cattell became our R.S.M.

On reaching Aldershot we were formed successively into platoons and companies. Reserve officers appeared as colonel, majors and company commanders, while platoon commanders, newly-commissioned second lieutenants from public school O.T.C.s, joined us daily. Somewhat elderly reservists with Boer War ribbons put up 'stripes' soon after joining, as quartermaster sergeants and sergeants. Where friends had enlisted in groups, generally speaking none would take stripes—an unwritten law which, in the event, took months to break down and which resulted in the emergence of natural leaders. This was a very good thing, as generally these men had been members either of the Boys Brigades or of one of the many Cadet Corps which flourished before 1914 in view of the German 'menace'.

These lads knew elementary section and platoon drills and were invaluable as section instructors. Once we were able to drill fairly well and intelligently as companies, the rest followed without much difficulty as all were keen to learn, although at first there were shortages of most essentials. The 6th Battalion (which, rumour had it, were originally part of the 9th Division, as were their neighbours in the near-by Talavera Barracks, the 6th Bedfords) was the only unit of the 110th Brigade to have khaki uniform. The 7th was issued with old fashioned red tunics with yellow facings and blue trousers, capped by Brodrick pillbox hats. As can be imagined, these deteriorated in appearance very rapidly. In camp at Bourley we and the 9th Battalion were given 'Kitchener's blue' serge uniform, with a fore-and-aft hat to match. A cheap civilian overcoat completed the outfit until, in November, old Lee Metford rifles and white pre-Boer War leather belts and cartridge pouches were added.

As the weather deteriorated with the approach of winter, Bourley Camp and surrounds became a vast polluted quagmire, in spite of strenuous efforts at drainage amid the lines of tents. Although latrine buckets were placed in position every night, occupants of the crowded tents had great difficulty emerging without treading on someone, and in bad weather anything could happen in the dark, if the culprits thought themselves unobserved. On pay nights, with strong beer at only a few coppers a pint, this evil was at its worst. Conditions in the camp became so bad that on Christmas Eve 1914 the 8th Battalion moved into Buller Barracks, the vacated Army Service Corps Depot in Aldershot, our platoon occupying some married quarters. Our breakfast on Christmas morning was cold tinned herrings, bread, and lukewarm tea tasting badly of stew; but, having raided the nearby Gun Hill coal-yard, and chopped up a few forms and table tops found lying loose around the barrack blocks, we kept reasonably warm on a dull, cold and showery Christmas Day.

Early in the New Year we queued for vaccination, and several days afterwards set out for Wokingham, doing exercises *en route* and sleeping in barns. By now, many of the men had terribly inflamed arms, made worse—in spite of repeated warnings—by drinking in the local pubs at night. My vaccination had not taken and, with several more lads in similar case, I performed mess orderly and other duties for the others, several of whom were evacuated to hospital. At Wokingham we were billeted in an old flour mill by the river and did more exercises, and I remember a long march and a billet in one of Huntley & Palmer's factories at Reading.

Our Company Commander was Captain Capper, a retired Regular officer but a fine soldier, with North-West Frontier and Boer War ribbons, who was at great pains to instruct us in the care of our feet, for which we had much cause to thank him in days to come, and in the matter of personal hygiene also.

We returned from Wokingham, but not to Buller Barracks—a pleasant surprise, for the battalion went into billets for a fortnight or so along the main streets of Camberley and Yorktown, and four of us found ourselves in wonderful accommodation, almost opposite the main gate of Sandhurst, with Mr and Mrs Wynn, whose butcher's and poulterer's shop, with its prominent Victorian portico, was still there in the mid-1960s. The Wynns couldn't do enough for us, but our evenings in their company were very limited, as we were constantly on night exercises in the neighbouring Blackwater area. A pleasant memory of our stay there was the occasion when Mrs Wynn took us to a service in the chapel at

Sandhurst. A soldier's daughter herself, she knew many of the college staff and we four were made most welcome, in spite of our shabby Kitchener's blue.

Around the beginning of March the battalion moved to Folkestone into billets on the Leas and along the Sandgate Road. Here we were issued with khaki, cap badges, shoulder brasses and Canadian-made leather harness and cartridge pouches, to which were added the standard valise, water bottle, entrenching tool and haversack; then, most important of all, the short magazine Lee Enfield Mark III rifle and bayonet. We now paraded proudly and with redoubled smartness, and marched incessantly for long route marches in full equipment. Our battalion band became a reality, and I'm sure that survivors of the 110th Brigade will never forget the long and arduous ascents of the hill on the Dover Road, with the 'Valiant Sailor' at the summit, and the Capel turn.

Towards the end of our stay at Folkestone, around Easter 1915, the first Canadians arrived at Shorncliffe Camp near by—the famous Princess Patricia's Canadian Light Infantry. They cut us out completely with the Folkestone girls, as their pay was six times ours, and the way they threw their money about staggered everyone. Moreover, our position was the worse for the reported defection of our company quartermaster sergeant, an old soldier, with the Company funds. Indeed, we were not sorry to move to Perham Down Camp on Salisbury Plain, near Tidworth, where we started to do our firing course on the ranges there. I recall that we were firing ten rounds at three hundred yards when news came of the sinking of the *Lusitania*. Our ammunition was American made, and was so bad that when I was of a party marking in the butts, bullets repeatedly went through the targets side-ways. Really, apart from experience gained in holding our rifles correctly and getting used to the recoil, our firing course was a complete waste of time, although we may have been eligible for an additional 3d. per day proficiency pay.

Incidentally, as a potential machine-gunner, I, with other enthusiasts, had for months past learned the Vickers gun by means of lectures and wooden models but, until some real weapons were forthcoming, the machine-gun section was not taken seriously by the battalion. However, several of us missed a long and tiring route march by attending a course in Tidworth on the Barr & Stroud Infantry range-finder. For some days we did brigade exercises, quite interesting at times, and in mid-June we had a Divisional Parade at the conclusion of which there was a grand march past in close column of companies. It was then that we knew that we were of the 37th Division, and we saw something of the other two Infantry Brigades 111 and 112. They were mostly Royal Fusiliers, Rifle Brigade or King's Royal Rifles. It was the only time I saw our divisional commander, and then only from a dusty distance. Our brigade left the Division and joined the 21st in July 1916.

In lovely summer weather we trained as a Division, the scheme being an advance on, and the storming of, the old town of Newbury, the defenders being one of our brigades. On the return exercise to Tidworth, our 110th were the defenders. It was all good fun, and may have been of some use to our officers. To augment our numbers, several pairs of us had to carry pole targets—silhouettes of six or more soldiers in the 'prone' position, fixed at intervals along a long pole. Across sometimes thickly wooded country, this became really hard work at times.

On our return to Perham Down, we of the machine-gun section were paraded and marched down to Ludgershall Station sidings. There we took charge of a number of kicking, bucking mules fresh from the Argentine, together with crates of mule harness and carriers. With the help of some of our Transport Section, who were also taking delivery of some more mules, we managed to get them to our transport lines, then in embryo form. For each company, one man who knew something about horses was transferred to the machine-gun section, and in our 'C' Company a fine man, one Bithrey, a gentleman's groom, took over the care of our mules. On the following day we paraded again, and took over from the battalion quartermaster four Lewis guns and a mass of ammunition drums and buckets to hold them. We had neither seen nor heard of these Lewis guns before and were terribly disappointed. We drew four heavy Vickers-pattern tripods on which to mount them, and started in right away with a newly-joined battalion machine-gun officer to learn them. Within a few days we had each fired a burst on the range, and began to see their good points, the chief of these being lightness and mobility.

It was now, when various deficiencies of kit were being remedied, that signs were not lacking that we should soon be moving. But where? France, or Egypt or Gallipoli, or even Africa? Rumour was rife.

I had been home on weekend leave once only, from Aldershot in November of the previous year, and now all leave was suddenly stopped. The married men, particularly, took this very badly, and there was a considerable amount of 'breaking out', especially on the following weekend. I was prevailed upon to go to Leicester with a man in our tent who invited me to stay on the Friday and Saturday nights with his family. The journey to Leicester went quite smoothly, but at the barrier there the following dialogue took place between my comrade and a Military Policeman who stopped him as he was handing his ticket to the collector:

'Is your name Collings?'

'No, it's Williams.'

'Right! You're the chap we want!'

And he was marched off, to return to camp at Perham Down with an escort sent to fetch him. I, left on my own, was not molested and, undecided what to do, went across to the Y.M.C.A. almost opposite the station. About half a dozen soldiers from the train were with me and we were all pretty hungry and thirsty. It was getting very late, but we managed to get lukewarm cups of tea and something to eat from the practically deserted canteen. Then we just sat or lay down where we were, and it was then that I found I had 2s. 3d. left and resolved to get the first train to London and back to camp. Suffice it to say that I reached Andover about mid-day and made my way furtively into our lines during the Saturday afternoon.

Our tent was deserted and I was sitting on the piled blankets outside in the sun when I was spotted by the orderly sergeant, who seemed very surprised to see me. In the event I found I hadn't been missed until that morning, and I got away with (I think) seven days Confined to Barracks. I supposed I was lucky, but everyone, without exception, had his problems just then, as it was now pretty certain that we were off to France very shortly. Captain Capper and other Reserve officers left and were replaced by younger men. Our new company commander was an American, one McCutcheon, who was the husband of Pearl White, one of the earliest film stars.

Weeks afterwards in France, a letter from home mentioned that the Eastbourne police had been round for me on that Saturday morning. It had upset them at the time, as naturally they thought that I was in trouble. I nearly was; but headstrong youth, I fear, didn't think of the possible consequences of indiscretions such as this just then.

By the end of July the battalion was lying at Houlle near St. Omer before going into trenches near Mont Kemmel for instruction.

APPENDIX III

NOTES ON OPERATIONS OF XXII CORPS
(Lt. Gen. Sir A. Godley)

Second Battle of the Marne, 18th July–7th August 1918, taken from the official history of the war, *Military Operations France and Belgium 1918, May–July*, Brig. Gen. Sir J.E. Edmonds (maps and sketches Maj. A.F. Becke), published MacMillan & Co. Ltd., St Martins Street, London, 1939.

1st July

Foch to Pétain and Haig. Directive No. 4, subject: 'Future operations' stressed importance of preventing any further German advance towards Paris or Abbéville. Haig replied: XXII Corps three divisions and motor machine-gun battery, covering Abbéville; could intervene on French front if necessary at short notice.

4th July

Foch considered indications of German offensive in Champagne early in July strong enough to warrant strengthening the French front east and west of Reims, although there were also signs of an imminent enemy push on the Flanders front (50km.).

10th July

Foch warned Haig that in view of coming attack in Champagne, he might need British reserves and asked for and obtained move of 12th Division (Third Army) and 18th Division (Fourth Army) to south of River Somme.

13th July

Foch asked for and obtained R.A.F. assistance—nine squadrons

flew south. 2.25 p.m. asked for a Corps H.Q. to take command
of British troops and that a second corps of four divisions be made
ready to follow. In absence of Haig in London, CUC CGS Lt.
Gen. Sir H. Lawrence arranged for despatch of XXII Corps H.Q.
and 51st and 62nd Divisions. On his return 2 p.m. on 14th Haig
asked for immediate interview with Foch. C.I.G.S. London
'phoned anxiety of War Cabinet and requested Haig to use own
judgement in complying with Foch's request. General Smuts
would come over and see Haig after interview.

15th July

Conference at Monchy-le-Châtel; Foch in high spirits; told Haig
German blows had struck east and west of Reims, twenty-six and
twenty-nine miles wide respectively, and that the situation was
satisfactory. This altered destination of first four British divisions;
instead of going to Chalons, would detrain Provins area, sixty miles
west south west, in rear of Ninth Army. Haigh still protested at
sending them, pointing out what was quite true, that an attack on
the LYS salient was imminent. Foch replied that it was necessary to
halt present German advance at all costs and that British divisions
would be in reserve and only used if absolutely necessary; also, if
British front was attacked, they would be returned at once. After
this explanation Haig agreed to allow the second pair of British
divisions, 15th and 34th, to proceed from First and Second Army
areas respectively. They were sent by rail to join XXII Corps.

15th–17th July

German offensive around Reims gained comparatively little
ground at great expense. On 16th Pétain ordered 51st and 62nd
Divisions to support the French Fifth Army. By 18th July, after
considerable confusion, the two divisions were concentrated east
and south east of Épernay in Fifth Army Reserve. Pétain also
asked for 15th and 34th Divisions, but Foch decided to keep them
at his own disposal and original detraining point, Chalons, was
changed. 15th Division detrained at Clermont, forty-one miles west
of Soissons, and 34th at chantilly. 15th Division concentrated
around Liancourt and 34th in Senlis area.

17th July

British CGB, in view of likelihood of strong attack on Second Army front at very early date, drafted letter to Foch for Haig's signature, asking for return of the four divisions forthwith. Before this was signed. Lt. Gen. DuCane arrived with letter from Foch stressing need for nipping fresh enemy attacks in the bud, and that moving troops from sectors where no attacks were immediately expected to deal with these would save far more serious calls, necessary in cases of deep penetration. He inquired, therefore, what Haig might need in the near future by way of possible assistance. Haig signed the draft letter as he thought it met the case, but told Gen. DuCane to tell Gen. Foch that, if the British divisions were needed to exploit any success of Foch's projected counter-attack, he was to use them.

18th July

Foch pleased at Haig's reply; he sent to tell Haig that his Marne counter-attack had struck and that it was of such magnitude that Haig need not fear any attack on his front, as all German reserves would be needed there. If he returned the four divisions now, they would be six days *en route*—too late for any Flanders battle and unable to assist in the Marne battle. Gen. Mangin's Tenth Army, attacking east of Villers Cotterets, took fifteen thousand prisoners and four hundred guns. At 10 p.m. on the 18th, XXII Corps received orders to relieve the exhausted Italian II Corps with the 51st and 62 Divisions, and after a long march they concentrated in the Montagne de Reims area.

20th July

These divisions attacked at short notice through the Italian Corps, instead of relieving them, as the latter were demoralised, and French Command considered them on point of giving way in a sector vital to defence of Reims bastion. The infantry of the two divisions had marched eighty miles in three days. Attack advanced line average of one mile against very strong defences. Foch gave permission for 15th and 34th divisions to be employed on Soissons side of German salient and for pressure here to be intensified.

Pétain: 'Everyone will understand that no respite must be allowed to the enemy until objectives have been obtained.' Braine (on River Vesle) Tenth Army, Fismes (River Vesle) Sixth. Airmen reported considerable German troop movements direction Fere-en-Tardenois and Oulchy-le-Château. also Ludendorff concluded that projected attack on British in Flanders would not now be possible.

21st July

Following German retirement from River Marne, in centre of front, French Sixth and right of Tenth Army made good progress. Left of Tenth Army held up by fresh German divisions and greatly increased artillery fire. Gen. Mangin decided to relieve the exhausted American 1st Division and French 38th African Divisions with the 15th and 34th Divisions respectively. With reliefs already in progress he would have four fresh divisions. On eastern shoulder of salient Gen. Berthelot had given orders for renewal of attack '*pousée sans arrêt*'—including 51st and 62nd Divisions.

22nd July

Attack partial failure. Germans bring up six divisions with four more to follow. Infantry 34th Division moved up by lorries, began relief of French 38th Division south west of Hartennes, completed by 3 a.m. on the 23rd. Maj. Gen. Nicholson assumed command of sector. 15th Division (Maj. Gen. Reed) relieved US 1st Division. Two French divisions separated the two British divisions. Germans had air superiority. On 22nd July Ludendorff ordered German 7th and First Armies to make preparations for retirement behind the Upper Ourcq with left flank on Marfaux on 62nd Division front.

23rd July

51st and 62nd Divisions advanced average one mile and took Marfaux. French 19th and 87th Divisions with 45 and 46 Brigades, 15th Division, attacked towards Buzancy; little progress; heavy losses. 101 and 102 Brigades, 34th Division, with French 58th Division attacked Parcy-tigny–Bois de Beugny–Tigny. 102 Brigade gained 1,200 yards. Disappointing day.

24th July

A German retirement under pressure enabled the French left centre to advance between Dormans and Ouchy-le-Château. Sixth Army advanced near Coincy, capturing ten field guns. Front of British 51st and 62nd Divisions reduced to three miles.

25th–26th July

Villemontoire stormed by 87th French Division Tenth Army; 51st and 62nd Divisions made considerable advance, reaching Chaumuzy–Bois d'Église.

27th–28th July

British 34th Division moved to right, to woods south of Villers Helon, 19th French Division right and 12th on left extended flanks. French Sixth Army capture Butte de Chalmont, overlooking Oulchy le Château; orders for 34th Division attack on Grand Rozoy–Beugneux sector. British 15th Division took over extra kilometre of front on their right from French 87th Division. They attacked and took Buzancy, but could not hold it.

29th July

101 and 103 Brigades, 34th Division with French 25th Division attacked high ground Beugneux–Orme du Grand Rozoy, including Point 189–Servenay. Objectives gained and lost. Line consolidated along Paris Line trenches—advance of 1.5km.

30th July

French re-occupy Grand Rozoy. Continuous gas shelling and heavy enemy artillery fire on 34th Division positions on Paris Line.

31st July

Reported Germans preparing to retire on Tenth Army front, but heavy machine-gun rearguards. That night 101 and 103 Brigades occupied outpost line along Grand Rozoy–Beugneux road.

1st August

15th British Division took and advanced considerable distance be-

34th. Division Graves, RAPERIE BRITISH CEMETERY VILLE MONTOIRE.

GRAVES OF 4th Royal Sussex men. RAPERIE CEMETERY, VILLE MONTOIRE.

34th Division GRAVES, CHURCHYARD EXTENSION BRITISH CEMETERY
OULCHY LE CHATEAU.

yond Buzancy, reaching Soissons–Cuiry Housse road. 101 Brigade (2/4th Queen's, 4th Royal Sussex, 2nd Loyal North Lancs) and 103 Brigade (5th Argyll & Sutherland Highlanders, 5th and 6th King's Own Scottish Borderers) attacked 04.49 hours; advanced beyond Beugneux Wood and Beugneux to Mont Jour and Buxy le Bras Farm. French 25th and 127th Divisions took over to follow up general German retirement to line of River Vesle at Fismes.

2nd August

34th and 15th Divisions ordered to remain in position and concentrate.

4th, 5th, 6th, 7th August

Both divisions entrained for British Zone.

Losses 24th July–2nd August 1918

| 15th (Scottish Division) | 165 officers, 3,351 other ranks | Total: 273 officers 5,718 other ranks |
| 34th Division | 108 officers, 2,368 other ranks | |

In appreciation of their services General Fayolle, General of the Allied Reserve of Armies, was moved to write a special letter to Sir Douglas Haig in which he said: 'Both of them by their dash, their courage and their devotion, have excited the admiration of the French troops—in whose midst they fought.'

Brig. Edmonds comments: 'They had indeed given of their best and worthily upheld the honour of the British Army in the ranks of our Ally, and in a country, in which the defenders had all the advantages. Their share, as well as that of the 51st and 62nd Divisions, in the first victorious Allied offensive of the War, has been fully and gracefully acknowledged in France, but almost entirely overlooked by their fellow countrymen.'

Note on final advance of 4th Royal Sussex on 1st August
(pp. 295–6)
1st August

About 5 p.m. it became clear that the line was not sufficiently advanced to cover the valleys on either side of the hill on which stood Bucy Bras Farm. In the easternmost of these valleys lay the village of Arcy, and here hostile action was causing considerable trouble to troops of the French 68th Division in Servenay, which stands at the head of the valley. Accordingly at 5.50 p.m., after consultation with Gen. Menvielle of that division, Maj. Gen. Nicholson issued verbal orders for an advance of three to four hundred yards to be made at 7 p.m. under a creeping barrage, as far as the Mont Jour objective on the right, but somewhat short of it on the left. This movement, in which the 68th Division co-operated, was successfully carried out against vigorous opposition by the German rearguards. *By 10 p.m. the 2nd Loyal North Lancs and the 4th Royal Sussex had captured a hill which dominated the German line of retreat, and touch was obtained with the 127th French Division south west of Mont Jour.*

With this success the operations of the 34th Division came to an end. At 10 a.m. on the 2nd, Gen. Nicholson received orders from XXX Corps to remain in his positions while the French 25th Division passed through, to follow up the enemy, who was now retiring. The whole plan was, indeed, already blue with advancing French. At 7 p.m. he was ordered to concentrate his division, and during the 4th, 5th, 6th and 7th August it entrained for the British Zone. *It had lost, since 24th July: 108 officers and 2,368 other ranks.*

Second Battle of the Marne, 15th July–6th August 1918

Total casualties: French 95,165, all ranks

                     British XXII Corps 16,552 all ranks

                     German 168,000

                           (inc. 793 guns and 3,723 machine-guns: 29,367 prisoners of war)

INDEX

Also Available From
Pen & Sword Books...

AVAILABLE FROM ALL GOOD BOOKSHOPS
OR TO ORDER DIRECT
PLEASE CALL **01226 734222**

OR PRE-ORDER ONLINE VIA OUR WEBSITE:
WWW.PEN-AND-SWORD.CO.UK

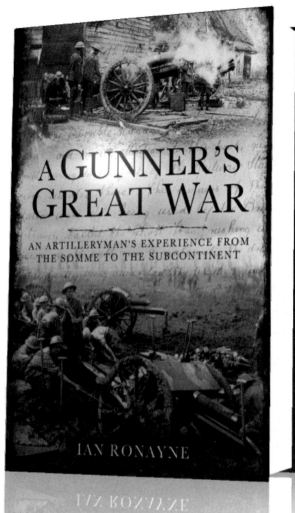

9781848846081 •
HB • 16 B&W plates •
192 pages • £19.99

If the First World War had not happened when it did, Channel Islander Clarence Ahier would almost certainly have led a mostly unremarkable life. But it did, and in October 1915, aged just 23-years-old, Clarence left his home and volunteered to join the British Army. He would spend the next two and half years serving as an artilleryman on the Western Front.

From the very beginning of his time at the front, he wrote a graphic and moving account of his experiences of war. The complete journal consists of around 25,000 words, with a focus on Clarence's experience during the Battle of the Somme, in the fighting around Ypres, and, after he was wounded for the second time, the journey to India and his time there as a member of the garrison. This will be supported by additional explanatory text.

WHAT THE CRITICS SAID:

'A Gunner's Great War is a graphic and moving account of an artilleryman's experience on the Western Front. An Interesting book for those who like artillery and WWI.'
English Heritage

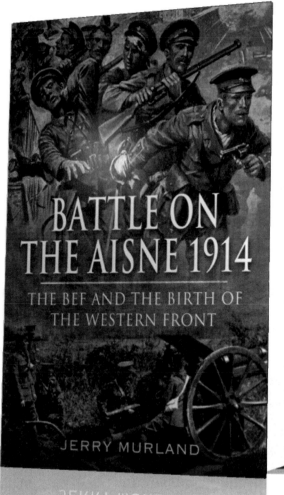

9781848847699 •
HB • 16 B&W plates •
256 pages • £19.99

The River Aisne featured prominently in August 1914 during the Retreat from Mons. A month later it was the scene of further desperate action when the BEF re-crossed it in their unsuccessful attempt to dislodge the German Army entrenched along the crest of the slopes on its northern bank.

Having already fought three major engagements and marched over 200 miles in a month, the battle proved hugely costly to the BEF. Indeed the three British Corps suffered losses of over 650 officers and some 12,000 men killed.

The author places the Aisne battles in their rightful context, both from the BEF and German viewpoints. In this detailed analysis he identifies the early deficiencies and lack of preparedness of the British Army staff and logistics organisation as well as friction among those within the command structure, all of which hampered effective operations.

WHAT THE CRITICS SAID:

'The author's narrative is clear, easy to read and engaging...the stories, quotes and anecdotes bring life to the proceedings and reveal weaknesses in British structure, tactics and command. Well worth a read.'
THE LONG, LONG TRAIL

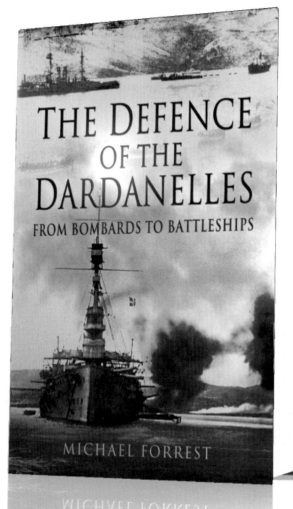

THE DEFENCE
OF THE
DARDANELLES

FROM BOMBARDS TO BATTLESHIPS

MICHAEL FORREST

9781781590522 •
HB • 120 integrated images •
272 pages • £25.00

The Dardanelles Strait, separating Europe and Asia Anatolia, was fortified in the fifteenth century with massive bronze bombards causing any unwelcome ships to run a truly formidable gauntlet. So it proved on 18 March 1915 when a powerful fleet of British and French warships attempted to force a passage to allow minesweepers to clear the Strait. The attack failed at the cost of three ships sunk and three more seriously damaged. The Allied inability to control the Strait necessitated and, crucially, delayed the disastrous Allied invasion of Gallipoli that cost the lives of some 250,000 men.

The author makes an in-depth study of the Turkish defences that caused such loss to the Royal Navy and French allies and reveals that the Ottoman army and Turkey's coastal defences relied almost entirely on the German firm of Krupp for guns. This choice was a crucial element to the successful defence of the Dardanelles. Using excellent illustrations he also examines the relative strengths of the Royal and French Navies and Turkish coastal defences.

This definitive work examines the flaws of Winston Churchill's strategy and identifies the inadequacies of pitting warships against shore fortifications. Damningly, the author's research proves that British intelligence sources had previously assessed that a naval attack alone would not succeed.

9781781590416 •
PB • 250 integrated images •
240 pages • £16.99

In 1916, Sir Douglas Haig, commanding the BEF, began his great offensive to drive the invaders off the ground they had been occupying for over a year and a half. The 'Great Push', as the offensive was advertised to the nation, began 1 July 1916. A glossy picture magazine was produced to inform the British public of the progress of the offensive. Over a four month period until the Battle of the Somme faded away in November the magazine appeared with the following advertising blurb:

'Sir Douglas Haig's Great Push; The Battle of the Somme; A popular, pictorial and authoritative work on one of the Greatest Battles in History, illustrated by about 700 wonderful Official Photographs and Cinematograph Films; By Arrangement With the War Office; beautifully printed on the Best English Art Paper.'

As is well known, the Great Push turned out to be little more than a nudge, but, for the sake of national morale, the British public had to be encouraged to believe that all was going well; especially in view of the horrific casualties wrecking the lives of families throughout the land.

WHAT THE CRITICS SAID:

'Another good photo reference in the Images of War series, and fascinating if you are interested in WW1.'
MILITARY MODELLING

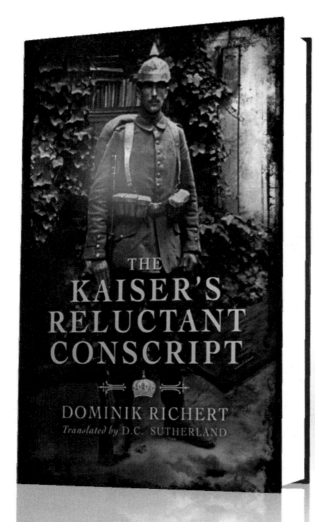

9781781590331 •
HB • 8 B&W plates •
288 pages • £19.99

In 1914 Dominik Richert was involved in fighting on the French border and was then moved to northern France where he was in combat with Indian troops. In 1915 he was sent to the East and took part in the Battle for Mount Zwinin in the Carpathians and the subsequent invasion of the western parts of the Ukraine and of eastern Poland. In 1917 he took part in the capture of Riga before returning to the Western Front in 1918, where he saw German tanks in action at the battle of Villers-Brettoneux.

No longer believing in the war, he subsequently crossed no-man's land and surrendered to the French, becoming a 'deserteur Alsacienne'. The book ends with his return home early in 1919.

This superb memoir gives a fascinating insight into the War as experienced by the Germans, and into the development of the author's attitude to it. Yes, Richert fights to survive, but he feels little respect for, or allegiance, to his own army or the society which sent him to war.

WHAT THE CRITICS SAID:

'This is an unusual, educational and absorbing memoir of an infantryman's Great War and I recommend it.'
THE LONG, LONG TRAIL

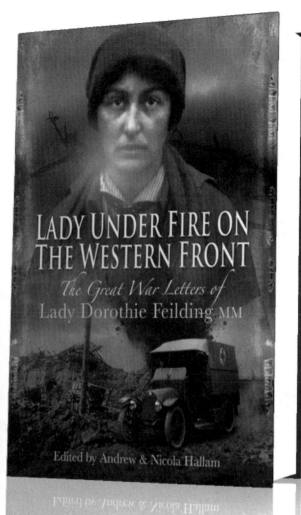

LADY UNDER FIRE ON THE WESTERN FRONT
The Great War Letters of Lady Dorothie Feilding MM

Edited by Andrew & Nicola Hallam

9781848843226 •
HB • 16 B&W plates •
240 pages • £19.99

Also Available as an eBook –
Epub: 9781844682140
Kindle: 9781844682157

When Britain went to war in 1914 Lady Dorothie Feilding, the twenty-five-year-old daughter of the Earl of Denbigh, wasted no time in volunteering for the Munro Motor Ambulance Corps. Spending nearly four years on the Western Front in Belgium driving ambulances, she had the distinction of being the first woman to be awarded the Military Medal for her bravery as well as the *Croix de Guerre* and the Belgian Order of Leopold.

Fortunately the hundreds of letters that she wrote to her family at Newnham Paddox, near Rugby, have been discovered and carefully edited by Andy and Nicola Hallam. These reflect the tragedy and horror of war and also the tensions of being a woman at the front contending with shells, traumatic wounds, gossip, lice, vehicle maintenance and inconvenient marriage proposals.

WHAT THE CRITICS SAID:

'Extraordinary letters written by an aristocratic heroine of the First World War...'
THE EXPRESS

'A useful addition to the relatively small collection of Great War works about those dedicated to easing the lot of the soldier on the Western Front.'
THE WESTERN FRONT ASSOCIATION STAND TO! MAGAZINE

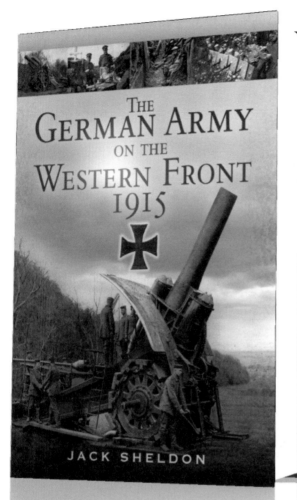

9781848844667 •
HB • 16 B&W plates •
336 pages • £25.00

Also Available as an eBook –
Epub: 9781783032266
Kindle: 9781783032259

With the Central Powers holding the initiative throughout, 1915 was the year that largely determined the way the remainder of the war would be fought. Constantly on the offensive in the vast open spaces of the Eastern Front, the German Army stood on the strategic defensive in the West. There, with minimal ground-holding forces and thanks to skillful deployment of limited reserves of men and guns, it repulsed with bloody losses every attempt by the Western Allies to drive it from occupied France and Belgium.

Shortages of weapons, equipment and ammunition forced both sides to tool up for what was clearly becoming a long war of attrition. Although the Western Front had stabilized by the end of 1914, this did not mean that tactical thinking and developments also stood still. Every Allied attempt to break the deadlock elicited a response from the German defenders, who brought the tactics of positional warfare to a high state of refinement. Trench systems increased in depth and complexity. The machine gun proved its lethality and the result for the Western Allies was one costly setback after another, with French losses reaching a staggering 1,000,000 fatalities by the end of the year.

This superbly researched book provides the clearest and most comprehensive German perspective yet on this period of the War. It covers such well-known actions as Neuve Chapelle, Ypres, where gas was used on a large scale for the first time, Aubers Ridge and Loos as well as the appalling clashes in Champagne and the Argonne Forest.

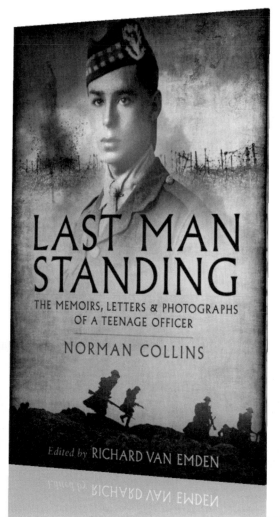

9781848848658 •
PB • Illustrated throughout
• 208 pages • £12.99

Also Available as an eBook –
Epub: 9781781597750
Kindle: 9781781597767

It hardly seems credible today that a 19-year-old boy, just commissioned into the Seaforth Highlanders, could lead a platoon of men into the carnage of the Battle of the Somme. Norman Collins, the author of this superb memoir, was this remarkable man.

Using Norman's own words, *Last Man Standing* follows him from his childhood in Hartlepool to his subsequent service in France. The book also covers such shattering events as the German naval assault on Hartlepool in December 1914 when Norman was subjected to as big a bombardment as any occurring on the Western Front at that time. Norman's love for the men under his command shine out in this book and his stories are gripping and deeply moving. They are illustrated by a rare collection of private photographs taken at or near the front by Norman himself.

WHAT THE CRITICS SAID:

'Enthralling memoir. These letters form the freshest part of this book, full of detail about kit and food that obsessed soldiers but which do not find a place in the history books.'
WHO DO YOU THINK YOU ARE?

'This is a harrowing tale of battle, loss and the horrors of war.'
SCOTLAND MAGAZINE

AN ANZAC ON THE WESTERN FRONT

THE PERSONAL REFLECTIONS OF AN AUSTRALIAN INFANTRYMAN FROM 1916 TO 1918

H.R. WILLIAMS

PRESENTED & EDITED BY
JOHN GREHAN & MARTIN MACE

9781848847675 •
HB • 16 B&W plates •
208 pages • £19.99

Having enlisted in 1915 and serving in the 56th Battalion Australian Imperial Force, Harold Roy Williams had only arrived in France, from Egypt, on 30 June 1916. He describes the horrors of the Fromelles battlefield in shocking clarity and the conditions the troops had to endure are revealed in disturbing detail.

Surviving a later gas attack, Williams' subsequent postings read like a tour of the Western Front. Following the Somme there was the mud and squalor of the line south of Ypres, the German Spring Offensive of 1918, the Battle of Amiens – frequently described as the most decisive battle against the Germans in France and Flanders – the capture of Villers-Bretonneux and, finally, the assault on Péronne. This is his graphic description of his service in the First World War.

WHAT THE CRITICS SAID:

'A remarkably candid and graphic account of his wartime service, this book details Williams' journey from the Somme through to the German offensive in 1918, his wounding at the Battle of Péronne, and his eventful turn home.'
BRITAIN AT WAR MAGAZINE